The Rise of the Masses

THE RISE OF THE MASSES

SPONTANEOUS MOBILIZATION AND CONTENTIOUS POLITICS

Benjamin Abrams

THE UNIVERSITY OF CHICAGO PRESS
CHICAGO AND LONDON

The University of Chicago Press, Chicago 60637
The University of Chicago Press, Ltd., London
© 2023 by The University of Chicago
All rights reserved. No part of this book may be used or reproduced in any manner whatsoever without written permission, except in the case of brief quotations in critical articles and reviews. For more information, contact the University of Chicago Press, 1427 E. 60th St., Chicago, IL 60637.
Published 2023
Printed in the United States of America

32 31 30 29 28 27 26 25 24 23   1 2 3 4 5

ISBN-13: 978-0-226-82681-3 (cloth)
ISBN-13: 978-0-226-82683-7 (paper)
ISBN-13: 978-0-226-82682-0 (e-book)
DOI: https://doi.org/10.7208/chicago/9780226826820.001.0001

Library of Congress Cataloging-in-Publication Data

Names: Abrams, Benjamin (Political sociologist), author.
Title: The rise of the masses : spontaneous mobilization and contentious politics / Benjamin Abrams.
Description: Chicago : The University of Chicago Press, 2023. | Includes bibliographical references and index.
Identifiers: LCCN 2022048795 | ISBN 9780226826813 (cloth) | ISBN 9780226826837 (paperback) | ISBN 9780226826820 (ebook)
Subjects: LCSH: Protest movements. | Revolutions. | Government, Resistance to. | Political participation. | Occupy movement. | Black lives matter movement. | Egypt—History—Protests, 2011–2013. | France—History—Revolution, 1789–1799.
Classification: LCC HM883 .A267 2023 | DDC 303.48/4—dc23/eng/20221027
LC record available at https://lccn.loc.gov/2022048795

♾ This paper meets the requirements of ANSI/NISO Z39.48-1992 (Permanence of Paper).

Contents

Introduction 1

PART I: THEORIZING MOBILIZATION 13
1. What We Know about Mobilization and What We Need To 15
2. Affinity-Convergence Theory 31

PART II: THE EGYPTIAN REVOLUTION, 2011 55
3. Egypt on the Eve of Revolution 59
4. The Anatomy of a Revolutionary Moment 71
5. The Fall and Fall of Revolutionary Egypt 91

PART III: OCCUPY WALL STREET 107
6. Globalizing the Revolution 111
7. Enter the Occupiers 123
8. The End of the Extraordinary 139

PART IV: THE BLACK LIVES UPRISING, 2020 153
9. From Tragedy to Uprising 157
10. Mass Mobilization for Black Lives 175

PART V: THE FRENCH REVOLUTION, 1789 197
11. Mass Mobilization against the Ancien Régime 199
12. The Development of Revolutionary Mobilization 215

Conclusion 229

Acknowledgments 247
Notes 249
Index 289

Introduction

On December 27, 2010, the Egyptian dictator Hosni Mubarak was celebrating his son Gamal's forty-seventh birthday. It appeared by all public suspicions that he was preparing to deliver quite a gift: succession to the Egyptian presidency. Mubarak—more than any Egyptian ruler in modern history—had established phenomenal levels of personal control over the nation, and Gamal was set to become Egypt's first hereditary ruler since its revolution in 1952. What Mubarak and his son did not know, however, was that within the space of a month, a new revolution would commence their undoing. Tunisians overthrew President Zine el-Abidine Ben Ali in the early days of January 2011, and Egyptians began their own revolution later that month. Within weeks, protests had erupted in Libya, Syria, Yemen, and Bahrain. This "Arab Spring" was met with a "Spanish Summer," during which the 15-M "Indignados" movement took the country by storm. Later that year this trajectory culminated in an "American Autumn" in the form of the Occupy movement, which spread around the world, triggering further contentious challenges.

It had been, as *Time* magazine declared, "The Year of the Protester." "No one could have known that when a Tunisian fruit vendor set himself on fire in a public square, it would incite protests that would topple dictators and start a global wave of dissent," the magazine declared.[1] What had we missed?

Most of what we know about mass mobilization concerns the activities of organized movements and activist networks. If we were to have used this knowledge to analyze the chances of a revolution in Egypt, our conclusion would have likely been that the country's social movements lacked organizational resources and that activist networks were too small and disempowered to pull off any serious challenge to the regime. This was also precisely what Egyptian activists were telling us: "Every political leader and activist I spoke with ... as well as analysts from across the

Egyptian political spectrum—saw no possibility of a domestic revolution in the near future," one report from 2008 concluded.[2] It looked, as leading opposition figures put it at the time, impossible for them to take on the regime and win.

When Egyptian revolutionaries *did in fact* take on the Mubarak regime in 2011 *and win*, the same established opposition forces who had only a couple of years earlier decried revolution as impossible were caught with their hands in their pockets. A Facebook event organized by a handful of young activists mobilized tens of thousands of Egyptians on January 25, more than established organizations' combined strength had in years. A couple of days later, when Mubarak's regime shut down the internet, cutting off even this loose avenue of coordination, hundreds of thousands more than had mobilized previously spontaneously took to the streets to face down the dictator.

In 2020, almost a decade later, it happened again. In the throes of a deadly pandemic during which people were being urged to stay at home, ordinary Americans poured into city streets to protest against police brutality in the wake of the Minneapolis Police Department's murder of George Floyd.[3] With movement organizations taken by surprise, masses descended on the streets of major American cities to partake in peaceful protest and police-provoked riots that spread to other metropolises nationwide, creating a wave of further mobilization. Once again we saw established, organized forces taking a back seat to mass popular uprisings.

But 2011 and 2020 are hardly unique instances of such spontaneous mass mobilization. Between 2011 and today, we have seen many more, similar mass risings. These include the 2013 Gezi Park protests in Turkey and the "June Journeys" in Brazil later that year, as well as the January 2017 Trump inauguration and Muslim ban protests in the United States. Still others are the *Nuit Debout* (Up All Night) protests in France, the early phases of the Hong Kong Umbrella movement, the 2018 Armenian Revolution, and the 2019–2021 Latin American protest wave. Conversely, puzzling periods of seemingly spontaneous popular protest also date at least as far back as the 1789 French Revolution. These popular eruptions have exhibited a kind of mobilization different from the type to which we are accustomed, demanding in-depth investigation for their own sake. This book seeks to explain why and how they take place, covering four different instances of spontaneous mass mobilization: the Egyptian Revolution of 2011, the Occupy Wall Street movement, the 2020 Black Lives Uprising, and the 1789 French Revolution. Drawing on these cases, as well as the rich history of scholarly research on mobilization, the book puts forward a new theory of spontaneous mass mobilization: affinity-convergence theory.

Explaining Spontaneous Mass Mobilization

Spontaneous mass mobilization occurs when large numbers of people partake in contentious politics without reliance on social movement organizations and their networks. When this happens—as we saw in Egypt—it can create enormous contentious political challenges ranging from mass marches to creative occupations, riots, and revolutions. Such challenges can occur alongside organized protest or in circumstances where movement organizations are passive or weak. When they do, we often struggle to explain why.

One major reason we struggle to explain spontaneous mass mobilization is because we lack a comprehensive theoretical framework for it. To find potential candidates, we have to cast our gaze far back in the history of social movement research, all the way to the classical theories of collective behavior in opposition to which mainstream social movement theory emerged. For many collective behavior theorists, almost all protest was presumed to be spontaneous and disorganized: a periodic expression of contagious psychological disquiet, subversive emergent norms, and the deviant predilections of those who refused to engage in institutional politics. This generalization was seriously at odds with reality and was rapidly discredited as the study of social movements took off. In its place came a vision of social movements as generally concerted and organized, rather than spontaneous and chaotic.

This vision formed the basis for mainstream social movement research over the course of the past half century, beginning with theories of resource mobilization, rational choice, and political processes, but broadening considerably to include studies of movement cultures, framing, strategic action, memory, and emotion, as well as instances of contentious politics that do not resemble social movements in their traditional form. With regard to mobilization, this trajectory has, for instance, explored how movement organizations and their networks mobilize affiliates in pursuit of their various goals, frame issues, cultivate membership, respond to structural shifts, and leverage resources. This research agenda, which is more fully discussed in chapter 1, has taught us an enormous amount about how mobilization generally works and tells us quite a lot about how social change can be meaningfully achieved by disempowered but determined and organized groups deftly navigating the political process. It is not, however, intended to explain situations where organized forces and their networks are relatively absent or inactive.

This book seeks to recapture spontaneous collective action as an object of study in light of the considerable advances we have made in understanding its more organized analogue.[4] We cannot reduce spontaneous collective action to atomized individual-level rational choices or psychological predilections, nor can we rely on purely structural accounts of movements' rise and fall. Rather, we need a theoretical approach that unifies the sociopolitical and sociopsychological dimensions of mass action, exploring how widely held individual characteristics interact in aggregate with large-scale structural shifts to produce mobilization.

The theory I develop in this book—affinity-convergence theory—draws upon our existing theoretical knowledge about mobilization of all kinds and places this knowledge in dialogue with an in-depth study of spontaneous mobilization across the book's four cases. The end result is an aggregate theory of mass action that demonstrates how individual predispositions for participation in a cause can be activated by emergent social conditions without the need for organized recruitment by movement networks.

Affinity-Convergence Theory

So how do these instances of spontaneous mass mobilization occur, and what keeps them going? In this book I argue that solving this puzzle requires the combined analysis of individual agency and large-scale sociological processes. There are a wide variety of factors that help predispose people toward participating in a cause. Some of these are primarily dispositional in nature, such as one's identity, perception of social injustice, and political attitudes. Others pertain to one's drives: the needs and interests to which a cause caters. Still others pertain to social position: their everyday patterns of activity, social status, resources, and obligations. I call these various predisposing factors affinities. In circumstances where these various elements of people's lives are highly compatible with a given cause, they possess an overall affinity for participation that renders them more likely to mobilize.

However, the existence of widespread predispositions for participation is not enough to guarantee mass mobilization. After all, people are predisposed toward all sorts of potential activities. Rather, those with affinity for a cause need a catalyst that helps turn predisposition into action. This catalyst comes in the form of broader sociological conditions of convergence, circumstances that encourage people to act on their affinity for a cause. These include opportune conditions, under which protest has a greater chance of succeeding or carries far lower risks than it had previously; exceptional conditions, in which the limitations on people's activities radically shift, enabling participation; and paramount conditions, in which

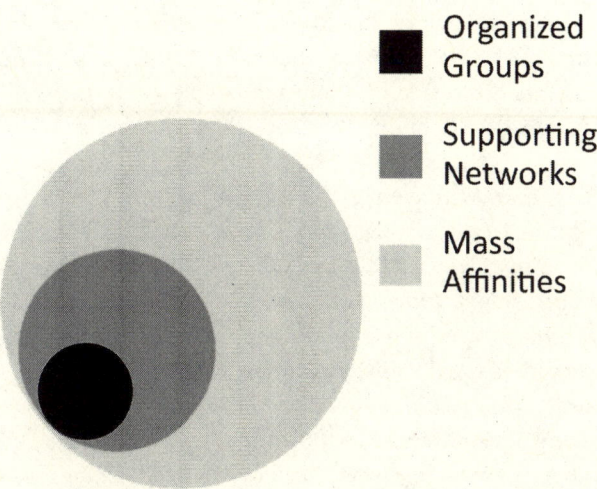

FIGURE I.1. A concentric representation of mobilization avenues.

participation becomes far more critical than it once was. These conditions manifest as alterations to social structures, such as a drop in repression; changes in physical spaces, such as the creation of a zone outside regime control; and shifts in framing, such as a disruption to established norms.

Where sufficient affinity for a cause exists among a large group of people in society *and* convergence conditions arise or are effected in that same society, the conditions for spontaneous mass mobilization are satisfied. This process is what I call affinity-convergence mobilization.

$$\textit{Affinity} \xrightarrow{\textit{convergence}} \textit{Participation}$$

Instances of affinity-convergence mobilization are a little mechanically different from the bulk of mobilizing structures employed by social movement organizations and their networks. Unlike members of organized movements and their supporting networks, affinity-convergence participants are far from a reliable or dependable element in mobilization. Although there generally exist dramatically *more* people with affinity to a cause than those within the reach of movement organizers (see figure I.1), such individuals do not possess the same kinds of concrete relational bonds as other participants and so are recurrently prone to other forms of activity, tepid participation, and simply dropping out. Even in circumstances where conditions of convergence are emphatically in place, a substantial proportion of people with a degree of affinity to a cause may still not elect to participate, owing to other intervening factors. As such, affinity-convergence theory should not be read as a deterministic model of individual choice or "collective" behavior. Rather, it is intended as an explanation and dissection of mobilized people's *aggregate behavior*: the combined consequence of many individuals' interactions with large-scale social forces.

Of course, affinity-convergence theory is far from a total explanation for mobilization in all circumstances. Conventional mobilization can and does occur in parallel with affinity-convergence mobilization, and even though affinity-convergence mobilization explains participation arising from beyond organized movements' regular mobilizing structures, the activities of activists and organizers can still play an important causal role in cultivating affinities or engendering certain convergence conditions. Moreover, when spontaneous mobilization winds down, it is quite often movement organizations—whether newly forged or long established— that pick up the mantle of social change.

Methods

In order to unpick the complex and interwoven dynamics at play in spontaneous mobilization, I needed to capture the interaction between social action and social structure. The intersection of these two elements can be very difficult to detect at the macrohistorical "birds-eye" level, commonly adopted in classic comparative research. To better access these points of intersection, we can combine a macrosociological perspective with finer-grain, within-case research methods, triangulating them to capture a process from multiple points of view. This approach is one I term "comparative history plus": a comparative historical approach to cases further enriched by the use of supplementary within-case methods that increase the resolution of our analysis. This is not a novel methodological intervention on my part, but rather shorthand for an approach already endorsed by comparative and historical sociologists such as Lachmann and Calhoun,[5] as well as mixed methods ethnographers such as Fu and Simmons.[6]

A "plus" approach to comparative historical research begins from the premise that historical sociology constitutes an attempt to trace the dynamics and processes of social change, rather than the exclusive subordination of sociology to the strictures of traditional historical inquiry.[7] As such, there is no specific reason that comparative historical sociology requires strict accordance to older traditions of historical argument and practice. With a sociological imagination, we can move beyond the interrogation of an array of already uncovered sources and actively develop new sources of primary data through methods such as interviews and digital/

physical ethnographic work. Much like "ethnography plus"[8] approaches that bolster classic ethnographic methods with facets of comparative and historical sociology, we can bolster the comparative historical approach with rich primary sources beyond extant historical artifacts.

The four cases covered in this book were selected because they all exhibited instances of spontaneous mass mobilization despite being highly distinct from one another. The first two are drawn from the so-called Year of the Protester: the January 2011 Egyptian Revolution and the September 2011 Occupy Wall Street protests. Though situated within the same wave of global mobilization and sharing some interesting connections, the sociopolitical circumstances in which these mobilizations took place were very different indeed. One was a revolutionary overthrow of an entrenched repressive police state in a developing country wracked by poverty and corruption, the other an autonomous occupation without clear goals in a world-leading economy and liberal democracy characterized by strong civil rights. The other two cases put the theory through the test of time, further assessing its generalizability. The first of these brings us up to date with the present day, examining the Black Lives Uprising: a wave of spontaneous mass protests in the United States that followed the murder of George Floyd in 2020,[9] establishing the utility of affinity-convergence theory in understanding contemporary protest. The second stretches far back into the history of contentious politics, all the way to the 1789 French Revolution, assessing the theory's applicability in an early-modern context where state structures, social life, and information flows were all highly different from the way they are today. By leveraging the differences between these cases (a "most different systems" approach to comparison), I was able to ascertain the commonalities underlying their shared pattern of spontaneous mass mobilization and trace its ascendance and denouement. It was especially important to trace not only the rise of mass mobilization but also how movements fared when the conditions supporting it faded. This enabled me to more precisely ascertain the conditions under which affinity-convergence mobilization could take place, contrasting it with periods of movement decline or shifts from spontaneous to organized mobilization.

My supplementary within-case methods range from highly extensive in-depth interviews and ethnographic observations to the interrogation of public and private archives,[10] as well as the scouring of social media sources and live protest footage.[11] It was through my engagement with these sources that I was able to gain a greater sense of how individuals, structures, and processes intersected. The balance of these various methods of data collection was individually tuned to each case.

The most historically distant of the book's cases, the French Revolution, was best served by conventional historical methods: the analysis of historians' accounts and other secondary materials in combination with archival sources. The latter were examined during two months of archival research in Paris and several further months of remote archival work. Historical texts and archival materials were in shorter supply for my other cases, particularly at the outset of my research in 2013. In the Egyptian Revolution and Occupy Wall Street cases, traditional historical methods were necessarily subordinated to primary data collection strategies. In the 2020 Black Lives Uprising, I had to depend on these strategies almost entirely, using them to develop an understanding of the case that would have otherwise proved elusive. In addition to work with secondary sources, I undertook two months of in-depth research in Egypt in 2015 (unfortunately curtailed due to security concerns), twelve months of ethnographic fieldwork with social movement communities in the United States (over a period of five years), and an extended period of digital ethnography and remote interviewing during the COVID-19 pandemic.

Interviews proved a most useful source of primary data, providing the opportunity to pursue specific questions for which answers were not available in the existing historical literature or publicly accessible sources. This helped me get "behind the scenes" of participation in contentious politics and understand the intricate ways in which individual microfoundations of mobilization interacted with macrolevel forces. There was also considerable worth in the experiences my interviewees had as participant-observers during the contentious episodes in which they partook, and their accounts were routinely very illuminating. I conducted a total of twenty-six interviews with those involved in Egypt's revolution, thirty-four with Occupy Wall Street participants, and twenty-four with participants in the Black Lives Uprising. These were conducted under conditions of blanket anonymity to protect individuals involved. Accordingly, they have been given pseudonyms when their interviews are referred to, and especially sensitive pieces of information are simply tagged "Anonymous."

Complementing the role of interviews was a variety of other sources of data. In the case of the Occupy Wall Street protests, I was able to acquire access to a privately held archive compiled during the protests as well as a litany of contemporary media reports. In the Egyptian case, I was able to draw on satellite footage, social media posts, newspaper articles, and a variety of other data points to contextualize and guide my research. Likewise, I was able to enrich my research on the Black Lives Uprising with live footage, police radio records, and other pieces of information that helped me verify or better understand events where participant accounts provided an incomplete picture, aided by the ubiquity of public footage and social media content. This also helped to flesh out what was on people's minds during the uprising and how they responded to emergent social conditions.[12]

What's in the Book?

The rest of the book is organized into five parts. Part I addresses the theoretical model, while parts II to V address each of the cases (the Egyptian Revolution, Occupy Wall Street, the Black Lives Uprising, and the French Revolution) in turn. Finally, a concluding chapter reflects on affinity-convergence theory in view of comparative findings from across all four cases.

Part I opens with chapter 1, which outlines the state of academic knowledge about mobilization and the pressing gaps in this body of research. Chapter 2 then offers a comprehensive explanation of affinity-convergence theory, situating it within existing theories of mobilization and explaining both affinity and convergence in depth.

Part II shows affinity-convergence mobilization in practice, explaining how the Egyptian Revolution of 2011 was successfully achieved, despite the very limited mobilizing capacity of existing organizations and activist networks. Chapter 3 investigates the context in which the revolution took place, detailing the affinities that predisposed Egyptians toward revolutionary mobilization and situating this alongside an analysis of other social and organizational factors. Chapter 4 examines the revolutionary moment of Egypt's "Eighteen Days" in detail, showing how sudden conditions of convergence triggered mass mobilization in spite of Egypt's weak civil society. Finally, chapter 5 considers the Egyptian revolutionary denouement, showing how postrevolutionary shifts in affinity and convergence ruled out further revolutionary mobilization.

Part III further explores the operation of affinity and convergence, with an in-depth analysis of the 2011 Occupy Wall Street movement. In contrast to the Egyptian case, in which a short, sharp peak in convergence conditions triggered rapid mass mobilization among those with affinity to the cause, the case of Occupy shows how affinity and convergence function in longer-running mass movements. Picking up where the Egyptian Revolution left off, chapter 6 explains how Occupy Wall Street emerged in response to the Arab Spring, showing how a loose band of anarchists sought to restage the conditions under which the 2011 revolutions took place, semisuccessfully achieving an array of convergence conditions. This chapter covers the period between February and October 2011, exposing

Occupy's organizational weakness, while explaining the synergy between the select set of convergence conditions from which the movement benefited. Chapter 7 then explores the sudden explosion of participation in Occupy Wall Street between October and November, explaining the broad spectrum of affinities underlying mobilization. Subsequently, chapter 8 analyzes the decline of the Occupy mobilization and the way in which the conditions of convergence underpinning its success were methodically undermined by Occupy's opponents, as well as accidentally subverted by shifts in movement activity.

Part IV examines affinity-convergence mobilization in the context of a highly pressing case from the present day: the enormous upsurge of popular protest in the United States following the murder of George Floyd in May 2020. This runaway movement posed more of a challenge to American policing in one month than organized protest had in the five years prior. Eschewing organized movements, Americans engaged in highly spontaneous forms of mass action, ranging from peaceful marches to disorderly protests, and responding to police repression with riotous reciprocation. This uprising gave birth to a wave of protest that has drawn in a wide array of protesters from around the world, with participation spanning ethnic and class lines. Chapter 9 examines the birth of the Black Lives Uprising, focusing on how police brutality–provoked riots in Minnesota's Twin Cities created conditions of convergence that spiraled into spontaneous riot and mass mobilization across the United States. Chapter 10 looks at how the dynamics of affinity-convergence mobilization operated during the uprising and how this gave rise to a renewed mass movement against police brutality during its decline.

Finally, part V turns to a classic historical case: the 1789 French Revolution. The revolution has proven an enduring test case for the generalizability of theories about contentious politics, and this section of the book tests affinity-convergence theory's utility for understanding early French revolutionary mobilization. Chapter 11 assesses the capacity of affinity-convergence theory to address the puzzle of French revolutionary spontaneity in 1789. Drawing on archival documents, historical accounts, and official records, the chapter carefully dissects the contentious powder keg of the Revolution's first year. In turn, chapter 12 surveys how affinity and convergence came to underpin French revolutionary mobilization in 1789, then traces the shift from spontaneous mobilization to more organized forms from 1789 to 1793.

Drawing together comparative lessons from across the four cases, the book's conclusion reiterates the contribution of its theory and cases, before moving to investigate an array of corollary questions. These include the relationship between organization and spontaneity, the impact of disruptive protest, and the role of repression and state opponents in shaping spontaneous participation. The chapter also briefly outlines some of the granular patterns and tendencies in processes of affinity-convergence mobilization occurring across cases in the book. I close by reflecting upon further areas for future research, such as the impact of convergence conditions on countermovements; the relationship between affinity, convergence, and *de*mobilization; and the potential routes to further improve affinity-convergence theory.

My hope is that this book will help all those who are interested in contentious politics better understand and explain spontaneous mass mobilization. For general readers and students, I hope to show how processes of spontaneous mobilization unfold, demonstrating how widely held personal attributes and broad social circumstances can conspire to create mass collective action in the absence of mass irrationality or hidden organizing forces. I also hope to convey that these processes are just as rare and fragile as they are powerful—liable to curtail when social circumstances change.

From a scholarly perspective, my aspiration is not only to improve our understanding of why spontaneous mobilization occurs but also to build some solid foundations for further research on the topic by offering a novel synthetic theory of spontaneous mass mobilization. In building affinity-convergence theory, I have tried to bring forward as much as possible of what we already know about mobilization and social movements and integrate it with the comparative lessons from the four cases in this book. I hope what I present proves a useful tool and a helpful framework.

I also hope that what follows will be of service to those readers who are primarily interested in finding out more about any of the four cases that make up this book. Accordingly, I have sought to ensure that each part of the book offers a solid contribution to our understanding of its respective case, rather than being exclusively subordinated to explicating and exemplifying affinity-convergence theory at every turn. I especially hope to have achieved this with regard to the Black Lives Uprising (a case that is, at the time of writing, still particularly uncharted by scholars), but I have tried to ensure that each case remains engaging for the nonexpert and informative and thought-provoking for the case specialist.

Finally, and not least, I hope that you enjoy reading this book.

PART I

THEORIZING MOBILIZATION

CHAPTER ONE

What We Know about Mobilization and What We Need To

After more than a century of systematic research on the subject, we already know quite a lot about mobilization. From foundational theories of collective behavior, through the organizational and processual models of the late twentieth century, to the networked theories of collective and "connective" action[1] today, a great deal has been written about the way mobilizations attract participants. Beyond the realms of sociology and political sciences, psychologists have developed a correspondingly sophisticated knowledge about why participants elect to join a mobilization. All of this research and theorizing has brought those of us who study mobilization to a certain level of consensus. Mobilizations by and large happen because organizers recognize and respond to regulated openings in opportunity structures by marshaling their resources, network ties, and cultural acumen to get people out on the street. Whether people show up for these mobilization efforts depends on how effectively organizers are able to recruit them.

For the most part, this kind of general idea suffices to explain a great deal of contemporary protest, from the orderly activities of large-scale membership organizations to less stable, more dynamic efforts of well-networked activist groups. There remains, however, a considerable lacuna: the phenomenon of spontaneous mass mobilization. It is not so much that this topic has been neglected by scholars as it is that past contributions pertinent to it have not been consistently cultivated as our field has progressed. Accordingly, it has not received the kind of systematic attention paid to organized and networked mobilization efforts. My goal in this chapter is to explain what we know about mobilization in a way that is equally attentive to our general knowledge about the mobilization activities of organizations and networks as it is to what we know about why ordinary people mobilize of their own accord.[2] Having completed the puzzle of mobilization as best we can, we can then turn our attention to the missing pieces.

Foundations

The beginnings of what we know about mobilization come from classical theories of relative deprivation and collective behavior. These perspectives did not conceive of organizations as constituting a core element in social movements. Rather, their advocates understood a social movement as "an instinctive effort to get for more men the things that have seemed to be good for some men," characterized by profound upsurges arising from the masses themselves.[3] "It is the momentum of the many," Albion W. Small wrote, in one of the first articles of social theory ever written on social movements, "hardly restrained by all the arts that the few can contrive."[4] Theorists consequently sought to discover how these surprising upsurges took form, turning to structural conditions, shared beliefs, and participant psychology.

Classical theories of relative deprivation attempted to offer cognitive models of why individuals might all collectively come to participate in phenomena such as a popular riot or revolution. The most influential iteration of the theory, found in Ted Gurr's *Why Men Rebel*,[5] advanced that in order to understand actions of social protest and rebellion, there were three general mobilizing factors one should investigate: "popular discontent (relative deprivation)," "people's justifications or beliefs about the justifiability and utility of political action," and "the balance between discontented people's capacity to act—that is, the ways in which they are organized—and the government's capacity to repress or channel their anger."[6] Of these three factors, Gurr's analysis prioritized the role of collective "relative deprivation"—the shortfall between the standard of living people expect from the social order and what it actually stands to deliver.[7] The consequence of this discrepancy was a perception of injustice among the groups in question, which served to underpin participation in collective action.

A second, related perspective—the collective behavior approach—describes a set of theories[8] engineered to explain all manner of uprisings, riots, religious movements, and even popular fads. These approaches made claims that would now seem quite radical, rejecting the notion that movements could be studied as "stable groups or established institutions,"[9] or that they accorded with a society's "common understandings or rules."[10] As Ralph Turner and Lewis Killian put it in their volume on the topic, far from being managed by established organizations, "collective behavior occurs when the established organization ceases."[11] If stable groups were to play a role, it was only to provide a point of contact and coordination around which these more disorderly mass outpourings could rally.[12]

Collective behavior theorists saw mobilization as taking place in unstructured conditions,[13] in which emergent norms suspended or otherwise altered everyday rules[14] and where established organizations lost a grip on individuals.[15] The process by which these crowds, masses, and mobs came together was sometimes referred to as "convergence," although relatively little work was done to develop this notion. Theorists also posited that there might be some form of dispositional vulnerability to participation in a social movement, which was suggested to arise from emotional, cognitive, or personality traits, such as a sense of "heightened frustration... relative deprivation, alienation, [and] spoiled or stigmatized identities," as well as, in the case of more charismatic causes, an authoritarian personality.[16] More than this, these theories even indicated that otherwise unconnected individuals' psychological and social traits could underpin spontaneous participation in collective behavior without, or even in defiance of, formal organization.[17]

Though these theories received little subsequent sociological development,[18] they remained an active topic of discussion among social psychologists. Despite their peculiar characterization of those who participated in collective action as deviant or disturbed, classical theories advanced two interesting ideas that are worth retaining. The first of these was the idea that individuals' psychological and social traits might in some way underpin or influence their participation in protest. The second was the notion that there might be certain structural circumstances in which this took place, dubbed "convergence."

While many among these early theorists of social movements advanced a vision of their participants as somehow disordered or psychologically disturbed, their younger colleagues were themselves actively participating in social movements and hence skeptical of such aspersions about their comrades.[19] Thus, a rising school of thought came to object to these classical models. Attributing social movements to the kinds of mass disorder seen in collective behavior theories was, they argued, irrational and illogical, particularly in the absence of supporting empirical work. Rather, such ideas constituted a theoretical straitjacket, and "an intellectual weapon to discredit mass movements... used by conservative critics."[20] Popular mobilization was, as William Gamson eloquently put it, "simply politics by other means... as instrumental in its nature as a lobbyist trying to get special favors for his group or a major political party conducting a presidential campaign."[21] Their rise and fall could be attributed to the deliberate agency of their organizers and participants, who approached protest strategically.

Organization or Spontaneity?

While classical theories of social movements were designed to explain unexpected mass protest, they looked ill-fitting when applied to large-scale, long-running organized movements, the likes of which became increasingly prevalent throughout the twentieth century. In these movements many participants entered into sustained trajectories of commitment to organized protest. Two organizational sociologists, John D. McCarthy and Mayer N. Zald,[22] sought to explain these movements by focusing on the role played by resource-mobilizing organizations. McCarthy and Zald's work sparked the beginning of a new dominant approach to the study of social movements, grounded in ideas about resource mobilization and organizational capacity,[23] which they crystallized in their own resource mobilization theory.

Resource mobilization approaches sought to consider how movements utilize their resources (such as money, tools, and supporters) and organizational structures to achieve discrete goals. For McCarthy and Zald, social movements constituted "a set of opinions and beliefs [representing] preferences for changing some elements of the social structure and/or reward distribution of a society," empowered by a clearly defined social movement organization (SMO), which constituted "a complex, or formal, organization which identifies its goals with the preferences of a social movement or a countermovement and attempts to implement those goals."[24] The rise of resource mobilization theories led to a shift in scholars' attitudes toward social movements, which were increasingly understood to be constituted by discrete sets of organizational activities pursued by a concretely affiliated collective.

Although resource mobilization theories are now well-established contributions to the mobilization literature,[25] these ideas were initially subject to considerable dissent and scholarly competition from an altogether alternate trajectory of research on spontaneity. The very same year as McCarthy and Zald published their seminal work on the topic, a scholarly debate raged in response to a volume issued by two Marxist sociologists, Frances Fox Piven and Richard Cloward: *Poor People's Movements*. Rather than the "purposive efforts of leaders and organizers," Piven and Cloward argued, it was disruptions to the underlying institutional conditions of a given society that gave shape (and gave rise) to contemporary protest movements.[26] In particular, Piven and Cloward evoked strands reminiscent of earlier "collective behavior" literature by emphasizing the roles of relative deprivation and disruptions to people's "institutional context." "Opportunities for defiance are structured by the general features of institutional life," they stressed, with these features "shap[ing] mass movements by shaping the collectivity out of which protest can arise."[27] The pair were in a great sense "spontaneists": followers of Rosa Luxemburg's contention that the core of revolutionary upsurge came from below. Accordingly, they argued that social conditions could readily create the sufficient conditions for unrest, a claim that they evidenced across four twentieth-century American cases.

Further defenses of spontaneity came from a rising collective of social scientists who sought to argue that, rather than acting purely in response to organization, people chose to mobilize for causes on the basis of their own rational calculations. Grounded in Mancur Olson's[28] "rational action" approach to collective action, theorists in this "rational choice" tradition tried to explain why mass participation in protest might arise from factors other than organizational force. These theorists, such as Anthony Oberschall and Karl-Dieter Opp, rejected both classical theories, which claimed that participants in protest were isolated from local organizations, and resource mobilization theories, which posited the opposite. Rather, they marshaled large-scale data sets to illustrate that there was "no consistent effect of integration into voluntary groups or into the community."[29] In other words, mobilization could arise from within organized groups or from beyond them. A key early example used to demonstrate this argument was the German Revolution of 1989 in which, these theorists argued, "protests occurred spontaneously, without any form of organization."[30]

Rational choice theorists were critical of efforts to explain spontaneous protest as a function of integration into organizations or to pathologize it as social dysfunction. Rather, they argued, protest could be predicted according to sets of "hard"' and "soft" incentive structures that determined the rational antecedents of individual action. While hard incentives constituted tangible goods derived from participating (such as monetary incentives, insurance against risk, and a better standard of living), soft incentives referred to intangible items (such as catharsis, entertainment value, normative expectations, sociability, and self-esteem).[31] They could also be "collective" or "selective"—applicable to all group members or only some.[32]

Rational choice theorists also argued that participants in protest possessed the ability for "spontaneous coordination," in which mobilizations based on common "interests, incentives, norms, and expectations," were galvanized by contextual factors, rather than organized mobilization strategies.[33] These included key political anniversaries, locations where protest was plausibly deniable, political developments that shifted incentive structures, and institutionalized meeting opportunities that incentivized further collective activity.[34]

Opportunities and Threats

Out of the various disagreements between resource mobilization theorists, rational choice theorists, and surgent spontaneists came a revitalized approach that sought to move beyond such debates. These came in the form of political process theories, many of which incorporated elements from the spontaneist and rational choice literatures, but with a retained organizational focus. These were advanced in a variety of evolving forms by a spectrum of sociologists, most prominently Charles Tilly,[35] Doug McAdam,[36] and Sidney Tarrow.[37] This structuralist, processual turn in the study of mobilization offered a vision of movements as "a sustained series of interactions between power holders and persons successfully claiming to speak on behalf of a constituency lacking formal representation," involving "publicly visible demands... with public demonstrations of support."[38]

The political process vision of mobilization drew on the concept of mobilizing structures—"the meso-level groups, organizations, and informal networks that comprise the collective building blocks" of a movement.[39] These structures help movements "bring people together in the field, shape coalitions, confront opponents, and assure their own future after the exhilaration of the peak of mobilization has passed,"[40] forming the bread and butter of organized movements' activities throughout a social movement's life cycle.

Peaks of mobilization, meanwhile, arose according to political opportunity structures: the political and institutional context of social change. Where these contexts were conducive, movements were more likely to find success exerting and/or building their mobilizing structures. In the broadest possible sense, periods of political opportunity constituted "*any* event or broad social process that serves to undermine the calculations and assumptions on which the political establishment is structured," including (but not limited to) "wars, industrialization, international political realignments, prolonged unemployment, and widespread demographic changes."[41] In their classic formulation, these tended to manifest in the form of "long-run transformation of the structures of power," rather than short-run shocks or strains.[42] Over time, the term "political opportunity" has become increasingly flexibly employed to refer to most periods of time where movements are able to contend more effectively, including drops in repression, extensions in franchise, elite vulnerability, or any other such moment on which organizers might capitalize. This process of conceptual expansion has been subject to criticism by both practitioners and detractors of political process theories.[43]

As work on opportunity structures gathered steam, a corresponding interest in the sociopolitical threats arose. Rather than considering threat to be solely a dampener on political opportunities, research on the subject has concluded that "a group may also decide to risk protest, even if opportunities seem absent, if the costs of not acting seem too great,"[44] such as in the context of looming future repression or when a conflict is forcefully escalated by a radical flank.[45] In contrast to the organizational dynamics of long-running political opportunities, the impact of threat is often weighted by ordinary citizens who mobilize in the form of highly motivated groups of friends, neighbors, or coworkers.[46] Some scholars have even argued that for this reason threats constitute a *greater* mobilizing force than opportunities.[47]

Networks, Communication, and Communities

Alongside the development of political process theories came a recognition that models of mobilization focused around a single organizational core were deficient for understanding how the process took place. "Too often, movement scholars write as if persons are unambiguously in or out of a movement... like the difference between members and non-members in formal organizations," Doug McAdam bemoaned in a 1986 article.[48] Instead, McAdam argued that when carrying out particular acts of protest, movements drew from "supportive networks" that did not necessarily consist of formal members, but were nonetheless clearly involved with and possibly even occasional participants in movement activities.

Thirty-five years later research on social movement networks has shown that they serve as a pivotal means by which variably organized movements can mobilize affiliated nonmembers on a scale far greater than their clearly defined members. These theories have successfully empowered those studying social movements to understand how activists and organizers mobilize those to whom they are connected. As Roger Gould noted in his review of the field, they have established that "if there are obstacles standing between sympathizing and participating, or between feeling neutral and sympathizing, a social relationship with someone who is already a participant helps to overcome them."[49] Belonging to such a network was theorized to endow an individual with "structural availability," the likelihood that they will be personally exposed to a recruiting attempt.[50]

Network analysis offers us a means to understand how resources are acquired and utilized during protest in contexts where organizations are constrained or struggling.[51] So too can the study of networks elucidate how the peripheral activities of movements help to inculcate perspectives and practices, ranging from repertoires of contention to collective identities, even when movements may not appear active in the streets.[52] These various elements of networked movement activity help to sustain what Suzanne Staggenborg has termed "social movement communities," which bridge movement organizations with the broader "networks of individuals, cultural activities, institutional supporters and alternative institutions" that help to propel a given cause.[53] Sometimes these communities are highly visible and public facing, yet in other instances they remain, as it were, "submerged" or "latent." Such "submerged networks," in the parlance of Alberto Melucci, engage in cultural production and informational exchange, spreading new norms and crafting new collective identities that may be leveraged in collective action. They range from fragmented, loosely coordinated forms such as cultural "scenes," webs of radical friendship, and spaces of association to more unified hubs such as "local free radios, bookshops, magazines."[54]

At their broadest, networked analyses of movement activity can extend to the everyday networks of communication in which individuals participate or to which they are subjected, such as mainstream television, newspapers, and social media platforms. While, as Mario Diani[55] has rightly emphasized, mutual engagement with a communications network is not consensually understood by scholars to in itself constitute a "network tie," these networks are still very important for our understanding of mobilization. Although mainstream media communications networks in a given society are only very rarely fully aligned with social movements, certain nodes or sectors within them may still be either movement-affiliated or temporarily appropriated by movement activists.[56] This may result in sympathetic coverage, the promotion of movement contributors, and, in the case of social media platforms, increasing exposure to movement affiliates or sympathizers. Under these circumstances, movement propaganda, calls to action, or even full-blown recruitment pitches can reach a far wider audience than they might usually be expected to were a movement mobilizing only organizationally brokered networks.[57] Even under circumstances in which a movement is not itself leveraging a wider communications network, certain shared networks may nonetheless help to create mediated contact between individuals and movements that promote the formation of further network ties.[58] Indeed, all three of the contemporary cases in this book involved communications networks drawing attention to movement activity or even—as in the case of Egypt in 2011—serving as a pivotal arena for publicizing protest events prior to the revolutionary period.

Culture, Shocks, and Disruptions

Intersecting with research on social movement networks and communications was a trajectory of research seeking to understand how cultural and moral factors encourage mobilization. Perhaps the most prominent outgrowth of this literature were social constructionist theories, which explain how movements actively reframe social reality as part of the mobilization process, most famously found in the work of Robert Benford and David Snow.[59] Herein, movement activists play a role as "signifying agents actively engaged in the production and maintenance of meaning," in competition or concert with other actors such as "the media, local governments, and the state,"[60] capitalizing on an array of "cultural"[61] and "discursive opportunity structures"[62] just as they might political opportunities. Shifts in framing may be carefully planned and executed by movement or nonmovement actors, they may be coincidental, or they may arise due to external factors, diffusing through interpersonal, spatial, and informational networks such as newspapers, television, and social media.[63]

Framing plays a crucial role in the mobilization process by giving "meaning to... relevant events and conditions in ways that... mobilize potential adherents and constituents, to garner bystander support and to demobilize antagonists."[64] These "motivational frames... function as prods to action," by promoting a certain interpretation of the situation at hand and ideas about how the world is or should be.[65] The rapidity and force of the mobilizing "prods" experienced by individuals can, in some circumstances, be very substantial indeed, as demonstrated by the power of "moral shocks."

Moral shocks constitute unexpected developments that evoke, as James Jasper's research on this topic puts it, "such a sense of outrage in a person that she becomes inclined toward political action, with or without the network of personal contacts" connecting the individual to a movement.[66] In these circumstances, participants' moral attitudes are galvanized in such a way that they actively seek out a given cause or spontaneously participate in political action. These are not the only kinds of serious shocks that can disrupt ordinary patterns of activity, as evidenced by Snow and colleagues' seminal study of "quotidian disruptions." Quotidian disruptions constitute situations (rather than frames) where "the taken-for-granted routines and attitudes of everyday life" collapse, arising from phenomena such as disasters, breaches of the social contract, resource crises, and shifts in social control.[67] Under these circumstances, the potential for people to participate in collective action may be dramatically amplified or suppressed by sudden or profound alterations to the status quo.[68]

Psychology, Identity, and the Individual

Alongside developments in the rest of the social sciences, social psychologists have conducted considerable work on movement participation and mobilization, drawing on experimental studies and large-scale social surveys. This work has returned to classical questions of collective behavior with a vigor and rigor far beyond that seen a half century ago. A variety of fine-grain models designed to account for individual-level participation decisions compete for dominance in the field. Many prioritize a single factor, such as research into the role of social identities in collective action,[69] the conducive effect of perceived injustice in mobilization processes,[70] and the role played by participants' perceptions of collective efficacy.[71]

A particularly well-established outgrowth of this literature among psychologists alone is the social identity model of collective action (SIMCA), established by Martijn van Zomeren and colleagues. While accounting for all three of the factors highlighted above, SIMCA posits social identity as the overarching variable in the mobilization process. In order for social identity to effectively trigger participation, there should also be sufficient levels of mediating "group-based emotions that bridge the gap between the perception of injustice and action... channeling broad social identities into more specific protest organizations."[72] Sociologists and political scientists such as Sheldon Stryker and colleagues have also sought to build upon social identity theories to emphasize how "shared beliefs about membership, boundaries and activities of a social movement held by movement members" can support or frustrate the organizers' mobilization efforts and activist involvement.[73]

The social identity approach tells us that where people strongly identify with a group that sees itself to be disadvantaged and capable of achieving social change, efforts to organize protests will occur. For group members, this is especially common when improving one's personal conditions appears futile without broader-reaching social change in the group's favor. People can also identify with groups other than their own, for example, by means of a common value system, a sense of solidarity, moral obligation or commonality, and other such psychological umbrellas.[74] In less organized instances of mobilization, however, the role of social identity can sometimes take a back seat. Researchers have noted that when we examine "collective protest and other socio-political schisms, such as... [2011] Tunisia, Egypt, and Libya," perceptions of injustice appear to play a greater role than social identity.[75] Other studies have instead foregrounded alignment between participant attitudes and causes, showing that its absence can sometimes invert the effect of social identity, making it predictive of opposition rather than support.[76] Psychological research on collective action thus points us to a trio of dispositional factors that result in positive participation decisions: a social identification with the aggrieved group, perceptions of injustice arising from relative deprivation, and attitudes that are aligned with the cause in question. Yet social psychologists do not claim to have all the answers. Rather, they maintain that, in the words of Katie Corcoran and colleagues, "a macro–micro link is needed to fully account for collective action," one that must "consider both social-psychological and objective structural effects."[77]

To this end, Bert Klandermans and Jacquelien van Stekelenburg's work on "contextualizing contestation" provides some highly useful directions for the integration of psychological and sociological factors. For Klandermans and colleagues, the metaphor of supply and demand (borrowed from the study of market economies) is a useful way to bridge these two elements:

> The demand side of protest refers to the proportion of the population in a society that sympathizes with the cause. The supply side of protest refers to the opportunities for protest offered to people. If there is no supply of protest, the demand might be high but nothing will happen. If, on the other hand, there is no demand there is no point in offering opportunities to protest. Mobilization is the mechanism that brings demand and supply together.[78]

Within Klandermans's supply/demand model, the mobilization process involves both the activities of organizers and the psychology of participants. First, people must sympathize with a movement. Second, they must "have been the target of mobilization attempts."[79] Third, they must possess sufficient motivation to participate, *and* fourth they must elect to actually do so.

Social psychological explanations for mobilization offer a variety of different, highly useful models of mobilization with attention to the role of efficacy, perceived injustice/grievances, identity, and sympathetic attitudes. However, despite a revival of dialogue between psychologists and other social scientists and promising novel research, much remains uninvestigated. Most pertinently, as Klandermans and van Stekelenburg have rightly noted, there remains an urgent need to "move from static decontextualized explanations of protest to more dynamic, contextualized models," grounded in the way that "the subjective experience of meso- and macro-level factors" actually play out.[80]

The Missing Pieces

For all that we know about mobilization, there is still a great deal that remains occluded. Work in the political process tradition has revealed much about how organized groups mobilize in accordance with the structure of political opportunities, but the approach remains grounded, as McAdam once put it, "on the assumption that movements only emerge over a long period of time in response to broad social, economic and political processes that afford insurgents a certain structural potential for collective action."[81] In this understanding, "participants are distinguished from nonparticipants on the basis of their greater integration into the established organizations" of a given community.[82] But what about when our unit of analysis is precisely those participants who lie beyond established groups?

Some former proponents of political opportunity theories have suggested that the notion of "opportunity" can be redeployed as a less heavily structured or organizer-centric concept. Tarrow, in his *Power in Movement*, advocated a shift away from traditional political opportunity theories to the more dynamic consideration of the "not necessarily formal or permanent ... dimensions of the political struggle that encourage people to engage in contentious politics."[83] These kinds of opportune situations might well be expected to have an impact on individuals' behavior comparable to the role played by threats in past popular mobilization processes.[84] Similarly, Neil Fligstein and Doug McAdam in their *Theory of Fields*[85] have advocated for greater attention to be paid to the "collective attribution" of opportunities and threats, rather than discrete structures of political opportunity per se, developing on an approach to mobilization set out by McAdam, Tarrow, and Tilly in the *Dynamics of Contention* paradigm.[86] Accounting for these more plural notions of opportunity invites us to move beyond the constraints of political opportunity theories and consider opportune conditions for mobilization from a more bottom-up perspective. On the one hand, certain sociopolitical contexts can play a structural role in accelerating the mobilization of individuals beyond the reach of movement networks, enhancing the chance that they will mobilize; on the other, certain frames can serve to encourage the widespread attribution of opportunities, threats, or other mobilizing constructions of reality. Even some physical spaces can vastly improve the prospects of successful participation.

Research on social movements' broader communities and networks certainly goes a long way to furnishing us with an enhanced view of mobilization, broadening the picture from the organizationally integrated to the more loosely connected. Even so, despite the advantages of a networked approach to mobilization, there are evidently pathways to participation which do not rely on network ties, and network theorists are acutely aware of this.[87] Florence Passy, in her analysis of two environmental social movements, the Bern Declaration and the World Wildlife Fund (WWF), found that only "about 59% of the Bern Declaration members and 49% of the WWF members were [i.e., became] connected to the organization" through any form of social tie.[88] When these criteria were tightened only to formal networks, figures fell to 5 and 23 percent, respectively. Likewise, a recent major test of the structural availability hypothesis in the specific context of mass mobilization could "not find any support for structural availability... [or] that people with higher levels of protest participation are more likely to hear about a demonstration through closed communication channels."[89] Similarly, a large-scale cross-national and cross-issue comparison of protests in Europe found that popular participants are "far more mobilized through 'open' mobilization channels like mass media, or friends and family, and far less by movements' mobilization efforts or organizational involvement."[90] Something else, beyond organizations and networks, appears to have also been at play in these cases.

Political process approaches to social movements have shown how movements are able to use formal organizational structures in order to mobilize their own members, and movement-network perspectives have demonstrated how affiliated individuals or groups in a movement network can converge around particular protests. But despite all this incredibly worthwhile and productive research, we are still left wondering about those who are not a part of any clearly defined movement network but nonetheless partake in mobilization. What of the Egyptian and French revolutionaries who ranged from young to old, middle class to impoverished, and city dweller to rural villager? What of the Occupiers of Zuccotti Park who involved apolitical painters, curious residents, visitors from across the world, and participants from political ideologies across the spectrum? What of the manifold Americans who took to the streets amid a deadly pandemic for an uprising in support of Black lives and against police brutality?

Cultural theorists of social movements have long clamored for renewed theoretical development in order to address situations where present perspectives cannot fully explain mobilization. As James Jasper put it in a review of the field, what the study of mobilization needed was "a theory of action," which considered "the [individual] microfoundations of social and political action" and built "from the micro-level to the macro-level in a more empirical way."[91] But where might we begin? The role of collective action frames in shaping mass behavior is certainly likely to play an important part in such a theory. So too are the dynamics of "quotidian disruptions" and "moral shocks," through which individuals are spurred to participate in movements by means other than networked outreach.[92]

There is also certainly much of value in psychological work on the topic of social protest. As van Stekelenburg and Klandermans note in their review[93] of the field, psychological analysis is ripe for combination with a (more sociological) analysis of the role of sociopolitical contexts in initial decisions to participate in collective struggles, an endeavor that I very much embrace in this book. Klandermans's own work on "mobilization potential," despite explicitly restricting itself to the category of "targeted sympathizers," has certainly helped us to understand how psychological dynamics interact with movements' own resources, framing activities, and capacity to generate protests.

Despite the excellent potential offered by work on the social psychology of mobilization, our present fusion of psychological and sociological research on social movements still favors a general assumption about agency in the mobilization process, namely, that mobilization is authored or enacted in the same way as a product might be marketed. Activists and organizers produce protests for which they leverage their resources to attract customers. In line with a marketized metaphor of demand and supply, mobilization is conceived of as a process in which "movement entrepreneurs" cultivate demand for certain protests or other collective actions and satiate that demand by supplying protests.[94] Unaffiliated demonstrators, by contrast, display differential participation behaviors than those within the orbit of a movement,[95] and those circumstances where "very little is needed to bring large numbers onto the streets" and protests arise "with minimal organization... [or] in the absence of any form of organization" remain very much a topic where "there are more questions than answers."[96]

If we are to revisit the agency of participants, where might we go from here? One route would be to reconsider collective behavior theories and retrieve their more valuable elements. The notion of convergence, for example, is ripe for more in-depth analysis and development, something I endeavor to offer in this book.[97] Much of this literature, however, proceeds from inaccurate first principles, namely, that "mass movements are not looking for pragmatic solutions to... any kind of problem" but instead are reflective of perverse and "deep-seated psychological tendencies."[98] It is thus an unfortunate reality that, while the problem of collective behavior remains pressing and important, the solutions offered by classical theorists are of limited utility today.

A comparatively promising direction is to reconsider the virtue of rational choice theories, picking up where Opp, Oberschall, and others left off in their analyses of spontaneity in the 1989 German Revolution. Some recent scholarship, such as Kira Jumet's sophisticated study of ordinary Egyptians' participation in protest between 2011 and 2013, has convincingly demonstrated the utility of doing so.[99] But might there still be more to spontaneous protest than the reintroduction of rational choice alongside political process theories? Even those who sought to apply the rational choice model to the German Revolution felt that more was needed, recommending that we instead develop "a new model of spontaneous mobilization," with attention paid not only to processual factors and rational action, but to "collective identities, moral and emotional dimensions of protest, and the informal structure of mobilization."[100]

Despite all that we do know about mobilization, we remain without an aggregate theory of mass action that bridges individual microfoundations and larger-scale social conditions to explain why those beyond movement organizations or networks spontaneously join mass mobilizations. The theory I develop in this book—affinity-convergence theory—seeks to address some part of this lacuna by building on the considerable corpus of what we know about mobilization and placing it in dialogue with the empirical evidence, triangulating the analysis of small-scale personal participation and large-scale sociopolitical shifts. The next chapter develops and explains this theory in depth. The parts that follow display the evidence that built it: a comparison of four highly different cases, all united by the phenomenon of spontaneous participation. I hope that what I offer will help make the puzzle of mobilization a little more complete.

CHAPTER TWO

Affinity-Convergence Theory

More often than not, the process of mobilization concerns organized forces. As we saw in chapter 1, these forces, whether revolutionary cadres, traditional social movement organizations, or movement entrepreneurs situated within wider social movement communities, are generally regarded as the principal agents in the mobilizing process. They make strategic and tactical decisions that compel, convince, or coerce people within their reach to participate in collective actions, drawing on their various skills, resources, and networks to do so.[1] This is why questions about mobilization often concern how movement organizers and activists use their resources, repertoires, networks, and strategies to mobilize participants.

Sometimes—and usually on quite pivotal occasions—people mobilize, but organized forces are caught by surprise. Such was the case in 2011, when protesters from Egypt to New York flooded city squares of their own accord; such was the case in 2020, when, despite being instructed to stay at home, ordinary Americans ventured out amid a deadly pandemic in support of Black lives and against police brutality; and in 1789, when radicalized French townspeople seized control of their country's fate in the first modern revolution. If we are to understand these momentous periods of world history, the many others like them, and those yet to come, we must begin from premises other than that organized forces mobilized people.

What if we turn this working assumption about participation on its head? What if, instead of tracing how causes mobilize people, we examined how people mobilize *for* causes? As we saw in chapter 1, classical theorists of collective behavior long entertained the notion that there might be certain social and psychological traits that could predispose people toward participation in protest, without the need for organizations or networked recruitment, in a moment of convergence. Working predominantly within the limitations of what has since been termed "armchair theorizing," collective behavior theorists made little further progress on this problem,[2] leaving open questions of how this so-called convergence took place and what the predisposing factors could be beyond irrationality or disorder.

A huge improvement on the collective behavior paradigm can be seen in the work of rational choice theorists, who begin with the assumption that people "do what they *think* is best for them [emphasis added]" according to a wide array of incentives and beliefs spanning social, moral, and economic factors.[3] As we saw in chapter 1, this perspective has offered a very important contribution to what we know about mobilization. However, rational choice approaches are concerned only with conscious decisions to participate in protest. Rational actor approaches can tend to neglect the *unchosen* elements of individual participation in protest, and the dynamics through which these elements operate are hard to recover if we only attend to satisficing behavior. For example, there exists a considerable array of factors that determine *how* individuals get into the position of being able to choose to participate in the first place. There are also numerous circumstances where people's decisions about whether to participate or their degree of participation are overridden by social circumstances that force their hand. To attend to these kinds of scenarios, it is necessary to take stock of both contingency and agency in human behavior.

It is here that we can turn to the life's work of Albert Bandura, whose experiments in the study of human agency led him to conclude that participants in any collective action must be regarded as having done so as "self-organizing, proactive, self-regulating, and self-reflecting" agents, responding to a series of different opportunities and fortuitous encounters yet constrained by the conditions of their everyday lives (a so-called social cognitive approach to human agency).[4] In contrast to theories of collective behavior and rational action, from Bandura's perspective participating in what we now call "contentious politics" is simply one of many competing paths any individual might choose to pursue, mediated by how conducive their personal traits and social conditions are to their doing so. His research found that mass behavior arises both through agents' conscious pursuit of incentives and through other social and psychological factors beyond the scope of their informed decision-making heuristics. These other factors predispose people to come into contact with a cause or group and so determine who is in a position to elect to join in.

Treating those who join spontaneous mass mobilizations as self-aware agents nonetheless circumscribed by their social and psychological traits allows us to reframe the mystery of collective behavior as a more approachable question of aggregate behavior. Whether any one individual comes to participate in a cause depends on what we might call their *affinity* to it:

the extent to which they possess a spectrum of personal traits (*affinities*) that predispose them toward the cause. Whether many people come to do so depends on how widespread these traits are in society. Whether an especially large number come to do so further depends on the *convergence* of favorable social conditions that allow a substantial proportion of the population to more easily act on these predispositions. I call this framework affinity-convergence theory.

$$\text{Affinity} \xrightarrow{convergence} \text{Participation}$$

Affinity-convergence theory dissects the problem of spontaneous mass mobilization, first tackling the issue of predisposition to participate in a cause (*affinity*), then tackling the problem of how shifts in social conditions can encourage people to act on these predispositions (*convergence*). In what follows, I explain *affinity* and *convergence* in detail, before detailing how they operate in concert.

Affinity

While social scientists have seldom used the term,[5] activists have deployed the concept of affinity[6] for the better part of a century, with the term's origins generally traced to anarchist organizing in prelude to the Spanish Civil War. The core tenet of affinity is that participants in causes generally "have something in common" outside of the organizational context "that is bringing [them] all together."[7] In the experiences of activist groups, it is often these commonalities, rather than adherence to organizational strictures, that form the basis of effective, enduring, and committed collaboration among participants in protest.

Activists most commonly use the concept of affinity to create affinity groups: autonomous groups formed on the basis of a wide spectrum of shared traits. In Spain in the 1920s, and later during the civil war, these tended to be formed on the basis of a shared workplace, social circle, or neighborhood, as well as emerging from common religious, literary, and political persuasions. When the concept spread to the United States in the 1970s, affinity groups often emerged around shared sexuality, place of education, and ethnicity.[8] More recently, affinity groups have been formed on the basis of an even wider spectrum of common dispositions. For example, during the 1991 Australian International Defense Exhibition (AIDEX) protest, affinity groups included Alcoholics Against the Bomb (an affinity group of alcoholics), the Perseverance Affinity Group (who, conversely, had all met at the same local pub), Screaming Trees (an affinity group of environmentalists), and the Aboriginal Bukra-bendinni Action Tribe.[9] Today many affinity groups forgo formal names and meetings altogether, existing as group conversations via email, text messaging, or encrypted communications platforms, as seen in the case of self-proclaimed affinity groups formed during the 2020 Black Lives Uprising.

Since its radical Spanish anarchist origins, the notion of affinity has also spread to the business world, where managers have supported the growth of "affinity networks," through which employees are encouraged to get to know others with whom their life experiences intersect. A plethora of companies from Motorola to McDonald's foster corporate affinity networks grounded in areas as diverse as race/ethnicity, gender, sexuality, age, skills, disability, job role, family type, military veterancy, living area, and religion.[10] Indeed, though once confined to activist circles, the notion of affinity has now become something we deploy in our everyday patterns of organizing, in corporate life as much as in protest.

A discernible link between affinity and mass mobilization first became apparent during my conversations with Occupy Wall Street activists in New York, who used the term to explain how they became involved in the movement's first popular assemblies. Without any organizational framework undergirding most of these initial meetings, the majority of those who showed up "were meeting each other for the first time," drawn to the movement on the basis of "affinities... from previous work."[11] As they pieced together plans for an attempted Wall Street occupation, the movement's earliest participants discovered that even though they did not know each other, they had lived their lives "in similar circles": some had come of age as student activists, others had long histories in radical labor unions, and still others had cut their teeth protesting New York City's many trade summits. These factors, in turn, predisposed them to spend their precious weekend evenings on the south side of New York City's Tompkins Square Park, with a few handfuls of other people, trying to work out what it would actually mean to "Occupy Wall Street."

The conditioning role of affinity is far from unique to the formation of protest groups. Studies on self-directed social networking have observed that even seemingly banal affinities between people can have a conditioning impact on their choices of social activity. In a yearlong experiment, Matthew Scott Smith and colleagues[12] created a small online community in which participants could give information on various personal attributes, ranging from handedness to profession, subject interests, restaurant choices, and even their preferred pizza toppings. Even when the participants in the study were unaware of the "loosely defined affinities... such as shared interests, hobbies, political views [and] preferences," which they had with others, their socializing decisions were nonetheless underpinned by them.[13]

The more I investigated the dynamics of the mass mobilizations that make up this book, the more I became convinced that affinity played a vital role in them. As my fieldwork led me away from the lifestyle activists of Occupy's early days and on to the lived experiences of the many otherwise ordinary people who participated in the movement, I began to realize that the concept of affinity was in fact pivotal to understanding their participation. This realization was only reinforced when I considered the lives of the Egyptian and French revolutionaries and the experiences of protesters in the 2020 Black Lives Uprising. Many activists lead a life enmeshed in organized political groups, radical social networks, or social movement communities, all of which are liable to pull them into a new conflict or cause at any moment. Ordinary people do not share these attributes. Although they might harbor political sympathies or radical inclinations, the organizational and networked landscape of their lived experience is, if anything, usually proscriptive of participation in protest.[14] While well-resourced and well-organized groups may sometimes attempt to forcefully permeate this landscape and obtain some new recruits, doing so is a serious exertion compared with appealing to the networks in which they are already embedded.[15] Rather, when ordinary people spontaneously descend en masse on the scene of contention, they tend to do so of their own accord, possibly even in defiance of the organizations, networks, and institutions that condition their daily lives.[16] The different affinities that underpin participation are thus central to understanding why and how they came to be there.

How might we draw all of this together and conceptualize affinity in the context of contention? In both activist and popular parlance, affinity generally constitutes a common ground between people that predisposes them to come together: shared practices, attitudes, places of living, identities, and so on. Things are broadly similar when we translate this concept to the level of an entire cause, whether a riot, revolution, occupation, or protest. Causes are composed of a large number of individuals as well as more or less clearly identifiable groups, each of which can be tied to places, ideologies, repertoires, activities, and so on.[17] Because of causes' broad scope, the potential points of intersection between an individual and a cause are more substantial than those that might occur between individuals alone. Thus, affinity to a cause might also entail living near the site of a mass mobilization, being available at the time, having certain skills or passions that the movement encourages or requires, and having the necessary resources or social status to permit participation.

36 | THEORIZING MOBILIZATION

■ Organized Groups

■ Supporting Networks

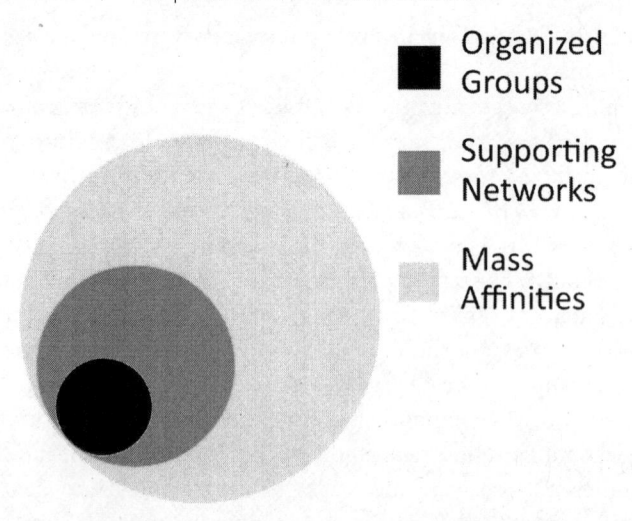

■ Mass Affinities

FIGURE 2.1. A concentric representation of mobilization avenues.

In view of the variety of factors that can lead to participation, *affinity* is broadly defined herein as having a predisposition to participate in a cause. I dissect this broad predisposition into specific *affinities*: the social and psychological factors that predispose people to participate. Because of its nature as mere predisposition, affinity to a cause is of course much more common than being part of an organized group or movement network. Yet, the comparative ubiquity of different affinities between individuals and causes is undercut by the fact that affinities alone are in no way a guarantor of mobilization. They are on their own simply indicative of the potential for spontaneous participation should the optimum conditions arise. This is depicted in figure 2.1, in which organizational membership, membership of networks, and affinities are represented in a Venn diagram. The size of each circle represents the maximum mobilizing constituency of each relationship, while the opacity represents the ordinary likelihood of a given individual participating.

The organized core of participants in a contentious episode—such as the (traditionally conceived) social movement organization (SMO)—are shown in black. These are dependable participants, substantially involved in a cause and highly likely to turn out. On the outskirts of this organized core, the middle circle represents broader movement networks. These are individuals who, although not part of an organized group per se, are networked with the group and supporting institutions or otherwise relationally integrated with the cause in some way, such as through a movement's submerged networks[18] or broader communities.[19] They are thus relatively easily recruited and likely to mobilize. By contrast, the outermost circle represents those participants who, despite not being members of the organized core or of supporting networks, possess the predisposition to participation, which I call affinity.[20] While they may be far more numerous than those with networked or organizational ties, they are usually highly unlikely to participate.

I have mentioned that affinity to a cause can be both social and psychological in origin. The social dimensions of affinity comprise the factors that predispose people to participate in a cause by biographical consequence. While potentially imaginable social affinities are legion, I found that the most influential social affinities across the four cases in this book generally belonged to one of four categories: patterns of activity, social status, resources, and obligations. By contrast, the psychological dimensions of affinity comprise those factors that predispose people to consciously seek to participate in or make contact with a given cause. Contrary to the claim that riotous, revolutionary, and protest participation appeals to the disordered or psychologically disturbed,[21] the psychological affinities that proved most common across the cases in this book were three core dispositional factors: social identity, perceived injustice, and attitudinal alignment. Along with these factors was the role played by other psychological drives: the various interests and needs that individuals seek to pursue that are extricable from contentious politics.[22]

SOCIAL AFFINITIES

Social affinities refer to an individual or group's conditions in the social world: their patterns of activity, social status, resources, and obligations. In comparison to psychological affinities, the role played by particular social affinities is often contingent and contextually dependent. Certain causes may draw heavily upon participant resources, while others might more readily appeal to people's everyday obligations. Causes may also differ with respect to the particular social statuses with which they are compatible. Similarly, causes that occupy a prominent urban space or disrupt the flow of everyday life will intersect with individuals' patterns of activity far more than those that are less disruptive in nature. Table 2.1 shows the four most prominent categories of social affinities borne out across my research on the Egyptian Revolution, Occupy Wall Street, the 2020 Black Lives Uprising, and the 1789 French Revolution. In what follows, I discuss each category in turn.

Table 2.1 Categories and Examples of Social Affinities

AFFINITIES	EXAMPLES
Patterns of activity	Jobs; pastimes; duties; residence; media exposure
Social status	Race; class; unemployment; gender; age; (dis)ability
Resources	Wealth; information; transport; tools
Obligations	Necessity of (+): eating; sleeping; security Absence of (−): child-rearing; long work hours

Patterns of Activity

Sometimes participating in a riot, revolution, or protest is simply a matter of being in the right place at the right time. The contexts in which people live, work, and elect to spend their time (whether physically or digitally) has a substantial impact on their likelihood of encountering and pursuing an opportunity for protest.[23] Patterns of activity concern exactly these kinds of factors: the structure of participants' everyday lives. When future Egyptian revolutionaries arrived at their regular Friday prayer sessions on January 28, 2011, many were not expecting to spend the day dodging bullets and clashing with the security forces. Perhaps unbeknownst to them, key mosques in Cairo were the intended starting points for marches to the city's Tahrir Square. Emerging from Friday prayers, it became all too easy to be swept up in the momentum and join the crowds descending on Tahrir. Likewise, when ordinary Parisians' daily routines led them across the city's Pont Neuf bridge—somewhere many were prone to cross several times a day—it was only a matter of time before some of them were swept into the revolutionary bands that also gathered there. So too in 2020 when the inhabitants of city blocks rocked by protests, occupations, and armed repression transformed, regardless of their own wishes, into participants in resistant and insurrectionary projects against the police and in support of Black lives.

Patterns of activity may also be digital in nature, something we are all especially aware of in the aftermath of the COVID-19 outbreak. One especially important form of digital activity is media consumption and engagement. While communications scholars have drawn attention to the way in which these patterns of activity can promote the formation of new network ties, they can also directly contribute to individual participation without the need for a prior movement tie.[24] Social and legacy media platforms can convey important information about a mobilization in progress by restaging events in the form of reportage, educating people about movement repertoires and plans, and conveying information about the kinds of participation available to people.[25] Someone exposed to footage of an ongoing protest in their city is liable to discover the location of the protest, the identity of the cause, and the kind of activity protesters are involved in—in other words, sufficient information to participate if one wished to.

Social Status

Supplementing the role played by patterns of activity is social status: the collection of factors that determine not only what an individual's options in life are likely to be but also what the likely outcomes of those options are. This entails factors such as one's class position, race, gender, age, and profession. Elements of social status serve to determine the institutional context of an individual's decision-making, which in turn structures and conditions their capacity to defy the dominant order.[26] Depending on the context of mobilization, an individual's social status can have a powerful effect on potential participation.[27] At the tail end of Egypt's revolutionary period, for example, it became unsafe for young women to go to large protests due to the danger of rape and sexual violence. Conversely, earlier in the revolution, Egyptian taxi drivers and downtown workers whose lives had been upended by the country's revolutionary process found themselves with an abundance of free time and consequently became a notable contingent of Tahrir protesters.

Resources

Just as movement organizations rely on their resources for effective mobilization, the same can be said of individuals. Personal resources are crucial in determining the capacity of potential participants to access, encounter, or otherwise participate in instances of mass mobilization.[28] Simple matters such as knowing about an action, being able to travel to it, and being able to risk arrest are determined by one's material and socio-organizational resources.[29] For example, when disruptions to the internet and censorship of official news plagued the early days of Egyptian revolutionary mobilization, access to satellite television was a highly advantageous resource for potential participants in Egypt's revolution wanting to discover more about the situation in Tahrir Square.

Possessing specific resources that a given cause requires can also condition people's opportunities for participation. The "Wall of Dads"—a litany of fathers in Portland, Oregon, who in July 2020 poured onto the city streets wielding leaf blowers—could not have done so if they did not possess a very particular resource. Similarly, those who participated in the early phase of the Occupy Wall Street protests—before the movement was financially self-sustaining—needed not only the resources to travel into Manhattan (sometimes from across or even outside the country) but also access to equipment, such as tents and blankets, and support in case of arrest.

Obligations

In contrast to resources, obligations constitute the everyday necessities that shape people's lives. The structure of an individual's obligations can produce affinity to a given cause in two distinct ways. First, an absence of competing obligations can predispose individuals to participate in mobilization. This is broadly reflected by the notion of "biographical availability," pioneered by Doug McAdam. For McAdam, biographical availability constituted the "absence of personal constraints that may increase the costs and risks of movement participation, such as full-time employment, marriage, and family responsibilities."[30]

While the factors McAdam entails in his work on biographical availability indeed often serve as barriers to participation, there are also other times where certain obligations instead serve as potential avenues through which one might come to mobilize for a cause. The presence of certain obligations can, when catered for or appealed to by a cause,[31] provide a powerful impetus for potential participation. Some of the most basic obligations are matters of nutrition, shelter, and security. It was no surprise, then, that food being handed out in Egypt's Tahrir Square and New York's Zuccotti Park proved to be quite an attractive prospect, not only for the destitute and starving but also for the merely peckish or pennywise. So too did some Egyptian revolutionary protesters arrive in Tahrir on account of the occupied square offering a greater sense of safety than the relatively anarchic state of the Cairo outskirts, replete as they were with suddenly established armed "defense committees" passing summary judgment on the conduct of those who passed through. Such participants possessed a favorable matrix of obligations, lacking those that impeded participation and possessing others that encouraged it.

PSYCHOLOGICAL AFFINITIES

In contrast to social affinities, psychological affinities refer to an individual's dispositions and drives (see table 2.2). While dispositions constitute

Table 2.2 Categories and Examples of Psychological Affinities

SUBCATEGORY	AFFINITIES	EXAMPLES
Disposition	Identity	Political outlook; allyship; demographic traits
	Perceived injustice	Senses of social injustice or relative deprivation
	Attitudes	Tastes; ideology; moral values
Drives	Interests	Cooking; art; learning; law-breaking
	Needs	Affirmation; solidarity; efficacy; emotional outlet

the factors that substantially determine participants' conscious political choices to support a cause, drives refer to those factors that determine the compatibility of their less-political interests and psychological needs with that cause. The difference between these two subcategories of psychological affinity can prove rather important. Alignment between a movement and an individual's interests and needs can allow those who do not necessarily identify strongly with a movement or even enthusiastically support its outlook to pursue participation. Conversely, being strongly disposed toward a movement can encourage people to mobilize even when doing so seems otherwise unrewarding or harmful.

Disposition: Identity, Perceptions, and Attitudes

Even should circumstances align to shepherd an individual toward a contentious action, a great deal often rests on their actually choosing to participate (or, at the very least, not choosing not to).[32] This decision primarily involves three dispositional affinities: identity, perceived injustice, and attitudes. While these are each distinctly different factors, the relationship between them is nonetheless a strongly complementary one, and there is a consensus among psychological researchers that these three factors tend to influence and amplify each other.[33]

Psychological research on group formation has time and again shown that one of the most powerful predictors of individual behavior is the person's social identity.[34] When applied to collective action specifically, research by van Zomeren and colleagues has shown that social identity constitutes a "key predictor of collective action," directly influencing it as a means by which one emotionally connects with a given cause.[35] One example of the power of identity can be found in the case of those who mobilized for Occupy Wall Street under the banner of "the 99 percent." This very expansive identity category (juxtaposed against a small Wall Street elite) proved highly appealing to ordinary participants in the movement. As one Occupier, Kevin, quite plainly put it in one of our interviews: "The 99 percent—that was what was really motivating me." Joining Occupy thus came to constitute participating in "the national moment against Wall Street," a collective rebellion against an unjust elite.[36]

Alongside the role played by social identity, an individual's perceptions of injustice also constitute a key element in the mobilizing process. The mobilizing role played by perceived injustice was perhaps most prominently heralded in Ted Gurr's work on "relative deprivation"—the perceived discrepancy between "the goods and conditions of life to which people believe they are rightfully entitled" and "the goods and conditions they think they are capable of getting and keeping."[37] Many of the Egyptians I spoke to were especially keen to express how important a shared perception of injustice was for their own participation in the country's revolutionary upheaval. One such revolutionary, Yusha, spoke eloquently of how "the oppression that has been put on us united us."[38] Even when the specific conditions of oppression differed, he argued, it felt as if everyone "suffer[s] from the same issues." Indeed, current psychological models place perceived injustice among the two most important disposing factors for participation in protest.[39]

Beyond the role played by identity and perceptions of injustice in disposing people toward participation in protest, "attitudinal affinity" also plays an important role in individuals' participation decisions.[40] It is not enough that individuals should identify with a cause and perceive that their conditions are unjust; they should also find its general tastes, ideology, and moral propositions to be, on balance, agreeable to them. Where an individual's attitudes and those that characterize (rightly or wrongly) a given cause reach a state of alignment, an individual becomes more inclined to mobilize in its favor.[41] The 2020 protests in the United States, for example, show a profound alignment between the nominal aims of the protests and those who participated. On the weekend of June 6 and 7, 2020, 92 percent of protesters in New York and 94 percent of those in Los Angeles cited police brutality and the Black Lives Matter agenda as key motivations for their participation.[42]

Drives: Personal Interests and Needs

In most scenarios, even particularly extreme ones, people's minds are seldom solely occupied with matters of contentious politics. They instead spend their time engaging in their various interests and fulfilling their psychological needs. Causes that fulfill these varied personal drives offer soft incentives that may prompt people to mobilize for reasons other than those we might expect, and movements can appeal to different groups within society by catering to them.[43]

Though people's interests are often diverse, there is often also a surprising amount of regularity to them. For example, 54 percent of Americans have sufficient interest in music to list it as one of their hobbies, with a similar figure (52 percent) attending at least one live show in a typical year.[44] It is no wonder, then, that mere rumors of a Radiohead concert at Occupy Wall Street prompted the crowds in Zuccotti Park to swell to three times their normal size within a matter of hours.[45] Subtler effects are often seen in the way that causes appeal to other kinds of interests. Occupy's kitchen, for example, offered the opportunity for aspiring and established chefs alike to cook whatever they so desired, an opportunity to which even accomplished restaurateurs took with aplomb.[46] So too did the movement's banners, pageantry, and autonomous orientation offer an excellent chance for artists to try their hand at all manner of interesting projects.

Take, for example, the case of Rose, an artist living in Brooklyn who initially showed little interest in Occupy Wall Street (further discussed in chapter 8). Though generally sympathizing with Occupy's ideas, Rose did not strongly identify with the movement and had never participated in any serious forms of protest before. She thus turned down several opportunities to participate: a sympathetic disposition alone did not prove sufficient for mobilization. It was only when she heard about an opportunity to fulfill her personal drives—an Occupy-run art session that appealed to her interest in crafts and puppet making—that she felt a desire to participate in the movement. She eventually went on to become one of the most dedicated Occupy activists in the city.

In addition to the opportunity to pursue a wide variety of personal interests, participating in a cause can prove the avenue for the fulfillment of crucial psychological needs. The 2011 Egyptian Revolution provided just such an outlet. Long-running anger against the government had been repressed by a wall of fear erected by the regime's repressive apparatus. When the revolution began, this "fear wall," as one participant put it, "just dropped."[47] By joining revolutionary marches, rallies, and gatherings—some of which were specifically dubbed "days of rage"—ordinary Egyptians seized on the opportunity to finally vent feelings that had been impossible to express in public for a very long time. It is likewise no coincidence that, at the height of social isolation during the coronavirus pandemic, the massive *collective* actions that arose following the killing of George Floyd drew so many people, an apparent majority of whom came from outside the African American demographics to whom the protests seemed most existentially intertwined.[48] In the words of one participant, "We had been super fucking isolated... we had stayed inside and had lost *so* much.... Everything had been shut down, so there was really nothing else to do."[49]

The mobilizing role of drives is not always as pronounced as dispositions, likely owing to the fact that their impact is contingent on their being catered to by the cause in question. While a long-running occupation might provide many opportunities to pursue diverse interests (as was seen during the 2011 Occupy movement), riotous gatherings can instead prove an ideal opportunity to meet otherwise hard to sate psychological needs (as shown in the 2020 Black Lives Uprising in the United States). However, contentious causes are sometimes not so widely appealing. On these occasions, the role of psychological drives in the mobilizing process is likely to be less pronounced. This was shown in sharp relief when Occupy Wall Street was forcibly evicted from Zuccotti Park. Without libraries to borrow from, kitchens to eat at, and musical performances to attend, everyday participation in the movement soon ebbed away.

Convergence

In an everyday context, affinities tend to have only a kind of latent or gradual coaxing property in relation to participation in collective action. Indeed, studies have generally found that "[pre]disposition toward participation matters little if the individual lacks the structural contact to 'pull' him or her into protest activity."[50] In the context of spontaneous participation, such "pulls" arise not from organized recruitment, but from other causal elements, producing sudden moments of coalescence around a single action or brief periods of contention lasting only days or weeks. These conditions of convergence activate people's affinities en masse, catalyzing their participation in contention. They constitute the situations, frames, and spaces that encourage individuals with affinity to a cause to participate in some form.

In considering how such conditions of convergence operate, we can begin by drawing on what we already know about contentious politics. Research on the structure of opportunities and threats points to certain kinds of contextual developments and sets of social conditions that are more conducive to successful political challenges.[51] If this is true for organized movements, then why not for individuals? We can envisage, for example, a variety of opportunity that instead of empowering organized groups, simply makes it easier for individuals to participate in a cause. Alternatively, we could point to moments when collective emotions can shift in response to political events[52] and novel attributions are attached to the situation at hand.[53] Still further, as Benford and Snow[54] have advanced, a shift in how an act of contention is perceived might be conducive to new or different kinds of participation. Likewise, as Snow and colleagues have noted, there can exist "ecological and spatial contexts and constraints" and arrays of "quotidian disruptions," which alter the conditions of participation in emergent mobilizations.[55]

In thinking about how these kinds of changes in conditions can affect participation, we can define convergence as constituting the sociological conditions that trigger or accelerate the mobilization process among those with affinity to a cause. In thinking about convergence, we can employ two further distinctions. First among these is the division between **subtypes** of convergence. Sometimes, convergence takes the form of **opportunity**, in which protest becomes more possible than it once was. Other times, convergence appears as a more **exceptional** instance of freedom or autonomy, where conventional forms of social action can be disrupted. At still other times, convergence occurs as a more **paramount** kind of phenomenon, activating participation as a consequence of its sheer significance. Thus we can subdivide convergence into three distinguishable subtypes: **opportune**, **exceptional**, and **paramount**. Each has distinct qualities.

Convergence with an **opportune** component has the effect of making participation in a cause more likely to yield positive results and less likely to inflict costs. This could take the form of a collapse in state repression, an emergent belief that change itself was achievable, or even a particular location with strategic or protective properties.

Convergence with an **exceptional** component has the effect of making participation more available to those with affinity to a cause. This could take the form of a collapse of the everyday social structures that guide or control individual activity in a predictable manner. Alternatively, a breakdown of the established norms and rules of social conduct could give way to a general sense of permissiveness. Particular spaces of protest might also take shape with a free or autonomous character, making protest more inviting.

Finally, convergence with a **paramount** component occurs when ordinary incentive structures are overcome or overridden. This can take the form of a particular situation that made participation more palatable on the basis of different structural incentives, or a cognitive frame highlighting the importance of participation in a "historical moment"[56] or in response to a "moral shock."[57] Alternatively, this component can manifest

Table 2.3 Taxonomy of Convergence by Subtype and Context, with Descriptions

CONTEXT	SUBTYPE		
	Opportune	*Exceptional*	*Paramount*
Structural (Situation)	Breakdown of repressive apparatus or regime cohesion	Disruption to the limiting structures of social life	Structural incentives are reshaped or inverted
Cognitive (Frame)	Sense that success is possible and achievable	Normative breakdown, state of exception	Sense of obligation or compulsion
Physical (Space)	Safe or strategically advantageous locations	Free spaces and autonomous zones	Locations of great collective importance

in material spaces that are of distinct cultural, historical, or otherwise symbolic import.

Mediating the role played by the different subtypes of convergence is the **context** in which it occurs. Sometimes paramount, opportune, or exceptional conditions of convergence arise from structural factors. At other times, they owe their origins to the emergence or transformation of cognitive frames. They can even be generated by physical spaces and their features. All three of these contexts proved pivotal across the four cases discussed in this book. Accordingly, we can further divide convergence according to its context: **structural situations**,[58] **cognitive frames**, and **physical spaces** (see table 2.3).[59]

STRUCTURAL CONDITIONS OF CONVERGENCE (SITUATIONS)

Affinity for a particular cause can be activated by the emergence of structural conditions of convergence. These are shifts in the structure of society caused by the collapse or creation of oppressive or constraining powers, economic circumstances, and alterations to the institutions that shape people's everyday lives.

Just as social movement organizations and activists may capitalize on "political opportunities," so too do individuals seize on moments when the opportunity for contention becomes more appealing or apparent.[60] These **opportune situations** entail periods such as a breakdown of state or elite cohesion, a suspension or decline in social control or surveillance, a relaxation of the penalties or decline in the cost of participating in social protest, and a crisis or dissolution of legitimate authority.⁶¹ Two particularly prominent examples of the opportune situations featured in this book are the ousting of state security forces from the streets during Egypt's revolution and the forced relocation of the entire French government to Paris, rendering it vulnerable to intervention by even the most disorganized cohort of disgruntled citizens.

Other periods share some elements with the loosely theorized notion of convergence that appears in classical work on social movements: such as the collapse or alteration of established norms, rules, and organized life.⁶² We might generalize **exceptional situations** as times when conventional rules, personal constraints, and expectations are suspended and experiments in contention become more possible and attractive. One prominent example of an exceptional situation in this book comes in the form of the 2020 coronavirus pandemic, in the early stages of which people's lives and schedules were enormously disrupted, leaving a substantial mass of young, healthy people furloughed, unemployed, or working from home.

We might also envisage a moment so powerful that rather than being only a disruption to a status quo, it becomes a **paramount situation**, during which the impetus for participation is somehow inverted. In such moments of historical or cultural importance, the structural obligation to participate can trump lingering fears or concerns people might have.⁶³ Such feelings of importance can be inspired by an array of factors, but perhaps the most common is a sense of threat.⁶⁴ One such instance occurred in Egypt when brigades of mounted brigands charged into a peaceful protest in Tahrir Square, swinging swords at protesters and tossing Molotov cocktails into the crowds. This repression attempt backfired, raising the stakes of participation by increasing levels of threat. With the fate of the country at stake, and the prospect of President Hosni Mubarak's bloody vengeance on the horizon, scores of ordinary Egyptians poured forth into the streets to defend the revolutionary cause, remaining there for days to come.

COGNITIVE CONDITIONS OF CONVERGENCE (FRAMES)

The cognitive conditions of a society can radically change the kinds of groups or individuals who might be drawn to protest. Just as causes may seek to engage with and reframe social reality for their own purposes, they can also be *subject* to radical shifts in the framing of social life.⁶⁵ Cognitive conditions of convergence constitute those moments when new frames take hold of large parts of a society's cultural consciousness and thus spur people from inaction to mobilization.

Opportune frames are characterized by an emergent sense of collective efficacy: the perception that a contentious accomplishment is possible or achievable.[66] In some cases, a sense of collective efficacy might emerge in response to domestic or world events, though they can also be consciously presented as motivational collective action frames by organized agitators that explicitly attribute a specific set of opportunities to the situation at hand.[67] The "We Can" movements, such as the United Farm Workers (*Si Se Puede*), Barack Obama's 2008 presidential campaign (Yes We Can), and the Spanish movement-party *Podemos* offer clear empirical cases of movements with well-articulated opportune framing centered around a notion of collective efficacy and discrete, attributed opportunities. These movements were able to mobilize a great many individuals who were by no means integrated into union, party, or activist networks. In other cases, frames arise as a consequence of developments in the real world. For example, in 2020 in the United States an opportune frame emerged following exceptionally promising signals that indicated a willingness of local authorities to tolerate protests and make reforms (something that turned out to be a misalignment between framing and reality).

Another key driver of cognitive convergence is the shift in a society's framing of norms and rules. **Exceptional frames** occur when the conventional connotations of taking contentious action are reframed in the public consciousness. Dissent becomes permissible, and the appeal of conformity to the diktats of "good citizenship" is in some way undermined. This, in turn, encourages those who do not hold strong activist commitments to turn their mind to the question of mobilization. Even where individuals do not consider contentious mobilization to be particularly appropriate, exceptional frames lessen the cognitive barriers to participation. Such a frame took hold during the French and Egyptian revolutions, encouraging even those who were unlikely revolutionaries to nonetheless participate.

At other times, a confluence of certain historical or cultural conditions can prompt the emergence of **paramount frames**. Such occasions are described by Jeff Goodwin and Steven Pfaff in their study of emotions and social movements, noting how identifying the "historical importance" of a moment appeared to reduce participants fears about becoming involved.[68] Tunisia's revolution served as a trigger for the emergence of similar conditions in Egypt, with the prospective spread of revolution offering a sense of destiny and direction to the growing and emboldened acts of protest that had happened over the past decade. For participants in Occupy Wall Street, this took the form of wildfire excitement about the movement's national momentum and global spread—even in the absence of a clear agenda or demands. In revolutionary France, the ringing of the revolutionary *tocsin* and passionate calls to arms established a paramount frame by presenting participation as a response to a unique, sudden crisis. Yet another instance of paramount framing emerged in 2020 in the United States, with mainstream cultural commentators and news outlets framing the protests as not only in support of Black lives but also as part of an existential struggle against fascism.

PHYSICAL CONDITIONS OF CONVERGENCE (SPACES)

Convergence may sometimes arise from or in certain spaces. As research on social movement geographies and spatiality teaches us, physical conditions (spaces, their features, and the people who fill them) can sway the tide of riotous, revolutionary, and contentious struggles and serve as a source of energy for an otherwise less robust cause.[69] First among the physical conditions of convergence are **opportune spaces**, which offer enhanced potential for contention by insulating participants from the risks or disincentives related to mobilization. This can take the form of ambiguous or impaired legal jurisdiction, the presence of physical protection,[70] and unique access to opponents, allies, or resources.[71] Such conditions were found in Egypt's Tahrir Square at the height of the 2011 revolution. Many of the participants I spoke to even advanced that they felt safer in Tahrir than they did in their local neighborhoods. In revolutionary France, the privately owned *Palais-Royal*, a gathering space identified with much early agitation in the French Revolution, offered similar insulation from oppressive intervention, serving as a "sanctuary" for "the new social forces that had to be mobilized."[72]

Exceptional spaces are those in which individuals feel more able to freely participate in protest enacted outside of their own networks or groups. In their study of democratic social movements in the United States, Sara Evans and Harry Boyte[73] have labeled such physical contexts as "free spaces," while others have termed them "autonomous zones."[74] These are spaces where participating in collective action is not contingent on a particular identity, ideology, or form of social eligibility and serve as looser points of contact and coordination among those with affinity to a cause.[75] Zuccotti Park and Tahrir Square constituted exceptional spaces par excellence. They were venues in which dominant social norms and rules were lessened in favor of a more liberating environment. These spaces permitted potential participants' passions or interests to take on a newly politicized or contentious character, making participation more immediate, attractive, and rewarding. In the case of Occupy, this took the form of the politicization of daily life: as part of the occupation, it became possible to draw, paint, sing, cook, clean, and even disagree politically in a fashion that still constituted participation in the cause. This was superimposed upon the initially boring, administrative, undefined character of Zuccotti Park, allowing participation in its occupation to be a lower-risk, lower-cost, and arguably less-transgressive act.

In contrast to exceptional spaces, physical conditions of convergence might also take the form of **paramount spaces**, featuring explicitly ideological or predefined sites with a unique cultural or historical character. This might take the form of distinct spaces, strongly associated with a particular ideological, cultural, or historical notion with which a great many people strongly identify. Past research has found that spaces such as Karl Marx Square in Leipzig were prominently identified in the German Revolution of 1989 as sites whose existence undergirded "a tacit coordination of individuals occur[ring] without any necessity for organization or mobilization."[76] Tahrir Square enjoys a similar function in Egypt.[77] Such spaces can also be instituted temporarily during an episode of contention, due either to contingent phenomena beyond the control of movement protagonists or to the deliberate activities of activists.[78]

Affinity, Convergence, and Mass Mobilization

Just as we know that powerful movement organizations and activist networks can create substantial mobilizations in their own right, affinity-convergence theory helps us understand why profound instances of mass mobilization can happen amid the relative absence or impotence of these forces. When combined, widespread affinities and conditions of convergence serve as *sufficient conditions* for the occurrence of spontaneous mass mobilization. This process is, of course, in no way mutually exclusive with causes' other mobilizing activities, such as those undertaken by movement organizations and their supporting networks, and such entities still play important roles in otherwise spontaneous episodes of contention. Rather, affinity-convergence mobilization helps to explain why people beyond the reach of these groups spontaneously participate in protest, creating truly massive instances of popular action.

But how exactly does the interaction between affinity and convergence operate? The initial hurdle or necessary precondition for a less organized cause to effect spontaneous mass participation is the presence of widespread affinity to it. Psychologically speaking, this means that a substantial proportion of the relevant population should be positively disposed toward the cause in question, such as by identifying with the cause, desiring a remedy to the injustice it purports to challenge, or finding its outwardly identifiable values and aesthetics generally agreeable. Further psychological affinity can be attained with recourse to drives: the needs and interests to which a cause can cater. Yet psychology forms only one element of people's predisposition to participate in mobilization. Widespread social affinity to a cause also constitutes an important part of overall predisposition. Here, more specific factors matter. For example, is a mobilization conveniently located? Does it cater to any widely held interests? Does participation require resources that many people have or that only a select few possess? Is it only realistically possible to participate if one is of a certain social status? Such questions further delineate the segments of a population from which mass mobilization may occur.

The kinds of affinities to which a cause appeals can emerge, change, or dissolve over time according to the social and political fate of a given society, the activities of antagonists, and the behaviors of those who create, maintain, and alter the shape of a cause. They are thus not entirely static. Just as the Occupy Wall Street and Egyptian revolutionary movements appealed to a much larger set of affinities after they successfully occupied urban space, the 2020 uprising in the United States appealed to a more extensive array of affinities as it snowballed from an individual memorialization to being also an antiracism protest, a more general protest against police brutality, and later a more general protest against the governing regime. Conversely, affinities can also fall away, leading to the frustration of further potential for spontaneous mass mobilization, as seen in Egypt after the replacement of the Mubarak regime (see chapter 5) and in the case of Occupy Wall Street following the loss of Zuccotti Park (see chapter 8).

Taken on its own, however, affinity is only a weak force. While affinity alone might prompt a small number of people to drift toward a given cause, for mass mobilization to truly occur there needs to be a catalyst. This is the role played by convergence: the shifts in conditions that push people with affinity to a given cause to take action. By changing the circumstances of a given society, whether structurally, cognitively, or physically, conditions of convergence shepherd people with affinity to a given cause to actually take part, activating their various affinities in favor of participation. This functions like a kind of collective catalyst, or invitation as some of my interviewees put it, that usher hearts, bodies, and minds toward the prospect of participation, eschewing the need for formal or deliberate recruitment processes. Opportune, exceptional, and paramount conditions hold the potential to amplify the advantageousness, availability, and importance of participation such that people's dispositions, drives, and social affinities guide them toward participating.[79] We can see an illustration of this interaction in table 2.4.

Table 2.4 An Illustration of Different Subtypes of Convergence's Catalytic Effect on Affinities

PREDISPOSING FACTOR (AFFINITY)	CATALYST (CONVERGENCE)		
	Opportunity	*Exception*	*Paramountcy*
Psychological dispositions (identity, perceived injustice, attitudes)	Advantage for action in support	Lowered barriers to supportive participation	Necessity of acting in support
Psychological drives (needs, interests)	Advantage pursuing compatible needs or interests	Broadened appeal of participation beyond contention	Importance of the context meets interests or needs
Social affinities (patterns of activity, resources, obligations, social status)	Advantage to socially proximate participation	Increased social compatibility with a cause	Increased social necessity of participation

Though many conditions of convergence rely on external factors such as state breakdown or weakness, others can be created by already mobilized protagonists in a contentious episode. For example, activists' framing activities and the spaces of protest that they create can in their own right underpin processes of convergence. Thus, in the absence of prevailing factors, a small number of skilled actors can still create the conditions for a very large mobilization, even when they lack the resources of an organized movement. We will see precisely such an instance in part II. Conversely, a wide array of other factors and actors can bring convergence conditions to an end, frustrating further mobilization. This might take the form of a regime-led effort at a return to normalcy, as we saw in Egypt (chapter 5), or a shift from spontaneity to organization that supersedes convergence-based mobilization with more dependable mobilizing structures, as we saw in France (chapter 12). At still other times, the energy underpinning certain convergence conditions can dissipate thanks to novel shifts in situations, frames, and spaces arising from new concerns and events, as we saw during the Black Lives Uprising (chapter 10).

Affinity-convergence theory is designed to account for spontaneous mass mobilization by drawing out the common factors in individual trajectories. In aggregate, it can be said that the presence of substantial affinity among a population and the emergence of conditions of convergence are both necessary for this particular type of mass mobilization. When both of these necessary conditions are met, the catalyzation of widespread af-

Figure 2.2

	Social Affinities	
	Patterns of Activity	Resources
	Social Status	Obligations

	Psychological Affinities	
	Dispositions	Drives
	Identity	Interests
	Perceived Injustice	Needs
	Attitudes	

Context	Subtype		
	Opportune	Exceptional	Paramount
Structural	Opportune Situations	Exceptional Situations	Paramount Situations
Cognitive	Opportune Frames	Exceptional Frames	Paramount Frames
Physical	Opportune Spaces	Exceptional Spaces	Paramount Spaces

Affinity Predisposes → **Convergence** Catalyzes → **Mass Mobilization**

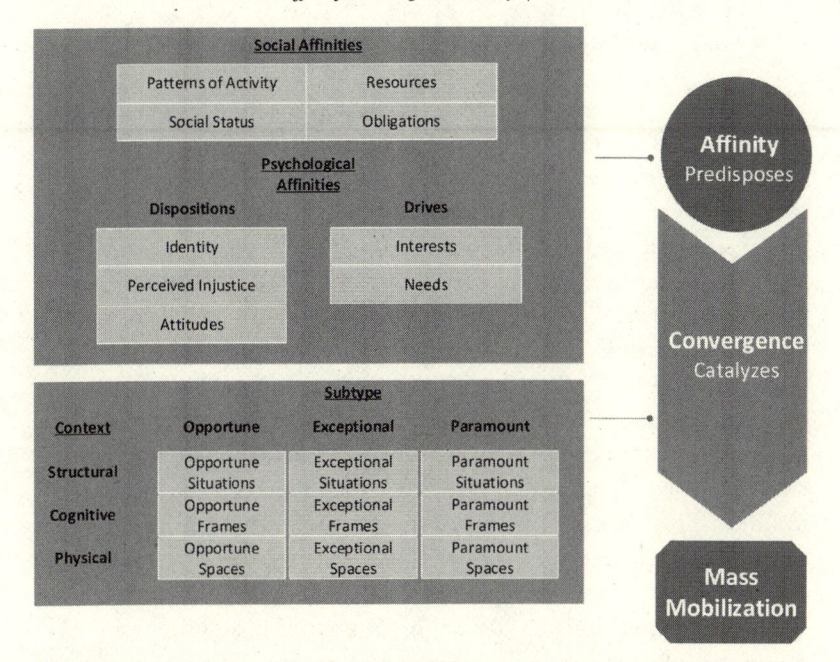

FIGURE 2.2. The overall interaction of affinity and convergence.

finities by conditions of convergence becomes sufficient for mass mobilization to occur (see figure 2.2). When they fall away, so too does the basis for spontaneous mass mobilization, as shown in the closing chapter of parts II–IV, which pays attention to how subtractive shifts in affinity and convergence had precisely this effect.

It may be tempting to use affinity-convergence theory in attempts to predict the behavior of an individual or small group. Attempting to do so rids the theory of much of its utility and can only be even contemplated with considerable caveats. First, it should be noted that, although convergence is a required catalyst for spontaneous *mass* mobilization, it is not strictly necessary for participation in the case of a single individual. Some participants may find their way to protest on the basis of other individual-level processes that are not significant in aggregate. Conversely, although the co-presence of affinity and convergence proves sufficient for mobilization at the mass level, it is not always a sufficient condition for participation at the individual level, owing to the possibility of highly individuated impediments to protest. This kind of microlevel "friction," as the philosopher of war Carl von Clausewitz put it, differentiates the subjective minutiae of the mobilization process from the way it functions in aggregate.[80]

Though I have so far presented affinity-convergence theory as part of a dialogue with existing work on mobilization and contentious politics, it is far from an exclusively bibliographic venture. The theory is, above all, a reflection of a wholeheartedly empirically led attempt to capture the intersection of social structures and individual agency in the midst of the hugely complicated process of unorganized mass mobilization. The model is thus derived from hundreds of hours of recorded and unrecorded interviews, extensive macrohistorical and archival research, ethnographic fieldwork, and careful comparison of common processes across highly different cases. Consequently, I would be remiss to declare the findings of this lengthy research process to be an all-encompassing theorization of all potential facets of affinity or convergence (i.e., the totality of potential factors that might generate or catalyze predispositions for participation). Rather, the constituent elements of each concept are derived from those factors that could be identified through the careful analysis of the cases in this book, in dialogue with existing social scientific research. There may well be factors that will have been eclipsed by my selection of cases or methods of inquiry but that play an important role in mobilization. These may be specific to certain historical or cultural contexts or be detectable only by specific methods. Some reflections on such factors can be found in the book's conclusion.

Much more about the operation of affinity and convergence will be uncovered in the chapters to follow. The rest of this book shows how this pair of mechanisms can help explain mass mobilization across a set of very different causes. Part II shows how affinity-convergence theory helps to explain modern revolutionary upheavals with an in-depth analysis of the 2011 Egyptian Revolution, while part III turns to the Occupy Wall Street protests later that year. Part IV turns to the present day, investigating how the 2020 Black Lives Uprising in the United States arose not from the domain of established organizational forces but instead out of long-standing affinities and sudden conditions of convergence. Finally, part V offers a test of affinity-convergence theory's generalizability beyond the confines of the information age, examining how it can shed light on historical cases through a study of French revolutionary mobilization in 1789.

PART II

THE EGYPTIAN REVOLUTION, 2011

On January 25, 2011, tens of thousands of Egyptians took to the streets in the first of the country's "Eighteen Days" of revolution. Demonstrations took place not only in and en route to Cairo's Tahrir Square but also all around the country. Although this was certainly remarkable, few expected that events would culminate in the overthrow of Egypt's longest-serving ruler in over two and a half centuries: the dictator Hosni Mubarak.

There exists an invariable temptation for the academic observer, particularly one writing a decade after the fact, to declare that Egypt's revolution was somehow inevitable. There are certainly factors that would assist an author with such aspirations. One could readily point to increasing decoherence among the Egyptian ruling elite: disunity within the ruling party, spiraling corruption, tectonic divisions and rivalries between the police and the armed forces, and the looming question of dictatorial succession, all compounded by Mubarak's faltering health. Alternatively, one could readily point to serious deficits in the country's economic condition that engendered increasing industrial frustration over the years. Through still another lens, one could note a shift in international relations that constrained authoritarian strongmen and made challenges more likely to succeed.

But even were it true that Egypt's social conditions were utterly unbearable and its regime somewhat less unified than it might seem, it would be a stretch for even the most enthusiastic observer to posit that the country was truly on the cusp of revolution. After all, Egypt was sorely lacking in the one area with which revolutions are generally associated: a coherent revolutionary movement. Instead, the country harbored a patchwork of resistance platforms, political parties, and opposition groups ill poised to launch a serious challenge to state power. Yet on January 25 the best efforts of only a handful of activists within Egypt's contentious political patchwork proved enough to set the stage for one of the most profound mobilizations in the country's history.

January 25 set in motion a massive wave of protest across Egypt. Within a matter of days protests in Cairo alone came to number in the hundreds of thousands, and the city's Tahrir Square was swiftly enshrined as a global revolutionary icon. With news networks broadcasting images of revolutionary masses filling the streets of Cairo, previously dour commentators exhibited a renewed excitement about revolution in the Arab world. A narrative emerged among global commentors that the Middle East and North Africa region was experiencing a new "Arab awakening," with Egyptians, like their Tunisian counterparts, finally casting off supposed political passivity.[1] What remained unclear, however, was precisely how and why this apparent awakening had taken place.

Early diagnoses suggested a "Twitter revolution" or "Facebook revolt" of Egyptians radicalized and recruited for momentous revolutionary *journées* via social media. This narrative drew extensively on the most immediate evidence of protest activity: the online record.[2] But almost as suddenly as it had arisen, the social media hypothesis fell flat. A first death knell came in the form of its public dismissal by the very same revolutionary protagonists that the narrative had posited were responsible.[3] Upon further investigation, it transpired that internet and mobile phone access had been shut down for the most crucial days of the revolution, and that a litany of prior and subsequent attempts to generate protest by means of online agitation had proven ineffective. Those of us seeking to comprehend Egypt's revolutionary crowds were thus sent back to the drawing board.

While academics, journalists, and other commentators had found themselves perplexed by the sudden appearance of Egypt's revolutionary crowds, they were certainly in good company. The country's activists, too, admitted a certain degree of nescience as to precisely why and how such an entirely unprecedented number of people filled the nation's squares and streets during this period. It was with this particular puzzle in mind—articulated with great emphasis by my Egyptian friends and colleagues—that I arrived in Cairo in the summer of 2015. Accordingly, with their considerable help, I was able to interview a diverse mix of revolutionary participants, ranging from initially hesitant apolitical types to stalwart political or religious devotees, as well as some of those who were skeptical about or even opposed the mobilizations going on.[4] I was incredibly lucky that my status as an outsider worked in my favor and laid the foundations for deep, meaningful personal conversations about why people joined revolutionary protests. These were conversations that my contacts often professed they would have felt unable to have with someone from their own community.

What I discovered was a set of facts that Egypt's revolutionary protesters had by then come to regard as banalities: that the notion that Egyptians had ever truly possessed a cohesive revolutionary agenda or were directed by an organized movement was an illusion, that the country's revolution was far more spontaneous than its hagiography had ventured, and that the highly specific conditions that had fostered it had long passed. I came to understand that participants in the revolutionary struggle were consistently unsure or unaware of what they would accomplish, who they were benefiting, and even who they were truly fighting. False representations, secrecy, masked allegiances, and total information disparity were rife throughout the Eighteen Days, and even the most active and well-organized revolutionaries had little control over the course of events they had clumsily helped to initiate and encourage. In place of a cohesive and well-organized movement came a profound convergence of Egypt's masses, drawn to Tahrir Square by long-standing affinities. A full suite of convergence conditions activated participation on the basis of a wide array of affinities, especially perceived injustice, antiregime attitudes, and collective national identity, as well as the revolutionary cause's intersection with Egyptians' everyday patterns of activity. It was a moment many had dreamed of but few had anticipated, constructed from the common ground Egyptians shared but did not know they had.

CHAPTER THREE

Egypt on the Eve of Revolution

Egypt's current state resembles a surrealist painting. It is difficult to decipher its components, challenging to comprehend its meaning. At the center of the painting there are dark, abrasive lines; most onlookers would see them as depicting anger, frustration and occasionally menace.

TAREK OSMAN, writing in 2010[1]

A decade prior to the Egyptian Revolution, President Hosni Mubarak stood all but unrivaled as the nation's leader. He had eliminated all major opponents within his own National Democratic Party (NDP), decapitated the military's political wing, and reorganized the nation's Ministry of Interior to function as more of an occupying force than a police force. After banning or imprisoning his most dangerous opponents, Mubarak had ensured, through a series of regulations and crackdowns, that any opposition parties he had not already made illegal were so heavily hamstrung that they were unable to compete. The Muslim Brotherhood, the nation's unofficial opposition, remained banned. Having secured himself against institutional threats, Mubarak's next concern appeared to be preparing a succession plan for his son Gamal, while making notional domestic reforms in order to appease growing criticism among Egypt's economic partners. Unfortunately for Mubarak, the first decade of the new millennium would give rise to an array of conditions that would in time set the scene for revolution.

Had Egypt by 2011 been somehow transformed from a country almost entirely consolidated by its ruler to one firmly accelerating toward revolution? Not so. Rather, the prerevolutionary decade played host to crucial changes in Egyptian politics and society that served to facilitate a wide variety of challenges to the Mubarak regime. That one such challenge on

January 25, 2011, actually took on revolutionary attributes owes its origins to certain key actors being inspired by events in neighboring Tunisia. That, furthermore, a torrent of revolutionary mass mobilization did indeed follow owes its explanation to the dynamics I elucidate in the next chapter. But before we encounter the dramatic stories of revolutionary agency and complex dynamics of mass mobilization, the very possibility of initiating *any* serious challenge to the regime must be explained. This chapter addresses precisely such a task, detailing the structure and emergence of a protorevolutionary situation in Egypt. I begin by detailing the widespread dispositional factors that leant some among the country's population a growing affinity for revolt, before tracing the emergence of widely acknowledged and visible, but largely weak and ineffective, antigovernment resistance in the run-up to the revolution.

Revolutionaries in Waiting?

One could be forgiven for thinking that all of the various organizations and associations detailed in this chapter would, come January 25, supplement their prior accomplishments by assuming the role of primary engines in Egypt's revolutionary process. Part of the mystery of the Egyptian Revolution, however, is that this was far from the case. While all of the groups outlined here did indeed (eventually) participate in the 2011 revolution, and some played very important causal roles, none of them exhibited the membership, resources, or mobilizing capacity necessary to carry forth revolutionary change. Rather, the element that sustained Egypt's eighteen-day revolutionary rising was assuredly the titanic host of ordinary citizens who mobilized for it on their own terms. But were the Egyptian people simply "revolutionaries in waiting"? Hardly. Despite the enormous protests that took place during the Eighteen Days, the overwhelming majority of ordinary Egyptians took no part in revolutionary mobilization.

That a revolution is carried through by only a relatively small minority of the constituent population is an unpleasant truth of almost all instances of the phenomenon. Perhaps more telling, however, is that truly momentous revolutionary uprisings are often differentiated from abortive revolts and ambivalent challenges by the fact that they (at least initially) enjoy far more widespread popular support than they do resistance. Accordingly, the puzzle for any social scientist seeking to explain the origins of mass revolutions is not to provide an explanation as to why the entirety of a country's population were somehow transmuted into budding revolutionaries just in time for the events in question, but rather why a small yet still large enough proportion of civilians might one day find themselves in the situation where they would countenance participating at all.

In the context of the Egyptian Revolution, we are faced with the question of why a considerable number of Egyptians were, by the tail end of January 2011, in a position to countenance publicly defying the Mubarak regime should the opportunity arise. Piecing together such a puzzle requires accounting for the emergent factors that provided so many otherwise ordinary Egyptians with affinities for revolutionary action. In the case of Egypt, the common ground undergirding my informants' decisions to challenge the regime in the revolution's early days almost always involved two psychological factors: strongly felt negative attitudes toward the regime and an entrenched sense of injustice. Though, as we will see in chapter 4, various other affinities would play important roles as the revolution developed, these two factors alone provided strong psychological affinity for revolutionary action among the Egyptian populace.

So why had such a conducive psychological disposition developed among so many in the Egyptian population? According to my informants, such a state of affairs had been brewing for quite a while, and by the time the revolution took place, Egyptians' attitudes toward the Mubarak regime had grown increasingly indignant.[2] "A lot of people did not like the status quo: the economy, education, health care," Ahmad, a middle-class Cairene, recalled.[3] "Corruption was a huge part." Indeed, it is hard to understate the poisonous effect of Mubarak-era corruption on how ordinary Egyptians perceived the regime. Almost everyone I spoke to raised this topic. "Of course, we all knew that the Mubarak regime was corrupt and that people's money was being diverted all over the place," one small business owner, Hazem, told me.[4] "You could see the corruption and *feel* it at all levels." State corruption had become nothing short of a total social fact, and a corresponding distaste toward the regime was rife. Even Mubarak's most enthusiastic supporters confessed to this state of affairs. "Mubarak and his family have had thirty years of the presidency... they stole the whole country," one NDP loyalist told me. "But we still thought that Mubarak was the best solution for *us*."[5]

Outside the wealthy and well-to-do, however, Egypt's kleptocracy offered no such silver lining, and the widening gulf between the regime's touted prosperity and the experience of everyday Egyptians engendered a palpable feeling that their situation was becoming increasingly unjust. Writing in 2010, the Egyptian political economist and journalist Tarek Osman observed that "within the many morbid symptoms of the fracturing of the social order and national regression, a shared feeling has emerged:

that 'something has gone wrong' (*fee haga ghalat*)."[6] The revolutionary participants I spoke to overwhelmingly concurred with such a sentiment. "What was happening on the ground socially and economically was screwed up. From my point of view, this wasn't what Egypt was supposed to be," Mustafa, a middle-aged professional, recalled.[7]

With the wealth of the country's elite seemingly soaring, the rest of Egypt's population was left feeling excluded. "They kept saying that GDP [gross domestic product] was growing, but people never felt any benefit," Hazem explained. Between 2000 and 2011, while Mubarak and the ruling elite had yielded the benefits of dramatic economic growth, ordinary Egyptians faced a 50 percent increase in poverty that left more than a quarter of the population below the poverty line.[8] Between 2008 and 2011 the situation became particularly drastic, with food inflation sending consumer prices skyrocketing by 47 percent between January 2008 and the end of 2010. Even relatively privileged Egyptians were feeling the pain, with university graduates making up just over 43 percent of the country's unemployment rolls in 2010.[9] Something had certainly gone wrong, and it seemed to be hurting everyone except the people in power.

A growing sense of economic injustice was not the only factor underpinning Egyptians' increasing sense of deprivation. The year before the revolution saw a forceful arrest of the past decade's semblance of political progress, most palpably displayed in the rigging of Egypt's 2010 parliamentary elections, deemed by observers to be "the most fraudulent in the country's history."[10] Every single political party was wiped out by the increasingly reviled NDP, almost all being reduced to either a single seat or no seats at all.[11]

"There had been a strong opposition [to Mubarak], but the results were as if there was no opposition at all," Mustafa explained. "It wasn't even smart!" he declared, still incredulous a half decade after the fact. "If [Mubarak] had wanted to play smart, then he could have won with a good percentage, but not 90-something percent!" Such farcical results were accompanied by widespread evidence of electoral malfeasance on behalf of Mubarak's party, widely publicized by mainstream Arab media organizations, such as Al Jazeera, and openly discussed online. After an apparent opening of electoral opportunities in 2005, 2010's parliamentary results led to the young Egyptians I spoke to losing all hope of electoral change. Not only had Mubarak's parliamentary power grab alienated almost every major political persuasion in the country from their organizational stake in the Egyptian state, but it had also convinced ordinary Egyptians of the futility of electoral challenges to the regime. "We knew for sure," Mustafa recalled,

Prerevolutionary Resistance

A CAUTIOUS BROTHERHOOD

Perhaps the most widely recognized element of Egypt's anti-Mubarak forces was the Muslim Brotherhood. Founded in Egypt in 1928, the Brotherhood is an invariably complex transnational society of like-minded Islamists. To even summarize its overall structure in any useful way is an exceedingly thorny task. In Egypt, the Brotherhood's home country, the group formed the most prominent organ for Islamist resistance to the Mubarak regime. This was carried out not only under the formal banner of the Brotherhood but also through a network of social organizations, mosques, companies, charities, study groups, and "independent" politicians who enjoyed greater toleration than the "official" Brotherhood was afforded throughout the bulk of the Mubarak years.[12] At the same time, the Brotherhood constituted a kind of parallel social order within the Egyptian nation, with its own internal networks, social expectations, marriage dynamics, and welfare system. "The social network inside the Brotherhood is overwhelmingly strong," one member of the group explained. "There is a broad social ecosystem that can help you be fulfilled with a lot of things [in life]—you and your family, your kids."[13] It was the Brotherhood's religious and social elements—over and above any political aspirations—that underpinned the involvement of the Brothers and former Brothers I spoke to in the organization. "I had no interest in politics.... I joined because I wanted to understand more about religion," another told me.[14] Once involved in the Brotherhood, my sources explained that it was usually the organization's social benefits that continued to appeal: "having a good job with a good salary, good pay, and good schools."

The Brotherhood's political operations, meanwhile, were fraught with intricacies and reversals throughout Egypt's prerevolutionary decade. Though formally illegal, Egypt's Muslim Brotherhood had long been considered one of the regime's more dependable opposition organizations, who would play by the rules expected of it by the NDP.[15] Thus, it was not uncommon to see the Brotherhood and NDP respecting one another's "red lines" or presenting the other with concessions despite a formally adversarial relationship. Perhaps the most high-profile instance of such dealing during Egypt's prerevolutionary decade occurred when the Brotherhood negotiated the outcome of the 2005 elections with the State Security Investigations Service, a process masterfully chronicled by Eric Trager.

The offer began with State Security chief Hassan Abdel Rahman contacting Brotherhood Supreme Guide Mehdi Akef, and expressing his concern that the Brotherhood might run for—and win—a large share of parliamentary seats, given the international pressure that the regime was facing to hold relatively open elections. Akef responded by indicating that he was willing to run for fewer seats so long as the regime didn't arrest Muslim Brothers en masse.... Over the course of a few meetings with State Security... [they] agreed to reduce the number of Brotherhood parliamentary candidacies from approximately 200 to 120, with the aim of winning 50 [to] 55 seats. In deference to the regime the Brotherhood further withdrew candidates from districts in which major NDP candidates were running. In exchange, the regime agreed to let some Brothers win, and to run the elections relatively fairly. The regime additionally afforded the Brotherhood unprecedented media access, including hosting Guidance Office member Abdel Monem Abouel Fotouh on public radio, and it permitted Brotherhood candidates to use the [group's] slogan "Islam is the Solution."[16]

The 2005 negotiations produced unexpectedly large election gains for the Brotherhood. A coalition of officially independent candidates representing the Brotherhood's platform managed to secure 20 percent of the total seats in the parliament (88/454). This was rather more than the Mubarak regime had bargained for; consequently, the Brotherhood's lease of generosity was almost immediately reversed, and mass arrests of Brotherhood members began soon after the elections. By March 2006 the number detained began steadily climbing into the thousands.[17] This process of repression certainly had its intended effect, encouraging the Brothers' leadership to withdraw from political life and sit out many subsequent protest actions. This change in orientation was much to the chagrin of the Brotherhood's activist-inclined youth members, most of whom were largely unaware of the intrigue that had underpinned this change of heart until Akef personally admitted it in a newspaper interview in 2009.[18] The Brotherhood's more radical members were further provoked when, in January 2010, the group's newly appointed Supreme Guide publicly declared that the group would not oppose Mubarak's son running in the upcoming presidential elections.[19]

THE RISE AND FALL OF KEFAYA

While the Muslim Brotherhood spent much of the prerevolutionary decade partaking in a complex political dance with the Mubarak regime, the rise of a public-facing anti-Mubarak movement was simultaneously taking place. This movement unexpectedly emerged from mass protests against the Iraq War in 2003. Immediately upon its declaration, the war sparked two days of mass protest in Egyptian cities that overwhelmed security forces. At its heart was a sit-in at Cairo's Tahrir Square, the central site of the future revolution. Within a year a coalition of activists, intellectuals, and cultural and political figures galvanized by the Tahrir sit-in announced the formation of a new cause: the Egyptian Movement for Change, or Kefaya. Kefaya (Enough) sought to unify a diverse and divided spectrum of Egyptian contentious actors into a cohesive movement to resist and oppose Mubarak while defending human rights. Kefaya's first protest, on December 12, 2004, constituted the first formal, well-established anti-Mubarak protest in Egyptian history, proclaiming: "No Extension of Mubarak's Fourth Term in Office, No to Mubarak's Succession by His Son."[20] Though this constituted merely three hundred Kefaya members protesting outside Cairo's High Court, it was the beginning of increasingly forceful, popular anti-Mubarak actions by the group, whose membership and supporters grew rapidly.

By the next year Egypt's first contested elections were planned,[21] and almost five thousand Egyptians had become "members" of Kefaya (a status attained by publicly signing its founding statement). "It might be remembered as the first sustained effort to bring together ordinary and elite Egyptians under a common project of resisting," the blogger Baheyya mused in 2005.[22] Small street protests evolved from previously stage-managed rarities to occasional but infrequent events. However, the forthcoming elections to the Parliament and presidency proved not only the summit of the Egyptian opposition's success but the harbinger of its decline.

While Kefaya officially advocated an electoral boycott, many of its supporting parties, the Muslim Brotherhood, and the popular opposition figure Ayman Nour were getting ready for full-fledged participation. Excitable commentators worldwide contrasted this moment with the revolutions of 1848 and 1989 in Europe. "The Arab Spring of 2005 will be noted by history as a similar turning point for the Arab world," conservative columnist Charles Krauthammer asserted, before noting with some caution that "we do not yet know, however, whether this initial flourishing of democracy will succeed."[23] By the end of the year, Ayman Nour had won an impressive 8 percent of the presidential vote, and the National Democratic Party lost 94 of the 404 parliamentary seats that it had previously controlled. Furthermore, amid widespread accusations of regime-led election rigging, Kefaya would organize its most momentous protest yet, with ten thousand taking to the streets of Cairo in open opposition to the regime in a protest spanning twenty-three governorates.[24]

The Mubarak regime was unsurprisingly unenthusiastic about this "flourishing of democracy" they had thus far entertained. In addition to its crackdown on the Muslim Brotherhood, the regime took pains to respond to the civil gains made by Kefaya and Ayman Nour's presidential campaign by engineering a harsh crackdown on political parties and civil rights protests. Nour himself was imprisoned and tortured on the basis of deeply suspicious and largely unevidenced charges of document forgery previously used to discredit his election campaign.[25]

Meanwhile, Kefaya not only faced a surge in police repression but was also plagued by emergent internal problems. In the wake of the election, the careful alliance that had constituted the movement's political support had all but collapsed, after Islamist factions became particularly dissatisfied by their lack of influence over Kefaya's operation. This combination of organizational weakness, a lack of support from major players, and stepped-up regime oppression would serve to cripple Kefaya's efforts to organize over the coming years.

THE EMERGENCE OF DIGITAL ACTIVISM

Amid increasingly harsh police repression of social movements and opposition parties came alternative outlets for young Egyptians' frustration. The first of these was a burgeoning blogosphere, fostered throughout the 2005 election year, and persisting well beyond it. Through the creation of anonymous blogs, Egyptians ranging from journalists to teenagers could circumvent regime censorship measures. Provocative articles, photographs, and reports abounded, with bloggers contributing new content daily. A new, alternative, unrestricted public sphere was brewing, though it was accessible only to any Egyptian fortunate enough to have an internet connection and, in the case of some blogs, literacy in English (itself a facet of social class). The conversations on these blogs would shape both activist and elite discourse during this quieter period of the revolution's prehistory.

In 2008 political resistance enjoyed a brief reprieve. Workers from El-Mahalla El-Kubra, a major industrial complex in the Nile delta, announced that they were planning to strike in April of that year. Two activists, Esraa Rashid and Ahmed Maher, created a page on Facebook, an increasingly popular social media platform among Egypt's youth (then with approximately eight hundred thousand users),[26] to bring together some kind of protest in support of the striking workers. Both had previously been volunteers with the youth wing of Ayman Nour's El-Ghad Party, while Maher had also been an active member of Kefaya's youth. Each had enjoyed successes organizing smaller protests in the past and were cautiously optimistic that they would manage a modest mobilization in support of the strike.

Rashid and Maher's page grew exponentially over its first few days and weeks, with followers numbering in the tens of thousands. Accordingly, the group's administrators swiftly reformulated the page as not merely a protest in solidarity with the April 6 strike, but a new April 6 movement. After a successful strike that day, the group's Facebook page served as a hub for discussion of radical and oppositional ideas. The page garnered a substantial following and online membership,[27] reaching over seventy thousand users (a sizable proportion of all Egyptians on Facebook) who were now exposed to a whole array of resistant and contentious ideas circulated and discussed on the page.[28]

While the April 6 movement's online popularity cannot be understated, it would be a mistake to consider the group as analogous to a mass social movement. In reality, the group was a collective of only a small number of activists, all already involved in Egyptian opposition politics.[29] Though the group planned anniversary strikes in 2009 and 2010, actions of any significance failed to materialize in both years. This was perhaps unsurprising, as the movement had come into existence by co-opting rather than organizing the set of strikes that had inspired its name.

THE NATIONAL ASSOCIATION FOR CHANGE

By 2010 Egypt's second ever presidential election (due in 2011) was fast approaching, and with Ayman Nour still in jail, Egypt's progressive movements needed a new candidate.[30] "[We] were looking for a guy who'd be internationally recognized, someone who was well protected... and could be presented to the Egyptian people as a possible candidate," Hakim, a progressive political activist, told me.[31] The chosen vessel for activists' enthusiasm was Mohamed ElBaradei, who was successfully persuaded to initiate a presidential campaign in February of 2010. An organization, the People's Campaign to Support ElBaradei, had already been set up on his behalf, but ElBaradei had bolder plans. Only days after touching down on the tarmac at Cairo Airport, he announced an anti-Mubarak umbrella group: the National Association for Change (NAC). This new organization appeared much like a more sophisticated redux of Kefaya. "The idea was to bring together everyone known to oppose the Egyptian regime," the activist and NAC member Wael Ghonim recalled.[32] Though it would not fully affiliate with the NAC, the Muslim Brotherhood took the unusual step of offering parallel support to NAC campaigns; these were strictly conducted, however, under the Brotherhood's own auspices. After all, the

National Association for Change was almost inseparable from ElBaradei's presidential campaign, which the Brotherhood was understandably reluctant to subordinate itself to.

The NAC set to work on a major public campaign demanding resolutions to some of Egypt's most high-profile political issues: ending the state of emergency, thus weakening police powers; a two-term limit on the presidency, thus preventing a Mubarak family dictatorship; and free elections,[33] thereby allowing for a shake-up of the deeply embedded political regime. These demands were reenforced by a joint NAC[34]–Brotherhood[35] petition, which reportedly garnered almost one million signatures. The petition was conducted with such sincerity that it had required those signing it to give their national identity information for verification and antifraud purposes.[36]

Not only did National Association for Change issue serious challenges to the Mubarak regime but also ElBaradei himself came to constitute a serious challenge to the regime's legitimating logic. "The argument *for* Hosni Mubarak in Egypt was that no one is better qualified," Mustafa recalled. "But actually, with the appearance of ElBaradei, no! *He* looked qualified to most people." Though ElBaradei's personal star would already substantially wane by 2011, the activities of the National Association for Change nonetheless served to popularize and legitimize public dissent against the regime, as well as normalize the public expression of attitudes that would have once been unsayable.

THE ANTIPOLICE MOVEMENT

While attempts to gather petition signatures continued, some young members of the NAC, who had offered their technical efforts to the petition process, embarked on an additional project: organizing around the murder of Khaled Saeed. Saeed had been tortured to death by Egyptian police officers in June 2010 after having been discovered possessing video material implicating those officers in illegal activities. His death sparked national outrage and inspired Wael Ghonim, an expat working in the tech industry, to create a popular Facebook page under the title "We are all Khaled Saeed." Ghonim had created the page as a hub for antipolice discussion and organizing after a horrifying postmortem photograph of Saeed went viral on social media.

Initially, Ghonim's page was used to organize a series of "silent stands" against police brutality. These appeared to be only somewhat successful. Ibrahim,[37] who attended some of the early "stands," recalled that these protests "did not last for long because the police came and asked us to leave." At his first such event, Ibrahim recalled "just standing over there, looking at the Nile, with our backs to the streets, wearing a black T-shirt and that was it.... We stayed for, I don't know, ten minutes maybe, and then police officers came and [said,] 'Yeah, you cannot stand here,'" and the event promptly ended. Nonetheless, it was from Ghonim's Facebook page, which had organized these generally underwhelming and minor actions, that Egypt's revolution would first be proclaimed.

Antipolice action was not always as restrained and civil as the small events organized by Ghonim and his associates on Facebook. One major source of radical antipolice action arose from a phenomenon known as the "Ultras." Notionally, the Ultras were groups of fanatical football supporters associated with Egypt's two most popular teams: Zamalek SC (Ultras White Knights) and Al Ahly SC (Ultras Ahlawy). Swiftly attaining tens of thousands of members between them, Ultras groups were organized into a series of local chapters and functioned as social communities, discussing football and attending games together. Because of their size and unruliness, they swiftly developed a reputation (alongside other Ultras groups around the world) for hooliganism and violence. This in turn provoked violent attacks by police, which served to create a considerable antipathy on behalf of the previously apolitical Ultras. One former Ultra I spoke to characterized his peers as "young guys who hate and despise the state security and the Central Security soldiers."[38] Violent confrontations between police and Ultras continued to intensify year after year, until the rivalry between the two groups reached a fever pitch, with Ultras even bringing improvised weapons such as fireworks and stones to events. "They were the only social group in the country who were [violently] confronting the police," my informant explained.

THE INSUFFICIENT NECESSITIES OF REVOLT

Even if they did not constitute a serious threat to the regime, Egypt's activists were content to have spent the prerevolutionary decade laying vital groundwork for some kind of future challenge to Mubarak. Ever since the Tahrir sit-in of 2003, organizers had routinely described their successes in terms of preparing and politicizing their peers in expectation of something bigger in the future. "Greater importance was placed on being present as a protest movement than on ideology," recalled Walid Shawky,[39] an activist affiliated with the April 6 movement. "We began in a moment in which there was little space or means for expressing political opinion, making the act of protest itself the center or core of the political protest," he explained. By 2011 this had in many ways been achieved. Protests had become an acknowledged feature of public life, in open defiance of the country's restrictive emergency law, and criticism of the regime was at an all-time high. Even though Egyptians were far from up in arms, it had nonetheless become socially acceptable to not only criticize and condemn Mubarak's regime but also to do so publicly, even in the face of criminal penalties.

As we have seen, there was indeed plenty to criticize, and it is perhaps unsurprising that antiregime attitudes were widespread in Egypt by the end of 2010, given the confluence of worsening conditions and increasingly effective and innovative activist efforts to legitimize dissent. Nonetheless, Egypt's immersion in revolution at the tail end of January 2011 came as a quite profound surprise to those very same activists. Even though the events of the past decade had instilled many Egyptians with a degree of underlying affinity for potential antiregime action, Egypt's anti-Mubarak forces lacked sufficient popular recognition, coalitional strength, committed participants, and mobilizing resources to reliably muster more than a few thousand people, let alone any kind of revolutionary challenge. Rather, Mohamed ElBaradei's National Association for Change was fragmenting, the Muslim Brotherhood was still paralyzed by repression, and digital activists had seen hardly any success turning out physical participants to their planned protests. With no sufficiently capable revolutionary movement, it appeared that Mubarak was destined to remain firmly in control.

Appearances, of course, can be deceiving.

CHAPTER FOUR

The Anatomy of a Revolutionary Moment

We were all suffering with the same stuff, we were all facing the same injustice.... [For] those Eighteen Days, it was pure, everybody just wanted change... nobody knew from where to start, who the leader was.... There were no objectives. We just wanted change.

YUSUF

We saw in chapter 3 how Egypt's gradually developing anti-Mubarak groups had, even at their apex, been totally outmatched by the repressive power of the Mubarak regime. Despite extensive regime repression and dismal potential for electoral reform, the notion of moving from organized resistance to the pursuit of revolution had hardly been countenanced by the country's beleaguered organizers. Yet a few short weeks into the new year in 2011, the country would witness its first grassroots revolutionary protest since 1919.

This chapter turns to the emergence, explosion, and denouement of Egypt's revolutionary apex: the so-called Eighteen Days. In what follows I deconstruct this period, with a primary focus on events in Cairo, showing how despite the rapid disappearance of organized activism, mass mobilization by means of *affinity* and *convergence* took center stage during the revolutionary period. I show how initial organizing efforts by a small number of activists operating beyond the purview of most established movements and parties were able to loosely focus the revolutionary energy brewing in the country. This disorganized array of contending, occasionally intersecting activists triggered a short period of popular mass mobilization largely beyond their control on January 25. I then detail how even this small vestige of activist direction rapidly vanished, and the revolution took on a life of its own amid its first major mobilization on January 28. From then on Egypt was immersed in an undirected revolutionary process. Though a coalition of online and offline forces created the conditions for protest, the nation's fate instead lay in the hands of ordinary Egyptians and their collective participation decisions.

From Revolution to Mobilization

In his long reign Hosni Mubarak had successfully maintained his grip on the Egyptian state, but he had antagonized a broad spectrum of enemies among the Egyptian public. "The revolution didn't just happen overnight," one participant told me. "It was spontaneous and chaotic and everything, but people had been keeping it inside themselves for years and years."[1] As we saw in chapter 3, one of the most prominent affinities that underpinned mass mobilization in Egypt's revolt constituted exactly these long-standing psychological dispositions—a widespread perception of injustice and antiregime attitudes, manifest in a common hatred of the police, a strong distaste with the regime, and horror over Mubarak's prospective maneuvers to install his son as president in a forthcoming September election. The primary elements of this collective distaste, however, differed according to participants' social status. For the poorest Egyptians, a pressing concern was the negative effects of the Mubarak regime's awful economic mismanagement. For the young middle class, human rights violations were particularly upsetting. Older professionals, meanwhile, were revolted by the corruption endemic in Mubarak's government.

"Events outside Egypt suddenly gave us the spark we needed," Wael Ghonim[2] recalled. With Tunisia's revolution underway, a similar fervor was brewing in Egypt and reached fever pitch when on January 14 news broke that the Tunisian dictator, Zine el-Abidine Ben Ali, was forced from the country. Online news articles were even published dubbing the two *Al-Shabihan* ("the Lookalikes").[3] There existed a plethora of parallels to draw between the two dictators, from their personal upbringings to their military careers and emergence from the bureaucratic shadows to create the savage police states that underpinned their regimes. As presidents, they had even both fostered the same public image: a personality cult that painted each as modernizing Westerners, ushering in a national break from an outmoded authoritarian past. Meanwhile, the pair ceaselessly enriched their families with kleptocratic malice, all backed up by two of the most severe security regimes in the world. Just as Mubarak's rise in Egypt appeared a template for Ben Ali's in Tunisia, so too would Ben Ali's decline serve as a powerful, paramount frame in support of further revolutionary agitation: the duo's shared history was again in motion. While this frame began to emerge in advance of Egypt's revolution, domestic events in Egypt would lend it greater and greater resonance as time went on, complemented by the emergence of a much wider array of convergence conditions.

The idea that agitation might spread was tantalizing: if revolution was possible in Tunisia, it yearned to be tried in Egypt. The "We Are All Khaled Saeed" Facebook page, run by Wael Ghonim, swiftly became a hub for discussion on the topic. After consulting with fellow activists involved in the National Association for Change (NAC) and the April 6 movement, Ghonim swiftly set about revising the plans for a small human rights protest he had been organizing for the January 25 public holiday, National Police Day. He would rename the event "January 25: Revolution Against Torture, Poverty, Corruption, and Unemployment."

Without established organizational resources or an extensive network of affiliates, Ghonim was forced to rely primarily on ordinary Facebook users and pages working "in parallel, without any coordination of effort." "The idea was that everyone had a right to advertise the day," he explained. Wary that Egyptians shared a perception of injustice but had radically different political persuasions, Ghonim stressed the need to keep the invitation to protest as broad as possible. "Let us focus from now until Jan25 on discussing Egypt's economic condition and our living standards," he implored those following his page. "We must reach out to the helpless layman who only cares about finding his loaf of bread... [and] refrain from elitist sophisticated talk so we don't end up only 1,000 or 2,000 on the street."[4] Ghonim was particularly mindful of the need to appeal to shared perceptions of injustice and broad-based attitudes rather than niche activist agendas. "I deliberately included poverty, corruption and unemployment," he recalled, "because we needed to have everyone join forces.... If the invitation to take the streets had been based solely on human rights, then only a certain segment of Egyptian society would have participated."[5] All in all, the goal of the protests had been presented such that the revolution sought on the twenty-fifth bore greater resemblance to a series of popular political reforms than the fall of a regime per se.

The general notion of a mass protest on January 25 resonated well beyond Cairo's small middle-class activist milieu, with invitations being shared by popular figures, humor pages, and even a 250,000-follower "Egyptian Sugar Cane Juice" fan page. To complement online work, thousands of flyers were cast around the streets by small cohorts of activists from the April 6 movement, while young Egyptians sent out mass text messages to their peers and even dialed random phone numbers, circulating news of the coming protest on January 25.[6]

By contrast, conventional organizing attempts were facing some considerable setbacks. While some small NAC-affiliated political platforms, such as Ayman Nour's El-Ghad Party and the Liberal Democratic Front, agreed to sign a statement in support of the protests, this seemed the summit of their supportive efforts. Meanwhile, Egypt's largest leftist party, Tagammu, openly opposed the protests, and the Muslim Brotherhood similarly declared on January 20 that it would not participate.[7]

By the morning of January 25, in addition to work on the ground, Facebook invitations to the protest had been shared with over one million Facebook users, one-tenth of whom had confirmed in advance that they would attend on the day.[8] However, it remained to be seen whether these online and offline organizing efforts would mature into action on the streets. "Unlike the Muslim Brothers... we did not have the same level of commitment," Mahmood, a highly involved activist at the time, recalled, "so our organizational capacity was limited to directing the marches [toward Tahrir Square]."[9] In the end, although the hundred thousand people "attending" on Facebook didn't materialize, a highly impressive contingent of approximately twenty-five thousand Egyptians descended from numerous gathering points across Cairo and its suburbs, supported by thousands more in Alexandria, Aswan, El-Mahalla El-Kubra, and Ismailia. As it became clear that the protest was going ahead, elementary steps were taken by Egypt's Ministry of Interior to block signal to individual activists' mobile phones, as well as to disable national access to Twitter and the then popular video streaming website Bambuser.com.[10] These were not entirely successful. In fact, authorities' attempts to block Facebook on January 26 disrupted other restrictions previously in place.

As crowds marched toward Tahrir Square, a heavy-handed police presence, live ammunition, and brutal attacks on peaceful protesters marked the day. Mariam,[11] a young woman who marched to Tahrir on the twenty-fifth, recalled that, although the crowds had been "very, very peaceful... the reaction was very violent." At around 6:00 p.m. that day, regime forces stormed Tahrir Square, beating faces bloody and brutalizing the peaceful crowd. As if to add insult to injury, 3G services in Tahrir Square shut down two hours later, leaving protesters trapped and communication lines cut.

"[With] how violent things suddenly became... I think this was the turning point," Mariam explained. The regime's extreme response to the protests led many to think that reform was impossible. "If they were hurting people like *that* in the streets, then they weren't going to do anything," she noted. Witnessing this transformation in real time, she recalled how, after bullets flew and protesters were beaten, the chants from the crowds making their way to Tahrir Square changed. "The chants began to say: 'The regime must fall,'" she recalled. Enraged and emboldened, protesters returned to their homes, while activists set about liaising with established opposition groups over the next two days. The failure of peaceful protest swiftly paved the way for violent confrontations.

The Masses Take Over

As excitement bubbled, Ghonim and his associates[12] tried to build an organizational coalition for a second protest on January 28. While the protest was officially billed as "The Friday of Anger: A Revolution against Corruption, Injustice, Torture, and Unemployment," many were already referring to it simply as Egypt's "Day of Rage." The day was shaping up to be altogether more eventful, and even more dangerous, than January 25. Energized by the events of the twenty-fifth and harboring a long-standing hatred of the police, the "Ultras" of Ahly and Zamalek collectively declared their readiness to fight for Egypt's future. Meanwhile, Brotherhood youth members passed word to activists that the group would be present at the protest's various starting points around Cairo, although they emphasized that they would not move unless they were accompanied by huge masses beyond their own membership.[13]

Patterns of activity constituted a particularly prominent social affinity that underpinned early participation in Egypt's revolution beyond groups like the Ultras and the Brotherhood. The enthusiastic cohort of relatively privileged youths who made up the revolutionary cause's early adherents did not have ties to the great masses of the country's poor and lower middle classes. However, the marching routes to Tahrir Square on January 25 and 28 intersected with many of the locales frequented during ordinary Egyptians' daily lives. Marches passed through major thoroughfares, crossed between shared or bordering neighborhoods, and—perhaps most importantly in the revolution's early days—started from prominent places of collective worship. As the marches rolled through city neighborhoods, residents, bystanders, and worshippers were enticed to step away from their routines and head toward Tahrir.

Members of Ghonim's group were careful to plan protest schedules around the Friday prayer sessions at the start of the Egyptian weekend. "Friday prayers were by far the largest weekly gatherings of Egyptians from all classes," he explained.[14] Accordingly, Ghonim and his peers made sure that the locations of the January 25 marches were announced promptly before midnight[15] on Thursday, January 20, so that people could discuss the event at prayers the next day. Similarly, protests on January 28 were deliberately scheduled to begin from mosques immediately after the Friday afternoon (*Jumu'ah*) prayer. In interlinking their demonstrations with Friday prayer sessions, Egyptian revolutionaries were able to present the opportunity for participation in the January 28 protests to Egyptians who lacked access to or sufficient knowledge of earlier digital agitation. "Reaching working-class Egyptians was not going to happen through the Internet and Facebook," Ghonim recalled.[16] He would unfortunately be prevented from seeing the fruits of his comrades' labor: by the evening of January 27 he had been arrested by agents of Egypt's Ministry of Interior. He would not be released until February 7. Almost simultaneously with Ghonim's arrest, at twelve minutes past midnight, a major shutdown of Egypt's internet providers commenced.

By the next day, mobile phone access in Cairo was dwindling, with networks eventually shutting down altogether in the afternoon. "Little did the regime know that this was the single largest promotional effort possible for the revolution," Ghonim[17] recalled. "Every citizen who had not heard of the uprising now realized that a major challenge to the regime must be under way." This created an exceptional situation, in which huge numbers of people whose routines and information flows had been disrupted decided, as Ghonim put it, "to take to the streets, some for no other reason than just to find out what was happening." As a leading Egyptian communications expert, Mohammad el-Nawawy, put it some days later, "The government has made a big mistake taking away the option at people's fingertips.... They're taking their frustration to the streets."[18] With the online space digitally blockaded, Tahrir and the paths leading to it would now constitute the only remaining avenues for Cairo's potential revolutionaries.

The events of January 28 were overwhelming. Hundreds of thousands took to the streets, progressing toward Tahrir Square from Friday prayer sessions across Cairo. Marches snaked through Cairo, originating from the city's many suburbs, just as they had on January 25, but this time with greater force, numbers, and determination. Protesters battled through lines and lines of the Egyptian police's paramilitary Central Security Forces, forcing their permanent retreat for the remainder of the revolution. With occasional exceptions, these were by no means organized revolutionary brigades. In fact, January 28 also marked the moment when activists who had helped set the stage for the revolution's early protests and online presence lost their last vestige of control over the proceedings.

Mahmood, who had been involved in organizing the day's protests, told me how the few activists who had been assigned to each protest site arrived only to realize that numbers were far too large for them to direct or manage. "We barely found each other, and we were just making sure that we were okay," he told me. Coordination problems only intensified once protesters reached Tahrir, and communication lines remained down. "Many of our ideas were unable to be put forward, because we definitely lost control," he explained. One could be forgiven for thinking that conflicts with Egypt's security forces and the burning of the National Democratic Party headquarters that day were examples of such lapses of organization. However, the contrary appears to have been the case. Another activist, also involved in organization on the day of the twenty-eighth, recalled how some carefully organized battalions of highly mobilized activists had agreed to burn the NDP headquarters that afternoon and entered Tahrir Square in the evening with "no other objective... except burning their HQ to the ground."[19] Indeed, Mahmood corroborated this story, recalling how some groups of protesters had planned and "prepared for a scenario in which to confront the security forces violently, using plastic shields and... Molotov cocktails." His own contingent of organizers, however, were disinclined toward such measures.

A short distance from Tahrir Square, in the impoverished streets of Boulaq Aboul Ela, a demonstration originating in the Giza district of Imbaba had been pinned down and brutalized by Central Security Forces. Witnessing this, locals sprang into action: "The people of Boulaq... closed from the side... and then they ambushed everyone and freed the demonstrators, [armed] with cables, with steel sticks, wooden sticks, they even used gunfire when [the police] started using canisters," Hakim recalled. Of all the people of Cairo, the city's poor had every reason to hate the police, who had long treated them with abuse and contempt. "The people who used violence, who burned all the police stations, were the poor classes... who were being harassed and being ripped off by the police, being used by the police," I was told.

Popular outrage against the security forces in the wake of January 25 meant that January 28's Friday of Rage offered the opportunity for what some of my interviewees dubbed "payback time," the opportunity to legitimately attack the police without social sanction. To the backdrop of this opportune frame, ordinary people across Egypt battled through lines of officers, fighting them all the way back to their police stations, many of which were subsequently burned down. Indeed, although many have depicted the events in Tahrir as a predominantly middle-class phenomenon, such a description is not so representative of the events of the revolution as a whole. As Neil Ketchley's authoritative study of Egyptian revolutionary violence notes, attacks on police were greatest in areas of high unemployment, with few college graduates, and a history of police repression.[20] This included those local to Boulaq.[21]

The successful defeat of regime forces on January 28 marked the shift from an opportune frame to a full-fledged opportune situation, one of the key conditions of convergence evoked in the Eighteen Days. Police stations were in ruins, the ruling party headquarters had been burned to the ground, and the regime's long-standing enforcers—the Central Security Forces—had been pushed off the streets. With the structural impediments to collective action removed, ordinary Egyptians finally had a chance to make their demands felt.[22] As Gamal,[23] a teenager during the time of the revolution, later recalled, "the fear wall" of social repression, in which people were afraid even to express their political opinions in private, let alone act publicly, "just dropped." "Before that people were very afraid to post on Facebook... [or] to talk in very intimate conversation," he explained, "because maybe someone with the neighbors was with the police or the government and would hear, and the police would come and take us."

The Uncertain Days

While many popular accounts of the Eighteen Days will present Tahrir Square as swelling to the brim throughout Egypt's revolution, the stark reality is that initial participation came in dramatic ebbs and flows. The day after the revolutionary events of January 28, satellite footage[24] showed only a tiny gathering in the square. Simultaneously, the Mubarak regime's attempts at damage limitation moved into overdrive. An image of a country under siege by vicious mobs was disseminated through all of the regime's communicative apparatuses. With internet and mobile phone connections interrupted, public panic, and an aggressive rumor mill, such a feeling was already on the rise. There was a serious danger of losing momentum.

"Misinformation campaigns are well orchestrated," surmised Pierre Sioufi, who was able to witness the dissonance between news reports and reality from his top-floor apartment on Tahrir Square.[25] "Families and friends are... pressurizing the protesters because they are now brainwashed by the Egyptian TV and the security forces' rumor spreading organism." The campaign had been incredibly effective, and almost all of the participants I spoke to explained how their desire to visit Tahrir early in the revolution had been kept in check by family security concerns.[26] These were exacerbated by missives received from retreating police and deploying soldiers alike that the jails were open, law enforcement had ceased, and help was not available. Domestic television networks repeated regime propaganda, leaving those without satellite television under the impression that the country had descended into criminal anarchy. The square was "empty, really empty," Hakim recalled.

To combat regime misinformation, a number of activists embarked on misinformation campaigns of their own. "We spread that there were maybe twenty, thirty demonstrations in Cairo heading to Tahrir Square, and actually there were around eight, or seven, I guess," Hakim noted. "We spread that there were huge casualties happening in different cities. We didn't know what was happening; we just spread everything in a very random way... this motivated people more." At times when the square was sparsely populated, some activists tried to prevent journalists from taking photos, while sending reports of inflated numbers. "We actually sent false pictures of the square," Hakim explained. "We had connections to international media publications... a lot of human rights organizations as well. This enabled us to spread huge false, and true, news." Established media organizations such as Al Jazeera "had a very important role," Hakim admitted. Indeed, at the time the network had reported three million protesters flooding Tahrir Square, a physical impossibility by a factor of 1,100 percent.[27]

Amid a confusing and chaotic informational environment, activists like Hakim worked hard to sustain the cognitive conditions of convergence from which revolutionaries had benefited on January 28. Their efforts comprised employing both opportune and paramount framing, pushing a notion of the revolution as a massive popular uprising through which the regime could be finally overthrown and a historical moment recognized around the world. One of these many attempts constituted a January 29 ruse to imply that the protests had garnered the support of the United States. Following a public statement by Mohamed ElBaradei that the United States needed to take a stance on the Egyptian Revolution, "we came up with [the news that Barack] Obama had a phone call with ElBaradei to discuss the current Egyptian situation, and President Obama expressed his solidarity with the Egyptian martyrs and people," Hakim explained. The activists researched White House press releases and prepared excerpts from a false statement in their style. It took until the next day for the White House to release a readout of the president's calls that contradicted this account.[28]

After three more days of disruption, on February 1 Mubarak appeared on national television in an attempt to deescalate the situation, offering to implement modest reforms and resign at the end of his term. In response, the number of protesters in Tahrir Square took a nosedive. This decline was reversed the very next day thanks to a sudden, unexpected attack by regime-aligned thugs, who had been mysteriously allowed through the military checkpoints set up around the square. The conflict became known as the Camel Battle, named for the camel-riding brigands who charged into the square wielding clubs, swords, and Molotov cocktails. News of the battle swiftly incensed the previously calmed passions of those who had hitherto remained at home.

With Mubarak again on the offensive and the stakes so high, participation in protest became utterly paramount. It was evident that the future of Egypt was at stake: stand with Mubarak, or stand with the people. This paramount situation was further reenforced by a regime ultimatum sent via mass text message to all thirty-one million Egyptians on the Vodafone network. Intended to persuade ordinary Egyptians to intervene in support of Mubarak, the message called on "Egypt's honest and loyal men to confront the traitors and criminals and protect our people and honor and our precious Egypt."[29] Such provocations appeared to have the opposite effect and only amplified the sense of compulsion that many Egyptians felt to defend their countrymen in the streets.

Just as Egyptians came to the aid of their compatriots in Tahrir Square when news of the Camel Battle spread, there were also many other instances of revolutionary mobilization on the basis of a shared national identity, an increasingly pivotal affinity as Egypt's contentious episode gathered storm.[30] Yusha,[31] a former soldier, recalled how during this period "people felt like they belonged to something." It felt as if "all of Egypt came to Tahrir Square," he explained. "We were all one side, all united, even if you were different." Yusha and his friends tried to capture this feeling in a banner they brought to the square the day of the Camel Battle. It read: WE ARE NOT MEL GIBSON AND THIS IS NOT BRAVEHEART. WE ARE JUST EGYPTIANS AND FREEDOM IS WHAT WE WANT.

Victory on February 2 also prompted the emergence of new physical conditions of convergence. Tahrir Square, having proved to be suitably defensible, became an opportune space for revolutionary protest. The square served to shield those who visited from otherwise dangerous conditions. Being in Tahrir "felt safer than when you left," Mariam told me. "Being there with the people? It made me feel safer." The newfound safety from regime attack that the now secured square provided attracted many protesters who would otherwise have never attended revolutionary gatherings. One older woman, Fatima,[32] even brought her adolescent daughter to Tahrir Square. "I took my daughter with me; she was twelve years old," Fatima explained. When I asked her further about safety concerns, she simply responded that "there were no police, so there was no violence: we were sitting and singing and chanting, and discussing with one another." It later transpired that she had even allowed her daughter to live and sleep overnight in the square unaccompanied.

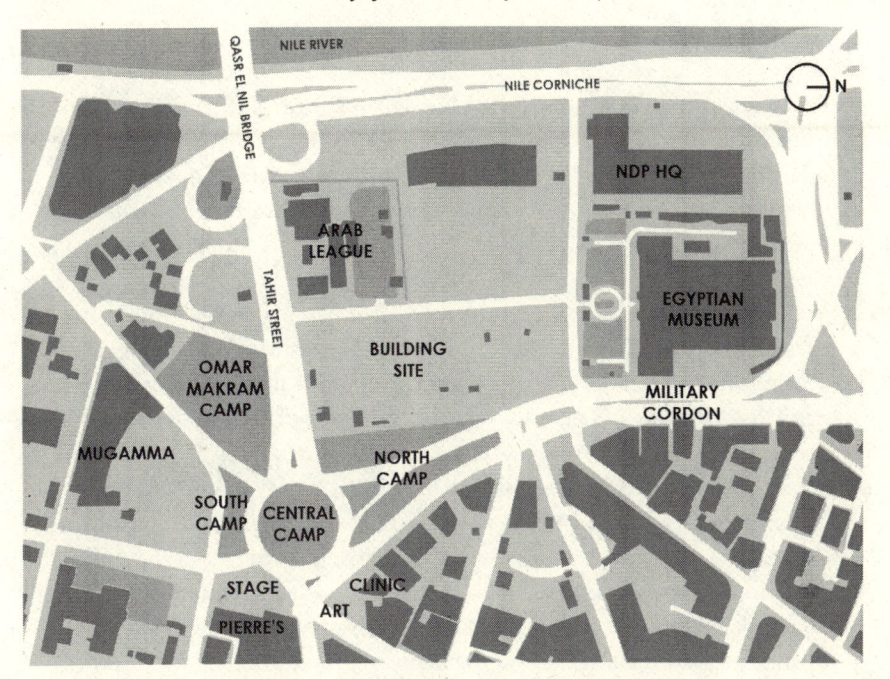

FIGURE 4.1. Labeled map of Tahrir Square and its environs.

The Revolutionary Square

In the wake of the Camel Battle, Tahrir transformed into a full-blown occupation. With thousands staying overnight, protesters set about creating organized common spaces (figure 4.1). By February 3 a central campsite arose in the middle of the Tahrir roundabout, with auxiliary camps emerging on the patches of grass and concrete encircling it to the north and the south, in the respective directions of the Egyptian Museum and the central office of the state bureaucracy, the Mugamma. Another satellite camp sprung up outside Tahrir's Omar Makram mosque, which had itself been repurposed for revolutionary endeavors. Tahrir's main camp hosted spaces for internet use, recycling, and even a nursery. Closer to the Nile, on Tahrir Street, food stalls and flag sellers set up shop next to a set of publicly accessible toilets and a nearby drinking-water tap. The north camp offered a newspaper board where the country's main dailies could be read and discussed. A sprinkling of cultural elites, intellectuals, Salafis, and political types also each set up their own enclave in the square for the purposes of debate, discussion, or simply passing time.

On the other side of Tahrir, closer to downtown Cairo, a makeshift stage was erected, from which public figures and other speakers would address the square. This part of Tahrir also featured another clinic, set up in a KFC restaurant, as well as a small space for public artwork. The square also played host to daily prayers for Muslims and Christians. These mass prayers not only proved popular cultural events and an excellent alternative to the otherwise disrupted prayer sessions elsewhere around Cairo but also allowed more pious followers of Egypt's two faiths to extend their time in Tahrir, free of the obligation to go and worship elsewhere. Equipped with a nursery, a clinic, an open-air mosque and church, and even an ersatz art gallery, the occupation of Tahrir meant that the Egyptian revolutionary cause was not only compatible with many Egyptians' daily patterns of activity but also actively appealed to the many obligations and drives of the capital's inhabitants.

Away from the street, a number of local buildings also fulfilled supportive functions. One such building was Pierre Sioufi's tenth-floor apartment, which became something of a haven for activists who found themselves overwhelmed by the masses in Tahrir. Pierre's place, with its seemingly unstoppable internet connection, became a nerve center for revolutionary media and played host to all manner of intriguing characters. One of these was Heba,[33] a teenage girl at the time of the revolution. "There were so many people everywhere sleeping... cooking... bloggers who knew Pierre just came up and wrote their blogs from there.... It was a hub for activist social media, and media in general," she recalled. The apartment also played host to foreign journalists, and many of the most iconic photos of Tahrir during the Eighteen Days were taken from its balcony.

Though the occupation was by no means a comprehensive operation, it was enough for Tahrir to persist and survive as a space of protest. "People just had to organize themselves. Things just went in a certain flow... the roles just kind of divided on their own, it was all very random," Heba explained. The flow of volunteers into the square was substantially guided by people's personal and material resources. For the older generation, delivering supplies to Tahrir served as a means of participation that saved their having to endure the harsh winter cold. For others, professional skills guided their engagement with the protest: doctors opened up clinics, bloggers set up media operations, and those who were physically fit came to take care of manual labor. "People just started doing something... and everyone started coming to help," Heba recalled. "Like, someone says I want to build a bathroom... and then he has a hundred people helping him. Things just happened very spontaneously."

Unlike the predominantly well-heeled contingent of revolutionary activists, with the time and resources to visit Tahrir almost every day, the bulk of those who participated in Egypt's revolutionary protests did so only occasionally and came from a very wide set of social backgrounds. Few were from the richer classes from which many of these activists hailed. As one visitor to Tahrir from Egypt's better off classes put it, "The majority of people from the top ten percent... wouldn't go and act *against* the revolution, but they were not happy about it."[34] By contrast, many of those who more regularly participated in the Tahrir occupation were instead workers from nearby neighborhoods, students, and the young unemployed from across the city. All of these groups were constrained by the realities of their social status, patterns of activity, resources, and obligations (the full matrix of social affinities). Accordingly, those who made up the popular presence in Tahrir on any given day would tend not to be intensely aware of developments the previous day. It was thus exceedingly difficult for revolutionary activists to establish any clear sense of rapport with the masses filling the square, let alone an aura of leadership.

The prospect of sleeping overnight in the square drew still different social groups than those who tended to participate in the daytime. One person who bore stark witness to this was Heba. After discovering Pierre's place, Heba began kitchen duty, handing out enormous batches of lentil soup to protesters in the square, keeping them warm and energized during the harsh Cairo winter. "When you're handing out the soup... you get to see all kinds of people," she explained. "There were definitely a lot of people from outside Cairo," Heba recalled, telling me how the events of January 28 had prompted a sizable number of rural Egyptians to leave their villages for the city. While some of the square's rural arrivals were those who had left their livelihoods and families behind, others brought their entire families to the square. "There was something special" about these people, Heba recalled. "They came all the way and... had to bring their families with them because if they left... their families would have nothing to eat." It was thus that some of the very poorest in Egypt were driven to Tahrir by obligation-based affinity: joining the protest meant access to food, water, shelter, and protection during a time of utmost uncertainty. Another group who became similarly bound up in Tahrir's occupation by dint of social affinity—this time, their patterns of activity—were the city's taxi drivers. With traffic blocked by checkpoints all over the city and no easy means to make money, many of Cairo's taxi-men made their way to Tahrir and stayed until the fall of the regime.

In the days following the Camel Battle, conflicts with Mubarak loyalist forces died down considerably. Egypt's defense minister, Mohamed Hussein Tantawi, even visited the square on February 4, and detachments of the armed forces appeared to begin providing some sense of security to the encampment. Without major new threats to defend against, and with plenty of time to bide, Tahrir took on a festive atmosphere. "The Square is in a party mood still.... Nothing really is happening but there is a sense of expectation all over," Pierre Sioufi mused in a February 5 post to his personal Facebook page.[35] Tahrir was evolving from a merely opportune space to an exceptional one, existing in the center of Cairo as some kind of militant fête. The square became a fashionable social venue, with self-determined deputations of its more radical contingents advancing to protest elsewhere, while ongoing discussions took place between the regime and the various political groups who had arrived at or formed in Tahrir. "We were all celebrating," Yusha told me. "These were the best eleven days of my life." He likened Tahrir to a "family party, but this family was about twenty million people.... You can eat for free, you can have anything you need.... People were singing with guitars and stages, it was like a carnival for ten days... everywhere, everyone was celebrating. The spirit—I like to call it the Tahrir Spirit—it was amazing." As Wael Adel, a civil engineer, recalled, this "festive atmosphere was a key element to drawing the high numbers that Egypt had rarely seen."[36]

Just as Tahrir became an exceptional space over the course of early February, so too did the nation's norms and rules seem to weaken in a more general sense. With the uniformed enforcers of the status quo gone and a seemingly magical atmosphere in the streets, an exceptional frame took hold in Egypt. This prompted many people who had never dreamed of joining a protest to join the revolutionary crowds swelling around the country. Many of the class, gender, religious, and political divisions that had long been prominent in Egypt seemed to break down before people's eyes. Fraternizing with a Muslim Brotherhood member, once a sinister prospect, was no longer taboo, intermingling with those of a different class was no longer considered a danger to one's safety, and joining a mass crowd ceased to be the frightening prospect it had once been. A long-standing fear of crowds had been ingrained in many young Egyptian women, yet this fear was suspended during the revolution. Rather, revolutionary participants of all genders explicitly recalled how the gatherings of the Eighteen Days had been incredibly safe when compared with other public gatherings, with incidents of sexual assault and collective harassment standing at virtually zero.[37]

After seven days of further protest, on February 10 Egypt's military finally played its decisive hand, in concert with regime elites. The Supreme Council of the Armed Forces held a meeting, from which Mubarak and his vice president were notably absent, and later that day announced:

> In affirmation and support for the legitimate demands of the people, the Supreme Council of the Armed Forces convened today, 10 February 2011... and decided to remain in continuous session to consider what procedures and measures that may be taken to safeguard the nation, and the achievements and aspirations of the great people of Egypt.[38]

"All your demands will be met today," General Hassan al-Roueini, told protesters in Tahrir. Meanwhile, Hossan Badrawi, the NDP party chief, told the international press that he expected Mubarak to "make an announcement that will satisfy [protesters'] demands." It appeared that Mubarak was being forced out. When Mubarak did take to the airwaves, however, it was not to satisfy demands, but to reiterate his current position in a speech strikingly similar to his plea on the eve of the Camel Battle. Mubarak remained steadfast in his commitment to rule the country and exert control over the constitution, while delegating everyday executive responsibilities to his vice president, Omar Suleiman. Immediately afterward, Suleiman took to the stage: "The door is open for more dialogue," he told protesters. "Return to your home and work."[39]

Protesters' demands had not been met that day. With hopes dashed and outrage at a high, the last great manifestation of the Egyptian Revolution was underway. One Egyptian chronicler recalled how within an hour of Mubarak's speech, "one group of protesters was moving to surround the Information Ministry... [while] another seemed determined to make the several-mile trek to the presidential palace."[40] By the next day, a Friday "of Departure" (the second Friday to be given this name), protesters had set up camp outside both locations in addition to seizing the offices of Egypt's state television stations, which in turn finally defected in favor of the revolution. The streets swelled with angry Egyptians. "And then," one journalist who had been covering the protests recalled, "with a short, lugubrious statement from Suleiman, it was over. Mubarak was out, and the military was in command."[41]

Affinity and Convergence in the Eighteen Days

The Egyptian Revolution's Eighteen Days stand as an excellent study of varying dynamics across the full spectrum of mobilization, but affinity and convergence play a particularly starring role. As this chapter has illustrated, Egypt's revolution was a coming together of a great many individuals, few of whom were acutely aware of the ideas, intentions, and agency of their fellow revolutionaries. Many of the participants I interviewed, even those who were well educated, informed, and connected, professed not to know how the revolution was organized, who was calling the shots, or what exactly was going on. Meanwhile, the activists and organizers with whom I spoke professed to be equally clueless about who their supporters were and why they had filled Tahrir. It seemed to them as if the great mass of people who had assembled there were compelled by an entirely separate force and merely intersected with the plans of the revolution's emboldened organizers.

Alongside my own interviews, other studies have confirmed that even though networks of friends and acquaintances would encounter each other once they arrived at Tahrir, "neither social nor activist networks played a large part" in the decisions made by nonactivists to demonstrate during the revolution.[42] It was only among more highly politicized individuals, already involved in activism, that contentious political networks appear to have played a significant role.

AFFINITIES

The initial affinities that underpinned participation in Egypt's Eighteen Days were widespread dispositions held by a broad spectrum of Egyptians whose social status placed them outside the ruling class and whose patterns of activity brought them into contact with the revolutionary cause on January 25 and 28. As time went on and revolutionaries repelled police and claimed space, an increasingly broad array of convergence conditions began to overlap and increase in intensity, with the revolution eventually exhibiting every single configuration of contexts and subtypes of convergence over its course. Accordingly, by the time the revolution reached its peak, an even wider array of affinities was also at play, including drives, obligations, and resources. This is summarized in figure 4.2, with illustrative examples drawn from the case for the aid of the reader.

Psychological affinities—especially the dispositions discussed in chapter 3—predominated at the outset of Egypt's Eighteen Days. Shared perceptions of the country's unjust conditions and shared attitudes about the nature of that injustice and who was to blame were ubiquitous among the revolutionary protesters I talked to. Incensed by electoral manipulation, economic mismanagement, and a general sense of relative deprivation, ordinary Egyptians in cities such as Cairo had become antagonistic to the Mubarak regime. This sense of injustice and strongly felt antiregime attitudes were further enriched by a strong sense of Egyptian national identity, one counterposed against the kleptocratic Mubarak regime and its brutal, repressive police state. This identity formed the basis of strong

Social Affinities

Patterns of Activity	Resources
Worship, neighborhoods	Supplies, skills

Social Status	Obligations
Cross-class, all genders	(+) Security, hunger (−) Family obligations

Psychological Affinities

Dispositions	Drives
Identity National identity	**Interests** Concerts, political discussion, rev. tourism
Perceived Injustice Deprivation, corruption, oppression	**Needs** Overcoming fear, expressing rage, collective celebration
Attitudes Antiregime hatred	

Subtype

Context	Opportune	Exceptional	Paramount
Structural (Situation)	Security forces' defeat	Digital and social disruption	The Camel Battle
Cognitive (Frame)	"Payback time"	Normative breakdown	Ben Ali's ouster
Physical (Space)	Tahrir's latter safety	Festival atmosphere	Tahrir's importance

Affinity Predisposes

Convergence Catalyzes

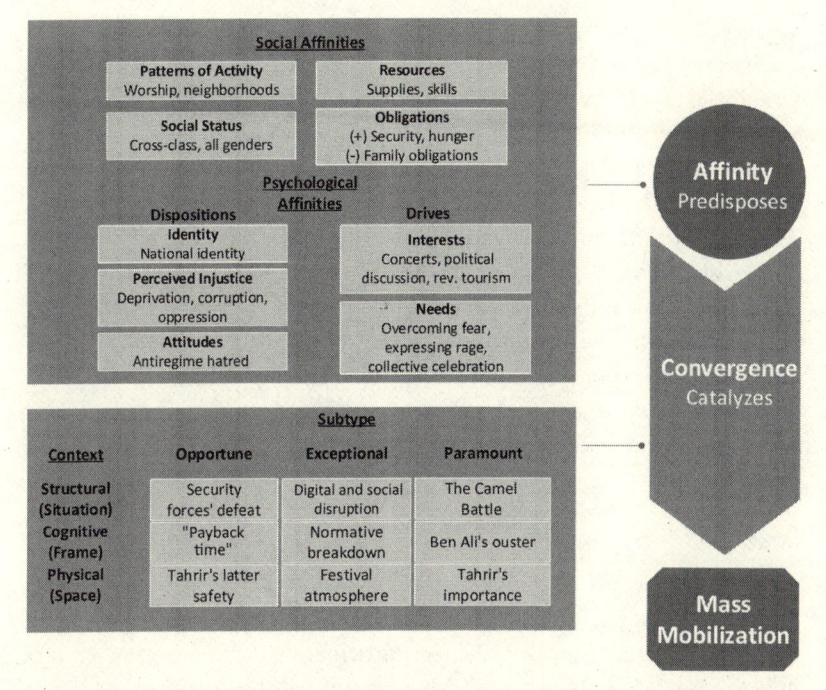

Mass Mobilization

FIGURE 4.2. Summary of affinity-convergence mobilization in the Egyptian Revolution.

solidarity among protesters with otherwise differentiated political and economic agendas. Just as the Mubarak regime had once united Egyptians in fear, the revolution came to represent a single national dream. As one of my interviewees[43] put it, "The dream united us. This dream of freedom, the dream of possible things that could happen, the dream of justice." Revolutionary protest drew substantially upon these affinities, which underpinned protesters' conscious decisions to visit the square or check out a march.

Accompanying the role played by dispositions were psychological drives. Early in the revolution, people's drives to express their rage, whether in the form of violent payback or peaceful protest, helped predispose participation in early clashes with the police; later on it was instead people's need for collective effervescence and celebration that attracted them to Tahrir. During this latter period (after the Camel Battle), people also sought out the Tahrir occupation in order to pursue their interest in the novel and exciting political and cultural goings on in the square.

Alongside the role of psychological affinities, social affinities also figured in Egypt's mobilization process. The most prominent of these was the intersection of Egyptians' patterns of activity with occasions for revolutionary protest. Where and how one lived, worked, and prayed played a vital role in the revolution's early protests by creating contact between potential protesters and the revolutionary cause, particularly vital for the revolution's early marches on January 25 and 28. As we saw earlier in this chapter, the intersection between people's patterns of activity and contentious gatherings helped swell the revolutionary crowds far beyond those who had already planned to attend, appealing to a broad spectrum of social categories across class, gender, and (latterly) religious lines. Of less prominence—but still notable at the height of Tahrir's occupation—was the role of obligations and resources, which shepherded new people into the square, whether they were seeking to be helped or to help out, so long as competing obligations, such as caring for family, did not get in the way.

CONVERGENCE

Activating Egyptians' affinities were several key conditions of convergence. The exceptional situation created by the revolution disrupted activity patterns in a way that further enriched participation. This occurred against the backdrop of an already established paramount frame—sparked by the success of Tunisian revolutionaries, stoked by the burning down of the ruling party headquarters on January 28, and dramatically reenforced by the regime's last-ditch assault on Tahrir Square on February 2. Likewise, the opportune framing of the revolution, expressed in the "payback time" of the poor and downtrodden, heralded a crucial chance to strike back at a corrupt regime and security state that had tormented people for decades.

Alongside the opportune and paramount frames that underpinned spontaneous revolutionary mobilization, corresponding changes in structural conditions in Egypt further increased the magnetism of revolutionary participation. When police were forced to flee the streets on January 28, this created an opportune situation for potential protesters, one where they could participate in revolutionary agitation free from the threat of secret surveillance or police brutalization. The regime's use of Molotov cocktails and mounted brigands in efforts to reclaim the square and rally its supporters on February 2 and (unsuccessfully) calling millions to arms against the revolution created the conditions for a paramount situation, in which people surged to defend the revolution and their country's future.

There was also something special about the physical conditions in Tahrir Square. Following the defeat of regime forces on February 2, Tahrir came to constitute an opportune space. It was at once visible to the world and protected from the regime. Participants were able to feel freer, more empowered, and physically safer than they would have elsewhere. This was bolstered by Tahrir's contemporaneous character as a paramount space, a location literally named "Liberation" in the wake of Egypt's 1919 revolution, and a classic site for momentous protests across Egyptian history. As Tahrir evolved, the square also exhibited exceptional features. Going to Tahrir ceased to be the pursuit of the dedicated revolutionary, and instead became an opportunity to pursue diverse interests, from collective prayer to musical concerts and nighttime festivals. For those who were less politicized, visiting the square offered a once-in-a-lifetime experience for revolutionary tourism or an opportunity for food and shelter.

Would Egypt's tremendous popular energy prove sustainable? We will see in chapter 5 how heightened conditions of convergence and widely held affinities progressively gave way to a process of mass demobilization, in which state powers were effectively able to rob the fledgling revolutionary movement of its contentious potential and disrupt revolutionary frames. Meanwhile, rising division among Egypt's victorious revolutionaries stoked the emergence of harsher divides among the very diverse coalition of actors who participated in the revolution.

CHAPTER FIVE

The Fall and Fall of Revolutionary Egypt

As important as they may be, mass mobilizations are hardly the sole engine by which revolutions or any other major contentious political processes are prosecuted. In fact, they are more often its fuel. Savvy players in the various arenas of revolutionary politics are able to leverage their resources, capacities, and other various attributes in order to engineer or capitalize on emergent political opportunities.[1] Two such players were Field Marshal Mohamed Hussein Tantawi, the head of the Egyptian armed forces, and his protégé, Director of Military Intelligence Abdel Fattah el-Sisi. With Tantawi at its helm, it was Egypt's Supreme Council of the Armed Forces (SCAF) that ultimately ousted Mubarak from power at the behest of the masses. It would be this very same group that subsequently presided over Egypt's so-called transitional period. Two years later, on July 3, 2013, Sisi would lead the SCAF in a similar seizure of power against Egypt's deeply unpopular first postrevolutionary government. While Tantawi had been willing to entertain the possibility of civilian rule, Sisi decided that military authority—chiefly, his own—would become permanent.

The ultimate story of the Egyptian Revolution was, alas, an assuredly unhappy one. After the country's eighteen-day uprising, any further revolutionary progress was swiftly curtailed, allowing the state structures that underpinned Egypt's dictatorship to remain largely in place. By the time I arrived in Cairo in the summer of 2015, the country had found itself firmly in the grip of a regime arguably even more entrenched and sophisticated than its predecessors. It remains so today.

So, how did Egypt's passionate, explosive revolutionary energy so rapidly fizzle out? Where did all the revolutionaries go, and why? Tracing the declining trajectory of Egyptian revolutionary mobilization following the Eighteen Days draws particular attention to two complementary explanations. The first of these concerns the Egyptian revolutionary movement's notable organizational deficits. Revolutionary activists were unable to capitalize on Egypt's revolutionary period to build an effective movement infrastructure, whether by way of formal organized bodies or broader supporting networks. Moreover, those preexisting organizations that halfheartedly partook in the revolution rapidly shifted their focus away from revolutionary change and toward institutional politics. In light of Egyptian revolutionaries' organizational failings, a second explanation becomes all the more enlightening. This explanation concerns not the orientation of organized movements, or their resources and capacity, but rather the fate of the hundreds of thousands who flocked to Tahrir Square from beyond such movements, their affinity to the revolutionary cause, and the cessation of the convergence conditions that brought them there. This chapter focuses on both of these explanations. First, I explain how and why revolutionaries were unable to build an effective mobilizing apparatus out of the Eighteen Days. Second, I detail the means by which Egyptians' affinities for revolutionary mobilization came undone and how the conditions of convergence that provoked their participation were thwarted.

The Activists: Where Did the Movement Go?

Before we get to the puzzle of how the Egyptian masses stepped away from the field of revolutionary conflict, it is worth explaining the organizational deficits that left Egyptian revolutionaries largely unable to mobilize on demand using conventional social movement strategies.

INSUFFICIENT MOVEMENT BUILDING

As we will see in the chapters on Occupy Wall Street, the 2020 Black Lives Uprising, and the 1789 French Revolution, periods of relatively spontaneous mass popular mobilization often provide incredibly fruitful conditions for movement building. Savvy organizers can seize upon these moments to recruit energized and radicalized newbies, while grassroots participants can form friendships, collaborative networks, and resource-sharing relationships. The comparative dearth of any of these activities in Egypt's revolutionary period cannot be overstated.

Although the occupation of Tahrir provided an opportunity for disparate groups across Egyptian society to come into contact, I was surprised to find that nobody I talked to purported to have made new social ties that stretched across social categories during the Eighteen Days. Rather, the kinds of connections revolutionary participants tended to make in Tahrir were almost always members of their social class and steeped in the same cultural, political, and religious inclinations. "If I didn't know [redacted] from the revolution, I would have known him another way," Yusuf (the participant quoted at the start of chapter 4) affirmed, when I asked him about the group of friends he had made during his time in Tahrir.

Despite a diverse array of encounters, there was little substantive cooperation and interaction that brought already divided individuals or groups together for more than an instant. When I asked my sources about the "times that people really came together," their answer was almost always the same: moments of collective opposition to the regime or experiences of a collective cordiality. Though I witnessed frequent vignettes about how bearded Brothers helped young women set up tents, or how atheists and Salafis fought together against the Central Security Forces, when these moments ended, the individuals involved would go their separate ways. Many only visited Tahrir for a day or two of the eighteen total, and no distinctive identity became clearly associated with being a protester there, except for the notion of representing the "Egyptian people" as a whole.

Despite these setbacks, activists still made conscientious attempts to build a formalized revolutionary coalition and platform for popular demands. "At some point after the twenty-eighth of January, there was talk that there was nobody to negotiate in the square, and that they [the regime] don't understand the demands of the people," explained Mahmood,[2] a member of the ill-fated coalition. "There were attempts on the side of the regime to meet young people, so that they can be considered to be 'the revolutionary youth,' [and] reach an agreement with them that was not representative of what people wanted." It was within this context that Mahmood and his fellow activists attempted to establish the Revolutionary Youth Coalition, a group that brought together diverse activists from various organizations in Tahrir and those involved in planning the protests on January 25 and 28.

The Revolutionary Youth Coalition was intended to be a broad-based group and saw its primary role as enacting a "block" on formal negotiation between the regime and any groups claiming to represent the protesters. "I remember our slogan was: 'No negotiation until the fall of the regime,'" Mahmood said. Nonetheless, regime outlets were keen to float potential concessions, having offered the coalition promises, including that the country's rigged 2010 parliamentary elections would be repeated fairly and that Mubarak would not run in a renewed presidential contest. Despite the coalition being recognized by the faltering Mubarak regime, their attempts to build popular participation and authority proved comparatively fruitless. "People in the square would actually stop and question us: 'On what basis are we actually represented in this? Why have you formed this coalition?' These people didn't know us... we were not known by the masses, so people did not trust us," Mahmood affirmed. In light of some positive postrevolutionary media depictions, the Revolutionary Youth Coalition would eventually gain some acceptance among ordinary Egyptians, but by this point they had forgone their most viable recruiting opportunity: the revolutionary occupation of Tahrir. Moreover, the coalition seriously fumbled any attempt to ride the Tahrir wave by announcing that it would demobilize shortly after Mubarak's ouster. The group proclaimed that their participation in protests would cease "in order to give SCAF and the government a chance to achieve the objectives of the 25 January Revolution, bring stability back and rebuild the country."[3] Activists involved in groups such as Kefaya, the April 6 movement, and the National Association for Change took a similar tack, seeking to use their rising public influence to shape civic debates and further the human rights agenda that they had adopted prior to Mubarak's downfall, rather than confronting the SCAF directly in the streets. It took until April 1 for these groups to manifest a formal effort to "Save the Revolution," by which point there was considerably less public interest in further revolutionary activism. Although around ten thousand Egyptians did attend the protest, it paled in comparison to the revolutionary crowds of the Eighteen Days.

COALITIONAL DECOHERENCE

While activists' efforts to build new movements during the Eighteen Days were met with little substantial success, many groups who already possessed organized platforms lost interest in the cause almost as rapidly as they had jumped on the revolutionary bandwagon. Even though diverse political groups did indeed eventually come together during the revolution, this coexistence never stopped each group from pursuing its own agenda. Rather, each participated in revolutionary protests for their own reasons and pursued their own interests. It just so happened that these interests were, temporarily, aligned. Once the Supreme Council of the Armed Forces replaced the Mubarak regime, each major faction was assigned their own military stewards and encouraged to work with the council behind closed doors rather than against it in the streets. The most formidable of these groups—the Muslim Brotherhood—was assigned to Tantawi, the head of the SCAF, and his right-hand man, Abdel Fattah el-Sisi.

With access to the "inside track" of Egypt's postrevolutionary politics, the nation's more established anti-Mubarak opposition parties and organizations were granted a considerable competitive advantage when compared with more radical, grassroots groups. However, this advantage was most pronounced in institutional political contexts and thus *outside* the sphere of revolutionary mass mobilization. Thus arose a relatively rapid shift in focus away from revolt and toward political competition. Only ten days after Mubarak's ouster, the Muslim Brotherhood had already announced its own political party, the Freedom and Justice Party, and many other revolutionary factions followed suit, either founding new political parties or rebranding and updating old political platforms for a postrevolutionary era.[4] The effect was that these fleeting but well-resourced revolutionary allies abandoned the revolutionary cause and transfigured themselves into institutional forces invested in the new order.

This divorce between radical activists and more formal political groups had occurred before around preparations for the 2005 election, and just as before, disunity provided space for repression and a withering away of support for social movements. There were now diverse outlets and avenues for Egyptians' common grievances, each proposing alternate, even contradictory, solutions.

The Masses: Where Did the People Go?

In contrast to the activities of organized forces, those who had comprised the revolutionary rank and file of the Eighteen Days experienced a rapid relaxation in the allure of further political participation. For the masses who had converged upon Tahrir in accordance with the affinities to which the revolution had appealed, Mubarak's ouster and the rise of temporary SCAF authority signaled an opportunity for calm. The structural context and mobilizing framing of events that had compelled them toward Tahrir faded away as a new political and discursive status quo took hold, with different opportunities, resurgent social norms, and markedly less existential stakes. Moreover, the underlying affinities that predisposed ordinary people toward revolutionary action were gradually unpicked as time went on. People's shifting daily activities and the pull of professional and family obligations actively dissuaded them from supporting further disruptive efforts, while their political attitudes, identity, and sense of injustice were transfigured by the shift from dictatorial to military authority and rising competition between postrevolutionary political causes. The fleeting conditions that had been so fertile for mass mobilization were fading fast.

CONVERGENCE THWARTED

To the chagrin of Egypt's revolutionary activists, the paramount situation that arose at the height of the revolution was short-lived. With Mubarak's overthrow, the existential battle for the fate of Egypt seemed to have ceased. The revolutionaries had won. Whether or not one was inclined to pursue further revolutionary change, the stakes had been definitively lowered. A realization dawned, both among firebrand revolutionaries and ordinary protesters: their participation in future protests—desirable as it might have been—was no longer as absolutely crucial as it had been during the Eighteen Days. "The first day after Mubarak was out... I went to Tahrir, but I didn't feel what I *was* feeling [during the revolution]," one revolutionary[5] explained. "I didn't feel *it* anymore. It was totally different: job done, finished, okay." From then on "I didn't participate in anything against the army during the SCAF," he recounted.

While a paramount situation on the scale of the grand showdown between Mubarak and the Egyptian people would remain unparalleled, there were nonetheless important but short-lived periods when the framing of protest activity (if not the actual structural dynamics of the situation at hand) once again took on paramount attributes. These were, almost invariably, elicited by moments of regime repression. Although these moments did not draw humongous crowds on the scale of January 28 and February 11, they were enough to inspire those Egyptians who still retained affinity with the revolutionary cause to return to the streets.

Just as the sudden importance of revolutionary participation faded away, so too did the sense that sustaining revolutionary mobilization constituted an opportunity to advance positive changes. With a planned constitutional referendum and parliamentary and presidential elections all within view, the draw of contentious political participation was considerably undermined by the tantalizing prospect of a functioning democracy appearing before Egyptians' very eyes. "People were like: 'It's not a good time stop the country, it's not very economically or political helpful,'" explained Gamal,[6] a university student at the time. "There was a parliamentary election coming up, and people were like, later we'll have the parliament, and the parliament will secure all our rights... we need to focus on the parliament, not on clashes [with the SCAF]." Of course, the collapse of opportune convergence conditions was not only a matter of framing but also the consequence of a situational shift. With the fall of Mubarak and the establishment of temporary military authority, the armed forces' sympathetic toleration of protest would rapidly fall away, leaving protesters in a situation in which they faced not only a resurgent police force but also a heavily armed military presence on the streets. The costs of participation were now considerably higher than they had been in early February.

The exceptional frame in which the revolution took place also dissipated, leaving behind it a renewed period of social division and spiraling rivalries between the country's different religious and political factions, each keen to claim a piece of the postrevolutionary cake. Moreover, the temporary conviviality that emerged during the revolutionary period was replaced with a postrevolutionary crime wave.[7] Protesting in the Egyptian streets felt markedly less safe and far more divisive than it had been before. One revolutionary[8] who spent his time intervening in the sexual assaults of Egypt's revolutionary and postrevolutionary crowds recalled how young women and girls attending postrevolutionary gatherings faced the risk of being sexually assaulted, gang raped, and even being physically torn apart in later manifestations, in a phenomenon known as *taḥarrush gama'ei* (collective harassment), colloquially dubbed "the circle of hell."[9] "I saw things that I didn't think I'd ever see in my life," he explained. "You'd find hundreds of guys around a girl, raping her, tearing her clothes with knives... you'd see a nine-year-old girl getting raped... [or] a sixty-year-old woman going to die because she couldn't breathe." He estimated that between November 2011 and July 2013 he personally witnessed more than 120 cases of these kinds of brutal assaults. On one occasion, his organization recorded eighty instances in a single day.

The conditions of convergence that supercharged Egyptian revolutionary mobilization rapidly ceased in the aftermath of Mubarak's overthrow. The conditions of opportunity, exception, and paramountcy that motivated many to spend their time in the streets during the Eighteen Days were replaced by new priorities, enhanced costs of participating, a return to life as usual, and a sense that further participation would be relatively pointless. Of course, there was nothing to stop these conditions—or weaker echoes of them—from returning in the future. Unfortunately for Egypt's revolutionaries, the decaying basis of mass mobilization did not simply occur in relation to convergence. The unraveling of the affinities that underpinned Egyptians' revolt against Mubarak served to even more enduringly undo the basis of spontaneous revolutionary mobilization.

AFFINITY UNDONE

With the Supreme Council of the Armed Forces' decision to oust Mubarak, the dictator's grip on Egypt had finally been relinquished. In the popular imagination, this had been attributed jointly to the Egyptian people and the nation's military. On the eve of Mubarak's removal, Tahrir protesters even chanted slogans asserting that "the army and the people are one hand." Thus, when the hand of the SCAF asserted its grip where Mubarak's once had been, many Egyptians saw it as a reflection of their own, guiding the revolutionary process in the best interests of the nation. The army, after all, was seen as having safeguarded the revolution against Mubarak, rather than throwing its lot in with the dictator.

"Throughout the revolution [people] were always talking to the military, saying... please guys, make him [Mubarak] step down," Hazem explained. "You expected the army to be on your side, and you were urging them to take action. So when they finally took *the action*, you were completely relaxed." While seasoned activists regarded the army with suspicion, the masses in Tahrir Square thought differently. "I heard people saying... [w]e shouldn't be leaving, we should stay to see what the SCAF will do, to see what the army will do. The revolution hasn't finished, it's only the beginning," Hazem recalled. Ordinary Egyptians, meanwhile, were skeptical. "There's no point, the military council took over... there's no opponent left, so why should you be staying?" people retorted. "You should go home now; there's nothing more to do. We'll leave it in their hands, and they should be taking over." "And," Hazem chuckled at the irony of the situation, "*they took over*."

With the military in control, the juxtaposition between an exclusionary, elitist regime and a common Egyptian identity was replaced by positive identification with an institution that was perceived to be close to the heart of the Egyptian nation. Military service is compulsory for almost all Egyptian men, and nearly everyone in the country knew someone actively serving. "We [Egyptians] will never accuse the army of not loving this country. No, they love it, and that's who they are," one former conscript[10] explained. "They think that Egypt is always in danger. Egypt must always be protected.... They are the protectors." The change in regime had effectively inverted the identity dynamics that had underpinned the revolution. Whereas under Mubarak participants saw the revolution as a conflict between the Egyptian nation and its dictator, under the SCAF further agitation constituted an assault on a vaunted national institution.

Even among those suspicious of Egypt's new military masters, the sense of injustice that had haunted Egypt prior to Mubarak's removal rapidly dissipated. As we saw in chapters 3 and 4, it was precisely the presence of these perceptions in Egypt's prerevolutionary masses that had helped swell the ranks of Cairo's revolutionary gatherings. With Mubarak gone and the promise from every single political outlet in the country that the revolutionaries' demands would be well and truly delivered upon, a new sense of optimism replaced the perceived injustice that previously characterized Egyptian social life. One postrevolutionary poll in June found that 83 percent of Egyptians believed that the country was getting fairer and freer, while 91 percent expected forthcoming elections to be conducted fairly.[11]

A shift in many Egyptians' patterns of activity, a rise in competing obligations, and needs the fulfillment of which could no longer be forestalled were all factors in the shifting affinities of Egypt's potential revolutionaries. "People needed to work, people needed to feed their families," Heba recalled. "If you were gonna keep going [to Tahrir]... then you'd get kicked out of your job... kicked out of university." Gamal similarly recalled how his family and friends rapidly lost interest in further revolutionary activity as the regularities of everyday life took precedence. Some would even complain about the goings on in Tahrir: "I can't import any products from outside! How are we going to live without police? How is my daughter going to go to the [leisure] club? My son has stopped his sports!" Such an attitude reflected the changing agenda of many ordinary Egyptians who sought to set revolutionary chaos aside in favor of a return to normalcy. People "were like... enough, *khalas*, Mubarak is out, let's move on to the political process," Ibrahim explained.

Without a unified enemy against which to juxtapose their political beliefs, Egyptians' political attitudes became increasingly competitive and divided. Ibrahim recalled how "divisions were happening between the masses of 2011... everyone was campaigning for his own side." One of the most prominent divisions was over whether the Muslim Brotherhood would make a fitting postrevolutionary government. Another, related issue concerned whether Egypt's constitution should be rewritten by an elected parliament or if military-commissioned revisions would suffice. The strong antiregime attitudes once held across Egypt were now replaced with a litany of nuanced political differences, each catered to by a different facet of Egypt's postrevolutionary political sphere.

The revolutionary cause was now out of sync with ordinary Egyptians' perceptions, attitudes, identity, and patterns of activity. As these affinities faded, Egypt's remaining revolutionary activists watched as their efforts to organize protest dwindled desperately. "We keep saying, where are the people who were there in the Eighteen Days, why aren't they here now?" Heba recalled, "but we never took the effort to know why they were there in the first place, and why they were interested." For Heba, the problem was that activists' priorities were simply unattractive to ordinary Egyptians. "Now we're asking for things they don't care about... these people just want to eat, they just want to live, but we just look in our own circles and say *we* want freedom.... [T]hey don't give a shit about that, they just want food, they want their kids to get treated when they're ill, that's all they want." She reiterated this point again later on in our interview: "It's not all of a sudden that we became a hundred people who protest. No, it happened gradually," she affirmed, "and it's because we kept neglecting the needs of the *actual* masses."

The End: What Happened Next

The revolution's first year passed without a repeat of the truly massive mobilizations seen during the Eighteen Days, but there were still sporadic instances of relatively substantial popular mobilization during this period. With only very occasional exceptions, these generally peaked in the tens rather than hundreds of thousands but still constituted substantial challenges for the SCAF. Perhaps the most notable was a series of clashes in November 2011, which drew many former revolutionary participants back to the square after about two hundred people conducting a small sit-in were brutally assaulted by SCAF enforcers. The response was incendiary but not as explosive as Egypt's earlier revolutionary process. Crowds flocked to Mohammad Mahmoud Street, between Tahrir Square and the Ministry of Interior, to defend the sit-in. Stark state repression rekindled the kind of paramount framing that had occurred during the revolutionary period. When friends, families, or news organizations "showed them the police brutality at Mohammad Mahmoud... people started gathering again," one participant, Abdul,[12] explained. Whenever the SCAF attempted to dismantle the sit-in, each time more forcibly than the last, more and more protesters made their way to Tahrir Square to support it, demanding that the SCAF hand over its authority to a civilian caretaker administration, rather than holding on to power until all elections were completed. The rising fervor associated with the Mohammad Mahmoud clashes was short-lived, however, with the whole affair lasting only six days, between November 19 and 24. The SCAF capitulated, appointing a handpicked civilian prime minister with whom they had previously worked during the Mubarak era, and that was it. Even limited concessions were enough to once again quell further protest.

Four days after the clashes, Egypt's extensive electoral period began, stretching from November 2011 to June 2012. During this period the character of Egyptian popular discourse swung decidedly away from revolution and in favor of party-political commentary. Media outlets that had provided much needed oxygen to postrevolutionary gatherings instead underwent election mania. With the country's democratic future seemingly secured, protest receded into the background.

After campaigns went into full swing, and the first round of polling for the new parliament opened, support for protests nosedived. "Public opinion is not in our favor now," Abdel-Rahman Samir, one leading Revolutionary Youth Coalition member, surmised.[13] Public exhaustion with revolutionary agitation had been compounded by the emergence of a new media narrative, which claimed that revolutionary activists and organizations were foreign agents attempting to bring down the country and "incite the Egyptian people to turn against its army." As protest attendance dwindled and Egypt progressed further toward the semblance of a presidential democracy, the case for revolutionary agitation became increasingly difficult to justify. After all, at the end of the election period, the Egyptian public had made their political sentiments felt a total of four times: once in a postrevolutionary constitutional referendum and three times at the polls.

Finally, in June 2012, the Muslim Brotherhood's Mohamed Morsi took his place as Egypt's first civilian president, definitively ending the transitional period and, for many, foreclosing the possibility of further revolutionary mobilization. In its place was a new battle, between Islamists on the one hand and secularists on the other. With the desire to resist the postrevolutionary Islamist government now high on the popular agenda, the same state forces many Egyptians had fought against in the postrevolutionary period—the military and the Mubarak-era judiciary—became allies against the Islamist cause. In the new conflict between Islamist parties and a secular state, the question of a renewed revolution was of comparatively little importance.

It took until 2013 for popular mobilization in Egypt to experience a renaissance on the scale of 2011. This time, however, it took the form not of a spontaneous uprising, but of a well-prepared, highly organized series of demonstrations, culminating in a preprepared military coup. Mohamed Morsi, Egypt's new president, had pushed the nation's postrevolutionary tolerance to its limits, successfully alienating almost all of the other major factions that had supported the initial revolution, as well as lingering supporters of the old regime. Moreover, he had lost the support of Egypt's judiciary, armed forces, and Ministry of Interior. It was against this backdrop that a massive petition campaign called *Tamarrud* (rebellion) was announced, demanding that Morsi step down and call early presidential elections, undergirded by the intervention of the Egyptian security sector, with command over approximately two million employees, half of whom were military or paramilitary in nature.[14] The most prominent faction was the Ministry of Interior, the same entity many Egyptians had rallied against on January 25. "Of course, we joined and helped the movement, as we are Egyptians like them and everyone else," one official with the Ministry of Interior told Reuters, referring to the institutional support given to *Tamarrud*.[15] With the enthusiastic organizing force of much of the Egyptian state behind it, the *Tamarrud* campaign became a well-mediatized, state-supported mobilization effort, complete with prominent newspaper coverage, widely disseminated action plans, and the nation's Ministry of Defense officials publicly and privately aggrandizing the movement on the world stage.[16] Far from exhibiting spontaneity, this instance of "elite-led mobilization"[17] successfully brought hundreds of thousands of Egyptians into the streets who, thinking that they were calling for a renewal of democracy, had instead become unwitting pawns in a military coup. Just as it had in 2011, the military stepped in and removed the regime, promising fresh democratic elections to follow. This time they never did happen.[18]

One month later, in August 2013, the "temporary" military regime under the thumb of then Secretary of Defense (and, later, President) Abdel Fattah el-Sisi remained in charge of the Egyptian state, with a rubber-stamp interim president supporting his whim. Meanwhile, loyalists to the deposed president, Morsi—largely members of the Muslim Brotherhood—had been making their disquiet felt in the streets. These protests were very different from the ones Egypt had seen during the revolution. One attendee estimated that around 95 percent of the protesters were members of the Brotherhood or other Islamist parties. "I had the sense that this was not the Egyptian people united together. No, a single party was protesting. It was uncomfortable," explained Fouad, a wavering Islamist at the time. One particular sit-in, at the Rabaa al-Adawiya mosque, had been going on for more than a month. It was Sisi's decision on August 14 to forcibly dispatch police and army forces to break up the sit-in, which was seen as the beginning of brutal efforts to consolidate power and deny the Egyptian people any future choice on who was to represent them. What transpired was a massacre. The large crowd of pro-Morsi protesters assembled at the Rabaa al-Adawiya and al-Nahda squares suddenly found themselves facing machine guns, snipers, and tanks. "I couldn't believe that all that noise was guns," one participant in the Rabaa protests recalled.[19]

"It was a new level, I've never seen before... Mohammad Mahmoud was child's play compared to what happened in Rabaa," explained Fouad, who took great pains to periodically loudly announce that he had never been to Rabaa between quietly explaining exactly what he saw. He suspected that the secluded commercial building we were in was being surveilled with long-distance microphones. "I found the Rabaa hospital full of injured people and corpses. I went to the front lines, where the troops were, and people [were still] chanting against them, very afraid they could open fire any time," Fouad explained. And open fire they did, claiming the lives of at least 817, and possibly over a thousand, pro-Morsi protesters assembled at Rabaa and associated occupation sites.[20] "There was so much [ammunition] fired," one eyewitness recalled. "I got out [of the mosque], and I heard an echo in my ears, a strange echo. I went back to the concrete where people were gathering... and they told me: 'You've been shot.'"[21] It transpired that my informant had been hit twice. One bullet—or perhaps shrapnel of some type—had only grazed him, but the other was a direct hit. At this point in our interview, he raised his shirt and showed me where the round had sailed straight through his body. His comrades rushed him to a hospital.

This was the last time he ever attended a protest, but the last day that many of those who protested at Rabaa ever saw. Though the sit-in had been armed, like many of the conflicts during the Eighteen Days, it had been largely peaceful, and the new regime's attacks on peaceful protesters would only escalate as time went on. "I had never seen such brutality as what I saw after Rabaa," Fouad told me. "I joined two or three marches after the Rabaa massacre," he said. "Whenever we started demonstrating, live bullets were shot, tons of people were killed." He explained how "machine gun batteries from the army and police" were rolled out on the streets and aggressively used at popular protests.

In the two years that followed, the Sisi regime continued to enclose freedom of assembly, expression, and association in Egypt, co-opting the state-run media for propaganda purposes, and heavily censoring private newspapers. The April 6 movement, once beloved for its role in resisting Mubarak and supporting the revolution, was soon banned, and activists and organizers were arrested for participation in the 2011 protests, which the regime has attempted to renarrativize as a mistake engineered by terrorist and foreign elements. Even the online space was closely monitored and controlled: in 2015 a twenty-two-year-old law student, Amr Nohan, received a three-year jail sentence for sharing an image on Facebook of Sisi wearing Mickey Mouse ears.[22]

It was at this point, in the blistering summer of 2015, that I arrived in Cairo as a fresh-faced PhD student with the intention of unraveling what had transpired during the revolutionary period. When I had proposed the visit back in 2012, I had not anticipated that, far from studying the vibrant life of a revolutionary nation, I would instead be required to fulfill the task of a mortician. The revolution was dead, and everybody knew it. In its place was nothing short of a reign of terror.

Armored vehicles toting heavy machine guns lurked around the corners of Cairo's city blocks, ready to mobilize at a moment's notice. Posters, banners, and flyers with Sisi's face lined the roads of the capital. Self-professed "honorable citizens"[23] strolled the city streets ready to report on anyone seemingly out of the ordinary. Before I had even touched down in Cairo, my contacts in the country advised me that the regime's spies were everywhere. It was imperative, they told me, that I avoid taking a taxi to and from the airport: these were used by the regime to work out where foreigners were staying and monitor them, something that would have placed my informants in serious danger. In fact, it was recommended that I avoid talking about my research at all while in the country and generally profess only to be a student "interested in Egyptian culture and society after the revolution."[24] Several colleagues had been ejected from the country and only narrowly avoided their research documents being seized, some after unpleasant treatment from the Ministry of Interior. Finding a "safe" location to conduct interviews was always a challenge. The threat of surveillance, I was told, was constant. While some people were quite content to have a conversation at home or even in public settings, others opted for eerily quiet roadside cafés on the outskirts of the capital, the husks of burned-out buildings since repopulated by new dwellers, dying business parks, and the quiet nooks of private members' clubs. This caution was often warranted: former revolutionaries, Muslim Brothers, and secular activists were being disappeared by the day. I was frequently told that the only reason my politically active interviewees were content to speak with me about their experiences was because, being a young foreigner with a paltry command of Arabic, I was one of the few people they could safely assume *wasn't* spying for their own government. Terror had reached such a point that many Egyptians now staunchly refused to trust their own countrymen. Researchers were also worried. Things were taking a very dark turn. Giulio, a colleague of mine from Cambridge, arrived in the country stalked by a looming fear that he was being watched.

By the time I left Egypt, things had gotten assuredly worse. My interviewees and personal contacts were becoming increasingly concerned about a wave of severe crackdowns being rolled out across the country. People were going missing, and nobody knew where they were. Giulio remained convinced that the regime was keeping tabs on him. I had hoped to return to Cairo for further research after a cool-down period, but the way things were going, it was looking doubtful. Things only got more desperate in the New Year. Amnesty International assessed that three or four people were being forcibly disappeared by authorities every single day.[25] Shortly after the fifth anniversary of the January 25 revolution, I became aware of one disappearance in particular. It was Giulio.

The intricacies of what followed are now a matter of public record, so I will retain the mantle of an academic and simply say that Giulio had been tortured to death. When his body was found at the side of a desert road, his fate became remarkable because he was not Egyptian. He was in fact one of many people picked up by the security forces on January 25 of that year, and thousands more have "disappeared" every year since.

"People are getting killed, and this time, brutally killed. This time, all the world is seeing them getting slaughtered and no one notices," I remember Fouad telling me during one of our interviews. His statement remains just as true today as it was then. For all the vocal interest world powers showed in Egypt's Eighteen Days, the reaction to its Eighteenth Brumaire has been a tinnitus-inducing silence.

PART III

OCCUPY WALL STREET

Although 2011 had heralded a surge of contentious energy in Tunis and Cairo, when the new year dawned in New York City, the metropolis's activists were exhausted. Amid an economic downturn, corporate bailouts, and legislative gridlock, President Barack Obama's promise of hope and change did not seem to have materialized. Meanwhile, it felt to many as if American protest since 9/11 had consistently achieved little and been met with harsh police repression. "I was tired of it," Larry,[1] one of the first activists to get involved in Occupy, told me on our morning phone call. "I had seen how it was worthless." The conventional tactic of meticulously planned marches and rallies that had predominated among organizers in the United States since the 1960s had worn seriously thin. Larry described how such events, often involving people in the tens of thousands, had failed to achieve any serious impact. "You look at it, and you can't even understand what's going on," he said. "It's just a mishmash of colors and all these different voices, and no real idea." Such events were just as uninteresting for activists as they were for their intended audience. Larry had put this to me quite forcefully: "I go to these events, and people yell at me about shit I already fucking know, *because I'm here*. I came here *because* I knew this shit already... there was no point!"

In New York's activist community, a sentiment similar to the one Larry had expressed was particularly palpable. Three major groups had long dominated the city's leftist organizing: the International Socialist Organization, the Revolutionary Communist Party, and, most prominently, the Workers World Party, mediated through a plethora of front organizations. After the 2008 financial crash, these organizations' antiwar mobilization had shifted in favor of questions of social justice and inequality. Their central repertoire involved enforcing a rigorously hierarchical structure and routinely reiterating old-school tactics from the 2000s Iraq War protests: a march, a stage, and a linkup with alternative news organizations such as Russia Today and Press TV for some additional reportage. There was often little scope for action outside of this preordained trajectory. Beyond these entities, there were the activities of various trade unions, Democratic Party–affiliated organizations, and civil society organizations. When these organizations did engage in street action (and this was rare), they were exceptionally constrained in their agendas and hierarchical in character.

Against this backdrop few could have expected Occupy Wall Street to succeed in New York, let alone inspire a global movement. In many ways, its genesis was a series of failures: a failure by its initiators (Adbusters) to adequately organize around their own call to action, a failure by New Yorkers Against Budget Cuts to seize the initiative, a failure by Workers World Party activists to cooperate and agree on a form of action, and then a failure to successfully occupy Wall Street itself on September 17. Instead, a dedicated group of hard-core activists, with the support of those who had marched on September 17, occupied Zuccotti Park after failing to reach either Wall Street or their backup target of the nearby Chase Plaza. Zuccotti Park was named for John Zuccotti, the then CEO of Brookfield Office Properties. Brookfield maintained the park as a "privately owned public space" as part of their obligations as the owner of a nearby office building, One Liberty Plaza, which had served as a temporary morgue during the 9/11 attacks. Far from seizing Wall Street, the Occupiers had made camp steps away from Ground Zero, less than a week after the tenth anniversary of the World Trade Center attacks.

So how, in the wrong place, without widespread support, and against all odds, did an occupation blossom, thrive, and finally disperse as something altogether more momentous? Occupy's early organizers had eschewed established leftist organizations, unions, and even other well-established social movements in favor of a radical anarchist framework: to "create a space," "take a space," "eliminate all rules for a second... and then decide what rules should really govern us as humans when we're interacting together."[2] Nonetheless, such a space persisted for almost two months, an autonomous enclave in one of the most heavily policed cities of the world, and remained active in the city as a decentralized movement. It inspired successful Occupy movements across the United States and the globe, persisting in American politics until the present day, with the bonds and identities forged during Occupy Wall Street reemerging to propel disaster relief efforts, early organizing efforts for Black Lives Matter, and even US presidential campaigns.

Despite the profound explosion of activity around Occupy Wall Street and the broader Occupy movement, it should be noted that the movement benefited from mass mobilization in a different way than its Egyptian inspiration. Rather than a short but extremely pronounced spike of mobilization within a highly concentrated eighteen-day revolutionary period, Occupy Wall Street attracted participants at a comparatively glacial pace, but it continued to mobilize people across a 228-day period spanning from the occupation's establishment on September 17, through its two-month peak in October and November, to a failed 2012 May Day strike that prompted the movement's dissolution. Egypt's revolution constituted a case of highly concentrated mass mobilization underpinned by highly distinctive structural conditions of convergence, as well as supporting cognitive and spatial conditions of convergence. Occupy, by contrast, saw mass mobilization occur more durably but less intensely. Its rise was underpinned only by spatial and cognitive convergence conditions, rather than widespread structural factors affecting a vast swath of the population.

The next three chapters elucidate the dynamics of affinity-convergence mobilization during this remarkable moment of spontaneous protest across the United States. Chapter 6 outlines the character and development of Occupy Wall Street, detailing how it emerged, sustained itself, and transformed over its first month. It tells the origin story of Occupy Wall Street, showing how the loose band of anarchists who planned the occupation sought in vain to plan an American analogue to revolutionary protests of 2011 Egypt, and how the occupation that resulted was buoyed by paramount framing elicited by police repression. This chapter covers the period between February and October 2011, explaining Occupy's early organizational weakness, while explaining the paramount framing from which the movement benefited and the exceptional, opportune space it was able to create in the city. Chapter 7 then explores the spectrum of affinities underpinning Occupy's surge in mobilization between October and November, which spanned every category discussed in this book, and details how these interacted with the movement's cognitive and spatial conditions of convergence, leading to the influx of a wide range of new participants in the movement. Finally, chapter 8 analyzes how these conditions came to a close, showing how the conditions of convergence underpinning Occupy's success were undermined by Occupy's opponents, changing circumstances, and the movement's transition to a spatially dispersed organizational structure.

CHAPTER SIX

Globalizing the Revolution

> *Our goal on September 17 was to have a General Assembly on Wall Street.... We're going to gather these people together, and we're going to take space on Wall Street, which should be literally impossible. And then we're going to have a conversation about how fucked up everything is. And that was it.*
>
> LARRY

On July 13, 2011, a quite different kind of protest was taking place in Cairo's Tahrir Square. In contrast to the misleadingly termed "Million Man Marches" that became quite popular in the revolution's denouement, this time the protesters stuck around Tahrir and didn't leave. They had arrived that Friday, July 8, as part of a long-planned protest organized by the Muslim Brotherhood and other political groups in favor of expediting the prosecution of former Mubarak officials. When the Brotherhood members and party loyalists went home, the activists elected to camp overnight. So began an almost monthlong occupation in the heart of Cairo. The proceedings generated considerable excitement in activist circles: would this be a "second Egyptian revolution"? Would the people of Cairo complete their overthrow of the Egyptian state? Activists from around the world flew to Tahrir to find out. Those who could not make the trip on their own watched excitedly from afar. One such observer was the Canadian "culture-jamming" collective Adbusters, whose members opted to try to establish a similar occupation in the United States. After all, if it had been so successful in North Africa, why not bring Tahrir to North America? And so Adbusters' media acumen sprung into operation.[1]

#OCCUPYWALLSTREET
Are you ready for a Tahrir moment?
On Sept 17, flood into lower Manhattan, set up tents, kitchens, peaceful barricades and occupy Wall Street.

From July 13 on this call was reiterated in various forms throughout the summer.[2] The Canadian activists' announcement was met with both excitement and confusion by New York City's organizers. "There was a kind of strange dynamic," Owen,[3] a veteran autonomist, recalled, "because Adbusters made this call to occupy Wall Street and picked a day, but they didn't really participate at all in what that would look like or how that would happen, so then people totally separate, with no affiliation whatsoever, had to figure out what to actually do with this day." An initial meeting in August was organized by activists working with New Yorkers Against Budget Cuts, who had been carrying out overnight protests at City Hall, which they had dubbed "Bloombergville" in mock honor of the city's mayor, Michael Bloomberg. The advertised program was for those interested in organizing around the call to occupy Wall Street to meet at the Charging Bull statue in downtown New York's Bowling Green, a short distance from Wall Street itself, in order to discuss the shape of the action to come.

When the meeting began, it was immediately apparent that the occasion had been co-opted by one particular faction of New York's political struggle, the influential Maoist group known as the Workers World Party, which had played a substantial part in Bloombergville. "What was advertised as an open assembly began like a rally," the anarchist writer Nathan Schneider recalled, "with Workers World Party members and others making speeches over a portable P.A. system to the hundred or so people there."[4] As my own contacts recounted, "people were not very happy about this."[5] "Anarchists started to heckle socialists, socialists heckled back, and the meeting melted down." Workers World, unable to control the crowd they had drawn, withdrew from the scene while a newly proclaimed New York City General Assembly (NYCGA) held its first meeting without PA systems, stages, or hierarchies, but instead sat cross-legged in a circle, deep in discussion for hours on end about the shape of things to come.

The early General Assembly was formed around three core principles: it would be horizontal, participatory, and autonomous—diametrically opposed to the hierarchical "rally" format common to urban activism at the time. Weekly meetings were planned, every Saturday, in the first instance at the city's Irish Hunger Memorial, then regularly at Tompkins Square Park in the East Village. Alumni of the Global Justice movement, now evangelical "horizontalists"[6] were on hand to facilitate meetings, drawing both from past experience and new conceptual approaches.[7] These meetings in Tompkins Square Park would bring together the breakaway Bloombergville protesters with activists who had spent time in Tahrir, Spanish Indignados, and an assortment of radicals from across the United States and around the globe.

Each early meeting of the pre-occupation General Assembly came with its own revelations, disagreements, and occasional progress. Gradually, the assemblies in Tompkins Square Park drew together some idea of what the action on September 17 (or S17, as it became known) would look like. Working groups were formed, managing matters ranging from outreach and tactical maneuvers to those such as food, art, and web design.[8] Anywhere between thirty and one hundred people attended these meetings on any given weekend, most of whom were drawn from New York's community of radical intellectuals and agitators in the autonomist and anarchist traditions, though with a sprinkling of socialists, libertarians, and relatively political newbies between them. As September 17 drew near, the NYCGA had carried out pilot studies, organized legal observers, medical training, and food and drink for the day. This was a sincere effort, even with its incredibly ad hoc method of organization.[9]

Because the early activists who planned the September 17 protests deliberately eschewed formal organizational structures, the planning process hinged considerably on participants' ability to trust one another. Consequently, meetings became considerably more successful over time as this trust grew. Initially, "the way people related individually, or politically, or organizationally couldn't work within the context," Owen mused when I asked him about these early meetings. "It was an interesting dynamic... or lack of dynamic between them." One of the meeting's early facilitators, Annie, concurred when I asked her about the same matter: "A lot of us were meeting each other for the first time," she said, "even though we had been in similar circles." Week by week, however, conversations and projects in pursuit of their shared mission created a situation where this initial stiltedness gave way to collaboration and connection. "We got to know each other really well through the planning process," Annie explained, "so by the time September 17 happened, there were really strong bonds and trust."[10]

Despite the considerable effort put in to planning September 17, there was no expectation that such an operation would succeed. As Larry recalled: "My perception of what was gonna happen was that the police were gonna come and just, like, beat the shit out of everybody and throw them out of the square and it'd be over—I was so sure of this." Nonetheless, the events of the day took a considerably different path. A momentous "snake march" had been organized, taking a train of about one thousand protesters (a rather disappointing turnout) around the Financial District in search of an occupation site.[11] As anticipated, Wall Street itself was blocked off, as was Chase Plaza, the primary backup target envisaged to play host to a potential occupation. Eventually, Zuccotti Park, one of the more undesirable backup locations on the edge of the Financial District, was proclaimed as a new target. The march made its way over, snaking through the streets toward its destination, flanked by hastily reconfiguring New York Police Department (NYPD) motorcycle brigades. Cardboard signs and homemade banners were displayed in place of the carefully prepared, ideologically curated posters that had characterized most major protests in New York at the time. A number of demonstrators could be seen carrying sleeping bags and other camping equipment.[12]

By the time the march had settled at Zuccotti Park, numbers had thinned to around two hundred. "There was nothing really happening, nothing to do yet," Owen recalled. "People were just sitting around, breaking off into little discussion groups or assemblies." These assemblies, as another early Occupier put it to me, "were various breakout groups… talking about the world that we wanted to live in, the world we currently lived in, with the [financial] crisis, and how we would get from one to the other: the question of transition."[13] These discussions continued late into the night—until 4:00 a.m. by some accounts—with a considerable proportion of those involved electing to sleep overnight in the park.

Despite activists' predictions of a swift and inevitable eviction, the NYPD seemed mysteriously repelled by the perimeter of the park. A plethora of peculiar theories were offered for why the occupation had been able to remain, ranging from legalistic explanations to theories of complex disputes among the city's ruling element. What was more readily apparent, however, was that Occupy's early agitators had succeeded: for the time being, an occupation was underway.

Occupying Wall Street

From the very beginning, a need for constant adaptation became a hallmark feature of Occupy Wall Street (OWS). Michael Gould-Wartofsky, then a student at NYU, recalled that initially, "in the absence of an infrastructure, life in the park was a continual improvisation."[14] The loosely associated group who had planned the march to Zuccotti on September 17 had succeeded in their general goal: they had marched, and they had occupied a location in the Financial District. There had been no expectation that they would be allowed to remain. Alongside the few who had participated in early planning meetings came a plethora of new "hard-ground" Occupiers,[15] who maintained the protest overnight, regular visitors who came by almost daily, and even everyday sympathizers who dropped in on occasion. There were no membership criteria and no real notion of a goal or mission statement, except that the occupation itself was worth sustaining.[16] OWS at this point existed not as a formal organization, or as a movement, but as an action, sustained by an undefined and unbounded community.

In the absence of a clear leadership or any new organizing structures, the occupation in Zuccotti came to operate in a similar fashion to the meetings leading up to it. The "Facilitation Working Group" who had served to organize the General Assembly meetings that planned the action on September 17 continued to facilitate those meetings, this time on a daily basis. A now much larger NYCGA, composed of whoever was willing to participate at the time, served as the manifest means of collaborative decision-making and would decide upon the occupation's most important matters by consensus. There was, however, a considerable difference between the General Assembly that had planned Occupy and the new assembly in Zuccotti: scale. Meetings prior to OWS had involved only fifty active participants at their peak, with about half of those who had showed up electing to speak. Even this had already proved unfamiliar for facilitators. "I had used consensus in different collectives and organizing spaces," one of the principal facilitators of the pre-Zuccotti assemblies noted. "I was pretty familiar with facilitation, although the size of the groups that we were working with was definitely something new for me... so we had to adapt as things went along."[17]

While the facilitation experts on hand had experience working with consensus, it had been in contexts generally involving fewer than even thirty people. By contrast, the new General Assembly in Zuccotti Park (or "Liberty Plaza," as it was also called) would eventually run into the thousands. Though there had been consensus-based mass assemblies before, such as in the Spanish Indignados protests of 2011, few had actually been used for the purposes of concrete, everyday decision-making, instead fulfilling the purpose of discursive hubs for a particular topic, often themed around matters such as education or the economy, while much smaller assemblies tended to confirm or refuse relatively uncontroversial, general proposals.[18] A consequence of the unmanageability of such a process was that General Assembly meetings were frequently decried by both their proponents and detractors as a chaotic or ineffective means of decision-making, a problem that only intensified as the occupation grew.

Nonetheless, much of Occupy's substantive work barely interfaced with these assemblies, taking place in smaller working groups. These groups would conduct the everyday practices of the occupation, ranging from crucially instrumental jobs such as operating the kitchen, facilitating meetings, and managing financial resources to nonessential elements such as roundtable Think Tank discussions. The activities of Occupy's plethora of working groups offered opportunities for participation to almost anyone who was sufficiently motivated to get involved. From planning protests to constructing complicated technological apparatuses, to chopping onions and sorting clothes, all manner of activities were constantly underway in and around the park, conducted by the autonomous working groups affiliated to the General Assembly. Some working groups, such as the Lightsource group, operated as progressive, low-profit start-ups, while others took the form of destructive and disruptive parodies of the entire process, such as the Thieves Working Group, nominally dedicated to stealing items from others in the park.[19] These working groups ranged from those lasting only a matter of days to others that would persist well beyond the NYCGA itself. They operated in a particularly autonomous fashion, without any clear central coordination except for the occasional request made to a General Assembly. One Occupier who became involved in a particularly large number of working groups recalled how "it was really hard to tell what was happening in a working group if you weren't in it.... I almost had no idea who any of these people were... [and] no one knew what I was doing really, except a few people."[20]

Throughout mid-September Occupy Wall Street remained a rather unexpected but ultimately low-profile disturbance in American public life. A good number of those who had already been aware of Adbusters' call and were plugged in to activist communities and networks possessed some awareness of the occupation, but the broader public in the United States and worldwide were almost entirely unaware of the disturbance in Zuccotti Park. Although the occupation's Media Working Group had built an impressive network of well-resourced photographers, livestreamers, bloggers, and Twitter warriors, with support from the technologically sophisticated Global Revolution collective, very little material was making its way into the daily newshole.[21] Though the protesters had the capacity to create stories, they were unable to capture the media's imagination. Fortunately for the movement, the New York City Police Department could.

Converging on Wall Street

The first serious public attention paid to Occupy Wall Street came one full week after the occupation was first established. On September 24, in the process of policing a small-scale Occupy protest, Detective Inspector Anthony Bologna (one of the senior officials on the scene, known as "white shirts") unleashed a can of pepper spray on a small crowd of peaceful protesters, standing inside a police corral on the sidewalk, almost all of them young women. This was the trigger for the first serious media coverage Occupy had received, with a recording of the incident spreading like wildfire online and being aired by progressive outlets such as MSNBC and *The Daily Show*.[22] The proceedings were also written up in a broad spectrum of major local, national, and international newspapers, including the *New York Times*. On the anniversary of the attack, the *Times* surmised: "We're not saying that Occupy would never have taken off without Inspector Bologna. But he gave it a mighty jump start last Sept. 24."[23] That week, Occupy Wall Street took up 2 percent of all US news coverage and won an array of new allies and public supporters.[24] The Bologna event was the first time that awareness of the occupation became seriously salient among a substantial proportion of the population and was a considerable boon to the movement. The park began to see a substantial increase in traffic, while sympathetic activists elsewhere even attempted a handful of small occupations in other cities. Spurred by the Bologna incident and the newfound attention the occupation was attracting, Occupy's General Assembly announced its first major mobilization: a march across the Brooklyn Bridge, designed to demonstrate solidarity between the two boroughs. The date was set for October 1, the start of the occupation's third week.

There is every chance that the October 1 march would have been a curio in the city's organizing history had it not been for the NYPD's decision to offer Occupy an even greater boon than it had on September 24. The occupation was not at this stage a substantial enough phenomenon to attract a great many people to its events and so had to rely on a few thousand protesters, who, despite including a smattering of first-time participants, were drawn primarily from New York City's activist community and a few sympathetic trade union members who had pledged to show up. This was at the time considered a major mobilizing effort. Little did the Occupiers know that it would form a comparative footnote when measured against the crowds their cause would later draw.

Once the march across the bridge was underway, a substantial contingent of the protesters, emboldened by the size of the protest, spilled off the pedestrian path and onto the bridge's main roadway below. A crowd of about eight hundred people successfully blocked the flow of traffic from Manhattan to Brooklyn and continued along the bridge. The result was a head-to-head confrontation with the NYPD. This was the point at which the NYPD began to engage, swiftly drawing up a police "kettle" to contain the masses gathering on the bridge. With nowhere to run, only a few protesters were able to escape the encroaching mass of armed officers. This left more than seven hundred protesters trapped in a police cordon as the NYPD methodically snatched, handcuffed, and arrested every single one.

The event constituted one of the largest mass arrests of peaceful protesters in the city's history, with the NYPD drafting civilian buses in order to cope with the numbers.

The NYPD's response to the Brooklyn Bridge march might have seemed like a tactical masterstroke to the department's sergeants, but it proved a strategic catastrophe. The spectacle was so profound that the American news media reported on it in droves.[25] The chief beneficiary of all this coverage? Occupy Wall Street. Looking into the arrests prompted further questions: Why had the NYPD been so heavy handed? Who were the protesters, what did they want, and why was their cause spreading? Was this the 99 percent's moment on the stage of history? With the American media searching for answers, Occupy Wall Street would account for 10 percent of all news coverage in the United States.[26]

This new attention and the public outrage coupled with it placed Occupy Wall Street at the center of American political life. In his own account, Michael Gould-Wartofsky concurred.[27] "As the news media spotlight cast its glare over Liberty Square, the occupiers found a screen onto which they could project their message to millions.... [F]rom the front pages of the dailies to the lead stories on the nightly news, participants were deftly translating the anti-politics and anti-capitalism of OWS into a new language, one that could be comprehended, copied, and ultimately co-opted by almost anyone." With its fully fledged entry into the mainstream of American consciousness, OWS became a focal point of national attention, and the cause célèbre among Americans dissatisfied with the status quo.

This shift in framing really mattered. Kevin remembered how prior to this moment he had been aware of the movement but had no desire to become involved and was in fact becoming increasingly apolitical. "I had been involved in protests since college and stuff, and I often felt embarrassed to be a part of it: I was like, oh, look at all these normal people going to and from work, and here we are just a bunch of weirdos, and they're just looking at us like a distraction or something." It was when considering the prospect of participating in Occupy that "all these feelings of shame and embarrassment from the past came up, and I was feeling this sense that it wasn't legitimate, it wasn't accepted, it was just this weird little bunch of radicals, or bunch of weirdos. And I knew I was one of them, but I didn't really want to be seen that way."

As attention to the movement grew, the public framing of Occupy began to take on a more paramount character. People like Kevin saw their feelings about participation changing. "Suddenly people were talking about it all over the country, and it really blew up then.... I started seeing that it was growing, and I started being interested in being a part of it," he recalled.

With the rise of a powerful, paramount frame, people who had been unsure whether to visit or participate in Occupy found themselves pushed toward taking that first step. "I started seeing that there was this national momentum happening," Kevin told me. "It was the excitement of the national moment against Wall Street and [for] the idea of the 99 percent—that was what was really motivating me." Clive,[28] an older participant in OWS similarly described how it "seemed to have some momentum that we hadn't seen in a long time," and that it was this momentum that attracted him and his wife to participate in a movement largely composed of much younger people. And so, in Zuccotti, the previously quiet park was swiftly inundated with new visitors from across the city and far afield.

The conditions of convergence that galvanized participation in Occupy did not only occur at the level of cognitive framing. The park itself served as an important space of convergence during the movement's growth. Zuccotti offered an exceptional space in which, at least notionally, the norms and rules of social and political interaction could be suspended in favor of an autonomous, self-organized community. Previously known only as one of New York's many banal concrete parks, and thereby not ideologically predefined, an occupied Zuccotti came to possess a remarkably open, participatory, and horizontal character in which any form of action could be reframed and reconstituted as part of a pluralistic repertoire of contention, offering potential participants with the possibility to engage without judgment or repercussions.

The swelling numbers in Zuccotti Park, the sympathetic attention it had received, and its seeming immunity to police dispersal, not to mention the raw momentum with which it was expanding, in turn lay the groundwork for a second condition of convergence in Zuccotti: an opportune space. The park became a mecca for radicals and anticapitalists of all stripes. Some even moved their entire lives to New York, temporarily or permanently, in order to join the occupation. Thanks to the protracted legal entanglements associated with dispersing occupied public spaces, it appeared briefly as if the occupation was unstoppable, lending radicals an arena in which contention could take place without exposure to conventional risks but with the spotlight of the global press firmly focused on them.

Where some chose to travel to Zuccotti, others began to organize emulations of the occupation in their own communities. A plethora of new occupations, modeled on Occupy Wall Street began to crop up. As the Federal Bureau of Investigation (henceforth FBI) noted in a then confidential report, by the weekend after the October 1 protest, "Occupy Wall Street protests have spread to about half of all states in the US, [and] over a dozen European and Asian cities."[29] The spread of occupations across America was only the start of Occupy's expansion. Many of those inspired by Occupy across the United States and around the world began planning for a global day of action on October 15. This action, initially organized by the 15-M movement in Europe, was now additionally energized by the surprise success of Occupy Wall Street. By October 15, Occupy had not just gone national, it was going global: protests were staged in over nine hundred cities, with occupations being attempted in almost every major city on the globe, and self-identified Occupy groups (of dramatically varying sizes and impact) eventually formed in 2,771 municipalities.[30] Occupy Wall Street on the East Coast was now mirrored by a similarly momentous occupation in Oakland, California, on the West Coast, as well as a major occupation in London. Also of note in the United States were major occupations in Boston; Portland, Oregon; Chicago; Seattle; Phoenix; and Washington, DC, each drawing between five and ten thousand protesters at their peak.

The rapid rise of Occupy in the public consciousness not only attracted individual participation but also encouraged a wide range of organized groups to flock to Occupy's side. Major new supporters included the 600,000-strong New York State United Teachers (the state's largest union), the AFL-CIO (the largest federation of trade unions in the United States), the Service Employees International Union (representing 2.1 million workers across the United States and over 400,000 members locally), and the (over one million strong) Teamsters. Other big unions, including the Transport Workers Union (TWU, representing 38,000 workers in New York alone, with 200,000 nationwide) and United Auto Workers (UAW), also threw their weight behind the occupation, while progressive icon Michael Moore personally offered to fundraise for the movement from his publication royalties. Big labor had thrown its weight—and, most importantly, its resources—behind a small occupation.[31]

The occupation was also connected worldwide. Occupy Wall Street's global public face offered a global audience the opportunity not only to observe and understand the activities of OWS (and later, other occupations) but also to participate from afar. This included social media accounts on Twitter, Facebook, and YouTube (underpinned by the occupation's Media Working Group), and even several newspapers, the most famous of which was called *The Occupied Wall Street Journal*.[32] By far the most participatory element of Occupy's online operation, however, was a regular livestream. "In the beginning we'd have this morning show, which'd be us opening gifts people had sent," Larry (one of the livestream's founders) had told me. Initially, this morning show also served as a means to share information about the occupation with an interested online community. Larry found himself "answering questions to [five to ten thousand] people in this chat... constantly providing information," ranging from information about bathroom breaks to complex details of meetings and live protest coverage. "I viewed it as a narrative," he explained. "I was a narrator in a story when I was livestreaming, so I'd be out and I'd be telling people what was happening around me, interacting with these people."

The livestream became a huge asset in its own right for the occupation, but it had a surprising additional benefit that was arguably even more powerful. The livestream had not just offered a narrative but started a conversation, with the streamer, the crowd, and the online community all exchanging information. "Having the viewers was like having five hundred researchers with me," Larry mused. The livestream would map protest routes on the fly, research police movements and vehicles (even calling police stations to find out additional information), and provide a wide array of auxiliary support over the course of the struggle.

This chapter has detailed the emergence of Occupy Wall Street and the movement's early development. In particular, it has drawn attention to three important conditions of convergence from which OWS benefited. The first of these was the occupation's character as an exceptional space: an open, participatory, and horizontal arena in which participation could take almost any form. The second was Zuccotti Park's role as an opportune space: an arena in which protest and dissent were at once protected and attended to. Finally came a paramount frame: a sense that the movement was summiting a national moment of collective resistance to the status quo. This framing primarily galvanized participation in Occupy on the part of people who already had clear dispositional affinities with the movement, whether a strong sense of injustice, sympathetic attitudes to one of the various ideological persuasions already participating, or a felt identification with the "99 percent" who were occupying the park. The next chapter details how these various convergence conditions interacted with the affinities held by those who flocked to Occupy and how, accordingly, a surge in participation took place as occupation matured into its second month.

CHAPTER SEVEN

Enter the Occupiers

To open up, then, how did you get involved in Occupy?
Interview question

Two weeks after Occupy's ascent in the public consciousness, the cause's mobilizing capacity would be put to the test by the owners of Zuccotti Park, Brookfield Office Properties, who attempted to evict the occupation on October 14. Brookfield argued that they needed to evict the movement in order to clean and conduct repairs on an apparently unsanitary and dangerous Zuccotti. A letter was officially delivered to the NYPD on October 11, and within moments an eviction had been agreed on between the two parties: it would take place on the morning of Friday, the fourteenth, alongside a new set of rules for any protests in the park that effectively prohibited any kind of overnight sleeping.[1] Occupiers met this challenge with a massive cleaning operation; more than three thousand people showed up for a hastily announced overnight sanitation session, leaving the park sparkling clean in time for the next morning. With its success, the eviction was halted, and the occupation was allowed, once again, to remain.

Occupiers' reassertion of control over Zuccotti spurred the movement even further, attracting a flurry of renewed participation. People came from college campuses, corporate offices, trade unions, delicatessens, almost all sections of society.[2] They came from different states, countries, and even continents. They could be radical anarchists, Democrat-voting liberals, Ayn Rand libertarians, or entirely apolitical. Some arrived at Zuccotti for love, some for ideology, some out of pure boredom, and some for a story. Some bore gifts, and others came in need. These often peculiar and fascinating trajectories were facilitated by the character of organizing at Occupy Wall Street. It was "like no one was doing any recruiting or outreach," Owen recalled. "I mean, it was happening [at] a small level, but it wasn't really the core of the movement." Instead, he explained, the occupation was like "an open invitation to show up: show up in the assemblies, show up in the occupation, show up in the working groups, it wasn't very organized." It seemed as if those who had found their way to Occupy from outside the movement's own networks converged of their own accord, but their pathways to doing so were notably variable.

This chapter outlines the underlying affinities that led many to OWS and discusses how they interacted with the conditions of convergence evoked by the movement. During Occupy, a wide array of affinities underpinned the pathways that new participants took. This is summarized in figure 7.1. In addition to a more general discussion of affinity and convergence, I trace two prominent interactions between participants' affinities and the case's convergence conditions. The first concerns the role of the occupation as an exceptional space in encouraging people to participate based on a diverse range of social affinities and drives. The second concerns how the occupation's characteristic as an opportune space and its paramount framing attracted participation on the basis of dispositional affinities. Finally, I consider some of the pathways that fall through the cracks of these general depictions, as well as cases of nonparticipation.

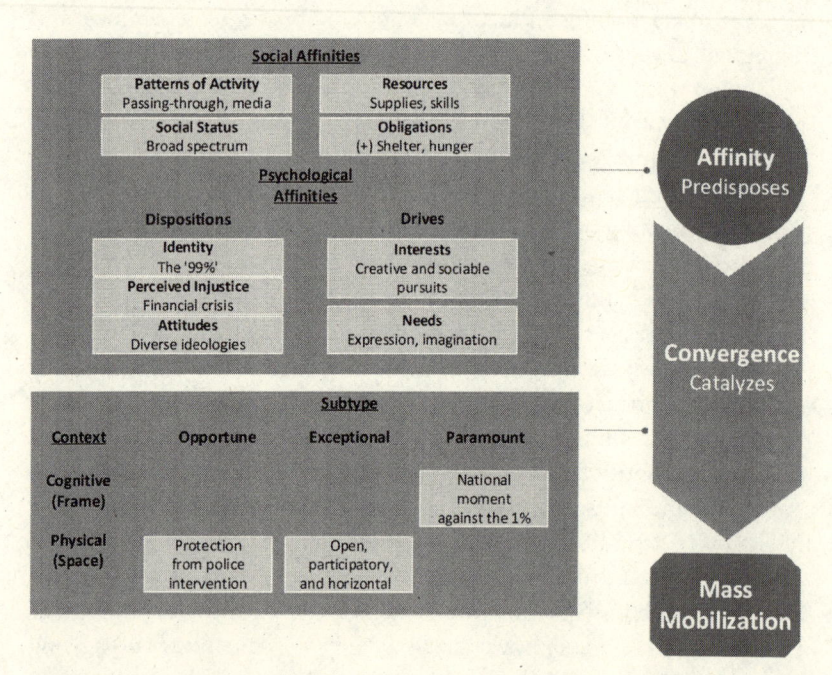

FIGURE 7.1. Summary of affinity-convergence mobilization in the Occupy Wall Street protests.

An Exceptional Space, Diverse Affinities

Even before Occupy was flung into the American public consciousness with paramount framing, the exceptional spatial characteristics of Zuccotti Park were already encouraging a degree of convergence. Zuccotti was a place with relatively undefined, unimposing material conditions. This was particularly important in galvanizing the participation of those with nondispositional affinities to Occupy. Visiting or participating in the occupation was not a disruption of some major urban landmark, nor was it located in a highly politicized place. Instead, Zuccotti's urban banality made the act of participating much less intrusive than other acts of participation, such as attending a meeting at an activist headquarters, marching across highways, or disrupting prominent urban spaces. Parks like Zuccotti were scattered throughout New York City. These privately owned public spaces existed mainly as corporate obligations, part and parcel with the building of new skyscrapers. To pass by or through Zuccotti came with no particular connotations. It was, as Jon Stewart of the popular *Daily Show* put it, "the park no one—even those of us who live across the street from it—had heard of until the Occupy Wall Street movement."[3] Enlightening his viewers, Stewart offered the following characterization: "Apparently, it's a park in Lower Manhattan where people from Wall Street would go to smoke around noon."

From this rather neutral grounding, it was possible for potential Occupiers across ideological, social, and structural divides to interpret and give meaning to the park in their own way. The park became a place where the norms and rules of social and political interaction could be suspended in favor of an autonomous, self-organized community. Jonathan Smucker, a thirty-three-year-old small business owner (and participant) at the time of Occupy, later attempted to give voice to this tendency in an article for the *Sociological Quarterly*.[4] "Zuccotti Park was a bastion of expressiveness, wherein participants could collectively (or individually) express emotions, creativity, values, opinions, and visions in countless ways," Smucker surmised, "without every participant having, necessarily, to grasp whether or how these expressions fit together into a strategic framework to achieve instrumental goals." The nature of this space was visibly and evidently apparent to those who were proximate to Zuccotti. I had asked Kristina,[5] an occasional visitor to the park, how she had perceived Occupy at the time. "It was very interesting," she had mused. "I could see how it would immediately be galvanizing to be a part of that scene and see so much happening around you. It was just people, flurries in every direction and tables overflowing with flyers, and information."

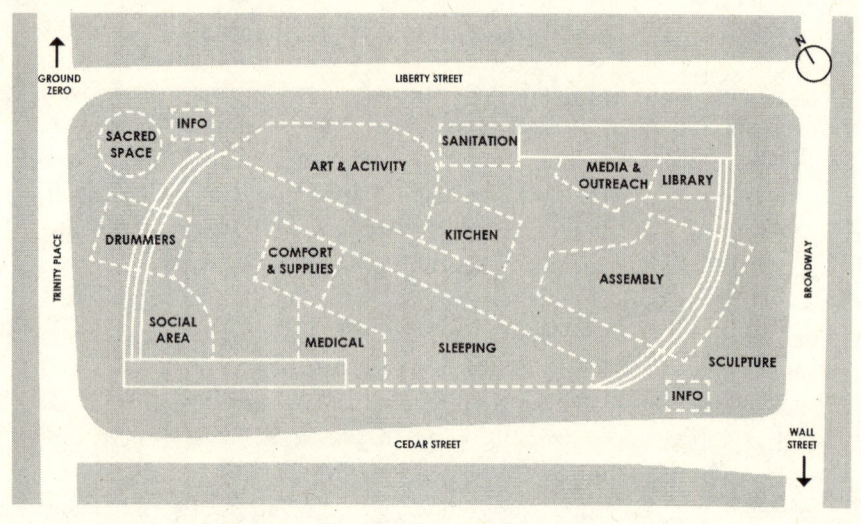

FIGURE 7.2. Labeled map of Zuccotti Park and its environs.

As the occupation became more established, the once banal Zuccotti took on a new, invigorated character as an environment for new associations, diverse activities, and the free exchange of ideas. Debates, cultural events, art exhibits, lectures, and musical performances were a regular feature, making the park a constantly bustling and vibrant environment. The park featured a busy kitchen replete with free food, a medical outpost, and a supply point for everyday comforts and other necessities (figure 7.2). There was always something going on, whether it was a social event, art workshop, religious ceremony, or musical performance on the park's north side, or a general assembly on its southern tip, next to the park's signature red sculpture. Passersby on every street corner were constantly tantalized by the occupation.

Zuccotti and its working groups also served people's more basic material obligations, acting as an access point for anyone in need of clothing, food, or basic medical care. The inhabitants, activities, and opportunities availed by this multifaceted space appealed to a diverse range of affinities, galvanizing all sorts of new encounters between ordinary New Yorkers and the occupation. Whether attracted by Occupy's cultural side, material necessity, or a curiosity about the space, many came to engage with the Occupy ecosystem. Along with those dispositionally inclined toward the occupation, the park attracted a substantial and frequently changing periphery of temporary participants, ranging from tourists and commuters to journalists and visiting celebrities. "You had thousands and thousands of people who would come in and out," Joe,[6] a journalist covering the movement, recalled. "The complete absence of any barrier to entry," he noted, "was one of the things that... really drew people in. They knew that they didn't have to show up all the time, and if they went even a couple of times, they'd probably start to see familiar faces." Many were content to spend a total of a few hours or days at the park, but others would be drawn into more protracted participation. Whether in confrontational protest or simply working together in the park, the everyday work of Zuccotti offered a plethora of chances to plug in.

Where the Zuccotti occupation differed drastically from most prior movements in the city was its psychological affinity with ordinary New Yorkers' drives, granting participants the opportunity to pursue their needs and interests. This ran the full gamut of emotional needs, passions, and interests. Moreover, doing so would be celebrated as valuable and important. There was something for everyone at Zuccotti Park. This exceptional space contained an open community, a litany of activities, and a platform for any faintly progressive cause one could imagine. The occupation also provided a protective environment. For the scores of homeless, drug users, and undocumented migrants, for whom the threat of arrest and fear of police was all too real, the occupation's role as a space of safety and autonomy allowed them to participate politically without the threat of violence or other negative consequences. These opportune spatial characteristics also eased the concerns of others who might have been otherwise hesitant about engaging with the occupation, such as inexperienced protesters and members of marginalized communities. It was in this context that a great many people who were previously apolitical came to participate in Occupy, despite not having a particularly strong alignment with the movement or its ideas. They "didn't necessarily even know that what they were doing was anarchistic," Annie explained. "They just knew that we had to feed ourselves and that we had to put up tents, to not get hypothermia: there were very practical questions."

Many of those who became involved in Occupy were in no way concretely connected with or tied to its early organizers, whose resources were neither extensive nor particularly effective as a mobilizing tool (as could be seen by the relatively poor turnout on September 17). "When Occupy Wall Street came around, suddenly all these people just came out of nowhere," David,[7] a member of these pre-Occupy networks, had told me. In my efforts to understand these people who "came out of nowhere," I discovered that they had been drawn to Occupy by a variety of affinities. These spanned the full breadth of social affinities, such as their patterns of activity, status, resources, or everyday obligations, but they also included their psychological drives: their creative passions and personal needs. One

Occupier, Ernesto, described this as how the occupation "took people in" and offered them purpose. Someone might be "a single mom, or a bus driver or whatever," who didn't feel as if their skills were valued in society, "[but] now you come to this revolution that everyone's talking about... and you feel valued there, and if you're gonna chop onions, you're gonna chop them with pride and honor." "It kind of validated you a little bit," said Kevin, who had participated heavily in sanitation work during the occupation. "It felt good to be part of something that was not just conceptual.... I'm doing this thing and it's important, and, you know, it's physical, we're helping take care of each other."

While some contributions in OWS often took the form of concrete actions, others were less material in nature. Even everyday conversations in the park could be constructed as contributing to the cause. One Occupier, Charlotte,[8] then a PhD student at a university in New York, had told me about how participating in conversations at the occupation's Think Tank working group, which held daily discussions in the park, prompted her to decide that she was going to participate for the long haul. "I was actually planning to move back to England," she explained, "but I came back quite quickly because I found the work that these people were doing really compelling."

It was because of the intersection of their individual affinities to Occupy and the convergence conditions from which the movement benefited that a great many new participants found their way to OWS. To give one particularly illustrative example, I recall Rose,[9] an artist living in Brooklyn, explaining how she became involved in the movement. Rose had first become intrigued by Occupy following news of the mass arrest on the Brooklyn Bridge. "I had never done activism before, so I didn't really think it was for me," she explained, "but I'm thinking, how can I contribute to this?" Rose considered collecting some donations in her building to support the occupation and posted a message on the building's bulletin board. This prompted another woman living in the building to tell Rose about a teacher at a nearby school, who had become involved in Occupy and was connected with the famous Vermont puppet theater Bread and Puppet. As Rose put it, "The word 'puppet' got in my brain, and I did decide to check out an Occupy action." It was after this action that Rose then decided to get more involved, splitting her time between Zuccotti and an activist art space in Brooklyn used by the movement. From her early artistic exploration, Rose rapidly became increasingly involved in Occupy, becoming one of its foremost artistic contributors. I would meet Rose for the first time at that same art space four years later, where she was coordinating a plethora of enthusiastic young activists preparing props for an upcoming climate protest. Rather than having been recruited to Occupy through organizational outreach or through activist recruitment efforts, it was Rose's affinity with OWS that formed the basis for her route to participation.[10] Although she did not consider herself political at the time, she enjoyed artistic pursuits, was curious about puppetry, and was particularly impressed by Bread and Puppet. It was on the basis of her desires to partake in artistic activity that she found her way to participating in the movement, galvanized by the exceptional space it occupied and the paramount frame it possessed.

In a great sense, Rose's narrative illustrates one of the profound vitalities of Occupy: it had something for everyone. Initially, the call to "occupy Wall Street," the notion of "the 99 percent," and the accompanying rhetoric were somewhat empty signifiers, onto which anyone could project a given desire, cause, or identity. This, in turn, provided the opportunity for the emergence of a community around the occupation with such great diversity that all manner of engagement became possible. In this exceptional space an artist could come to paint, a librarian to curate, an intellectual to debate, the homeless to eat, and anyone could affiliate to whatever group or section of Occupy they felt most drawn. This, in turn, allowed the occupation to become a potential stopping point on the paths its participants, visitors, and associates were taking through their own lives, in order to satisfy their desires, needs, and obligations. While some, like Rose, were in the arts, these unusual participants came from all walks of life. Ernesto,[11] a particularly socially active Occupier, explained to me how Occupy's participants ranged from "single moms and bus drivers" to "Wall Street people that switched over, lawyers, and doctors that got radicalized by this movement," alongside other "professionals who wanted to dabble, who had read a Gandhi book, or an MLK book."

While some of those drawn to Occupy became quite actively involved, others provided ancillary support. This could involve donating resources or looking out for activists' welfare. These were seldom the committed leftists that one might expect. I remember Ernesto talking about two such individuals, Maggie and Fred, although he and others have assured me that there was a plethora of similar people, each with their own reasons for assisting. "For Maggie... it was more like 'I wanna take care of you,'" Ernesto explained. Maggie had appeared one day in search of Occupy's "leader" to donate some spare avocados and had, on a whim, invited some of the kitchen staff to visit her Midtown Manhattan apartment any time they needed a shower or to do laundry. When they showed up, Ernesto and his fellow Occupiers were greeted not only with a shower and a laundry service, but brand-new clothes, sweaters, internet access, and a delicious home-cooked meal, topped off with a parting gift of three or four perfectly rolled joints, hidden inside a film canister. Though Maggie felt unable to participate in Occupy's more contentious actions because of her own health issues, she kept a file of newspaper clippings and saved recordings from television shows on the topic, helping in her own small, tangential way.

In contrast with Maggie, "for Fred it was more like 'I wanna show you off, and I wanna invite my friends over,'" Ernesto recalled. Fred was a well-to-do Italian American with a house in Manhattan, who would invite Ernesto or other Occupiers over as "revolutionary" guests of honor at his fancy dinner parties. At first, Ernesto recalled, "I realized it was an exchange," in which his presence at a dinner party was to be compensated through small favors and occasional financial support. However, over time, Fred and other such "Occu-mamas and Occu-papas," as Ernesto dubbed them, became crucial support for Occupiers who became homeless after the eviction of Zuccotti. "He took in these two kids," Ernesto recalled. "One in particular was this seventeen-year-old kid, walking barefoot after the park got evicted; it was raining, and Fred's like, you're coming home with me." When I asked if this was common, Ernesto explained, "A lot of those folks, I think, after meeting us, took in a lot of folks that were in trouble, a lot of folks that were like me, or worse off.... [T]here's a million stories like that."

While Maggie may have simply been looking for somewhere to donate her spare avocados, and Fred might have just been interested in finding a new dinner guest for his intellectual soirees, both became integrated into the struggle around Occupy, serving as supportive struts for the movement as a whole. This was underpinned by their personal resources and psychological drives: having things the occupation needed and seeking out social stimulation that Occupiers could have provided. In this context, the exceptional character of OWS made it a more attractive location for food donations than a food bank and a more interesting source of stimulating conversation than a popular café or university lecture. Thus, the relatively commonplace affinities that Maggie and Fred had with Occupy—their resources, interests, and needs—were focused more directly on the occupation. Had Occupy not seemed so exceptional, we can imagine that Maggie might have visited a homeless shelter, and Fred might have simply invited someone else to dinner. The pathways people like Rose, Maggie, and Fred took to participating in Occupy tended to be individuated and unique, but they had the remarkable effect of bringing a very large number of unconnected or disinterested people into contact with a movement they would not otherwise have countenanced participating in.

Paramountcy, Opportunity, and Disposition

In contrast to those with an initially picayune interest in Occupy, people with strongly aligned dispositional affinities to the movement—attitudes, identities, and perceptions of injustice—were most strongly catalyzed to participate by the paramount framing surrounding OWS and Zuccotti's status as an opportune space for contentious activity. With the occupation's growing status as a cause célèbre of radicals worldwide, Zuccotti Park became not only a vital linchpin of protest but also a pilgrimage site for many who felt a dispositional affinity to the movement. "People who lived on the other side of the planet or country quit their jobs and hitchhiked to join the occupation," Annie recalled.

The park's opportune qualities, when coupled with Occupy's paramount framing, served as a catalyst for those who had a strongly felt identification with the movement, whether the highly motivated like Ernesto or the more curious like Kristina. As Kevin noted: "For a lot of people the park had become a home: it had become a community for people who didn't have homes; it became a mecca for the disenfranchised and the angry, [for the] victims of the 2008 collapse who had come from all over the country." Of course, this identification wasn't only open to those on the political left. "It wasn't just one particular ideology," Kevin cautioned. "It was people who felt that very radical change needed to happen, and a lot of them were just developing their political consciousness for the first time." Participants ran the gamut from right-wing libertarians dedicated to ending the federal reserve through the mainstream centrist persuasions, all the way to anarchists and communists more closely aligned with those who had planned the September 17 action.

One of the earliest Occupiers to follow this trajectory was Ernesto, who had been living on the other side of the country at the time Occupy got started. "I was working at this nursing home," he recalled. "I was washing the tables, and there was the news, and there was, like, a bunch of people in some park... and some guy gets on the TV and says, 'Anybody who wants to come, we need help... just come.'" For Ernesto, who was passionate about immigrant rights and was seeking new opportunities for activism, this invitation was all he needed. "Within the next three days I had already made up my mind. I borrowed my sleeping bag from my uncle [and] told him, 'I'm going to NY tomorrow.'.... I got to New York with $200 in my pocket, and I didn't know shit, I didn't know anybody in New York, I didn't know where Wall Street was." Explaining why he felt so driven, Ernesto mused: "I wasn't here to find myself.... I was here because I heard the drums, and I went toward the drums."

Experiences similar to Ernesto's often followed the explosion of public attention Occupy Wall Street received in October. The "drums" Ernesto heard when he first came across fleeting news of the protest had been amplified tenfold by the paramount frame that emerged around Occupy, reaching a crescendo with the escalating successes of and threats to the movement. Vast swaths of new participants, already aware of or interested in Occupy, chose to either become involved or further escalate their involvement. In addition to the extensive range of affinities that had characterized the occupation's appeal to ordinary New Yorkers, a very particular set of dispositional affinities had now been catalyzed by this further convergence condition: Occupy was framed as the de facto struggle against the dominant economic and sociopolitical order in the United States and, soon after, across the globe.

A general image of an Occupier swiftly crystallized, and the movement became clearly identified as a platform for antigovernment, antipolice, and anticapitalist rebellion. For some, these amplified characteristics would be the necessary preconditions for their own routes to involvement, with this new awareness of Occupy and its intersection with their political identity driving their decision-making. This occurred at both individual and collective levels. The New York Transport Workers Union spokesman Jim Gannon, when explaining why the union had unanimously voted to support OWS in the wake of the Bologna incident, stressed this in no uncertain terms: "It's kind of a natural alliance," he told a local newspaper reporter. "On many levels, our workers feel an affinity with the kids."[12]

The affinities that drew people like Rose to Occupy differed greatly from the ones that drew Ernesto. In Rose's case, her affinity with the occupation was not substantially underpinned by dispositional factors. She did not think of herself as having any fundamental compatibility with Occupy, of which she was only marginally aware when she began her pathway to participation. By contrast, Ernesto's affinity with Occupy arose fundamentally from his disposition. He had felt some kind of connection to the occupation, having "heard the drums," as he put it, and pursued them doggedly, just as many others did once the profile of Occupy's opportune space and paramount framing had been raised in the news media. Dispositional affinities often gave rise to different pathways to participation than the more diffuse set of social affinities or drives encountered in narratives like Rose's. Where affinities arose from identities, perceptions, and attitudes (rather than social status, patterns of activity, resources, or drives), mobilization was often a very deliberate process. Consequently, rather than stumbling into connection with Occupy, individuals such as Ernesto, with strongly felt affinities, actively sought out connections with OWS, ranging from participation, to emulation, to auxiliary support or engagement.

Rose and Ernesto's narratives neatly demonstrate two different poles of participation in Occupy, each pulling on different kinds of affinities and appealed to by different conditions of convergence. In many cases, things are not so extreme. Take, for example, the case of Kristina, a young magazine editor who visited Occupy occasionally during the protests and whose mobilization drew on perhaps the greatest variety of factors of anyone I interviewed. Kristina recalled how she had quite consciously sought out Zuccotti from a standpoint of curiosity. "I was interested in seeing what the fuss was about," she told me. "There was a lot of interest in what this young, ragtag group of people were about to accomplish, there was a real sense of promise... so one Saturday I went down there like a bit of a cultural tourist.... I didn't know what it was going to be like, but I wanted to be present for whatever it was." In this explanation, Kristina alludes to the paramount framing of Occupy and the movement's appeal to her interests as motivating factors for participating. Another element in her decision was the idea that visiting the occupation might be professionally productive, something catalyzed by its characteristics as an exceptional space. "I imagined it being something like MacDougal Street in the sixties in New York, where the next Bob Dylan is rolling up and down with a guitar and singing a beautiful protest anthem," she explained. Furthermore, she also possessed a degree of identification with the occupation and an attraction to the opportune space in which it occurred: "I really wanted to see if there was something there that maybe I could be part of on some level," she told me, "something that could be inspiring, that would make sense."

It is also worth remarking on the role of obligations, one social affinity not yet discussed in relation to Occupy. Unlike other social affinities, those drawn to OWS out of obligation were just as deliberate as those drawn by disposition. One illustrative example of this comes in the form of the New York homeless, who eventually became a very substantial contingent of the "hardgrounders" who slept overnight in the camp. "I mean, they had a lot of amenities down there, you know," André,[13] a formerly homeless activist in his later years recalled. "There's an infrastructure on the streets of New York City to get food, you know: homeless folks realize there's a hundred pizzas going... folks started gathering." As the harsh New York winter drew closer, a substantial proportion of the park's homeless visitors found themselves spending more time in the camp. One regular participant, Jack,[14] estimated that of those regularly sleeping in the park, "a third of the people were homeless," and that about "seven hundred more" would regularly show up at mealtimes. Many found themselves drawn into participation with the movement. "Once they were here, they tended to become more politically active... [and] contingents of people who were normal New York City homeless were now caught up in Occupy Wall Street."

Mobilizing an Occupation

A variety of conditions of convergence acted as a catalyst for the affinities between Occupy's participants and the movement. While at its zenith, Occupy's paramount framing attracted new participants with dispositional affinities of which they were well aware, the occupation's gradual growth was underpinned by a very broad spectrum of social affinities and drives, empowered by the occupation's character as an exceptional space, with low barriers to entry, making participation by those not strongly disposed toward the movement more palatable. Occupy's character as an open, pluralistic space in which participation could take many forms drew in many new Occupiers who were not highly political or die-hard activists when they first encountered the movement. Finally, the protection from police repression afforded by Zuccotti's opportune characteristics allowed those at risk of violence, arrest, or eviction to see the occupation as a refuge and even a home.

For Occupy, an affinity-convergence-driven mobilization process offered a means by which an initially marginal and isolated action could gain traction, even with very limited resources and no capacity to produce clear demands or distinct ideological propositions.[15] One Occupier[16] I interviewed even joked, "It seemed kind of bizarre that there was momentum about organizing around the financial crisis, you know, three years after it had actually hit." But where it lacked the means of organizationally sophisticated social movements, Occupy offered opportunity, hope, and possibility in the most populous city in the United States. Anyone could contribute, anyone could visit, and there were no membership criteria and no obligation to do anything more than you wanted to. Crucially, in persisting for almost two months, Occupy also had the time for these affinities to be activated more gradually. For many who became involved, finding their way to Occupy took time, relying on opportunities, discoveries, and chance encounters that are not guaranteed to occur in the same way as contact with one's regular social network. Nondispositional affinities were powerful for Occupy, particularly because the occupation also had the luxury of time and initially very few obstacles to its persistence.

The stories in this chapter only give a snapshot of the different pathways through which those with affinity to Occupy Wall Street came to participate in the movement. Nonetheless, their pathways are indicative of the routes taken by a great many more. Among those I interviewed, I encountered former employees of Wall Street banks, political journalists, music critics, seasoned activists from other cities, former homeless, filmmakers, students, and all manner of others who had taken their paths to Occupy guided by affinity, rather than becoming integrated through organizational recruitment or activist networks.

Equally, the very notable importance of affinities in the case of Occupy should not be taken to mean that other factors were irrelevant or unimportant: interpersonal ties with other participants, activist networks, and even organizations all played a role at various points in the movement, particularly in its later stages. One example is the litany of organized labor unions in New York that encouraged their members to participate in Occupy and even provided resources in the movement's later days. Likewise, the band of activists who planned the occupation and helped establish it in Zuccotti Park were well integrated in New York City's social movement communities. So too would have been many of those who heeded Adbusters' initial call. Among the contacts I have discussed so far, those who encountered Occupy directly through networks include individuals such as Annie, Owen, and Larry, all of whom became involved in Occupy by drawing upon their contacts in New York's activist and anarchist communities.

It is also worth briefly considering those who did not participate in Occupy, despite possessing some degree of affinity to the movement. Among these, the most notable were the local residents of the Financial District. During my fieldwork, in order to get a sense of the Zuccotti area and those who lived there, I spent two months living in the Financial District, about a five-minute walk from the park. During this time, I held regular conversations with a wide range of district regulars across the social spectrum,[17] as well as the residents of the luxury Financial District apartment complexes and the employees of major corporations whose offices were only steps away from Zuccotti. While their daily patterns of activity might have predisposed them to perhaps fleetingly spend time at the park or encounter Occupy activists, a great many tended to actively avoid the site instead. This was particularly pronounced among those living close to Zuccotti, who managed to avoid the occupation with an exacting effort. To further understand this phenomenon, I conducted an interview (unrecorded at the subject's request) with one such local resident, who had lived very close to the park, in one of Wall Street's $1.7 million condominiums, a short distance from it. In our conversation he explained how his friends and colleagues in his building and small business owners working around the park had felt remarkably repulsed by Occupy. Though they may have had some kind of small affinity to the occupation with respect to their coinciding everyday patterns of activity, these individuals lacked any substantial affinity to Occupy in any other regard. In fact, psychologically, their identities, perceptions, and attitudes were actively dissonant with participants in Occupy, making the prospect of their own participation substantially more unlikely.

In some contexts, even when participants did have seemingly promising dispositional affinities to the movement, their participation was frustrated by intervening social factors. A number of those I talked to had passed up their initial opportunities to participate in Occupy because intervening issues had presented themselves, only to participate when they later became biographically available. The similar lack of social affinity was true of individuals among the poorer African American communities in the boroughs of Brooklyn and Queens, one of the rare instances of a group deliberately targeted for movement outreach by Occupy's working groups. In some cases, this lack of affinity to the movement was later compensated for when a greater number of conditions of convergence compounded: the exceptional space of Zuccotti attracted far more participants once it had also developed the characteristics of an opportune space and still more when it was contextualized by a paramount frame.

Accounting for these instances of temporary and permanent nonparticipation offers substantial benefit for our understanding of affinity and convergence. The case of the Financial District locals highlights how simply having affinity to a cause in one particular respect can be rendered insignificant where others are lacking or counteracted by an actively oppositional stance. Cases of temporarily frustrated participation show that an absence of social affinity can present a similar impediment. Finally, cases of initially reluctant participants who mobilized following the addition of further convergence conditions indicate that the catalytic effect of convergence is intensified by the presence of multiple conditions.

The dynamics of participation in OWS appear quite different than those found in Egypt's revolutionary Eighteen Days. Fewer coinciding conditions of convergence—none of which were structural in nature—meant that the kind of spiking participation seen in downtown Cairo was not reproduced in downtown Manhattan. Instead, a sustained space of convergence with both exceptional and opportune qualities gradually attracted participants with a wide range of affinities to the movement, a process that was accelerated once the movement became broadly framed as a highly distinctive, paramount scenario. The exceptional space of Zuccotti was important in catalyzing the participation of those with compatible drives or social affinities, whereas its opportune qualities appealed more precisely to those with strong dispositional affinities toward the movement. So too did the paramount framing of the movement, which attracted those who identified or sympathized with the movement, as well as those sharing a sense of injustice about the status quo.

Because of the presence of a relatively select array of convergence conditions, tendencies in the catalytic relationship between convergence and affinity become especially legible in the case of Occupy. Even more enlightening is the fact that the spatial and cognitive conditions of convergence associated with the movement occurred over a relatively long period, during which they appeared both separately and simultaneously. In light of these relatively unique attributes, I have attempted to use the case as a prism through which processes of affinity-convergence mobilization can be looked at in a more dispersed, individuated fashion. In the case of Occupy, the cause's exceptional space seemed to primarily catalyze participation among individuals who foregrounded their social affinities and drives when discussing their involvement. By contrast, when opportune and paramount conditions came to the fore (along with ongoing exceptional conditions), an increasing number of participants attributed participation to their dispositions as well. It is hard to say how generalizable this pattern may be. I return to its discussion in the book's conclusion. More generally, the pathways to participation discussed in this chapter help illustrate how aggregate behavior unfolds not as mere mob mentality but as individual agency under evolving conditions. The next chapter, by contrast, shows just how fragile those conditions can be.

CHAPTER EIGHT

The End of the Extraordinary

> *Occupy Wall Street—it's hard to talk about it as an organization.... The action of Occupy Wall Street transformed into this never-ending, many-headed beast of a thing. But it wasn't really an organization, and it wasn't really a movement, and it wasn't really a moment, it wasn't any of these things. And so, it became really complicated.*
>
> ANNIE

> *[Occupy] was maybe the best networking event for progressive and radical folk in recent memory; there are now people who know each other because of it who are able to work on projects whether they're called "Occupy" or not, that are involved in a whole range of issues from economic justice to climate justice to anything else.*
>
> NOAH

By November 15, 2011, almost two months after its emergence, Occupy Wall Street seemed titanic. With hundreds of occupations worldwide, a month of news cycle dominance, the active support of the United States' major unions, and a war chest of hundreds of thousands of dollars in New York alone, Occupy seemed unstoppable. By this point major marches on the streets of New York were a weekly event, with battles between police and protesters stretching from Wall Street to Times Square. OWS and other US occupations enjoyed an incredibly supportive online community and considerable public goodwill. Even some among the 1 percent had bent their ear and opened their wallets, with the CEOs of Ben & Jerry's joining Occupiers in Zuccotti Park, with an offer of $300,000 and plans, along with a coalition of other CEOs calling themselves Occupy's Movement Resources Group, to raise $1.5 million more. As well-resourced organizations flocked to join the growing movement, they brought new spaces of their own. "A whole new set of people came in with ties to the NGO [nongovernmental organization] world," Annie recalled. "They got an office space on Broadway, and then announced... at the assembly: this exists. Sign up with your working group, and we'll, like, create shifts to allow access."

"So we had an office now," Ernesto recalled. "Of course, it was gonna create problems."

The influx of resources, office space, and money to the Occupy movement at the exact same time as numbers in Zuccotti were surging led to a serious outflow of actual organizing work from the park and into private spaces. By the tail end of October, "most working groups simply became focused on their own work and didn't go to the general assemblies," recalled Juan,[1] a participant in the Spanish Indignados protests who had joined the Occupy Wall Street protests along with his entire family. He explained how—complete with their offices, finances, and increasingly insular character—these "groups began to become so internally focused [that] they became almost like a job."

"The office, definitely, it was weird. It was a little bit corporate, right? A little, like, 'Show up for work,'" Kevin recalled.[2] There was a standing expectation that the groups using the office be formally registered and commit to maintaining the space and administering the building. This included admitting and refusing people seeking access, turning away those who were not deemed to have legitimate business on-site.

Of course, this new organized side of Occupy was highly attractive to many of those who had become exhausted by the chaotic dynamics of the occupation itself. As the occupation grew in size, it had also become increasingly difficult to use Zuccotti as a productive activist workspace. With thousands of participants flowing in and out of the park on a daily basis, General Assembly meetings were becoming increasingly difficult to manage. Consequently, work began to amend the General Assembly model to include a "Spokes Council," named for its structural similarity to the spokes of a wheel.[3] The Spokes Council brought together spokespeople[4] from Occupy's varying working groups, as well as caucuses of traditionally marginalized groups. The idea was that each group would nominate a rotating spokesperson for any particular meeting, resulting in a meeting consisting of twenty to thirty spokespeople rather than the masses of people attending General Assembly meetings. While the General Assembly would remain the sole forum for the substantial political and strategic matters pertaining to OWS, the Spokes Council would control the approval of budgets and capital expenditures, as well as the ratification of working groups and caucuses rights to representation on that council. These new meetings were to be held away from the park, in indoor spaces around the city, and would be focused on the regular business and administration of OWS itself.[5]

While Occupy's working groups were becoming estranged from Zuccotti, they were also establishing novel ties with other occupations in what has been subsequently dubbed the global Occupy movement. Two of the most prominent networking efforts were known as Occupy Together and InterOccupy.[6] While Occupy Together served as a general overarching hub, spreading news and information on the activities of the various occupations, as well as integrating with Meetup.com to offer people the chance to plan new occupations, InterOccupy served as a coordinating hub between existing Occupy groups. Initially, InterOccupy was a conference-call planning group, consisting of various working groups at occupations in New York (OWS), Pennsylvania (Philadelphia), Michigan (Kalamazoo), California (Los Angeles), and Oregon (Portland) that had participated in some experimental conference calls held between occupations. Over time, as many occupations lost access to physical space, InterOccupy shifted into the role of technical and communications support for protest actions and collaborative projects, and continued to play an impressive role in post-Occupy work.

While InterOccupy and Occupy Together offered some opportunities for connection between Occupy activists, neither was particularly well known, engaged with, or understood by ordinary participants in the occupations. Attempts to build an official Occupy Wall Street network of these more ethereal, fleeting participants were entirely glacial. Even something as simple as an email list proved very difficult to get off the ground. "We could not send a fucking email to a list until six months after we were evicted," Munroe,[7] a member of Occupy's "Tech-Ops Committee," bitterly recounted. Consequently, the vast bulk of coordinating activities during Occupy took place on an individual or small group level, rather than in formal interoccupation networks. This meant that the spread of occupations throughout the United States was almost mimetic in character, with attempts at new occupations emerging from communities of grassroots organizers who attempted to mimic OWS in their own fashion and inspiring others to join them.

Although OWS and its affiliates appeared to be getting ever more entrenched and had carried out a slew of successful actions, the movement was also becoming more fragmented. While numbers in the park had swelled to thousands, a great deal of the actual activity had moved elsewhere. Some working groups were barely visiting Zuccotti at all, preferring to meet at bars or in other public spaces, while others even registered as organizations in their own right, spending their days in office space donated by major unions, instituting strict proceedings, and maintaining tight circles of trust.

And so, at its organizational height, with hundreds of thousands of dollars in funding and a great deal of popular support, it came as a great surprise to the Occupiers that November 15 was the day OWS would be evicted. New York's mayor, Michael Bloomberg, in tandem with mayors of major cities across the United States and supported by intelligence gathered by the Department of Homeland Security, the FBI, and several other government agencies[8] that had been surveying occupations across the United States, ordered police to descend on Zuccotti. Under the cover of dark, NYPD officers raided the park, seizing and destroying the resources within it and ejecting its residents. The area around Zuccotti was then swiftly reoccupied by a semipermanent police presence for many months afterward. Occupy Wall Street had lost its namesake.

Occupy without an Occupation

The seizure of Zuccotti robbed Occupy Wall Street of its central constitutive space. The park had proved vital in attracting the masses to OWS, and its loss deprived the movement of one of its key points of access. Now deprived of the exceptional, opportune space that Zuccotti had come to constitute, drawing in new participants outside of the scope of New York City's organizing scene would prove to be difficult. So too would maintaining the casual flow of participation that had sustained Occupy over the past two months without a daily point of contact between the movement and potential new participants. "Without that center, people started [to be like], okay, well,... I got my shit to take care of, I need to make rent," Liam, a longtime Brooklynite and well-connected Occupier, explained.[9] Accordingly, both novel and persistent participation from beyond the movement's core began to decline.

The eviction loomed large in the memories of many of the people I talked to as the point at which Occupy began to falter. Emily,[10] a young woman who had been keeping a diary during the occupation, pulled it out and read to me the following entry:

> I used to go to Liberty [Zuccotti] almost every day even just to touch base for a few minutes.... They've taken that away now. So it's as if they've taken my spiritual home, the space that made me feel connected to something bigger than myself.... It was a truly magical time, that period when Liberty Plaza grew, morphed, transformed every day, a time when we felt that anything is possible.... It had been the space that inspired me to believe, to have faith, then poof, it was gone. I still can't help but feel disconnected now that there's no physical space to hold

on to, to congregate, to meet up.... There are ways to plug in, but I just don't have that same sense of urgency or compulsion that was driving me before the eviction.

Accounts like Emily's were not uncommon. Without the occupation the vast spectrum of disaffiliated individuals who would flow in and out of the park on a daily basis had nowhere to gather, and the enormous variety of ideological factions who had participated in the movement no longer had a shared project to sustain. The eviction "scattered the community physically *and* theoretically," one Occupier, Noah,[11] explained. In its absence the movement began to drift apart.

"People were shattered by the fact that they were evicted from the park," Liam recalled. "Once the park was cleared, I heard universally about people going back to their apartment and being depressed.... They were like, what the hell am I doing?" For many of the "hard-ground" Occupiers who had dropped everything to hold space in Zuccotti, the loss of the park was simply gutting. The situation was even worse for those who joined the movement while they were homeless. These were some of the most committed Occupiers, and they had lost not only their community but their place of living. "There were lots of people who came to Occupy because the system had failed them, and they didn't really have other places to go," Noah recalled. "Being able to have a space and hold space was a much more pressing and less theoretical concern for them than it was for some other people who were involved in the movement."

For the office-dwelling contingents among the movement and its burgeoning periphery of organized affiliates, the loss of Zuccotti was considerably less concerning. "People could start meeting in a quiet, calm place," Kevin recalled. "I felt like we needed a certain amount of structure and discipline. I was frustrated with how long everything took, I was frustrated with the endless discussions; I wanted more doing, less talking." Accordingly, the loss of the park proved a vital step in shifting OWS away from the kind of dynamic participatory mass movement it had been in Zuccotti and toward a more conventional model of organized activism, buoyed by hefty funds and prominent allies.

Fading Framing

It would take more than an eviction to vanquish the massive burst of organizing around Occupy Wall Street. In this sense, a fragmentation of the movement into smaller groups that had prompted concerns during the occupation of Zuccotti now became an asset. Occupy was no longer just an action; it was the network of all of the activists, sympathizers, movements, and organizations that had been drawn to, and then sustained, that action. With Zuccotti gone, it was the Occupy network that picked up the torch, and, at least initially, the masses were still willing to come to its aid. What followed was, if anything, an intensification of OWS's activity in the month following the November eviction.

The eviction of the park had shattered OWS's core space, but it served to briefly amplify a different convergence condition: the paramount frame that had contributed to sustained mobilization since October. Like many of the other instances of police repression during Occupy's life cycle, the eviction drew a great deal of attention to the movement and its struggles. The movement's two-month anniversary protest, long scheduled for November 17, was supercharged by the loss of the park as the paramount framing around the movement was temporarily heightened. More than thirty thousand (by NYPD estimates) took to the streets of New York.[12] Even with the loss of the park, the strength of this frame ensured that new participants continued to find their way to Occupy. Likewise, the movement's considerable resources and relatively recently won organizational allies were still ready for sustained contentious activity.

Even when the stream of new participants slowed over the winter months, the movement's day-to-day operation still persisted, its funds were still readily in use, and General Assembly meetings were regularly scheduled. Nonetheless, it appeared that shift from occupation to organization came with an inertia greater than many Occupiers had anticipated. "When I look back at my emails and all the videos I was making, I was just getting started around the time the park got evicted, I was just getting into it, and I didn't have any sense of defeat around that time," a member of Occupy's Media Working Group recalled.[13] "I felt like they can take the tents out of the park, but they're not going to stop this movement; it's still growing, it's all over the world.... But when you look back you can see that it was really the beginning of the end."

Initially, some elements of the network of new and old activists formed during Occupy came together to try to recreate a Zuccotti-style occupation. The first major attempt at this came on the three-month anniversary of the initial protests, targeting Trinity Church's Duarte Square on December 17, and was swiftly foiled by the NYPD. A second attempt to reoccupy Zuccotti occurred on January 1, 2012, and was again shut down by police forces. Another attempt to retake Zuccotti took place nine days later and was rapidly curtailed. Finally, on March 17, Occupy's six-month anniversary, another attempted major reoccupation failed to take Zuccotti. With the hope of a new occupation in New York lost, other occupations across the country winding down, the movement's public-facing activities entering a winter hibernation of sorts, and the presidential electoral cycle now in full swing, the paramount framing that had underpinned so many people's initial participation in OWS also faded away. Gone was the sense of a mimetically spreading movement of occupations, the sympathetic media coverage, and the sense that the movement was gaining pace. Accordingly, popular excitement substantially diminished. Without its physical and cognitive conditions of convergence, the capacity of Occupy actions and activities to compel and mobilize those beyond its own network seemed less and less effective.

During the movement's winter hibernation, activists sought to conserve energy in favor of a far larger action in the spring. The movement's big public return was to be a May 1 general strike, which they would call "Occupy May Day," planned to occur across 135 cities in the United States. "While American corporate media has focused on yet another stale election between Wall Street-financed candidates, Occupy has been organizing something extraordinary: the first truly nationwide General Strike in U.S. history," a rousing announcement on occupywallst.org proclaimed.[14] "The Occupy Movement has called for A Day Without the 99% on May 1st, 2012. This in and of itself is a tremendous victory. For the first time, workers, students, immigrants, and the unemployed from 135 U.S. cities will stand together for economic justice." "I've never seen people work so hard as they did in the run-up to May Day," Charlotte recalled. "Every night of the week, people were going and sitting in meetings and planning and preparing and organizing.... People were dedicating their entire lives to this. And it was quite extraordinary."

Despite the hard work of so many activists and organizers, there was, of course, no general strike on May 1, 2012. There was a plethora of reasons for the event's failure: its overambitious, rushed, and vague planning; activist fatigue from constant failed Occupy-themed actions; the impossibility of a general strike without consensus among the nation's many trade unions; and many more. "There was a breakdown of those relationships around mayday in particular," Annie had recalled, speaking of trade unions' dissatisfaction with Occupy around the May Day strike. One labor organizer[15] with whom I spoke offered a similar sentiment. "The whole thing broke down quite dramatically," they recalled. Not only was it the case that "very few... groups in Occupy who were involved in the Mayday planning meetings were actually trying to do real outreach," but the formal organizations that had attached themselves to the movement and did have the resources to conduct outreach and recruitment for the day were fighting an uphill battle. "The sort of structures that go into place with labor organizing conflicted radically with what should have been a more community-based organizing model," they said. "It dissolved spectacularly."

By May Day a sense of discomfort with the Occupy operation had become palpable. "The bubble was ready to burst," Ernesto recalled as we sat in the back room of his bustling apartment in Brooklyn. Shortly after the action, it did. "We're beyond this, we don't need Occupy, we don't need the word, it's not a group, [and] we don't need this shit," Ernesto and his friends concluded. Soon enough many others concurred. "Phase 2, 'after-Occupy,' started when May Day hit," he concluded.

Beyond Wall Street, Beyond Occupy

September 17, 2016, was the fifth anniversary of Occupy Wall Street, but what remained? It was with this question in mind that I had taken a trip down to Zuccotti Park that evening. When I arrived, the park was hardly bustling, but it held a good number of alternative-looking types in their various uniforms of activism: printed tees, dreadlocks, hand-woven brightly colored garments, and figures clad all in black made appearances. There were a number of familiar groups in the square, and even some familiar faces—I learned later that I had just missed Rose and Joe. The day's activities had been planned to give space to a number of organizations, each staking variably dubious claims to the Occupy legacy. One such group, Occu-Evolve, had thrown a lot of energy into the day, but, as in the previous year, it continued to be ignored by everyone who showed up. They were assembled by the park steps wearing T-shirts bearing the slogan BECAUSE OF OCCUPY, planning a grand march for the day's end, which never materialized.

As I approached the park, an older man in a stars-and-stripes cowboy hat, standing at a table covered in posters and a stack of Guy Fawkes masks, noticed my bewilderment and extended a hand. "Hey!" he said with a grin. "Welcome to Occupy." No sooner than I had thanked him for his welcome, he had diverted his gaze back to an older woman he had been conversing with earlier. "Seven dollars each. These? They're fifteen," I heard him say, "and I'll sign them. We only made five of these, they're collectible; they'll be worth much more in the future." I was unable to ascertain exactly what his role in the production of these posters had been, though my hunch was that he was not their creator: he certainly did not seem to sense any irony in trying to sell Occupy Wall Street merchandise for its speculative future value.

So where did Occupy go? In the years following Occupy Wall Street, both conventional leftist organizations and Democratic Party affiliates attempted to incorporate the language and symbols of Occupy into their work, with varying success. These attempts to assume and employ the Occupy "brand" have been seen in efforts such as the 2015–2016 Bernie Sanders Democratic primary grassroots campaign (which prominently featured an endorsement from "Occupy Wall Street" at its kickoff), the highly successful "Occupy Democrats" media organization, and a wide variety of other platforms that leveraged the movement's reputation to appeal to a wider public, but not for the purpose of contentious mobilization.

Meanwhile, the organizational and networked relationships developed during Occupy Wall Street continued to evolve as newly minted activists returned to their communities and began to organize for other issues. "Everyone went back to their people, took a little piece of that revolutionary gospel, and sang it," Ernesto explained, "and the best part about that was that we were still connected." Ernesto described how former Occupiers would "start building these little bubbles back in [their] community," around local interests and issues, and how, thanks to the connections former Occupiers built during OWS, "little by little, those bubbles [would] get bigger," before eventually "crashing into each other" and creating new social movements of their own.

Along with the formation of new associations, network ties, and even formal organizations in the wake of Occupy's decline, another key outgrowth of the movement was a new social identity, that of the Occupier. To be an Occupier connected you not only with participants in Occupy movements in different states, and even countries, but created a firm standpoint from which to maintain and continue the relationships one had formed during OWS. While to some extent this simply emerged from the bonds and trust formed during the occupation, it was also imposed upon many regular visitors to the occupation by external forces. "I think the fact that the cops treated anyone who was there as fair game... meant that they had to become a part of—they *were* part of—the collective experience, whether they wanted to or not," one of the journalists covering Occupy, Joe,[16] had told me. For Joe, it was his arrest that cemented his identity as an Occupier. "There was just a sort of way in which, even if you attempted not to become a part of the [Occupy] story, for almost all of us that happened at one point or another," he explained, while describing how all but one of the journalists he had met covering Occupy came to identify with the occupation in some way. Even once the conditions of convergence that underpinned OWS ceased, this identity proved a pivotal affinity on which future mobilizations could draw. This would long outlast the struggle around Occupy Wall Street and continued to manifest in the years to come.

The first major recombination of Occupiers came in response to the deadly and destructive Hurricane Sandy, which had made landfall in New York at the end of October 2012, one year after Occupy had been at its highest point. Countless civilians had been left stranded in their homes, many without food, water, or electricity, and some surrounded by floodwater. Local and national responders, though somewhat prepared for the storm, were woefully poor in response, and the situation seemed dire. It was a critical flashpoint, and Occupy had just the network: it was time to Occupy Sandy.

Despite its name, Occupy Sandy was not an occupation. Instead, the use of "Occupy" by organizers was a clear statement of identity and acted as an activation of the affinity, network, and organizational ties that had been built during Occupy. Coupled with the social media resources built around OWS, a movement of some sixty thousand volunteers was assembled within a matter of days, initially consisting of members of post-Occupy networks, and growing to include new participants as well. By the time it had ceased activity, Occupy Sandy had raised over $1.36 million and would lay claim to the title of "the largest civilian-led disaster relief effort in American history."[17] It was so outstanding of an effort that the Department of Homeland Security commissioned a full report on its activities and how it was able to outperform established disaster relief organizations, NGOs, and even the Federal Emergency Management Agency (FEMA) in its impact.[18] The *New York Times* commented that, since 2011, Occupy had "wandered in a desert of more intellectual, less visible projects, like farming, fighting debt and theorizing on banking.... [I]t is only with Hurricane Sandy that the times have conspired to deliver an event that fully calls upon the movement's talents and caters to its strengths."[19]

Since 2012 the networks of activists and actual resources that coalesced during Occupy Wall Street have found themselves involved in a plethora of struggles and movements that do not bear its name, but which it has bolstered nonetheless. While discussing contemporary activism in the United States with Noah, he explained to me just how much these movements and organizations were connected to OWS. "There's a huge amount of folks who've been involved in pretty much everything you've mentioned"—the People's Climate March, Flood Wall Street, Black Lives Matter, Rising Tide, Occupy the Pipeline, and Fight for 15—"who were alumni of Occupy Wall Street. That manifests both in terms of the tactics that are employed and also in terms of the larger systemic analysis that you see," he explained. Another Occupier[20] told me how the OWS bail fund had provided support in the wake of the shooting of Eric Garner and indigenous rights struggles in South Dakota.

Occupy's activity and potency have stretched not only well beyond Wall Street but also well beyond Occupy. This runs from the massive reunions of the Occupy network such as Occupy Sandy, to political movements such as the Sanders campaign, to new intersectional ventures around income, race, police brutality, indigenous rights, climate change, and all manner of other matters. Indeed, OWS had played a part in the formation, discourse, and praxis of a great many individuals, organizations, and social movements. This array of diverse entities remained associated and networked with one another long after the worldwide Occupy movement and Occupy Wall Street itself had wound down.

Even today networks, groups, and associations that trace their origins and goals to Occupy are active in New York City. Perhaps the most recently prominent, the Metropolitan Anarchist Coordinating Council (MACC), was founded after the election of President Donald Trump as an attempt to resist the state's encroachments on civil liberties. The group featured working groups, general assemblies, and a consensual decision-making process, many of the hallmarks of the Occupy movement. I asked one of the group's founding participants about these similarities.[21] "That was intentional," she explained. "There was a direct connection." Many of the key organizers "involved in starting MACC were also part of Occupy Wall Street, and we drafted all the structure documents... to create a somewhat permeable open-door space," she explained. The group has played a number of roles over the past few years, most recently during the COVID-19 pandemic. MACC brought together hundreds of people in New York communities around "mutual aid, the politics of care, and abolition." Reflecting on OWS's legacy, she concluded: "Occupy was this moment in which the emperor had no clothes, people could see the system more clearly. Nothing has been the same since then." Even though Occupy Wall Street fell well short of the "Tahrir Moment" initially advertised, the movement created something their Egyptian inspiration lacked: a massive interconnected network of radicals, activists, and organizers who have continued to fight for a better world over the past decade. "Everyone that I know is still active in some way," the MACC organizer explained. "In pretty much every area, every sector of society, there's some kind of pushback, some kind of resistance."

Though the conditions of convergence that sustained Occupy dwindled, participation dried up, and society moved on, the network that crystallized from the movement has remained in place, ready to deploy for a just cause, a common aim, or a critical juncture. While Occupy veterans have taken radically different directions from one another, they can be traced throughout much of the past decade wherever fitting causes have arisen, whether for Sanders or Sandy, to defend immigrants against deportation or stand up to the Trump administration and the far right, to resist police brutality or provide mutual aid. Occupy may be long gone, but its legacy lives on.

Eric Garner	Billy Ray Davis	David Joseph
John Crawford III	Samuel DuBose	Calin Roquemore
Michael Brown	Michael Sabbie	Dyzhawn Perkins
Ezell Ford	Brian Keith Day	Christopher Davis
Dante Parker	Christian Taylor	Marco Loud
Michelle Cusseaux	Troy Robinson	Peter Gaines
Laquan McDonald	Felix Kumi	Torrey Robinson
Tanisha Anderson	Keith Harrison McLeod	Darius Robinson
Akai Gurley	Junior Prosper	Kevin Hicks
Tamir Rice	Lamontez Jones	Mary Truxillo
Rumain Brisbon	Paterson Brown Jr.	Demarcus Semer
Jerame Reid	Dominic Hutchinson	Willie Tillman
George Mann	Anthony Ashford	Terrill Thomas
Matthew Ajibade	Alonzo Smith	Sylville Smith
Frank Smart	Tyree Crawford	Alton Sterling
Natasha McKenna	India Kager	Philando Castile
Tony Robinson	La'vante Biggs	Terence Crutcher
Anthony Hill	Michael Lee Marshall	Paul O'Neal
Mya Hall	Jamar Clark	Alteria Woods
Phillip White	Richard Perkins Jr.	Jordan Edwards
Eric Harris	Nathaniel Harris Pickett	Aaron Bailey
Walter Scott	Benni Lee Tignor	Ronell Foster
William Chapman II	Miguel Espinal	Stephon Clark
Alexia Christian	Michael Noel	Antwon Rose Jr.
Brendon Glenn	Kevin Matthews	Botham Jean
Victo Emanuel Larosa III	Bettie Jones	Pamela Turner
Jonathan Sanders	Quintonio LeGrier	Dominique Clayton
Freddie Gray	Keith Childress Jr.	Atatiana Jefferson
Joseph Mann	Janet Wilson	Christopher Whitfield
Salvado Ellswood	Randy Nelson	Christopher McCorvey
Sandra Bland	Antronie Scott	Eric Reason
Albert Joseph Davis	Wendell Celestine	Michael Lorenzo Dean
Darrius Stewart		Breonna Taylor

George Floyd

PART IV

THE BLACK LIVES UPRISING, 2020

The list you have just read details some of the most high-profile police killings of Black Americans in the six years before George Floyd's murder by Minneapolis police on May 25, 2020.[1] The total number for that period, when limited exclusively to those not found to have been armed with any discernible weapon, stands at 346.[2] Black people are roughly three times more likely to be killed by police than whites across the United States and as much as twenty-two times more likely in some major cities, such as Minneapolis and Chicago.[3]

In the years between 2014's Ferguson, Missouri, protests that brought the Black Lives Matter movement to public prominence and America's 2020 uprising, the nation's police departments had collectively held a Roman candle to the public mood and somehow managed to avoid igniting something bigger. They had given Americans three hundred and forty-six opportunities for outrage (following hundreds more in years past), and for the most part, small-scale, orderly, peaceful protests had been the result.

So what changed in 2020? Why was it that this time, Americans responded to police brutality not with small episodes of disorder or regulated orderly organized marches, but with an uprising that will go down in history as a pivotal moment in the nation's politics? The answer to this question lies in no inconsiderable part in unpicking the phenomenon of popular spontaneity that characterized the surge of protests following Floyd's death. In the two chapters that follow, I pursue just such a task. Chapter 9 examines the birth of the 2020 uprising, tracing how chaotic yet peaceful protests in Minneapolis cascaded into police brutality–provoked riots across the Twin Cities, which in turn galvanized popular spontaneity elsewhere, spiraling into a similar pattern of spontaneous protest, police-provoked riot, and mass mobilization across the United States. Drawing on qualitative interviews with participants, published eyewitness testimonies, livestream footage, social media posts,[4] government documents, and media reportage, this chapter traces the progression of the uprising's first two months through an indicative selection of the cities it touched: Minneapolis, Atlanta, Seattle, and Portland, Oregon.

Counterbalancing the narrative content of chapter 9, chapter 10 turns its focus to the specific dynamics of affinity and convergence that played out during the uprising, detailing their role in fomenting popular mobilization without reliance on movement organizations and their networks. It shows how the exceptional state of affairs stemming from the COVID-19 pandemic combined with emergent paramount and opportune situations arising from violent showdowns with police forces to catalyze greater participation in protest, as well as discussing the role of preemptive local concessions and federal authoritarian threat in framing participation as first opportune, then paramount. The chapter also discusses how certain claimed spaces in cities like Seattle and Portland provided opportune and exceptional physical conditions for participation in protest. These various convergence conditions interacted with a wide array of social and psychological affinities. Social affinities included belonging to the young and precariously (un)employed, possessing skills or tools useful to protesters, and the absence of obligations such as pandemic shielding and in-person jobs, as well as where people lived and the media they consumed. Psychological affinities ranged from protesters' need for social stimulation and catharsis to a dispositional triad of identities, perceived injustice, and attitudes oriented around antiracism, civic outrage, and opposition to the police. The chapter closes by detailing how new forms of movement organization emerged directly from protest activity during the uprising and how they have persisted over time.

Because of the novelty and contemporary politicization of this case, it is necessary to issue some caveats to the reader before we move on. First, I must note my own positionality: the movement for Black lives is one I have long supported and something I have protested for on both sides of the Atlantic, both prior to and during the 2020 uprising. Doing so was made considerably easier by the fact that I am a white male scholar from the United Kingdom, factors that meant I was never directly targeted by law enforcement and had far fewer reasons to fear being targeted. At the same time, I am not a movement activist, nor am I affiliated with any movement organizations. I am not privy to any special knowledge or access beyond that accessible to any other qualitative researcher. I, like so many others, was simply a fleeting participant in the cascade of protest that year.

Despite my personal dispositions, I have steadfastly refrained from glamorizing what took place in the summer of 2020. Rather than present a narrative of purely peaceful protests carried out by orderly citizens (and

I would not be the first to do so), I have instead attempted to convey how the protests' predominantly peaceful element interacted with and was buoyed by instances of disruptive, unruly, and even riotous contention. As other cases also show, these facets of movement activity can be crucial in shaping the convergence conditions under which further protest takes place.

Second, and equally crucially: this is far from a fulsome history of the uprising. In explaining how 2020's upsurge of mobilization took place, I have drawn indicatively from snapshots of cities across the United States. These cannot possibly substitute for the definitive or entire story of the 2020 uprising. There are several instances where my narrative spotlight swings away from invariably important events: the prehistory of Portland's Fed Wars and the dramatic showdowns in Washington, DC, in May and June; the response to the shooting of Rayshard Brooks in Atlanta; the evolution of protest in Seattle over the course of June; and, ultimately, the entire course of events in cities like New York, Chicago, and across most of the US's fifty states. Rather, I have leaned into sections of the narrative most pertinent to understanding the dynamics of affinity-convergence mobilization and focused on sites where my interviews proved most revealing.

With these caveats dispensed with, we begin in Minneapolis.

CHAPTER NINE

From Tragedy to Uprising

> "I didn't do nothing serious, man. Please, please, please: I can't breathe. Please, man, please, somebody?... I can't breathe... the knee on my neck...
> "I'm through, I'm through...
> "I can't breathe, officer...
> "Don't kill me...
> "Please, sir. Please. Please. Please. I can't breathe."
>
> GEORGE FLOYD, May 25, 2020

A little after midnight on Tuesday, May 26, 2020, the Minneapolis Police Department (MPD) announced that they had arrested a man the previous evening who "appeared to be suffering medical distress... [and] died a short time later."[1] Soon after, at 1:46 a.m., a young woman named Darnella Frazer told the world what really happened: "They killed him right in front of cup foods over south on 38th and Chicago!!" she wrote on Facebook, uploading a ten-minute video of the man's arrest and murder at the hands of the MPD.[2] This man was George Floyd.

It would have been immediately clear that the police report looked like a cover-up: the footage showed an officer kneeling on the handcuffed Floyd's neck for almost eight minutes, long past the point of unconsciousness, amid calls from the crowd directly alleging that he was killing Floyd.[3] The video spread like wildfire.

In response, organizers in the Twin Cities of Minneapolis and St. Paul spent a sleepless night setting up and circulating a Facebook event inviting locals to a 5:00 p.m. protest at the site of Floyd's killing: 38th Street and Chicago Avenue. This was somewhat of a fraught task, as the United States had been struck hard by the COVID-19 (Coronavirus) pandemic, and governments and civil society organizations were for the most part encouraging people to socially isolate. The Minneapolis protest was set to last for two hours and would be kept COVID-secure by its organizers, who had received assistance from the city in procuring personal protective equipment for attendees. "We want to see those killer cops prosecuted and convicted for what they've done. They need to be held accountable. And the city needs to be prepared for a multimillion-dollar payoff for this family," Nekima Levy Armstrong, one of the members of an ad hoc coalition of local community organizers coordinating the Facebook event, declared.[4] An accompanying "Virtual Protest" was called by Black Lives Matter chapters around the country (this was less a demonstration than a link to a livestream of events in Minneapolis).[5]

The various Facebook invitees from around the city were not entirely on board with the protest plans. "Question: Would it make more sense to protest outside the 3rd precinct?" one person asked at around 8:22 a.m. "May I suggest delaying the protest to tomorrow due to the severe weather warning for tonight?" asked another.[6] Yet a third contended that "[i]t would be an additional crime against the people in our community (on top of the police killing) for outsiders to show up."

"We've got all kinds of messages... saying, Oh, can you do it tomorrow? Can you make it a car parade?... I know y'all mean well, but just trust that we know what we're doing, we're going to do the best that we can," Nekima told her Facebook friends on a livestream at lunchtime that day.[7] By this time, however, plenty of people had taken action on their own. Small crowds had already gathered at both the Third Precinct and the intersection of 38th and Chicago, while people across the United States started "doxing" (researching and revealing personal information about) the various officers involved in the arrest. As the video spread from person to person—posted to social media networks, exchanged in WhatsApp groups, and even appearing on the news—public fury brewed. Hours before the protest was supposed to start, thousands were already on their way to both locations.

The speed with which the event at 38th and Chicago had been planned meant that there was no real order of ceremonies or definitive direction, and instead multiple groups showed up planning to make their voices heard. Meanwhile, what passed for the "official" organizing coalition had a great deal of trouble managing the event. At the Minneapolis Third Precinct, things were even more unstructured. Without a clear set of coordinators, protest simply took its own form, mostly—at first—shouting, chanting, and marching. After about an hour, as people continued to pour in to both sites, things began to heat up.

At 38th and Chicago, organization was collapsing, and emotions were running high. A truly diverse sample of people had showed up, across a wide range of demographics. Arguments were breaking out in the crowd. "Hey, please don't film THAT, okay. We're out here to protest, not to make us look bad. Y'know what I'm sayin'?" Trahern Crews, a local Green Party activist, cautioned another livestreamer who was pointing his camera phone in the direction of some commotion.[8] "Usually our protests are a little more organized than this," he explained to his own audience, "but it happened so quickly, we had to get a quick response, but people just came out to get busy."

Many of those gathered at 38th and Chicago wanted to link up with the other protesters at the Third Precinct. Meanwhile, the event's organizers and some family members were busy trying to keep everyone at the intersection. They were "upset that people are starting to march. They want to stay right here," Crews told to his audience. Conflict between the marching contingent and the organizing contingent escalated as a roadblock set up by organizers began interfering with the flow of the march. One person approached Crews as he was streaming and asked who was responsible for the roadblock. "The organizers who've been out here since ten o'clock!" he exclaimed.

"Well, tell the damn 'organizers' that they're making our people vulnerable up front!" came the reply.

"Keep marching! I'm telling everybody to keep marching right now!" a young Black girl with a megaphone cried out. "No matter WHO tries to stop you."

"Tell them to bring their ass back [here] or stay the FUCK out," someone among the organizing crowd retorted.

By about 6:15 p.m., it became clear that the marching contingent had won out, so the rest of the crowd at 38th and Chicago joined the march and headed to the Third Precinct. By the time they arrived, the crowd at the precinct had become especially rambunctious. Some of the organizers who had lost control of the protest at 38th and Chicago arrived shortly after 7:15 p.m., and made best efforts to calm down the crowd at the station. "Hey, y'all quit that. Hey, you don't need to break nothin'.... That ain't the way to get it done," one of the older community organizers on the scene said over the megaphone as he gestured toward the smashed glass door to the police station. "They gon' get that fixed. That ain't gonna get Floyd back."[9]

The people gathered around the precinct did not seem to find this a compelling argument. "They *can* fix that door, we *won't* get our brotha back!" one protester cried. "They're looking for ANY excuse to kill us."[10]

"Ain't no winning them back, man, ain't no winning them back," one of the organizer's associates said to him. "Damn, the kids! They went at the police station!"

A few minutes later, yet another organizer made an effort to stem the tide. "Hey, yo yo yo yo yo, y'all need to quit destroying their property!" he said. "Quit destroying their property! We're not here for violence. Quit destroying their property around back! We're not gonna win if we..."[11]

But the error had already been made. "They're breaking police lines at the back?" one person said to another. Another voice chimed in, "You goin' out back?" And another: "I'm going to the back." And so, a steady stream of people began to peel off the front of the demonstration and make their way around to the back of the building, where various graffiti tags had been sprayed all over the station walls and police vehicles. It was not in fact as violent at people might have thought. A crowd of mostly young people milled around the entrance. A few stones had been thrown. The only notable damage was to the electrics outside the building, which had been kicked and pulled at. One enterprising participant was severing the building's communications cables. Police in riot gear and gas masks stood just inside the doors.[12]

"I don't know how many of you guys've been outside America, but I've been outside of America at a riot *and* a protest. These motherfuckers are ready," a man at the doors told the crowd. "We ready too," an assertive female voice replied. "I'm gon' fuck shit up! I don't care—I don't give a FUCK—I can go to jail. Fuck all y'all," another shouted as she advanced on the precinct's doorway.[13]

Over the course of the next half hour, vandalism intensified as protesters pelted the building with bricks, bottles, and eggs before turning their attention to parked police vehicles nearby, first on the road and then in the station parking lot. "This is the END. This is the END. We took enough of this. We didn't care then, [but] we got our foot down now," one protester shouted into a nearby camera. "If you're black, you should be out here. We all out here whether it's peaceful or not. They not peaceful with us!" another exclaimed. "Minnesota nice, my ass," a third chimed in. "This has been going on far too long. Let us SHOW how we Black people really get down."[14]

It was then that the police response began in full force. Riot troops deployed from unmarked white vans, firing tear gas canisters and other munitions at both protesters and civilian press.[15] Having cleared the crowd, reinforcements pulled in armed with heavy-duty batons and gas grenade launchers, again attacking the press on the scene before advancing on the fleeing crowd. Soon the air was thick with tear gas.

"The police have turned Lake [Street] and Snelling [Avenue] into what resembles an urban war zone," one reporter decried. Nonetheless, "there's hundreds of people still out here."[16] A series of small fires burned on the grass banks nearby, ignited by the red-hot canisters lobbed by police.

So far any vandalism had been carried out by a small but eclectic minority of the younger people in the crowd. To those who had not taken part, such an incredibly harsh police response seemed appalling. "Our shit was peaceful. People who had nothing to do with our protest fucked their shit up, and they want to come after us?" one protester shouted. "If it's war they want, we'll give them war. If they don't want to give us peace? Hey, peace killed our brotha. Sitting down, not doing shit killed our brotha. We not gon' get him back? They not gonna get their cars back, they not gonna get their building back, they don't get their shit back."

Another woman, in tears, cried: "I just want them to listen to us, but they're not gonna listen. They didn't listen. Why is it that they didn't listen, bro?" She turned away from the camera and advanced on the police lines, the air thick with nerve agents: "WHY DIDN'T YOU FUCKING LISTEN?"

As the evening drew on, police repression hardly let up. Protesters were bombarded with tear gas and shot with "less lethal" marker rounds (so called because they are potentially *still* lethal when targeted at the head, groin, or upper torso).[17] A small contingent of a few hundred protesters continued facing down cops near the precinct, with one or two people even shooting paintball guns at police and pellet guns at the station windows.[18] Others, deterred from reaching the precinct by the police line, smashed the windows of nearby businesses instead. Rage was bubbling.

The Power of Riot

Word rapidly spread about Tuesday's fractious protests and the overbearing police response. Many had been watching along on livestreams, while others heard from families and friends. Still more found out when footage of the protests and the subsequent wave of police repression hit the nightly news. Community discussions online and in the streets swirled with potential protest locations for the next day.

I talked to Whitney,[19] a young white woman living in the city, who told me how she first heard news of the commotion on the evening of Tuesday, May 26. "My roommate came home, and she's like: 'People are *pissed*. People are *really fucking upset about this*.' ... It was a big deal." She had initially decided not to attend the Tuesday protests, but this realization changed her perspective. "When she said people were *pissed*, I was like: oh *wow*, maybe I *should* try and get out there... this is something I should try to make time for. It was seeming that this was becoming a really big thing."

Curiously, upon first hearing news of Floyd's murder, Whitney's immediate reaction had been simply that the killing constituted "just another police murder in Minneapolis," a tragically regular event to which she had become habituated. "[The police killing of] Philando Castile had happened a few years ago," she explained, "[so] I was just like, 'Aw god, not another one.'" It was only when she heard about Tuesday's events that she decided to forestall her other commitments and join in.

Those who had witnessed Tuesday's events firsthand were similarly affected. "Look at this shit, yo," Shay, a middle-aged mother, tearfully told her friends on Facebook Live before work on Wednesday morning, pointing to news footage of Tuesday's events.[20] "That was us yesterday. I was proud to be a part of this protest. Naw, I didn't throw shit. But I wanted to. I wanted to be this angry." She added: "I am tired of this shit. I'm tired of going to another vigil, another march.... I understand Malcolm X: [We want justice] by any fuckin' means necessary."

The next day an even larger body of protesters descended on the streets of Minneapolis without instruction or formal leadership. Some went to the house of the officer who had killed Floyd, others returned to the Third Precinct, and still others made their way back to 38th and Chicago for a second day. The pattern from May 26 repeated itself: those who gathered at 38th and Chicago marched to join protesters at the Third Precinct as the evening arrived, being joined at both locations and en route by many local Minnesotans who had just finished their day's work. Unlike the previous day (in which the MPD response occurred only after protesters breached the parking lot), this time police were engaging in proactive repression. Lines of police encircled the precinct, with sniper squads on the rooftops armed with a variety of "less lethal" antipersonnel ballistics.

"We had shut down pretty much all of Lake Street," recalled Chase,[21] a young man who grew up in the north of the city, "and it was pretty peaceful.... Nobody was doing any property damage, there wasn't any rioting, it was nothing." Yet as evening began, police assaults suddenly intensified. "One of the first things I remember seeing [was]... ten or so cops on the roof of the precinct sniping people with 'less lethal' weapons," Whitney recalled. Police began firing rounds widely across the crowd of protesters, even as many participants were still arriving. "Within fifteen to twenty minutes of me being there... they shot something at me. It whizzed right behind me." Armed only with a camera phone and a desire to see what was going on, Whitney had almost immediately been targeted by the rooftop snipers. "I felt that they had shot at me intentionally for filming," she recalled.

A series of pops and cracks filled the air. Chase turned to his friend and cried out, "They're fucking shooting at us!" Then, he recalled, "this wave of tear gas just came over us, you know. They didn't tell us to move. They didn't say anything. They just started shooting at us." The protesters—unsurprisingly—sought to respond in whatever way they could. Some among the crowd gathered up rocks and bricks in shopping carts from the nearby Target superstore, while others hurled them at police. Protesters also set up makeshift barricades with the disused carts, and an ersatz medical pavilion was pulled together at a nearby church to tend to injuries.[22]

As the evening progressed, there was another sea change in events. "Once it got dark out, like, the dynamic changed," Chase said. "It was in response to how the police were acting." He described how people were "getting tear-gassed and pepper balled, and getting the shit kicked out of them by the police," who advanced heavily armed and clad in riot gear. "In all honesty, I don't think it would have gotten violent if they didn't start shooting at us," he remarked. This time, police escalation would be reciprocated.

As one group of protesters ran away into the night, those who returned to the streets did so in force. One man showed up with a rifle the size of his torso and a hundred-round magazine, declaring, "We gotta protect *us* against those who are *supposed* to protect us.... I know what's up. I'm shooting back if they shoot at me. If they shoot y'all, I'm shooting back. If they got y'all down with their knee in your neck? I'm comin' for 'em."[23] Others had the same idea, and, making their presence felt, fired volleys of shots into the air across the city. People began shooting fireworks at police lines, and elsewhere the crackle of weaponry echoed across the darkening sky. Soon it would be joined by the blaze of buildings.[24]

While police were pushing enraged protesters away from the precinct, one group had broken into the nearby AutoZone (automotive accessories) store, setting it ablaze. Other people followed suit at locations across the city. As midnight arrived, multiple buildings were aflame, and gunshots were still ringing out across South Minneapolis while the police hunkered down at the precinct. Their victorious skirmish at the station had cost them control of the streets. And so, the Minneapolis riots began.

TAKING THE PRECINCT

Amid the chaos on Wednesday night, there was a certain sense of jubilation. "Everyone was walking around with shopping carts from Target, and they were like, 'Hey, I've got a cart full of goodies, you want anything?'" recalled Devin,[25] a man living near the Third Precinct who joined protesters that night. "It felt more like a festival than a protest.... There was just this very charged energy." He took pains to reiterate just how unlike the stereotype of riotous danger things felt. "I did not feel unsafe," he affirmed emphatically. "Never—not once that evening—did I have a concern for my safety."

Even the Tuesday protest's community organizers were feeling energized by the proceedings. "They burning down the facade of Minneapolis having progressive values. They burning it down," Nekima said, gesturing to some rioters behind her shortly after midnight on May 28.[26] "They're changing the narrative, honestly, just by being out here.... I think they [the MPD] [are] hearing us now."

For all of the emphasis placed on nonviolence by activists who had hastily cobbled together protest plans for May 26, Tuesday's repression and Wednesday's riot seemed to have had an empowering effect far more profound than any vigil might have had. "To see my hometown on fire, and the anger of the generation below me, how [they were] filled with anger frustration, love, and hate?" one Minneapolitan grandmother I interviewed[27] asked rhetorically. "I was filled with pride. I was absolutely filled with pride. I knew, right then, that is the generation... that's gonna take this thing home." When I pressed her on this feeling, she explained: "It was just like, okay, you know, the revolution is starting. We had all these young Black people, we had white people that are supporting us... unity, you know. It's finally happening!"

By Thursday morning, as sunlight crested the husks of burned buildings and reflected off the streets of shattered glass, Minneapolitans had gained the upper hand and were ready for round three. "I pulled out my gas mask... and I pulled out all the [military] gear that I had," one veteran recalled.[28] Huge protests filled the streets of South Minneapolis throughout the day, remaining extremely cordial save for the occasional, isolated act of vandalism or property damage. Some set about redistributing items looted the previous night, setting up water and refreshment stalls. Others spent their time tidying up, sweeping streets and boarding up businesses. By the Third Precinct, the parking lot of the nearby Target became a base of operations, with the looted store's supplies retrieved and put to use by the people gathered there. With so many protest locations, police were stretched incredibly thin, and city administrators encouraged them to defuse the situation by pulling away from the precinct.

"It's been really beautiful watching so many people from so many different backgrounds coming together today," Andy Hobday, a local youth livestreaming the event, mused a little while before 9:00 p.m. that day.[29] About ten minutes later, the crack crack crack of police ordnance echoed across the lot. A group of officers had resumed their position on the roof of the precinct from the previous day, while a new battalion of officers swooped into the intersection by the station. Canisters and marker rounds began their descent onto the crowd, as shouts and screams rang out.

"See, this is what I fucking said," Hobday complained bitterly. "No issues *until* the police show up. None. Fuck that, yo; it's about to get fucking heated, people are fucking pissed.... I've been on this stream for fucking four hours. Peaceful. Until the police show up."[30]

"Fuck you!" Hobday shouted at the officers. "See, this is what they fucking do," he explained to the stream. "Sun goes down, people were fucking chilling, and now they're out here firing on civilians. It's absolute fucking bullshit, man."

"Are you fucking surprised when people start burning shit down? No. Because the police are out there shooting at everybody. It's fucked," Hobday surmised. "People are coming out heavier tonight. It's about to go down." His observations proved correct. Unlike the night of May 26, when police successfully scattered protesters, and the night of the twenty-seventh, when authorities had retained control of the area around the precinct, by the night of the twenty-eighth, residents were ready to respond in kind. Peaceful protesters stood on the front lines with their hands raised, chanting, "Hands up. Don't shoot." People with gas masks and protective gear filled the middle ground, soaking up police munitions, while farther back protesters with laser pointers began blinding police shooters. From elsewhere people began launching fireworks at the station, successfully hitting the marksmen on the roof. Some of those who had retreated upon the arrival of the police used the opportunity to light fires around the nearby area. Peaceful protest and riotous rebellion were hand in hand. And it was working.

A little after 9:55 p.m., police pushed into the street but were met by a huge crowd of people rushing over to confront them. "There's way more people here now than there was earlier... they're not gonna be able to take down 5,000 people all at once!" Hobday observed. The huge crowd, undeterred by police repression, successfully pushed back lines of officers and marched right up to the precinct, hurling projectiles at the station's windows. The closer they got, the clearer it became. The precinct had been abandoned. In disbelief, protesters made their way into the station, seizing trophies and setting fires.[31] Soon enough, amid a chorus of cheers, the building caught fire. "Burn! Burn! Burn!" the crowd started shouting, as the building went up in a blaze. Victory was in the air.

If one were to rely on mainstream media accounts or social media commentary in relation to the events in Minneapolis that night (and later on in cities throughout the United States), it would become tempting to strike a contrast between "peaceful protesters" and "violent anarchists," or to differentiate between "community members" and "outside agitators" (distinctions explicitly employed to successful political effect by the Trump administration[32] and then uncritically reiterated elsewhere),[33] or even to strike a racialized contrast between Black demonstrators and white rioters (a distinction favored by liberal city officials and media talking heads).[34] But what the summation of firsthand footage available to researchers shows is entirely to the contrary of such analyses. Participation in the peaceful and "riotous" portions of the day was not at all mutually exclusive, and both portions were of a thoroughly mixed ethnic composition. Peaceful protest and violent[35] tactics co-occurred during the riotous portion of the night, and their combination was a central feature of how the masses contended with the police. This continued until the victorious burning of the precinct, after which the vast majority of participants that evening became celebratory and cordial. The sheer elation of protesters in the streets of Minneapolis that night was so distinctive that it is hard to put into words. The fireworks that people had been shooting at police were almost instantaneously redeployed—this time for their intended purpose—to the background of elated chants of "Whose streets? Our streets!" People started hugging one another in the streets, professing their love for one another, sharing looted refreshments and sporting the most enormous grins.[36] The people of Minneapolis had won.

The Rise of the Masses

As people across the United States watched the victory of Minneapolitans over their police force, something began to change. Even celebrities were weighing in: "Seeing people looting and goin' extremely outraged... makes me feel like: YES, finally. Finally, motherfuckers is gonna hear us now," the celebrity rapper Cardi B told her tens of millions of social media followers after the events of the May 28.[37] Ordinary people were no different. Even though I never specifically asked my interviewees in other cities about the burning of the Third Precinct or the Minneapolis riots, people kept making reference to them. "You don't see the kind of uprisings all the time that we saw with George Floyd [in Minneapolis]," a Seattle protester, Cameron, explained.[38] "It was sort of like a moral obligation, in a way, to engage with that moment politically." Similarly, one Atlanta protester, Mason,[39] told me how they "saw the video of the third precinct burning down and I was like, wow, this, this is actually happening, people are actually making change right now. It's not a pipe dream." It was at this moment that "I was like, yeah, there's just *no way* that I can ethically sit this out. This is the time," they explained.

Another protester, Avery,[40] in St. Louis, Missouri, recalled how "all types of people were coming out and demonstrating solidarity with the Minneapolis uprising," following the burning of the precinct. Yet another, in Philadelphia,[41] explained how seeing "the burning of police precincts" in other cities set the tone for their own future mobilizations. And so, the Minneapolis uprising sparked a flurry of further mobilization across every single state over the course of the weekend of May 29 to 31, well and truly dwarfing the initial half dozen cities in which solidarity demonstrations had been announced.[42] It was during many of these mobilizations that the pattern established in Minneapolis was replicated across the country. Swelling protests cascaded into conflicts with the cops, sparking riotous behavior that then galvanized further mobilizations.

In Atlanta a relatively small peaceful protest on May 29 escalated exponentially. After a march around the city in the afternoon, the crowd was halted by police as they advanced near the CNN headquarters downtown. "They had brought in military vehicles and were pushing back on the crowd," the journalist Hope Ford recalled. "That started to agitate people."[43] Soon after police began snatching people from the crowd, provoking a spate of sporadic vandalism and thrown projectiles, reciprocated by police use of pepper spray and further incursions.[44] Just before 8:00 p.m. officers and heavily armored vehicles advanced in full force, making very aggressive arrests. Protesters, in turn, responded by smashing the windshields of a fleet of police cars blocking their path of retreat. As the sun set, police fired volleys of tear gas at protesters and deployed heavily armored riot squads to suppress them.[45]

Initially, the protesters wavered. The crowd seemed to dissipate somewhat, and some people began heading home. Then something quite unusual happened. People started showing up, not just in such a volume as to replace the protesters who were leaving, but in waves that further swelled the crowd. Even though it was around 9:00 p.m., it seemed that people had stopped what they were doing and come out to face off against the police. "In the last hour or so we've seen people park in the parking lot across the street... and they've actually come to join whatever is happening," Ford reported from the front lines of the protest. The crowd continued to grow as protesters smashed shop windows, brawled with the police, and set fire to law enforcement vehicles late into the evening.

"Seeing a peaceful protest get turned into violence by the police felt like: we've seen the narrative in the media of what the police are doing;

we've seen that secondhand [in Minneapolis]; now we're here and we see it firsthand.... I don't think there's a way to turn a blind eye to that when it's right in front of you," said Mason, one of the protesters who had left home to join the evening's commotion. A similar story unfolded in cities across the United States that same night, with an all but identical pattern as in Atlanta unfolding in Washington, DC, Indianapolis, New York, and Portland, Oregon. The next day (Saturday, May 30), Seattle, Salt Lake City, Oklahoma City, and others across the United States followed suit, along with an even larger variety of peaceful protests in cities around the country. A nationwide uprising had begun.

By the time the month drew to a close, America's rising wave of mass mobilization for Black lives showed no sign of stopping. Rather, popular participation in protest only seemed to be on the increase. Over the course of the next month, contention would spread to over two thousand municipalities in the United States, and constitute a total of 8,700 protests across 74 countries worldwide.[46]

In the city of Seattle, protesters assembled multiple times over the course of the last weekend in May, the most significant of which occurred on May 30, even though the sole protests planned for the day constituted a couple of Facebook events posted online. The first was an event spontaneously posted by a local white woman with no discernible organizing experience, proposing a midday protest at the Seattle Police headquarters.[47] The second had been set up by a local antiracism educator whose brother had been killed by Seattle police in 2016; it was scheduled for 3:00 p.m. at downtown Seattle's Westlake Park.[48] The city was still officially under a COVID-19 "stay at home" order and, amid a ranging pandemic, its various established civil rights organizations had not proactively arranged anything for the day. Rather, the mood of local organized groups was highly epidemiologically cautious.[49] "We can NOT overstate the risks to protesters and to the community at large because this one woman felt inspired to do her own thing and start a FB event. More than 3,000 people are going/ interested. WE ABSOLUTELY DO NOT RECOMMEND THIS EVENT," the Washington State chapter of the Poor People's Campaign told its membership.[50] The local Black Lives Matter Seattle chapter[51] took a similar stance at the time, publicly stating: "We have heard your calls for action in response to the murder of George Floyd and other recent victims of police brutality... [but] decided that the situation is too dangerous for us to encourage greater attendance at these in-person protests."[52]

The people of Seattle thought otherwise, and many thousands took to the streets over the course of the day. While some specifically participated in one protest or the other, many more took to the streets without strict accordance with either event. Police recorded that "demonstrations began to grow across the entire city," with crowds more than doubling in size beyond those that had initially assembled at the two event locations.[53] In response, police sought to contain the protests with the full force of their riot munitions. And just as it had in Minneapolis and Atlanta, their strategy backfired. The crowd pushed back, setting fires, looting buildings, and even tossing Molotov cocktails at police lines.[54] By 5:00 p.m. a two-night curfew had been hastily called, and two hundred National Guard troops were mobilized to support police forces. As appeared to be happening all across the United States, police repression would see popular reciprocation.

When the weekend ended, the protests didn't. Instead, the city of Seattle saw another huge, spontaneous mobilization of its denizens on Monday, June 1, with thousands of people pouring into the streets during working hours and thousands more joining them shortly thereafter. "Discipline? I mean, there wasn't [any]," Cameron recalled. "The group was way too big to be coordinated... it was very [much] just 'let's just go this way' as a huge group." Eventually, after passing by an array of locations in the city, the approximately seven thousand protesters began to make their way to Seattle's East Precinct, in the fashionable Capitol Hill District.[55] Eventually, lines of confrontation were drawn. The police closed off the street in front of the protesters, blocking their path at the intersection of Pine Street and Eleventh Avenue.

This was a location with a history. "The intersection is Seattle's OK Corral," wrote Eric Scigliano, the former riot reporter for *Seattle Weekly*.[56] "The place where stormin' crowds and cops go to stage their showdowns." For quite some time the crowd and the cops stood toe to toe without major incident, but it was clear that the police were preparing for something. Officers on bicycles pulled back from the front line, and others in riot gear and gas masks began unloading in their place. Heavy-duty pepper spray dispensers were being readied, and other riot munitions began to be deployed among officers. Some protesters who had brought umbrellas made their way to the front of the crowd, trying to use them to shield the crowd from what was anticipated to be a hail of noxious chemicals.

And then it happened. In a moment shared on live video across the globe, officers reached over the barricades and seized a solitary pink umbrella from a young woman at the front of the crowd before coating her in pepper spray. Seconds later other officers on the line followed suit, dispensing thick sprays of mace over the peaceful crowd and unlinking the barricades behind which they had been standing.[57]

"Let's just try to deescalate, let's deescalate this, let's just try to bring this down, guys," local journalist Omari Salisbury was saying just moments before the police assault began. Almost immediately, a jet of pepper spray hit him squarely in the face. "Goddamnit, they got me... I've got pepper spray all over me... the barricade is up, the officers are going with the spray.... I've only got [vision in] one eye!" he exclaimed. Things only got worse: "There's flash bangs, these are flash bangs.... Goddamnit, it's the tear gas, it's the fucking tear gas. Police, STOP! Holy shit, tear gas is everywhere. Oh shit... [wheezing] oh shit... oh shit... oh my god. Oh shit... Medic! Medic! Water! Medic! Somebody! Fuck. I need help! I need help!... Help me!"[58]

This was a scene witnessed by some 128,000 people and only one of many extremely disturbing pieces of footage circulated following that evening. The sheer level of brutality on display by the Seattle Police Department was breathtaking. And just as in other cities, the repression on display didn't suppress protest activity; instead, it made the moment seem all the more paramount. In response to surging repression against peaceful protesters, people poured into the streets every single day that week, ready and willing to face down the cops if necessary. "I remember soaking up basically every Hong Kong [protest] documentary I could," recalled Hayden, a first-time protester in early June, "to figure out, like, what the hell happens once you're [out] there."

Despite demonstrators' overwhelmingly peaceful conduct, police routinely unleashed riot munitions. But protesters came ready: lines of umbrellas were used to deflect munitions and shield against pepper spray, earplugs were handed out to help protect against flash-bang grenades, and street medics showed up in droves to provide aid to the injured. Every day saw smarter and smarter tactics being employed, as well as an increasingly broad spectrum of attendees. By day five, even city council members were attending the protests, but police were unrelenting in the barrage of munitions they unloaded on the crowd. Still, the protests didn't stop. People kept coming.

Eventually, the demonstrations proved such a drain on police resources and so disruptive to the city's administration that the protesters began to gain the upper hand. By Monday the city of Seattle formally instructed police to abandon the East Precinct. When demonstrators showed up on June 8, they found the precinct—and the Capitol Hill area surrounding it—abandoned. "Suddenly, there was this moment where this area *was* the world we were trying to imagine: a place without police," Cameron said. Over the course of the day, the area around the precinct "became like this spontaneous community," in which people began organizing themselves. "Was there a meeting where everyone got together [and said,] ['Let's] occupy this?'" she asked rhetorically. "No! There were far too many people for it to be like that. It was a sort of spontaneous moment where we actually had a place where we didn't have to have police."

As more and more people came to the area, questions began to be raised as to the fate of the precinct. Some among the protesters advocated burning it down, replicating what happened in Minneapolis, but in the end the general mood settled on precisely the opposite response. Rather than engaging in property destruction, arson, or vandalism, the protesters ended up refashioning the area as a safe haven, free from police brutality and the chaos that had been wrought in the streets. Soon enough it had not one but several names: Free Capitol Hill, the Capitol Hill Autonomous Zone (CHAZ), and the Capitol Hill Occupied Protest (CHOP) were among the most popular.[59]

Much like the 2011 occupation of New York's Zuccotti Park, the area around Capitol Hill became an important space of convergence for participants in the uprising until their eventual eviction on July 1. The space created breathing room for tired and traumatized protesters, drew in a wide array of new participants, and—crucially—allowed protesters to network and organize, taking what had been a remarkably decentralized and spontaneous movement in the city and giving it a modest degree of regularity, coordination, and structure. This move was partially emulated in cities such as Minneapolis, New York, Atlanta, and Portland. We will return to these occupied spaces and their mobilizing role in chapter 10.

THE FED WAR

In nearby Portland, Oregon, a story similar to other cities in the United States had been unfolding: peaceful protests, aggressive policing, riotous reciprocation, mass mobilization. For the better part of thirty-five days between May 28 and July 1, the city had seen constant protests, although numbers dwindled from tens of thousands in early June to only a thousand or so by the second half of the month. But over the course of July, this dwindling of protest would be substantially reversed. "Operation Diligent Valor" was about to be unleashed.

At the command of the Trump administration, various units of federal agencies were dispatched to the city, clad in military-style camouflage and armed to the teeth with heavy-duty riot munitions. By midmonth, reports began circulating that the agents were snatching peaceful protesters off the street, performing the abductions from unmarked vehicles. This news was highly alarming. National media outlets even began to warn that federal agents' activities in Portland may be the prelude to "an attempted coup" by the Trump administration.[60] It is worth recalling that simultaneously with his deployment of federal agents in Portland and elsewhere, Trump was strenuously declining to pledge that he would leave power if he lost the 2020 election. Trump's opponent, later president, Joe Biden, had voiced such fears in the weeks between Trump's declaration that he would use federal agents to quell the protests and the time they showed up in Portland. "This president is going to try to steal this election," Biden declared plainly, dubbing the eventuality his "single greatest concern."[61] Elected officials across the country, from the city level to sitting members of Congress, condemned Trump's assault on Portland. At every level of elected official, the move was described in terms such as "dictatorship,"[62] "an attack on our democracy,"[63] "the activity of a police state," and the practice of "authoritarian governments."[64] It was, as one representative put it, "unconstitutional, dangerous and heading towards fascism."[65]

What had previously been the tail end of a conflict between protesters and their various local police bureaus—one that had been dying down amid increasing normalization of protest activity and progressive concessions by local government—was suddenly reframed as something greater. This paramount framing of the struggle in Portland as part of an existential battle for the soul of America against a dangerous president preparing for a power grab was highly impactful. It not only reinvigorated participation among those already attracted to the struggle against police brutality and for Black lives but also actively broadened the constituency of participants even further. With the perception of a more generalized threat, scores of liberal Oregonians who had been relatively disinterested in the struggle for Black lives instead showed up in an effort to resist authoritarian incursions.[66] Such opponents to the president were certainly in ample supply in Multnomah County, the region where Portland is situated: Trump had won only 17 percent of the vote in 2016 and would win only 18 percent in 2020.

And so, people came. Protesters swarmed the federal agents' outpost at the Mark O. Hatfield US Courthouse and flocked from the suburbs. They joined the protests not as civil rights campaigners, leftists, or radicals but as ordinary people: mothers, fathers, and military veterans concerned by the sights they had seen playing out in the national news. This renewed upsurge in mobilization and the period around it became known to the various participants I talked to as "the Fed War(s)" and to others around the United States as the "Battle of Portland."

War was a fitting analogy. "I've been to war zones on two continents. I've been shot at and I've been shelled once, and I can honestly say that… ranks as among the most frightening things I've ever experienced," the conflict journalist Robert Evans recalled of his time in Portland. Reports of posttraumatic stress disorder (PTSD) and severe injuries were commonplace among the protesters I talked to, something Evans's own reportage also found.[67]

Despite the fact that protesters were up against devastatingly well-equipped presidential paramilitary platoons, something curious began to happen. As participation snowballed into the thousands and thousands, federal officers' resources began to run thin. Munitions were exhausted, tactics were counteracted, and, soon enough, the protesters started winning. The very same federal forces who had been aggressively snatching people off the streets in the middle of July were only a week and a half later virtually besieged in their headquarters by protesters who had established a semipermanent presence in the nearby Plaza Blocks park.

Things reached a peak on the weekend of July 24 to 26, when protesters—by now consistently numbering thousands every day and around six thousand people as late as midnight on Saturday—successfully brought down the heavily reinforced metal and concrete fence the federal agents had erected around the courthouse. What followed was panic: federal officers armed with automatic rifles and laser sights poured out of the building, and Portland Police were called in to assist. The cops and the feds gave it everything they had, hurling so much tear gas into the vicinity that it felt impossible to breathe, even for those protesters wearing heavy-duty gas masks.

With the prospect of what might happen the *next* weekend doubtless looming over the heads of all of the officials involved, it was shortly after this showdown that the Trump administration and the state of Oregon reached a joint agreement on the demobilization of federal forces in Portland. Federal forces would stay in the city but would step back from their invasive tactics and high-tenor public confrontations with citizens. The protesters had won their showdown with the Trump administration, but as the masses of liberal volunteers went home, their mission seemingly accomplished, the issues of Black lives and police brutality still loomed large. As the last major episode in the Black Lives Uprising came to a close, contention would shift from mass mobilization to sustained struggle.

CHAPTER TEN

Mass Mobilization for Black Lives

So far we have heard about how an explosion of mass mobilization took shape following George Floyd's murder by Minneapolis police and explored the huge upsurge of popular protest that followed. But what were the factors that predisposed people to join these contentious uprisings? How did the Black Lives Uprising develop over the longer term, and where is the movement today? This chapter answers all three of these questions in turn, beginning with the dynamics of affinity-convergence mobilization during the 2020 uprising. Next, it explores how protesters sought to maintain mobilization, how they interacted with more established forces, and how the alternative structures and relationships they developed have persisted.

Convergence Conditions

In analyzing the conditions that helped catalyze mass protest during the Black Lives Uprising, one cannot help but begin with the exceptional situation created by the COVID-19 pandemic. Only 25.6 percent of Americans were going to their workplaces, with the remaining proportion either out of work or working remotely.[1] Disruption was particularly strongly felt by young people, whose daily routines had been eviscerated by the pandemic. Approximately 57 percent of those between the ages of sixteen and twenty-four were enrolled in education systems seriously disrupted by COVID-19.[2] Among those in the same age bracket who worked for a living, between April and June, 24.4 percent were unemployed (up from 11.3 percent in 2019), and 35 percent were on reduced hours.[3]

"People were, like, stuck at home, and a lot of people didn't have to go to work or were laid off," Chase[4] recalled. "They were available to be out there." Maria,[5] a young Black woman from Seattle, similarly contended that "the context of COVID" was pivotal in people's turnout to protest.

"I think that's the main reason why you saw a lot of people out in the streets," she argued. "A lot of people who were out of work had nothing better to do, [and] a lot of people working from home were able to go out and still be employed." This sentiment was further confirmed by Gray,[6] a Portland protester, who presented their participation decision in striking terms. "While I was inspired [by the protests], I was also... bored shitless, you know what I mean?" they recalled. "There wasn't really anything to hold me back. I was unemployed, and it was coronavirus: a pretty good combo of having nothing to do! So, yeah, it became what stuff I *had* to do."

These kinds of observations and anecdotes peppered my interviews with participants in the 2020 uprising, but it is worth noting that its coincidence with the pandemic's disruptive zenith was far more pronounced among those who were likely to feel insulated from its perceived dangers.[7] Older supporters of the movement to whom I spoke cited the pandemic as a reason they felt *unable* to participate in the streets, something similarly reported by other activists involved in the movement. "So many people... had to quarantine, as they had a high risk of dying from COVID," Riley,[8] an Atlanta protester who eventually became very involved in the movement, recalled, "Older generations that felt like it was their duty to [participate] couldn't because they were at high risk." For older people, COVID-19 thus offered a motivation *and* socially permissible justification for nonparticipation. The particular quotidian disruption caused by the pandemic thus simultaneously created an exceptional situation in which potential participants' biographical availability was radically amplified and had a knock-on effect on which social demographics had the greatest affinity for participation.[9]

In addition to the exceptional situation created by the pandemic, there were also plenty of opportune and paramount conditions that facilitated participation. Right from the outset, widespread and widely publicized statements by local elites expressing sympathy or even making preemptive concessions conveyed to people that their mobilization would be well received (an opportune frame). In Minneapolis, for example, the city almost immediately acknowledged the injustice at hand, and all four officers involved in the killing of George Floyd were fired before protests on May 26 were fully underway.[10] Similarly, in Atlanta the city's police chief publicly announced that she would instruct officers to give the protests latitude and even joined the crowd herself on the protests' first day.[11] Officials across the country made similar statements, condemning the killing of Floyd and announcing that they would respect the rights of protesters. Some city police even "took the knee" in solidarity with protesters (an antiracist gesture that, given how Floyd had been murdered, looked rather puzzling coming from police officers). Thus, the framing of participation gave protesters good reason to expect that they would not suffer undue participation costs and were likely to extract concessions.

"There was a lot more hope that things might actually change because it was just such a bigger deal," one Minneapolis activist recalled.[12] "The city council at the time was sounding much more open to at least shifting some of the police budget and maybe rethinking how they do some stuff, which was new." Similar sentiments were raised by protesters in other cities. Blake,[13] a Portland protester whose participation began early on in the uprising, explained how he had felt "a great opportunity... to try to realize the things that I believe in... the opportunity to be a part of the movement."

In stark contrast to the opportune framing of protest participation, the situation on the ground in many cities was swiftly revealed to be one of serious hostility. It soon transpired that police departments would be extremely repressive in their treatment of protesters, attempting to push them off the streets by sheer force. Much like the responses seen in Minneapolis, Atlanta, and Seattle (discussed in chapter 9), police departments around the country took a highly repressive stance. Many states even called in the National Guard. By engaging in brutal repression of May's protests seeking justice for George Floyd and an end to police brutality, city and state authorities created the conditions for a far more existential struggle between police and local civilians. Such showdowns between law enforcement and the citizens they policed became paramount situations, in which protesters felt all the more compelled to participate.

A pattern emerged in which, as one of my interviewees from Seattle, Billie,[14] put it, "over and over again, every time they escalate... it just turns out worse for them." More people—not fewer—came out in response. "The whole purpose was that we're protesting the fact that the police could do whatever they want," Maria explained. "So if you go out and protest that, and they [still] do whatever they want, and you just stop protesting? You've given up the game! That's... literally the only reason we *can't* stop."

Soon enough the tide began to turn, and protesters not only proved resilient to police incursions but even scored material victories: occupying spaces, destroying police targets, and winning control of the streets. These victories in the face of repression created an opportune situation for further participation. "When this all started, I was very much like, Why do they have to burn things down? Why do they have to loot?" Whitney[15] recalled of her experiences in Minneapolis. One might think that such objections would have pushed her away from participating once the Third Precinct was burned, but the event had the opposite effect. It left her "wanting to continue to be involved, wanting to get out there again, because this is obviously becoming way bigger than anything else I've ever been involved in, in my life." "I remember feeling... really powerful," Hayden[16] recounted, "and feeling like there was some momentum." Gray made the same observation about the impact of riots in their city:

> Everyone was less scared. Everyone was more like, "Oh! We have numbers." A lot of times, you have to see shit to believe it's possible. Even if it's something as simple as a bunch of people can... destroy a building. They *can*, but you don't really believe that until you see it happen. So it definitely... validates any desires you have.... Oh, yeah, I can actually get involved.

As May's signals of elite support gave way to June's reality of stepped-up repression, and the Trump administration positioned itself in direct conflict with the protesters, the framing of protest activity replaced its opportune elements with a more paramount character. Drawing on a longer-running trajectory of resistance to the Trump administration and concerns about a potential coup in the upcoming 2020 elections, the uprising was reframed as facing down the threat of fascism, dictatorship, and authoritarianism. This framing reached its zenith when Trump directed federal agencies to respond to the protests by force, quashing the sovereignty of governors and mayors across the United States. In an attempt to suppress the wave of contentious mobilization already in motion, Trump announced on June 2 that he would be "dispatching thousands and thousands of heavily armed soldiers, military personnel and law enforcement officers" to cities across the United States in order to quell the protests, starting with Washington, DC. If local authorities refused to deploy National Guard troops and "an overwhelming law enforcement presence" to "dominate the streets," Trump declared, "I will deploy the United States military and quickly solve the problem for them."[17]

"I thought for sure that would scare people, but instead it would have the complete inverse effect," one Portland protester recalled of Trump's intervention.[18] "It felt like everybody was like: Oh, *hell* no!... It was pretty crazy to see." "It felt like a threat of immediate danger," Gray recalled. Cameron, in Seattle, talked about how Trump's declaration "brought the kind of [police] brutality that is commonly used against indigenous people or Black people" to entire communities, broadening the appeal of participation by introducing serious threats to everyday life. "That freaked a lot of people out, because they were kind of like: Whoa, hold on... I thought I was safe, because I'm white, but holy shit, maybe I'm not safe anymore."

Trump's intervention also broadened the appeal of participation to those who were motivated not by racial justice or policing issues but rather by opposition to the administration. This was particularly the case in Portland, which saw a dramatic incursion of federal forces in mid-July. The incursion revitalized the paramount frame first promulgated in June by creating a full-blown situation on the ground. "One hundred percent it felt like Us versus Trump," one Portland protester argued emphatically.[19] "It felt like... [Trump was] just trying to make an example out of us and show the rest of the country what could happen if you don't stay at home." The situation in the city was "completely derailed because of... Trump's shit," Gray recalled. There were "thousands of people who showed up... purely because they felt like what they were doing was sticking it to Trump."

The impact of these combined situational and framing dynamics helped to override people's potential concerns about participation, thereby strengthening the mobilizing impact of the exceptional situation created by the pandemic. As Cameron put it: "I *was* exercising more caution in terms of going out, because I didn't want to get [COVID] and then bring it home to these other people that I live with. But once George Floyd happened, and [we] saw... this giant wave of action, we felt that it was almost like a moral obligation to engage with that moment politically, despite the risk of COVID."

In addition to the various situations and frames that helped underpin convergence, occupied spaces played a role in certain cities. Seattle's Capitol Hill occupation (CHOP) is perhaps the most high-profile example, but other occupied sites also arose during the uprising. These included Minneapolis's George Floyd Square, at the intersection of 38th Street and Chicago Avenue; New York City's City Hall Park (renamed Abolition Park by protesters); Portland's Plaza Blocks park;[20] and Atlanta's almost monthlong occupation of a Wendy's that had been burned down during the protests. What these spaces had in common was that, much like those seen during the Occupy movement, they served as areas in which people could interface with and participate in the movement without exposing themselves to the risk of police brutality, arrest, or the many other potential dangers associated with street protest. They were thus opportune spaces in that they offered a highly favorable balance of risks and rewards for protest participation and exceptional spaces in that participation in them had extremely low barriers to entry and could take forms far beyond conventional acts of protest. In CHOP joining the protest "was this kind of lower-stakes way of still resisting and still saying... 'No, I don't agree with this [police brutality],' or 'I agree with the protesters'... without hunting down where a protest is, or having to wear special black [bloc] clothes, or putting yourself actually in front of a police officer," Billie explained. "There were... a lot of people there all the time, so it was easy to just feel like you could go.... I didn't think twice about it." Others concurred. "People forget that's a form of protest, right?" Maria explained on a late-night call. "There were people who wanted it to be about... organizing ourselves, doing different workshops and stuff, but there were a lot of people who were there to just chill and relax." At its height participating in CHOP felt like "it was a party," she explained. "There was free shit, there were events, there was a band playing, there was a stage. Riot Kitchen came out with food... we talked on the ground, we read zines."

Even in Portland, where aggressive actions by federal agents and law enforcement made the space notably less opportune than others, its exceptional characteristics still drew in substantial public participation. One of the most popular ways to plug in to the Portland occupation was to visit its famous Riot Ribs outlet, a protest kitchen run by a former Black Panther, and make a small donation to mutual aid efforts while doing so. The Portland journalist Robert Evans recalls how the outlet became "so beloved in Portland that even local politicians who had been negative about the protests were hard pressed to say a single bad word about them.... The ribs made local dining news, and protesters would often wait in line through clouds of tear gas to get them. They were pretty darn good."[21] But Riot Ribs was not just a kitchen; it consisted of all manner of services that helped sustain protest activity and mutual aid efforts across the city. It was not uncommon for people to show up to the park for lunch and gradually find themselves more and more involved in the proceedings elsewhere.

The intersection of these situations, frames, and spaces during the uprising served as highly propitious conditions of convergence for continued mass mobilization without reliance on established organizational structures. The exceptional situation of the pandemic massively increased people's availability to protest and reduced the availability of alternative pursuits. Mobilization was further galvanized by the creation of a variety of paramount and opportune situations that further incentivized participation, reenforced by frames that drew attention to (and even magnified) these incentives. Moreover, as time went on and attendance at marches decreased, occupied spaces provided new avenues for participation with lower barriers to entry and/or lower risk to participants. But as we will see, the kinds of people mobilized during this period were quite distinctive—diverse by some demographic metrics but highly specific in others. Certain social affinities played a highly particular role in galvanizing participation, even though the protests also appealed to more generalized dispositions and drives.

Affinities in Action

While the various conditions of convergence that developed over the course of the uprising help us understand the nationwide mass mobilizations of late May and early June, as well as in the mobilizations in Portland in July, such an explanation is incomplete without an examination of the social and psychological traits that predisposed people to participate in the first place. Some of these were long-running factors, such as social status, one's place of living, and perceptions of injustice that had been in place for much of the Trump administration. Others concerned more recently developed predisposing factors, such as attitudinal alignment around the idea of defunding the police and needs for social stimulation that had gone unfulfilled due to the social isolation to which many were subjected in 2020. A sketch of the most pivotal affinities and convergence conditions at play during the uprising can be found in figure 10.1, after which the rest of this section considers the role of affinities in greater depth, exploring how they predisposed participants in the 2020 uprising to partake in its various protests.

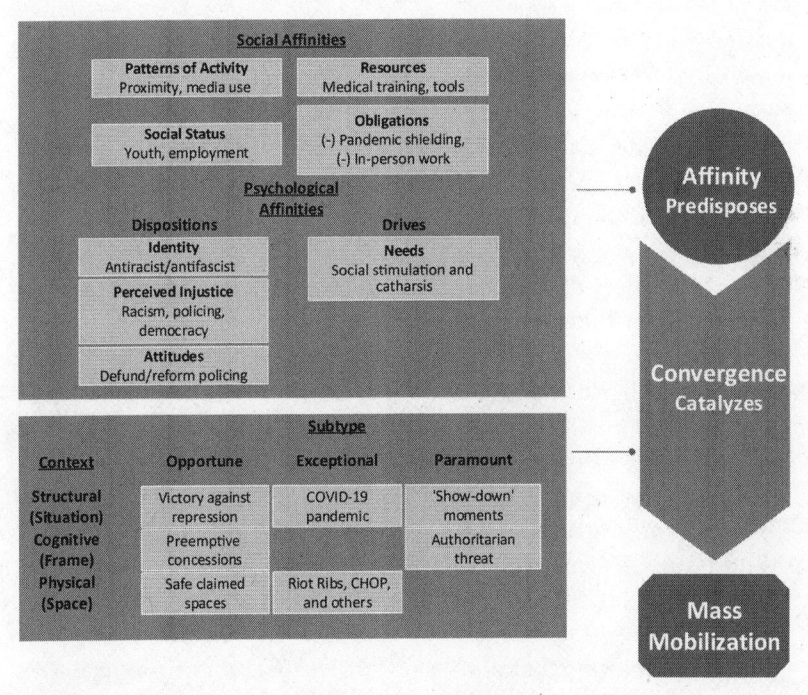

FIGURE 10.1. Summary of affinity-convergence mobilization in the Black Lives Uprising.

SOCIAL AFFINITIES

Perhaps the most distinctive social affinity underpinning mobilization during the uprising related to people's everyday patterns of activity. This was a factor routinely reiterated among participants in the sudden unruly protests of May and early June. "It's one thing if you have to drive across... the state or across the country to do a protest, but when it happens in your backyard, you don't really have a choice, do you?" Chase told me. Whitney had said something similar, frequently explaining that "the proximity to where I live" was one of the most significant factors in explaining why she decided to participate. "I was like, well, oh, shit, this is basically in my neighborhood. I should probably get out there," she explained. Even people who felt otherwise disinclined to participate (though supporting the general sentiment of the protests) described how they found themselves drawn into temporary participation because they would be "walking past every day," and inevitably "spend twenty minutes stopping," standing with the protesters and surveilling the police response.[22]

Complementing the important role played by physical patterns of activity were people's digital patterns of activity. In the circumstances of stay-at-home orders in cities such as Seattle (and a general confinement to quarters set in place by the pandemic), platforms including online and TV news, interpersonal messaging services, livestreaming, and social media became crucial information conduits. Protests were proposed and discussed through social media platforms, such as Instagram and Facebook, spread via messaging apps, such as WhatsApp and Signal, liveblogged on Twitter and TikTok, and livestreamed on Twitch, Facebook/Instagram Live, YouTube, and other platforms. "There's so many people [online]: you don't have to be connected to any group or be politically involved at all; you just have to see something on... like a drag queen's Instagram story... [or] on someone's Instagram page, and show up," Maria said. "Every day to every week, people on Instagram would constantly have a slideshow of different protests to go to.... Through just word of mouth you could get thousands of people to show up if you did so on the right social media [platforms]."

Another particularly important affinity driving mobilization during the 2020 uprising was participants' social status, especially youth. Although the uprising was demographically diverse in many respects, the most notable skew in participation involved the young. Some of this was a consequence of the pandemic: not only did being a young person suppress many of the epidemiological risks of participation, but it also increased the likelihood of being the subject of disruption to one's ordinary social patterns (as discussed in the prior section on convergence). Meanwhile, young people—particularly those in Generations Y and Z—were also in an excellent position to rapidly ascertain information about protests owing to the far greater digitalization of their social and economic lives compared with older generations and their familiarity with the technological tools most commonly employed by protesters.[23] Of course, youth was not the only element of people's social status that proved important in conditioning participation. Those who were subject to unemployment and underemployment were highly biographically available during this time. As one Seattle protester explained: "I had been laid off... this meant was that I now had a lot of free time that I could use to... be more engaged politically.... I think a lot of people in the United States were similarly able to do that."[24]

People's physical ability was pivotal in determining their capacity to endure the highly violent police actions that characterized many of the uprising's protests. Many participants talked about how incapacity brought about by tear gas exposure stopped people from coming back to protests. For people with disabilities, physical participation in the uprising was often similarly prohibitive. "I'm disabled and chronically ill so... I can't be on the ground all the time... [it] takes a lot out of me," one Portland activist explained in a press interview.[25] Lennon, a disabled person in Minneapolis with whom I spoke about the subject, similarly explained how, despite their best efforts to participate from a distance, physical participation in the kinds of protests the city was undergoing was simply not possible for them. "It's not the easiest," they surmised, "[but] I can donate money, I can call... and stuff like that." This marked a common pattern among those with impairments that prohibited street participation: while their able-bodied comrades faced down police in the streets, disabled, ill, or injured participants were assisting from afar.

Because of the rapidly evolving situation during the uprising, protesters were frequently in need of aid from their fellow citizens. Consequently, possessing certain resources provided a variety of avenues into protest participation. The most common resource-based affinity during the uprising was possession of medical training and supplies. Medics were a frequent appearance in protest footage, and a surprisingly large proportion of participants in the uprising credited their initial participation decisions to wanting to put their medical resources to good use. A SWAT paramedic in one city[26] even told me how he refused to work with police during the uprising and joined the protesters as a volunteer riot medic instead. "How could I in good conscience go out on the line with the guys that are shooting [civilians]?" he posed. "They were calling me from work, like, 'All hands on deck, we need everyone to come in!'... I was like, Well? I have other things I have to fucking deal with." When I asked why he made the decision to stand up against a police department he had worked with for many years prior, he simply stated: "I have a particular set of skills... so I just took what I had, and I helped out." An even greater array of resources provided pathways into participation as tactical requirements became more diverse. One particularly evocative example arose in Portland, where a so-called Wall of Dads was proposed, in which men who owned leaf blowers were invited to show up to the city's nightly showdown with federal agents and use them to repel tear gas fumes. It proved quite a surprise when leaf-blower wielding gentlemen did in fact show up, in droves.

In contrast to the role of resources, people's matrix of obligations had a strongly bifurcated mobilizing effect during the uprising's high point. While the absence of obligations such as pandemic shielding to protect relatives, housemates, and oneself, as well as freedom from in-person work obligations, proved important in predisposing participation, positive obligations had a comparatively muted role. Early on the uprising was unable to offer much at all that helped people meet material obligations, save for a few isolated opportunities to engage in acquisitive looting. It was generally only when movement activity became more developed and generated an excess of resources that participation began to arise as a positive consequence of obligations (and still only rarely). This tended to occur in the context of occupations such as in Seattle and Portland. One such example concerns the participation of Portland State University (PSU) students in the city's July "Fed Wars." The PSU campus was situated steps away from the front line of the July protests and the camp at Plaza Blocks park. After the university cafeteria was shut down, PSU students began to make a pilgrimage to Riot Ribs instead, getting drawn into the protests in the process. The students "started going to Chapman [Square] every day and eating at Riot Ribs," Hayden said, which in turn put them in touch with other protesters and exposed them to the situation at the federal courthouse. They were like, "What the fuck is happening? I never thought I'd be out here!" she recalled.

PSYCHOLOGICAL AFFINITIES

In tandem with the various social affinities that predisposed people to join the uprising was the conditioning role of people's psychological drives and dispositions. Drives played a particularly bifurcated role in the uprising, with people's needs being important in the early unruly days of mass protest, while the pursuit of their interests had virtually no impact on mobilization until well after its peak in May and early June.

A great many participants I talked to drew attention to two particular needs that the uprising helped them meet: social stimulation and emotional catharsis. People's need for social stimulation was fundamentally bound up in the conditions of the COVID-19 pandemic. It is worth recalling that many people across the United States had spent the better part of the spring in various forms of isolation imposed or undertaken in order to combat the coronavirus pandemic. To people stultified by these conditions, the opportunity to join a mass popular protest was a rare chance to break free of these conditions and experience some degree of collective effervescence. As one participant put it, "We had been super fucking isolated... we had stayed inside and had lost *so* much.... Everything had been shut down."[27] The protests were an opportunity to act collectively in pursuit of a worthwhile cause, a moment when the sheer atomization to which people had been subjected could temporarily be reversed.

By contrast, participants who mobilized seeking catharsis saw in the clashes with police and unruly protests of the uprising's early days an avenue by which they might strike back at a system against which they had long felt powerless. We saw such instances of emotionally charged mobilization in chapter 9, but the tenor and force of this feeling was perhaps most eloquently exposed by one Minneapolis protester, speaking the night after George Floyd was killed: "I feel hurt, I feel betrayed, I feel not safe, and honestly, I feel like I'm not wanted in this country at all. Fuck the state, fuck this city. I feel like I'm not wanted in this country. I feel underrepresented, I feel fucking pissed off," he said. "I feel like I want to fucking burn some shit down right now. And honestly? I don't wanna see no police, because I know I'm gonna fuck some shit up when I do."[28] Gray, one of the Portland protesters, offered their own observations of why people sought out clashes with the cops or riotous mobilizations. "I think it's all about emotion, honestly," they reflected. "Are you upset? Are you angry? Do you feel unheard? Rioting *is* the language of the unheard. That's what you do."

Just as in other cases in this book, dispositional affinities played an important role in the uprising, although their operation was in some respects subtly different from what one might anticipate in a movement with such a prominently racialized public image. With regards to the role of identity, perhaps the most consistently referenced form of identification underpinning involvement in the uprising concerned participants' political identities, rather than racial ones.[29] These political identities were grounded in shared progressive values, such as being antiracist and antifascist, that had become increasingly mainstream among the younger sections of the US population. This tendency among my interviewees was also reflected in survey data on protest participation, which found that non-Black minorities participated in the protests at roughly the same rate as Black participants, and that whites participated at roughly half the rate of Black people. The consequence for protest demography in many cities across the United States was that a considerable proportion of the protests were majority white.[30]

Protesters' departure from racialized identities in favor of antiracist identities was reflected in many of the interviews I conducted. "I came out in defense of Black lives, for my Black comrades that were out there getting their ass kicked by the cops," said Riley, a white protester. Blake, who also is white, explained how identifying as an antiracist ally underpinned his and other white people's decisions to consistently participate: "We're supposed to be showing up! If it's filled with white people to the fucking brim? That is a great thing. Because we're supposed to be showing up as allies, as people who are invested in this. It would be sad if it was just people of color, because that would mean that white people still didn't give a fuck." Similar feelings of compulsion were felt by protesters who identified strongly as antifascist. Mason explained how the antifascist identity he and his peers harbored prompted them to "employ every available option in reducing the power of fascists," ranging from participation in the uprising to anti-Trump mobilization.

Complementing the role of participants' political identities were perceptions of social injustice. These took the form of a racist society and a rising police state in America, both of which were signified by Floyd's death and against which the uprising's dramatic mobilizations were counterposed. These perceptions were not particularly new observations among the youth protesters who joined the uprising, many of whom came of age near the advent of the Trump administration and whose adult political lives were dominated by a normalization of resistance to the status quo. During a stretch of interviews with anti-Trump protesters conducted in 2019, I found very similar themes being articulated more than a half year before the uprisings occurred. "I was such an institutionalist center-left person... and now I'm like... we need to burn a lot of shit down and start over," one future protester in Washington, DC, told me.[31] Prior to the radicalizing effects of the Trump era, she recalled how she "would never question what a local cop was doing, and now I'm like, fuck the state, fuck the police, fuck everybody: don't give them a budget, everything sucks.... I had my eyes opened."

When the Trump administration threatened military action and sent federal agents into the streets of cities such as Washington, DC, and Portland, a further group of participants found themselves mobilized by a sense of democratic and civil injustice. Once "we were facing what felt like an existential threat, it [also] became a protest against overstep by the federal government... against violence by the state against all people, and silencing dissent," recalled Jordan, a journalist who joined the protests in Portland.[32] This in turn attracted a set of more mainstream liberal participants who had not previously been drawn to join the protests.

As public discussion around police brutality and racial justice developed, discrete political attitudes began to play a distinctive role in the mobilizing process. Certain popular demands or well-recognized ideas resonated particularly well with participants, and actions that elevated them proved virtual guarantors of a good showing. By the middle of June, these alone seemed to have the power to draw crowds. As Maria put it, "You didn't need to have any political will yourself; you just needed to be like, my imaginary group wants to have a protest, and we want to make these three demands.... So everybody come. And then thousands of people would come."[33] "It really was just like any group of people that wanted to get people riled up could pretty much do it around that centralized message of defund [the police]."

The kinds of protesters who were maximally predisposed to participate in the uprising were those with both social and psychological affinity to the cause. These tended to be young, geographically urban, and digitally connected people with strong antiracist sentiments. This was also precisely the group of people whose participation in the uprising endured the longest. During the height of local and national convergence conditions, however, people with a less comprehensive set of affinities played a pivotal role in swelling the crowds to a size far beyond what this narrower demographic could have achieved alone. These ranged from residents and laborers drawn into protests because of where they lived or worked to anti-Trump liberals concerned with authoritarian threats, and from people seeking social or emotional fulfillment to college kids in need of a meal. Beyond its foremost protagonists and later custodians, the uprising's casual participants reflected a notably broader segment of American society.

Mobilizing beyond Organizations

Witnessing an upsurge of protest that defied the auspices of clearly defined preexisting organizations was disorienting for many. For example, in the wake of the June 1 showdown at the East Precinct in Seattle, the city's mayor, Jenny Durkan, proudly spoke of her planned meeting with the "organizers of the protests" and had the meeting widely publicized in the local newspapers. Almost immediately after her announcement, it was revealed that the so-called organizers were entirely unknown not only to the protest's participants but also to *any* local organizations at all. Moreover, they did not appear to have had any role in protest planning.[34]

Mayor Durkan was not alone in her misapprehension of where the protests were coming from: people all over America were grasping for a way to support or engage with the movement. Well-meaning donors sent millions of dollars to groups that not only had nothing to do with the protests but also were directly opposed to many of the protesters' demands.[35] Others looked toward their local Black Lives Matter chapters or the national organization with the assumption that these groups were coordinating the protests. The notion that these were Black Lives Matter protests connected to the official Black Lives Matter (Global Network) organization had been widely publicized by large-scale media organizations and government officials. In cities across the United States, including Seattle, this was incorrect. "Despite various media reports, Black Lives Matter Seattle/King County has had no role in any of the protests that have occurred in the greater Seattle area," the group announced in a June 3 press release. "We cautioned our communities not to participate in protests due to COVID-19... [and] didn't want to encourage people to risk their health protesting."[36]

This pattern of relatively subordinate activity from organized groups was the case across the United States. Throughout the month of May, of 1,429 antiracist protests recorded in the Crowd Counting Consortium data set, 1,316 were not associated with an organized group, and only 33 were reported to have been organized by either self-professed Black Lives Matter groups (25) or NAACP chapters (8).[37] A similar but less extreme pattern was seen in June, with 83 percent of protests not reported as affiliated with a named organization (5,583 of 6,653).[38]

This general stepping back of established organizations during the uprising's early days created space for the development of new tactics and forms of association, as well an exceptionally open-ended and diverse program of action. "What's great about this [movement] is that we can all be doing different shit and still believe in the same end goal or motivation," Mason mused. "I don't want to have the same tactics as everyone else because if we're all doing the same thing, we'll be very predictable.... I think the beautiful thing about this is that people have the freedom to protest how they want and express themselves in ways that feel right to them." Alongside the huge outpourings of peaceful protests filling America's streets and constituting the overwhelming majority of actions, riotous acts of property damage, clandestine direct actions, and creative occupations also played key roles throughout the uprising, giving the movement an operational breadth unrivaled by its contemporaries. Using these strategies, protesters were able to steadfastly resist police repression, take out targets of symbolic importance, and prepare the ground for further peaceful mobilization. Even though actions causing damage to property or harm to officers constituted only 4 percent of antiracist demonstrations across the United States over the course of 2020, during critical periods the use of such tactics was notably higher. During the actions at the end of May, for example, protests injuring police or causing property damage were three times as frequent as during the rest of the year and constituted as much as 39 percent of major protest events (where crowds numbered more than one thousand people).[39]

ORGANIZING AMID MOBILIZATION

Precisely because of its spontaneous character, the 2020 uprising gave rise to an incredibly significant and important exercise in movement organization. One of the most remarkable elements of the uprising was the way in which organizational forms drew on the various affinities that had led protesters to participate in the first place. One woman who had heard about the protests on social media but knew nobody else who was going recalls how she put out a call on Twitter for other people in the same position.[40] After finding "four other random women ... I reached out and they didn't know each other either, so I started a group chat, and that became our affinity group," she said. Over time, as the group continued going to protests together and planning further involvement, the bond between them became ironclad. "Those women, I would take a bullet for," she told me, "and I don't even know their real names!"

Affinity groups became an effective way of concretizing the pathways that had led people to participate in the uprising in the first place, turning participants' shared personal characteristics into common ground for further organizing. Over time, as protesters became aware of other commonalities they shared beyond the reasons they mobilized, even more new affinity groups emerged, which then fed into new activist projects. "The thing with affinity groups is they're ever evolving," Riley explained. "You know one affinity will stop [mobilizing people], but the people that are still coming out ... will join another one [affinity group]." He explained how once his political views shifted from being liberal to more radical, he was able to find a new affinity group that helped him sustain his involvement in more direct action–oriented protests in Atlanta when liberal mobilization was dying down. Later on, as those protests also slowed, he and some peers from the movement formed a new homelessness activism affinity group based on their shared participation in the protests that summer.

In Portland protesters drew on a hybrid of mutual aid and affinity group organizing styles, forming a wide array of self-professed "blocs" organized around various services or resources that people could help provide to protesters and marginalized community members. Eventually, more than seventy different self-professed blocs emerged, so many that someone had to start a "Bloc Bloc" to keep track.[41] Blocs broadened the appeal of participation in the uprising to all manner of constituencies. Keen gardeners, for example, could join the city's Plant Bloc, video game enthusiasts could join the Gamer Bloc, the unemployed could find help from the Job Bloc, and those looking to perfect their pandemic sourdough could join the Bakers Bloc. Blocs were also formed across social categories, such as the Jewish Matzah Bloc, the religious Faith Bloc, and the local-area Beaverton Bloc, focused on one of Portland's commuter cities. Others were concerned with the more practical elements of protest coordination, such as the Snack Bloc, one of many groups who brought provisions to protests; the Badger Bloc, who made shields for protesters; the Rides for Protesters Bloc, who helped to provide transportation; and the Bail Bloc (also known as DefenseFundPDX), who helped to provide arrestee support. To form or join a bloc, one need only think of "any way that you can help people," Blake explained. "The thinking is like: This is a thing that I can do. Now, how can I make this help *everybody*?"

The use of the term "bloc" began in part as an in-joke by protesters amused by reports warning about the involvement of a group called "the Black Bloc" in the protests, or, as President Trump and his allies called them, Antifa.[42] Though "black bloc" more accurately describes a tactical decision to wear black gear that obscures one's identity, and "antifa" is in fact a variably used contraction for the term "antifascist action" (or occasionally, just "antifascist"), it is accurate to observe that antifascists employing black bloc tactics did play a role in the protests. In stark contrast to press depictions of formally constituted "Antifa" groups supporting the uprisings, several participants explained how the emergence of coordinated black bloc protesters during the uprisings in cities such as Atlanta, Portland, and Seattle was a facet of repeated mobilization and practical necessity rather than conscious organizational efforts.

Because police are believed to use loud clothing to identify protesters for arrest or munitions targeting, wearing black is not uncommon at protests with a heavy police presence. Because of the conditions of the COVID-19 pandemic and the heavy use of police riot munitions, wearing face masks and other full-body coverings was also commonplace during the uprising. The need to conceal one's identity was further exacerbated when protesters became concerned by stories of far-right groups monitoring livestreams to select targets for retaliatory harassment. Consequently, some participants recalled how they eventually took on the appearance of black bloc protesters without realizing it. One particularly illuminating example was recounted by Mason, who recalled how, while preparing for an action, he noticed that "my friends and I were getting into all black clothing." "Oh, that's new, that's interesting," he had thought. "We, without calling ourselves [a name], or without joining any sort of organization, one day, we got into the clothes... stepped out the door, looked around at each other, and we were like, Oh! *We* are 'Antifa.' *This* is the boogey man that has been in the news." He took a moment to pause, then let out a chuckle. "Who would have thought, in your own backyard?"

Beyond the auspices of explicitly delineated blocs or affinity groups, a great deal of movement activity occurred through everyday person-to-person interactions between people across the country who simply wanted to participate in whatever way they could. Because of the conditions of the pandemic and the extremely heavy police presence in most cities, face-to-face organizing meetings were generally unfeasible.[43] Consequently, many unaffiliated movement participants made use of a broad array of information and communications technologies to plug in to the movement. These ran the gamut from traditional social media, such as Facebook and Twitter, to anonymous group chats on platforms, such as Telegram and Discord, and heavily encrypted communications using platforms, such as Signal. Also employed were other, less widely discussed services, such as the local crime-reporting app Citizen and a litany of police scanner apps.[44]

Many people would be plugged in to multiple platforms simultaneously or seamlessly pair online activity with actual physical participation. For example, some participants would show up to a protest action while actively monitoring a livestream from someone else at the event, all while coordinating their activities using encrypted messaging services. Meanwhile, people at home (perhaps in other states altogether) would monitor police scanners and publicly accessible surveillance cameras, feeding information on police movements to those on the ground. After an action, physical protesters and digital supporters alike would discuss the uprising's progress on social media and online chat rooms, reflecting on tactics, highlighting potential threats, and sharing ideas for the next day's mobilization. As the summer drew on and mobilization waned, movement cyberstructures developed around the protests remained in place, creating scope for individuals to rapidly resume ad hoc coordination where necessary and providing a backbone on which a longer-running movement community could develop.

After the Uprising

By the end of July, the Black Lives Uprising appeared to be racking up an impressive array of victories.[45] In Minneapolis the city council pledged to "defund and dismantle the police department," and not only fired but charged and eventually convicted Derek Chauvin, the officer who murdered George Floyd. The three other police officers on the scene have since been charged with "aiding and abetting second-degree murder and manslaughter" and convicted of two other offenses related to the murder, for which they will serve jail time.[46] In Portland Mayor Ted Wheeler pledged to cut police budgets for the first time in years (by approximately 3 percent), diverting the money to support communities of color.[47] In Seattle—perhaps most remarkably—the city council pledged to defund its police force by 50 percent and reinvest the money in public services.[48] Cities including New York, Los Angeles, Chicago, Philadelphia, Baltimore, San Francisco, Milwaukee, and Austin, Texas, followed suit, announcing their own reductions in police funding following the protests.[49] On a national level, a bill known as the George Floyd Justice in Policing Act was passed in the House of Representatives.[50] Its provisions included scores of restrictions for federal police and local police departments receiving federal funding, restrictions on the transfer of military equipment to police, and new federal investigative powers for police misconduct.

Unfortunately, what seemed like a surge of full-throated progress was in fact largely aspirational.[51] While the scope of the bold pledges and measures proposed by city governments was widely heralded at the time, as mass mobilization petered out and national attention shifted, many of these victories were quietly reversed or dampened. Pledges were watered down, bills were tied up in the legislative process, and some measures were abandoned altogether. At other times pledges were systematically undermined by the people who had made them: Seattle's promised 50 percent reduction in funding was transmuted into an 11 percent cut, and the city's mayor, Jenny Durkan, subsequently clamored for a net increase in police numbers. Portland's Ted Wheeler refashioned himself as a "tough on crime" mayor, bragging that he was diverting federal funds to "support the police bureau," and that the effect of any cuts was minimal, producing "no reduction in police officers on the street." Meanwhile, substantial tranches of the money allocated to communities of color remained unspent.[52]

At the same time, the evaporation of the various conditions of convergence that helped galvanize mass protest earlier in the year left protesters increasingly demoralized. "A lot of folks are baffled that there are police shootings and killings regularly, even here in Georgia, and it's the same stuff that would have mobilized thousands back in the day. But now? Nobody. Not even a flyer would come out for stuff like that," Mason sighed. Cameron concurred: "Things are still happening, but nobody's looking anymore because the sensational element of the murder and the highest points of sensation have passed." She explained how the July concessions won by protesters "for a lot of us was not even close to the end" of their involvement in the movement, "but in the American public consciousness? It was the end." By August 2020 broadly antiracist mobilizations had dwindled to just under 1.3 percent of June levels, rendering them virtually unrecognizable in scale.[53]

THE RETURN OF ORGANIZATION

For all of the dynamic new organizing efforts that arose from the uprising, most have flown under the radar of public consciousness. Rather, established mainstream organizations proved the uprising's primary beneficiaries. Chief among these groups was the national Black Lives Matter organization—also known as the Black Lives Matter Global Network Foundation (BLMGN)—often used as a shorthand for the broader movement against anti-Black racism and police brutality. While in some cities local BLM chapters raised hundreds of thousands of dollars in their own right, BLMGN received the overwhelming majority of donations. Despite the fact that the group appears to have had no role in mobilizing the uprising (something reflected in my participant interviews and the group's annual report for 2020), BLMGN raised a stunning $90 million over the course of 2020 and attracted an almost fiftyfold increase in sign-ups to its email list. "We are no longer a small, scrappy movement. We are an institution. We are mature. We are a growing entity developing its stake in the philanthropic world," the group proclaimed in its annual report. "Our sights are set on diving into work at the levels of policy, community investment, arts and entertainment, and research," the organization boasted, announcing the foundation of a new political action committee (BLM PAC) and an array of exciting new partnerships with Sprite, *Hamilton: An American Musical*, and the Working Families Party.[54]

Regrettably, more than three-fourths of donations received by BLMGN went undisbursed by the end of the year, and the group generally refrained from engaging with the uprising that had skyrocketed its popularity and filled its coffers, instead avidly pursuing its new organizational and electoral agendas. They "aren't really helping us but are benefiting from the momentum," Blake complained when I asked about the impact the national Black Lives Matter group had. The leadership of a great many local BLM chapters concurred with this sentiment: "It would be irresponsible to take credit for the demonstrations that have taken place simply because they are in the name of BLM," stated the Seattle/King County chapter.[55]

The relative lack of involvement of BLM nationally led many local chapters to break with the organization's approach. Chapters in cities such as Washington, DC, Philadelphia, Atlanta, and Seattle, though seldom organizing protests in the uprising's early months, actively sought to fulfill auxiliary support roles. This ranged from using the groups' digital platforms to raise awareness about the protests all the way to actively employing their funds to support protesters by providing bail or purchasing equipment. After mass mobilization died down, breakaway BLM chapters and those that had independently procured funding took on a renewed role in supporting the development of other small-scale postuprising projects. In Atlanta, for example, protesters recalled how their local BLM chapter became pivotal in assisting the various causes that emerged from the uprising with financial and logistical support once mass enthusiasm died down. "They're great people," Riley recalled. "Black Lives Matter [Atlanta]... did step up, and, you know, help us out." This reflected a more general pattern of new activists (whose involvement in the uprising's more autonomous method of coordination had engendered a certain suspicion of formally organized groups) beginning to develop better working relationships with established leftist and progressive organizations. "There's every number of criticisms for them, but they show up," Mason mused. "The truth is that right now, we don't have a very deep fucking bench, and they, for whatever reason, are there at actions.... It's kind of like, if you brought ten people to a protest with fifty people.... Maybe that's okay."

In contrast to the increasing proximity between local racial justice organizers and postuprising activist projects, BLM chapters engaged in supporting the new movement that formed during the uprising found themselves increasingly at loggerheads with the national organization. By December 2020 local chapters numbering more than half of the national organization's remaining affiliated branches had left in protest, rebuking BLM for "intentional erasure" of grassroots activity and neglecting local organizers and activists both financially and democratically.[56] One leader of the BLM chapter in Philadelphia castigated the group for having "nothing to do with what we're doing on the ground.... We had an uprising here in Philadelphia... did you see any BLM network broadcast about that? No one reached out."[57] By 2021 multiple chapters had either changed their name (removing Black Lives Matter) or considered doing so, and many had explicitly disavowed the national organization in favor of supporting local community organizing efforts that arose out of the uprising.[58]

THE MOVEMENT TO COME

Even though the movement that came out of the uprising was denied the tens of millions of dollars donated to established groups, it has benefited from an enormous influx of freshly minted activists, as well as the steadfast support of experienced racial justice activists who eschewed prior organizational fealties. It is a movement dedicated not to electoral politics or discrete midrange reforms, but to policing abolition and steadfast antiracism in a way that informs a far wider array of struggles beyond these topics. It is one that refuses to limit its tactical repertoire, elides traditional organizational structures, and continues to innovate constantly, even when mass mobilization ceases. It might appear that the uprising is over, but the movement it has generated has only just begun.

Even if the scope of elite concessions has been scaled back vastly since the victories won in the summer of 2020, the activists forged in its fires are taking matters into their own hands, employing an array of creative and diverse direct actions to further a fundamentally different vision of society than the perceived police state they had combated that summer, drawing to a considerable degree on socialist and anarchist ideas. When wildfires hit the state of Oregon, activists armed with the respirators and protective gear they had accumulated fighting police stepped in to help provide relief. As an epidemic of eviction, homelessness, and hunger festered across the United States, the uprising's emergent blocs, mutual aid associations, and affinity groups turned their resources to the task of providing care. When it struck the country that President Trump might actually pull off a much-rumored coup plot following his loss in the 2020 election, veterans of the uprising were among the most active grassroots elements planning a response.

"The reality is that there is still a very active resistance... against the police state," Cameron told me. This was something many of my interviewees were keen to convey. Another protester concurred, explaining how, even though protests had subsided, the movement's "level of sophistication has grown" substantially since the uprising began. "The infrastructure is in place that if things were to kick off again, there'll be a very good response," Mason affirmed. It appeared that widespread participation in the summer of 2020 has had the effect of "building a nucleus" for further contention, as Blake put it during a conversation about the future of the uprising. He explained that the uprising had generated "a strong, large, somewhat cohesive group of *revolutionaries*" in the cities it touched. When the next moment came, he asserted, they would be ready. "There's going to be another highly, highly televised murder or other things are going to happen," Blake concluded, "and it's going to *swell*."

PART V

THE FRENCH REVOLUTION, 1789

In the early years at least, once we have accounted for the efficacy of pamphlets and journals, and the spoken propaganda... there still remains an element of spontaneity that defies a more exact analysis.

GEORGE RUDÉ[1]

It was with these words that George Rudé ended the last substantive chapter in his history of *The Crowd in the French Revolution*, which remains to this day one of the most famous scholarly works on the revolutionary mobilizations that beset Paris between 1788 and 1795. This part of the book begins where Rudé left off: trying to understand the element of spontaneity that he identified as a matter historians might be inclined to leave "more particularly to the province of the sociologist."[2]

Thankfully, historians have disobeyed Rudé's suggestion and have instead helpfully returned to the topic a great many times since *The Crowd*. I thus arrive at the case not only equipped with a sociological theory to explore, but with the benefit of sixty more years of in-depth research into the social and contentious history of the Revolution. It is guided by the wisdom and insight of the many historical studies before and since *The Crowd* that I approach the French case. Even so, to obtain a thorough sense of the case, it was necessary to delve somewhat into the primary material. Visits to the Parisian police archives, the *Archives Nationales*, and various outposts of the French National Library, as well as surveys of the wide variety of archival material now remotely available to scholars sufficed to familiarize me with the Revolution in a way that made the question of popular mobilization far more accessible than it would have been otherwise. Properly dissecting such voluminous archival material, however, is a task that often requires decades, rather than months, of delving, so I refer to such material sparingly. Rather, it is overwhelmingly the thoroughly concerted, critically interrogated, and empirically detailed work of historians that guides my analysis of the French case.

Accordingly, this part of the book does not attempt to uncover some utterly new, undiscovered segment of the French Revolution, nor does it attempt to retell the full history of the case. I refrain from offering a new account of its *marche générale* that does not substantially disrupt or oppose already extant historical narratives, and instead draw from the considerable literature on this case in composing my more specific assessment of affinity and convergence in the Revolution. The Revolution is thus a *shadow case study*, designed in the first place to test the generalizability of the theory I have advanced over the course of this book *and*, having passed that test, to further enrich theory building by drawing attention to contextual continuities and divergences.[3] By examining the social struggles of the French masses, we can determine not only the utility of my approach beyond conventional cases but also how the dynamics of affinity and convergence mobilization may vary across time and context.

The two chapters that follow trace the course of French revolutionary mobilization during the Revolution's most spontaneous year—1789—before examining how affinity-convergence mobilization was progressively supplanted by organized mobilization processes. Chapter 11 pays particular attention to how the convocation of the Estates General and subsequent showdown between the king and the Third Estate in 1789 established the situational groundwork for revolutionary agitation on the basis of long-standing affinities. Chapter 12 then surveys the affinities and convergence conditions that characterized revolutionary mobilization by the end of 1789. These included perceptions of injustice stemming from the country's dire economic condition and broad antiseigneurial attitudes, along with participants' social status, economic obligations, and daily patterns of activity. These affinities were activated by emergent convergence conditions at a number of critical junctures throughout the year, with various configurations stretching across almost the full gamut of opportune, exceptional, and paramount situations, frames, and spaces.[4] Looking forward from the end of the Revolution's first year, the chapter closes by exploring how affinity-convergence mobilization was first hybridized with and then supplanted by organizational strategies as the Revolution progressed.

CHAPTER ELEVEN

Mass Mobilization against the Ancien Régime

They cannot raise supplies, but they can raise mobs.

EDMUND BURKE[1]

The year 1788 had not been a good one for the Kingdom of France. King Louis XVI and his ministers were facing numerous hurdles: bankruptcy, an increasingly dissatisfied class of nobles, a despondent peasantry, and rising popular tumult across the country. Addressing these manifold issues was the backdrop to Louis's decision to indulge a convocation of the nation's Estates General, France's formal constitutional and legislative advisory body. This was, in fact, the King's second attempt to employ a long-ignored institution: one year earlier he had reconvened the Assembly of Notables, which had not met since 1626. The principal difficulty was that, despite the dire economic situation, Louis had been unable to levy new taxes because of the reluctance of local courts (*parlements*). Calling the Assembly of Notables in 1787, and later the Estates General in January 1789, was a means to force the *parlements*' hand by appealing to some form of representative legitimacy. The body was dominated by the power holders of the feudal order: France's clergy and nobility comprised the First and Second Estates (chambers), respectively. The body's Third Estate was to be elected from among the common people and would be twice as large, though equally powerful, as either of the other estates. France had not had an election since 1614, and as such the process generated a considerable degree of national excitement. "Citizens, the nation is in danger!" one election pamphlet read. "Domestic enemies, more dangerous than foreign armies are secretly plotting its ruin."[2]

A Fateful Election

In line with the procedural tradition of the Estates General, France's many urban and rural districts were invited to elect representatives and submit *cahiers de doléances*—lists of complaints and requests drawing attention to popular grievances and potential reforms. This process involved public meetings across almost every parish, professional guild,[3] township, and city in France over the course of the early spring. These meetings allowed ordinary people to engage in public political debate and make public political demands, often for the first time in their lives.[4] People who had hardly or never been in contact before were suddenly invited to meet and discuss their intersecting and differing grievances, ardently discussing the possibility of changing the structures and policies of the feudal regime.[5]

The *cahier* meetings became spaces in which aggrieved Frenchmen across social and structural divides could come together and express their frustrated attitude toward the status quo. Participation was open to all Frenchmen over the age of twenty-five who paid any tax whatsoever, numbering roughly five million in total, about 20 percent of the population.[6] People spoke of "breathing a new atmosphere," experiencing "the finest days in our lives," and inhabiting a place of political freedom that had not existed in France for two centuries.[7] It was, in short, an entirely unrivaled opportune situation for political association among the struggling masses who had lived their entire lives under the thumb of an aristocratic order (even if, at this point, the very poorest were still notionally excluded from the process). In this protective context for political dissent and discussion, all manner of new political and social proposals were catalyzed, ranging from grand reforms to the most picayune or unfeasible proposals. One parish, Vitry-sur-Seine, simultaneously demanded "the total suppression of all [feudal] privileges," "the price of bread to be fixed at a lower price," and "the selling of grain by weight," but also requested with the same force the "total destruction of all rabbits" and the "total abolition" of the right to keep pigeon coops.[8]

As the electoral historian of the French Revolution, Malcolm Crook, has noted, these meetings "mobilized the French people in an unprecedented fashion."[9] It was these meetings, Crook declared emphatically, that "created the first generation of revolutionaries." They created a space in which an ordinarily politically excluded cross section of the French people were able to reflect critically on the awful state of the country and suggest solutions to their every political and social plight. These new democratic spaces proved popular, and many cahiers called for regular convocations of the Third Estate and the continuation of local meetings. Though the king was staunchly opposed to such proposals, the meetings were nonetheless de facto continued by their participants, well beyond the electoral period, becoming new political spaces accessible across the entire country.

While across France municipal and local groups were meeting and formulating popular demands, the people of Paris faced comparative repression. They had been denied the right to compile cahiers, denied the right to meet with their noble and clergy counterparts, and permitted only a single day to assemble. In response, on their single allotted meeting day, groups of citizens across the sixty municipal districts of Paris almost universally declared open resistance to these edicts. "On the morning of 21 April [1789] men who had never been accustomed to act together politically met for the first time to transact business for which there were no precedents," the historian Robert Rose details in his exposition of the Parisian elections.[10] "Within a few hours, from one corner of Paris to another, these ad hoc assemblies, varying in size from two dozen to almost five hundred members, had each improvised modes of procedure." Rebuffing any royal authorities and emissaries sent to oversee their meetings, Parisians instead autonomously appointed their own representatives and decided upon their own practices. These assemblies, in themselves acts of popular resistance to royal authority, would persist in their operation until July 1790, much longer than the single-day existence envisaged for them. They would even reconvene in some of the Revolution's most quintessential mobilizations (or, in French revolutionary parlance, *journées*).

The Extant Precursors of Revolutionary Mobilization

ACTIVISTS WITHOUT ADHERENTS

Though participation in the Revolution's early popular meetings was certainly an organic popular phenomenon, this is not to say that those who attended were not subject to activist influence. Achieving such influence, however, was no easy task. In the Revolution's early days, France's revolutionary activists lacked both numbers and organizational capacity. Without a formidable organized movement at their disposal, they had no other choice but to thrust themselves into contact with the nation's masses by whatever means they could. A wide variety of differently motivated revolutionary agitators made their way to the nation's electoral assemblies, cafés, and even street corners, but they also employed a tactic that would amplify their reach even further: the popular press. One of the procedural quirks of convoking the Estates General had made it possible for publishers to subvert the harsh restrictions usually placed on the French press.[11] Publishers who had previously been concerned about the possible ramifications for expressing political opinions in the public press "issued a flood of pamphlets to a public roused by the forthcoming meeting of the Estates-General."[12] Among these pamphlets were the words and agendas of revolutionary activists, disseminated across France to a politically ravenous public. There were, however, limitations on the efficacy of this strategy. During much of the Revolution's first year, agitators depended on printing houses and distributors to circulate their provocations, having not yet assembled proper publishing operations of their own. Where writings were considered to be out of step with popular opinion or likely to otherwise imperil the publisher, requests for publication were flatly refused. One quintessential revolutionary pamphlet, *La France Libre*, was initially rejected by so many publishers that it took its author months to so much as have it printed.[13]

As time went on and revolutionary activists developed better relationships with publishers, agitant pamphlets and improvised briefings evolved into full-blown emulations of professionally produced newspapers. Such was the volume of material being circulated that it became impossible for authorities to effectively censor or prevent their circulation. One hundred forty new periodicals were started in Paris alone, thirty-four of which persisted beyond one year of reportage.[14] The increasingly politicized French electorate (and even those who could not vote) consumed these pamphlets ravenously, with gatherings forming to discuss their content in the nation's many cafés, workshops, wineshops, and taverns, and even as crowds in the street where they were read out loud for the benefit of the illiterate. Their recipients were not afraid to act on their content, not only against political elites but also against editors who fell out of popular favor. The editor of the popular *Mercure de France*, for example, was confronted by a crowd who had poured forth from one Parisian café after having read his most recent edition. Having judged it to be too conservative for their liking, they descended on his house and demanded that he entirely rewrite the next week's issue on pain of being strung to the rear end of a donkey and paraded through the city streets.[15]

While revolutionary activists were clearly fervently operating throughout the Revolution's earliest days, they lacked any formidable organization of their own. One prominent activist at the time recalled that the republican cause was furnished with "such slight resources" that there were "no more than ten [activist] republicans" in Paris as late as July.[16] Moreover, French revolutionaries worked in an informationally limited environment, where the success of their calls to action were highly unpredictable and ultimately determined by public inclination. For example, several days before the Parisians defied royal edicts on April 21, a pamphlet titled "*Arrêtés concernant le choix des électeurs de Paris par un assemble de citoyens*" (Decrees Regarding the Choice of Paris Electors for a Citizens' Assembly) had been circulated, imploring citizens to disregard their official instructions and instead to elect their own president and officers and stand in protest.[17] A model Declaration of Rights was included, based on the American revolutionary model. Yet only a selection of the capital's assemblies referred to this material in their decision-making; some referred to other documents, and still others made no mention of their inspirations. As one in-depth study of revolutionary electoral contestation concluded: "A hidden hand was certainly manipulating events, [but]... not enough, nevertheless, to explain the virtual universality of the districts' revolt, with only six out of the sixty... failing to upset the official regulations."[18]

POPULAR PREDISPOSITIONS

Though many of the dynamics underpinning popular mobilization would emerge only later in the revolutionary period, some of the affinities that characterized those who chose to mobilize for the Revolution's early days were well established. As the historian Bailey Stone has outlined,[19] "the uprising of the country's humbler folk had certain roots in the [A]ncien [R]égime." Even before the mass revolutionary risings of 1789, bitter unrest had served as the backdrop to everyday French politics, touching almost every region in some way.[20] Lynn Hunt's work on local revolutionary politics advances three particular antecedents here: economic vulnerability, antipathy toward social elites (antiseigneurialism), and familiarity with revolutionary activity elsewhere.[21]

Perceptions of Injustice

Although social historians note that there existed "deep internal divisions" among France's urban population, as well as substantial competing interests between the rural and urban sectors, for much of 1789 these otherwise divided classes were united by a long-standing sense of injustice.[22] The cost of France's economic woes had predominantly been borne by the poorer classes, while France's richer citizens at least appeared to still enjoy a life of luxury. This sense of relative deprivation formed the basis of concerted episodes of popular violence inside and outside the capital, stretching back to December 1788.[23] France's peasantry were particularly aggrieved at the unjust extraction of their produce by their feudal overlords during a time of profound economic hardship. Conversely, the nation's urban classes were incensed by the escalating price of the very same bread and meat withheld from the rural peasantry. Amid a time of mass unemployment and a sharp divergence between prices and wages, the hoarding of bread and meat was a cause of deep concern, propelling incensed populaces across the nation to seize upon the plump stores of aristocratic profiteers.[24] Bread, in particular, was 60 percent more expensive than its standard cost by February 1789, taking its cost to the point at which the poorest in France would fear starvation.[25] By July 1789 the price would rise higher still, and an average day laborer supporting a wife and two children would have spent 96 percent of his income on bread alone.[26] As time went on, the price would continue to increase, taking conditions from dire to deadly. The situation was particularly bad in industrial towns, where steep price rises and obstinate elites set the backdrop for novel surges of popular mobilization.[27]

Attitudes

This shared sense of injustice was accompanied with attitudinal alignment in the form of the recognition of a common enemy. The aristocratic classes found themselves in the crossfire of poor urbanites and rural peasants, articulating their allied but potentially contradictory demands: the peasantry could not sell their produce for enough, and the urban classes could not afford it. This "hatred… for the lords was not a thing of [only] yesterday," Georges Lefebvre noted in his classic history of the Revolution's beginnings.[28] Indeed, antiseigneurial inclinations had been a periodic occurrence in France's history and reflected long-underlying disputes between peasants and landholders dating back to the institution of serfdom. The common solution to both peasant and urban problems was to eliminate the extractive element, constituted politically as the aristocracy, their taxmen, and the collection of feudal dues.[29] With the affinities of a shared sense of injustice and compatible attitudes as to how it might be solved, the urban and rural classes would later seize upon the confusion and uncertainty of Parisian revolution and partake in their own offenses on the French social order.

The Parisians with whose exploits we associate the Revolution's central story also harbored more specific attitudinal affinities that would stoke the capital's role as a revolutionary powder keg. Notably, unlike the provinces, Paris was largely isolated from the rest of France, making the prospect of famine, invasion, or any other such incident all the more daunting for its populace. Periods when these issues arose often prompted profound popular panic, making matters ranging from the (suspected) hoarding of grain to movements of troops especially provocative to the capital's populace during the Revolution's early years.[30]

Patterns of Activity

One of the most notable affinities held by Parisians related to their patterns of activity. The roughly six hundred thousand Parisians present in the city in 1789 were regularly drawn to some particular centers of rendezvous in which revolutionary activity would routinely occur.[31] The most prominent of these were the shopping arcades of the Palais-Royal (discussed at length later) and the markets of Les Halles, as well as the city's dozen bridges, most particularly the Pont Neuf, the most heavily trafficked bridge in the city at which "if you waited... for an hour, it was said, you could meet whomever you wanted."[32] It was upon the Pont Neuf and on Paris's other bridges that revolutionary bands and popular mobs would sweep up whomever was passing by into whatever form of action in which they were engaged. Concentrated precisely around these bridges, and the city's center in general, were not—as today—the houses of the rich and well-to-do, but those of the poor, the needy, and the desperate: the foot soldiers of the coming revolution. This was far from a novel phenomenon— the city's bridges and markets had long functioned as contact points for contentious mobilizations, having played a similar role in the popular riots of May 1750. Arlette Farge and Jacques Revel's meticulous dissection of one 1750 riot recounts how a contentious "whisper ran from stall to stall in the market square where it was magnified like an echo chamber."[33] All of these various points of intersection were in the middle of the city and were usually a ten-minute walk from either one another or from some critical center of urban power. When one reads that, for example, a revolutionary crowd swelled at Les Halles and made its way to the Hôtel de Ville (City Hall), it might well have done so in less time than it has taken you to read this chapter. Thus, the particular geography of Paris made it such that people who frequented these various key sites in the center of the city were highly liable to encounter opportunities for revolutionary mobilization.

Social Status and Obligations

There was a considerable contingent structurally ripe for revolutionary mobilization among the nation's less fortunate souls, should the thought occur, the time come, or the place emerge. The roughly 20 percent of the population who attended the *cahier* and electoral meetings across France held a particularly strong affinity for revolutionary participation in the early days, being massaged into contact with other grievance-holding Frenchmen as part of the convocation of the Estates General. Another social category that became increasingly prone to revolutionary mobilization as time went on were the nation's economically precarious, who "had no classical education" and generally "worked with his hands as an artisan, kept a shop, or was employed in some minor clerical post."[34] This included a great many individuals in France's major cities, not so poor as to be totally denied access to the political sphere, but poorly resourced enough to be vulnerable to the slightest reconfiguration in economic or political conditions. These classes were so frequently overtaken with revolutionary fervor that they were later given a nickname by contemporary observers—the *sans-culottes*—inspired by the fact that they seldom donned the formal breeches (*culottes*) worn by members of the upper classes. As time progressed, this nickname served as the backbone for a form of popular identity that reached a crescendo both in Paris and the provinces by 1792.[35]

While men's engagement in revolutionary mobilization often arose as a consequence of the structured commitments of everyday life permitted by their social standing—their work, their political rights, and related facets of male sociability that came with a certain status—female revolutionary participation was considerably different in character.[36] Excluded from the heights of commercial and political society, and instead expected to participate predominantly in casual labor, housekeeping, and child-rearing, women were thus seriously unlikely (in the early days, at least) to be roused to revolutionary action in the clubs, cafés, and assemblies of the city. Rather, it was the local neighborhood, busy intersection, and central market that proved the most fertile grounds for female revolutionary mobilization, containing within them dynamic and animated arenas for continuous feminine sociability.[37] So too did women's particular domestic roles as the individuals responsible for feeding their families and communal roles as the principal vendors of urban foodstuffs give them a particularly strong sensitivity to issues relating to prices and shortages of food.[38]

A Revolution in Motion

It was grounded in the various affinities of France's budding revolutionary masses that some early spontaneous revolts of the French people began to emerge. At first, these took the form of protracted rural unrest throughout the months of March, April, and May 1789. Originating as episodes of collective looting and attacks on hoarders, these would solidify in March to include the popular de facto abolition of local taxes, dues, and charges in the more radically inclined communities. Indeed, some communities had even declared themselves entirely free of their feudal obligations and organized hunting parties to steal from noble estates.[39]

In the capital, meanwhile, conflict among France's newly elected Third Estate and the king was reaching fever pitch. By June its representatives executed an incredible challenge to royal authority. Frustrated that their demands were being ignored by Louis XVI, they had started the legislative process unilaterally, inviting members of the other Estates to join them in their legislative deliberations. By June 17 they had formally declared their sovereignty as a National Assembly of the French People, initiating a full-scale power grab. In the subsequent days, hosts of supporters flocked to the Palace of Versailles,[40] excited by the proceedings and fueled by rumors of an impending armed assault on the assembly by royal forces. France's press, assemblies, and streets quickly became incensed, as pamphleteers urged radical action and notably inflamed political meetings and gatherings spread across the nation.

The thousands who flocked to Versailles were sustained, in a great sense, by a common (and justified) fear of an aristocratic conspiracy: the Revolution's downtrodden protagonists believed that they had gained much by the emergence of the National Assembly only days earlier and feared a sudden reversal of fortune.[41] This was assisted by the activities of revolutionary rabble-rousers in the public spaces of Paris, most particularly those in the city's Palais-Royal, which would prove pivotal in the coming July days. When royal forces were employed to repress the Third Estate and its supporters, troops instead refused to fire upon the National Assembly and the thousands who stood in its defense. With this attempted purge having failed, Louis was forced to formally recognize the Assembly on June 27, effectively sundering his sovereignty in the process.

RURAL REVOLT

A more widespread test of the French people's capacity for mobilization came in the month of July. With the situation at Versailles remaining precarious, revolutionary agitation had begun to crop up in the public spaces of Paris with rousing news, revolutionary slogans, and calls to action arising across the city's cafés, bakeries, and street corners.[42] Such fervent activity also found its way to the provinces, where these encouragements were met with major insurrections of revolutionary peasants on an unprecedented scale: grand popular attacks on feudal manors and castles became rife, complemented by a spate of lynchings directed against nobles. Law and order entirely broke down in some districts as thousands of peasants mobilized into armed forces. This became known as the *Grande Peur* (Great Fear).[43]

Despite its name, we now know that the Great Fear was not an anarchic, disorderly response to panic and hunger (an image better suited to riots of the winter of 1788–1789), but instead a more distinctly political instance of contentious mobilization. As the historian Peter Jones noted in his study of the peasantry, "By the summer, hunger and desperation had ceased to be the dominant factors behind the peasant offensive. They had been replaced by an awareness that the entire social order was crumbling, and by an opportunistic desire to strike while the iron is hot."[44]

The tenor and commonality of rural political demands had been galvanized by the drawing together of disparate provincial grievances during the convocation of the Estates General. "The experience of drawing up the cahiers helped country dwellers to formulate their grievances, while the... electoral assemblies taught them who their allies and their enemies were likely to be," Jones wrote.[45] The points of assembly for cahiers and elections functioned as opportune spaces in which like-minded individuals could gather on the basis of their common concerns before formulating and indeed pursuing collective actions that spoke to them. Moreover, these early assemblies and meetings at which cahiers were drawn up were also possessed of exceptional qualities. This was particularly so in rural contexts, in which the assemblies became spaces that temporarily freed peasants from what cultural historians have termed the "matrix of cultural reproduction and stability" that characterized much of rural life at the time.[46]

Nonetheless, it was not merely the existence of conducive spaces of convergence that powered the enormous upsurge in the French countryside. Lefebvre, in his history of the Revolution, distinctly emphasizes the impact of the French political process on mobilizing the peasantry: "One can hardly exaggerate the echoes produced by this event [the convocation of the Estates General] in the countryside. On hearing of it the peasants concluded that, if the king invited them to set forth their grievances, it was because he meant to give them satisfaction."[47] We might conceptualize this "collective state of mind," as an opportune frame, in which peasants considered the convocation of the Estates General as a collective opportunity to act on their complaints. Such an interpretation is further corroborated by John Markoff's in-depth analysis of peasant democratic and protest activity, which found that, "although the deputies of the Third Estate were more gradualist than the countryside wished... peasants had come to believe that rural action against seigneurial rights had a good chance of paying off."[48] Markoff continued: "The trajectory of anti-seigneurial actions shows that rural action was not merely a blind and angry reflex. There may have been anger, but the uprisings developed as the moment seemed opportune and faded as goals were achieved."

Despite its contentious component, the Great Fear was certainly still underpinned by a genuine sense of alarm around a potential aristocratic conspiracy or reaction against prior peasant insurgencies. Research on the spread of this rural panic depicts it as almost contagious, radiating through the roving bands of migratory workers and dispossessed vagabonds: they became the carriers of "popular fears and prejudices, news and rumors of great events, of violent political changes, of great disasters natural and human."[49] These framing activities were further perpetuated by rumors circulating across the full breadth of France's social strata: "these included bourgeois, priests and monks; postal couriers... and village curates, local officials and gentry... even the government sub-delegates and mounted constabulary were no exception."[50]

MOBILIZING THE CAPITAL

Profound instances of spontaneous revolutionary mobilization were certainly not an exclusively rural phenomenon. The French capital was fast becoming a contentious hotbed, known for sudden splurges of mobilization, arising as if from nowhere. At this time, the most infamous space from which revolutionary agitation would spring was, by far, the city's Palais-Royal. Indeed, along with the city's bridges, cafés, and street corners, the Palais-Royal would serve as perhaps the most important space for Parisian revolutionary mobilization throughout 1789. It was a rather novel public space in Paris, which had emerged in the 1780s as a forum or agora of sorts. Its owner, Louis-Philippe II, Duke of Orléans, had seized the initiative to open his palace to the public, building a grand series of arcades in and around its picturesque gardens, with great galleries containing all manner of coffee shops, restaurants, markets, boutiques, theaters, operas, and other establishments where Parisians might meet, shop, and generally spend their time.

"During the revolutionary period, different political factions each had their favorite café in the Palais Royal," Kevin Hetherington remarked in his sociological examination of the Palais during the Revolution.[51] The Palais-Royal, however, was home to more than a bourgeois public sphere and commercial society. Indeed, though at its center beautiful gardens bloomed, and the great and the good would associate, the Palais was also home to a plethora of seditious theaters, cafés, and small meeting places, while "in the newly built arcades, prostitutes would rent small shops with rooms above, in order to be able to provide sex for their clients. Streetwalkers would mingle with the fashionable crowds and dress up to disguise their intent... [and] the bookshops sold not only the latest Enlightenment works, political pamphlets, newspapers and journals, but alongside them pornography and seditious writings." It was, Hetherington's in-depth study of the Palais declared, a "heterotopia," an exceptional space, in which all manner of people of different origins, backgrounds, and inclinations could associate freely and indulge in joint experiences. Such a space was crucial to early revolutionary mobilizations. Take, for example, the experience of the Parisian bookseller Nicolas Ruault on the evening of July 10, whose anecdote shows how a mobilization could take form in the environs of a café at the Palais, leave its premises on some revolutionary venture, and pick up participants as it steamrolled through the streets of Paris.

> After dinner I went to the Palais-Royal, the singular noisy meeting-place at this moment of rumor, fear and alarm. I saw at the rear of the garden a crowd of people in front of the curtains of the cafe Le Caveau. It was a company of artillerymen, regaled [by the crowd] with liquor and shouts of "Bravo." I made my escape via the rue de Richelieu, [where] I soon met this same crowd, leading these gunners to the Champs-Elysées; they were more than a hundred [artillerymen], well packed, arm in arm with French guards, women, and workers. They would say to the public who saw them pass: "We are friends, fear not," and were applauded. I was enveloped in this crowd, my will forced, called to arms by this popular movement; a white-haired artilleryman gave me his hand, I shook it, saying "Bravo," like the others. He said, looking at me: "Are you crying?" "Yes," I replied, "and it is [tears] of joy." ... Joy was universal among everyone along the streets and quays. It felt like a party.[52]

THE FALL OF THE BASTILLE

Throughout the Revolution's first year, thousands would congregate at the Palais-Royal throughout the day, and thousands more would do so at night. The space thus played a quintessential role in cultivating popular revolutionary agitation in the early days of 1789.[53] In July it took on a particularly starring role. Indeed, "[i]f the French Revolution can be said to have begun in any single spot at any single moment," the historian James Billington argued, "it may have been in the gardens of the Palais-Royal at about 3.30 in the afternoon of Sunday, July 12, 1789, when [journalist and politician] Camille Desmoulins climbed up on a table and cried *Aux armes!* to the milling crowd."[54]

And to arms they took! Ordinary Parisians, joined by defectors from the French military corps and a variety of neighborhood guardsmen, pinned leaves from the Palais gardens to their chests and raised the alarm all around the capital.[55] When a detachment of soldiers at the royal palace of the Tuileries attempted to employ a cavalry charge to put a forceful stop to the growing crowds, it seriously backfired. As Micah Alpaugh's detailed chronicling of the protest recounts, "attempted repression led to the escalation of a conflict Parisians likely felt they could not afford to lose... [and] offered no compromise."[56] Such a characterization is directly reenforced by official reports at the time, which stated that the instance of repression confirmed "to the capital's citizens the dangers now confronting them: all who saw this scene have raised alarm as far as they can."[57] The situation had become utterly paramount: either the king's forces would crush the Parisians, or the Parisians would have to confront the king.

Hundreds of marches spilled forth all around the city, and citizens began arming themselves for coming events. Those individuals who could attend the Parisian assemblies rapidly assembled themselves into a militia (which would later become the National Guard). The host of agitated Parisian citizens stormed the armory jail of the Bastille before serving as judge, jury, and executioner for the conservative mayor of Paris and the commander of the Bastille's defending regiment.[58] By July 15, as the commotion intensified, Parisian assemblymen moved in concert with the masses, declaring the city to be a democratic revolutionary Commune, complete with a new mayor and an independent military force in the form of its newly heavily armed citizens. With the situation becoming inextricable, the king formally met with the Paris Commune two days later, accepting the revolutionary cockade (with the red and blue of the city of Paris superimposed atop the traditional white of the Ancien Régime), and thereby symbolically endorsing the revolutionary process.

Crucial in understanding the scope of spontaneous participation in revolt during the July days is the realization that for the people of Paris, public episodes of protest or riot were not regarded as entirely extraordinary. Rather, as Farge and Revel's work on Parisian popular mobilization finds, "riot was accepted as a recognized part of the social scene," as far back as the early eighteenth century, and "this sense of familiarity reappears from one uprising to the next right up until the days of July 1789. People knew instinctively how to react."[59] Even without access to direct information on what was happening, the populace of Paris would have had a good idea of where to go should they wish to participate in an urban mobilization, either to an initial staging post such as the Palais-Royal, or to busy thoroughfares, such as the city's markets and bridges.

The storming of the Bastille and de facto victory of Parisians over the king's forces would be the first of many events subsequently given the moniker of "revolution" by contemporary observers, but it was not the only instance of momentous revolutionary activity to have taken place in July. Indeed, many of France's major towns had mirrored the example of the capital and done away with established authorities in favor of revolutionary uprisings and new, local self-governance. Of France's thirty major cities, only ten were not in some way brought under the control of their revolutionary populace.[60] So too had smaller towns and villages across France been, as Jones eloquently put it, "busily engaged [in] their own Bastille-style revolutions."[61] The local groupings and new power arrangements that emerged were in no way subordinate to the victorious Parisian government and would subsequently come to disregard national authority in accordance with an enormous spectrum of radical and antiauthoritarian agendas as the Revolution progressed.

THE MARCH TO VERSAILLES

A further test of revolutionary mobilizing capacity came in October 1789. Following rumors of a banquet at Versailles in which the new national tricolor cockade had been insulted by the king, his wife, and his court, along with soaring bread prices over the past few months, Paris was becoming an incredibly tense place. On the morning of October 4, that tension broke. Women congregated in the public markets around Paris, most forcefully in the central thoroughfare of Les Halles, where they constituted not only the majority of clients but also the vendors. Expressing their discontent about the price of basic essentials, numerous women at the market stalls declared their intention to march to the Hôtel de Ville and request that the newly instituted Paris Commune address their concerns. Between one and two thousand women made their way from Les Halles to the City Hall as early as 8:00 a.m., and the crowd steadily grew in size over the subsequent hours, as news of the event radiated out from the central market to the various districts from which its patrons hailed.[62] The crowd became increasingly rambunctious, procuring armaments, attacking buildings, and issuing threats against the newly established Parisian authorities.[63] It was at this point that some among the crowd proclaimed that their intention was to procure bread from the royal palace at Versailles.

It was around 11:00 a.m. that, as the commotion raged, some individual—perhaps enterprising, perhaps merely alarmed—elected to ring the City Hall's *tocsin*, or alarm bell, an activity strongly associated with times of danger and commotion in the city of Paris.[64] With the citizenry called to arms, bells rang across the city, and people poured into the streets. The various citizens who had volunteered for the National Guard began to descend on the Hôtel de Ville, ready to defend the city against potential external aggression. But when the citizens and guardsmen of Paris arrived, they found not an invading army, but their fellow civilians demanding action. With only a fragment of the guard having arrived, and the situation at the Hôtel de Ville growing increasingly heated, the most widely respected guardsman on the scene conferred with his fellow volunteers and duly agreed to escort the uproarious crowd to Versailles, later explaining that he feared that the increasingly irate and increasingly heavily armed Parisians at the Hôtel de Ville would proceed in taking the capital if he had not.[65] In addition to the substantial contingent of guardsmen, the crowd that set off for Versailles numbered around seven thousand people, many of whom had arrived on the scene in response to the tocsin.[66] Seizing arms and bread on their way, the masses set off for Versailles, preparing a deputation to confront the king.

When the Marquis de Lafayette, the supposed but belated commander of the National Guard, arrived at the Hôtel de Ville later that day, the tens of thousands who had not already marched to Versailles demanded that he lead them there to join their comrades and fellow citizens. When they arrived, Lafayette officially opted to support the masses against the king, occupying the grounds of Versailles and effectively besieging the palace.[67] As the situation escalated, even more people traveled to Versailles, demanding the relocation of both the king and the National Assembly to Paris. The Assembly members were quick to acquiesce: by October 6 Louis XVI was relocated to Paris, accompanied by a sixty thousand-strong procession (approximately one-tenth of the capital's population), and followed soon after by the entire governmental apparatus. The "Second Revolution" of 1789, as it became known, was complete, and with it, France's national trajectory would be forever altered.[68]

CHAPTER TWELVE

The Development of Revolutionary Mobilization

This chapter begins by drawing together the affinities and conditions of convergence that developed throughout the 1789 revolution, before detailing how the dynamics of mobilization shifted in the years following revolutionaries' victory in October 1789. I characterize the Revolution as having progressively transformed from a revolution underpinned primarily by the dynamics of affinity-convergence mobilization to one in which highly organized forms of mobilization became dominant. During the process of this transition, instances of hybrid mobilization occurred, in which revolutionary forces sought to control or replace spaces of convergence with factionally controlled clubs and other gathering spaces, built an organized propaganda apparatus to instill political predispositions in sectors of the populace, and even gained the ability to cultivate convergence conditions by leveraging limited control over elements of state power.

Affinity, Convergence, and Mobilization in 1789

The revolution of 1789 owes substantial thanks to the spontaneous mobilization of individuals and groups that held no formal political association with one another until they mobilized. The Revolution's first year was thus distinctly characterized by the spontaneous torrents of mobilization which surged through the nation's streets and roadways on some contentious mission or other.

The overall picture of affinity-convergence mobilization during this period is one in which ordinary French men and women were drawn into participation in revolutionary politics through a mélange of social and psychological affinities. Strongly held antiseigneurial attitudes and visceral perceptions of injustice helped foster a dispositional affinity to revolutionary participation. While those privileged enough to be deemed taxpayers were provided with access to political hotbeds, such as the cahier meetings and local assemblies, other people's patterns of activity were still liable to produce encounters with contentious political action in the café, wineshop, bridge-crossing, or market. Moreover, ordinary people's obligations to feed their family were sometimes afforded a political recourse in the form of taking by force from political foes.

Helping to convince people to act on these various affinities were underlying conditions of convergence: opportune and exceptional situations and frames, taking stock of a weak French state and unparalleled political freedom, aspects that were all the more amplified in certain opportune spaces, such as local assemblies and the vibrant radical heterotopia of the Palais-Royal. At other times, one could be drawn into contention by surprise, finding oneself in a radical gathering outside a café or burbling in a market square. At times of greatest importance—or threat—such as during the failed repression attempts of July 1789, people found mobilization especially paramount. Even in less truly imperative situations, the sound of the tocsin ringing across town would imply the paramountcy of rushing to the aid of one's fellows.

Figure 12.1 shows a synopsis of the most pivotal affinities and convergence conditions in 1789.[1] The remainder of this section explores them in depth, detailing how each contributed to the mobilization process.

	Social Affinities		
	Patterns of Activity Locality, leisure & commercial activity, media		
	Social Status (Initially) Taxpayers	Obligations (+) Acquiring food	
	Psychological Affinities		
Dispositions			
	Perceived Injustice Hunger, starvation, poverty		
	Attitudes Antiseigneurialism		

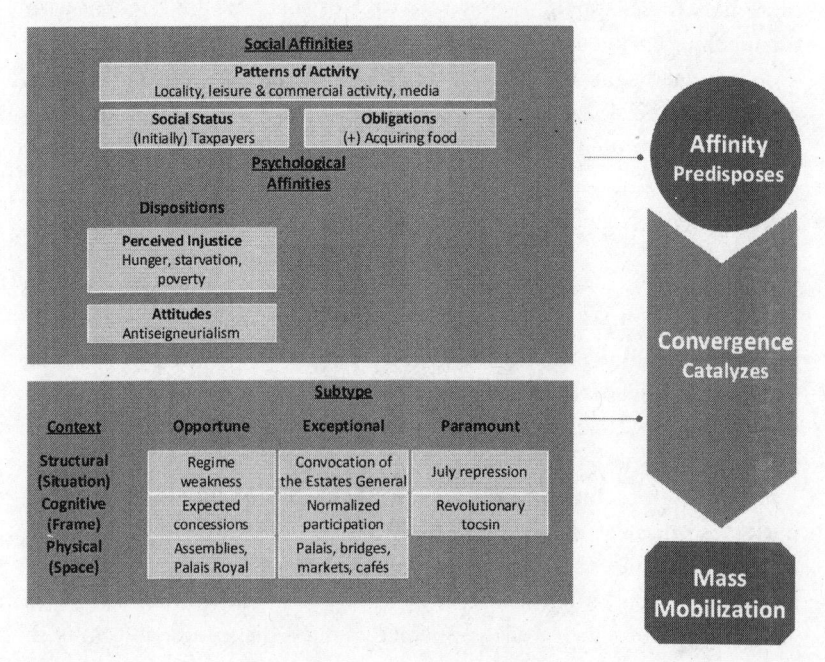

		Subtype	
Context	Opportune	Exceptional	Paramount
Structural (Situation)	Regime weakness	Convocation of the Estates General	July repression
Cognitive (Frame)	Expected concessions	Normalized participation	Revolutionary tocsin
Physical (Space)	Assemblies, Palais Royal	Palais, bridges, markets, cafés	

Affinity Predisposes → Convergence Catalyzes → Mass Mobilization

FIGURE 12.1. Summary of affinity-convergence mobilization in the 1789 French Revolution.

AFFINITY

When we further interrogate the matter of who became swept up in collective action during the Revolution, we see an incredible breadth of participants. Rural peasants, vagabonds, and migrant workers in the provinces were mirrored by the petite bourgeoisie of France's merchants, craftspeople, and other such traders in the towns and cities. Likewise, the nation's plebeians—be it millers, bakers, garment-workers, sailors, market-sellers, soldiers, or the toiling classes—were frequently drawn into revolutionary agitation. What they had in common, however, was affinity: by sharing political dispositions, reading the same newspapers, frequenting the same marketplaces, or living in the same district, they were able to spontaneously come into contact with the revolutionary cause when the conditions for mobilization were ripe.

Early mobilizations owe a great deal to an array of affinities in place long before the Revolution. These are discussed at length in chapter 11, and generally included material disadvantages that made direct political action a preferable recourse; a sense of grievance that motivated such action; and sudden spatial proximity to revolt for the dwellers in the Paris *faubourgs* (suburbs) and market regions. In Paris and across the nation, other shared material obligations and corresponding political grievances, such as hunger and poverty among ordinary people, were also reflected by a longer-standing attitudinal alignment characterized by a hatred of the aristocratic classes. In a great sense, as Bailey Stone's history of the Revolution's genesis affirms, townsfolk, peasants, and Parisians had been imbued with a "psychological preparedness for an active role in the politics of 1789" as a consequence of their shared material desperation.[2]

Perhaps as a consequence of the increased importance of face-to-face encounters and physical proximity during the 1789 time period, social affinities were also particularly important in the Revolution's early years. In Paris and other major cities, merely living or working near a protest thoroughfare gave one a certain proximity to revolutionary action that could manifest in political participation, something to which the depositions of the women who marched to Versailles in October attest. Indeed, participants often described feelings or, indeed, concrete experiences of being compelled by the crowds that swelled and assemblies that convoked for one revolutionary end or another. As one woman on the march to Versailles, Marie-Rose Barré, noted in her formal deposition, it was when crossing the Notre Dame bridge at approximately 8:00 a.m. on October 5 that she encountered "about a hundred women who told her that it was necessary for her to go with them to Versailles to ask for bread there."[3]

She had found "this great number of women" so irresistible, the deposition noted, "that she decided to go with them." Such a sentiment was not uncommon. Another woman, Françoise Miallon,[4] recalled how she had left her house "around ten o'clock in the morning... to go about her business, she was drawn by a crowd of women who were passing through the rue Montorgueil [near the Les Halles market], and ushered to Versailles," arriving at 5:00 p.m. that day, where they decamped at the palace, lodging with a local café owner.[5] Indeed, police investigations into the October mobilizations found a great many Parisians who recounted that they had been "carried away by the crowd"[6] to participate in the march to Versailles.

At least initially, the activist beneficiaries of these mass mobilizations had little ability to actively engineer them. As Rudé noted in his seminal study of revolutionary crowds, "The *menu peuple* [ordinary people] of Paris were no more helpless accessories, willing to stage an insurrection for the sole benefit of the constitutional monarchists in October, than they had been... for the Paris Electors in July. While they might share the general alarm... they also had their own particular preoccupations."[7] These preoccupations generally concerned the scarcity of bread, a general lack of funds, and a distaste for the conspiracies of the aristocracy, which they shared with their beneficiaries in the Assembly.

Over the course of the Revolution, the central affinities underlying mobilization shifted from those that were in equal parts social and psychological to those more squarely underpinned by psychological factors. One exception was people's shared patterns of activity, exemplified in the reading of the new political periodicals that proliferated across the country. This is because the new periodicals were precisely the means by which new grievances, attitudes, and identities were instilled in the French population by an array of activist propagandists. These affinities thus came to be as a consequence of attempts by revolutionary factions to induce dispositions in the otherwise unpredictable masses, with the hope that they would come to serve a more pointed purpose in future mobilizations. Indeed, they would.

The kinds of attitudes generated by the revolutionary press became more complex as factionalism among activists and politicians in the National Assembly came to leave its mark on French politics more generally. The notion of an aristocratic, or Bourbon conspiracy was a particular favorite of revolutionary publishers and found much traction with the French people. A changing political culture would also cultivate the emergence of common attitudes and, far more distinctively than in the Revolution's early days, collective identities, whether as equal citizens in defense of their fundamental rights or a dedication to one particular revolutionary ideology or another, supported by provocateurs in the popular press or at one's local club. Another transformation that occurred was that drives such as a need for sociability and an interest in current affairs became more important in predisposing individuals toward revolutionary participation. As the Revolution consumed more and more of French culture, the spaces in which such things were likely to be available were increasingly the very same cafés, theaters, and taverns that were being repurposed as revolutionary hotbeds and political clubs.

CONVERGENCE

When we consider where the grand upsurges of the Revolution's first year came from, it is worth situating the affinities underlying French mobilization within the situations, frames, and spaces of convergence that served to activate them. As William Doyle astutely noted in his history of the Revolution's origins, there had existed a plethora of grievances, complaints, common sufferings, and "serious deficiencies" of grain affecting the nation for the two decades prior to the Revolution.[8] The key difference by 1789 was that these deficiencies had placed the state's capacity at breaking point, prompting a shake-up of the long-persisting structures around France, creating both a highly opportune situation for political discontent and a thoroughly exceptional frame in which the normative scope of political participation was profoundly widened.[9] Prior to this, the vast majority of the nation's denizens were hardly able to naturally gravitate toward the time-consuming process of revolution, being otherwise occupied and largely excluded from legitimate political articulation.

Insofar as there was any initiatory shift in situations and frames underlying the Revolution's early contention, it can be said to have occurred in response to the convocation of the Estates General. The notable shift in belief structures that accompanied this new democratic process gave rise to an exceptional situation and an aligned exceptional frame through which the underlying affinities of a great many of the French people for political participation were activated in favor of revolutionary participation during the 1789 rising. This was particularly true of the toiling classes and petite bourgeoisie, of whom Stone wrote that the "consciousness raising tasks of electing delegates... [and] drafting protests to the king" would lay the foundation for their role as "the brawn in most of these uprisings."[10] Contemporaneous with this shift toward exceptional convergence conditions was the emergence of an opportune situation. Indeed, for Stone, revolutionary mobilization during this early period was "only made possible by the breakdown of a government overtaxed by its grandiose international mission."[11] A great many other historians of the Revolution also consider the power of the central government to have effectively broken down in the period of 1788–1789, with a collapse in government competence across areas such as fiscal capacity, constitutional authority, social support, and, most crucially, the instruments of physical coercion.[12] Consequently, peasants, Parisians, and paupers were free to associate, assemble, and act in ways that had been previously restrained, and as this realization dawned, the framing of participation shifted to reflect reality, taking on similarly opportune characteristics.

Paramount frames and situations also played a key role in revolutionary mobilization, particularly during the periodic emergence of revolutionary *journées*. Announced by the ringing of the tocsin, a quintessential alarm bell of revolutionary activity, a journée signified a moment at which change became possible for the masses of Paris, and when one would be assured of a substantial enough crowd to impress the collective will in some regard or other. Lefebvre characterizes these journées such as those in July 1789 as "popular excesses... [and] irruptions of popular violence," in which "passionate feelings, the fear, the frenzy for fighting, the thirst for revenge" all became possible.[13]

Finally, we cannot forget the Revolution's spaces of convergence. Though enough has already been said in chapter 11 on the pivotal role of the Palais-Royal in Paris as an exceptional space, its exact character is worth qualifying. Part of the reason that the Palais played such a role in the early days of the Revolution is because of the intersection of two complementary spatial attributes of convergence: its unstructured, libertine, exceptional character and the physical security from regime forces it opportunely provided. Beyond the Palais, spaces such as the Pont Neuf bridge offered the unassuming character of a banal urban setting—nobody would suspect someone frequenting them—but they could nonetheless easily give shape to revolutionary mobilizations at any moment. Wineshops, cafés, and other public gathering places likewise proved crucial environs for the generation of revolutionary activity. These spaces were ubiquitous across France, particularly in Paris. By 1788, the capital played host to approximately twelve hundred cafés, one for every five hundred inhabitants (more than four times as many per person than any US city today).[14] Lynn Hunt identifies as central "the revolutionary ambiguity" of these spaces of convergence, which created the conditions for popular politicization from the bottom up. "Once men began to discuss public issues," she explained, "their social and economic interests became more apparent to them; freedom engendered questions about equality."[15] In a more sociological parlance, it was once people converged in these places that they would reflect upon their shared political interests and, potentially, engage in revolutionary agitation.

There were also more distinctly opportune spaces, which attracted consciously political types alongside sympathetic protorevolutionaries. In the Revolution's early days, these included assemblies to draw up cahiers and appoint deputies to the Estates General. After 1789 these were gradually supplanted by more organized popular committees in Paris and the provinces. Nonetheless, in the early days, the importance of these spaces for the convergence of the revolutionary masses was still vital. Indeed, during this period revolutionary politics necessitated assembly, discussion, and debate about questions of common importance. It was thus pivotal to claim and create secure and free spaces.[16]

For all of the efficacy of affinity-convergence mobilization during the 1789 revolution, it was nonetheless dependent on highly unwieldy forces. In a context where activist provocations were constant, forceful revolutionary mobilizations that aligned with activists' agendas were a comparative rarity. Moreover, the dividing line between a riot and a revolutionary mobilization was sometimes exceedingly thin during this early period. Sometimes—as in July and October—the originating sentiments of popular mobilization could be relatively divorced from its consequence.[17] At other junctures the popular mood could be far more radical than that of contemporary political activists. Activists, however, are quick learners, and accordingly their efforts to build an *organized* movement out of the sporadic revolutionary activities that had so far graced the French nation showed both an adaptation to the dynamics of spontaneous mobilization and a concerted effort to render it more dependable.

Organizing the Masses

Though the events of 1789 had seen France's revolutionaries and their allies in the National Assembly prove victorious over royal authority, they were far from in control of the revolutionary process. Rather, it was predominantly the more ordinary so-called *menu people* of Paris and the provinces who directed their own protest activity, as well as various assembly factions who would temporarily fasten their fortunes to these mobilizations.[18] For the bourgeois assemblymen who the revolution of 1789 had benefited, the novel associations of the *menu peuple*—the poorer, unestablished, ordinary constituents of French society—proved an unwieldy phenomenon. Having associated autonomously under their own auspices (with often different or less specific goals from the beneficiaries of their actions), they had proved useful in the revolts of July and October of that year but had been excluded from much of the beneficial concessions granted as a consequence. The agendas of the revolution's victors and its protagonists on the ground were thus in danger of diverging.

A means of remedying this division availed itself in the form of the establishment of political clubs and societies, as well as a reconstitution of two of the elements that had previously been so helpful in rousing Parisians to action in 1789: revolutionary publishing and local spaces of association. These entities, though means of association for the *menu peuple*, were usually under the auspices (and ownership) of members of France's bourgeoisie, many of whom were aligned with the more radical wings of the National Assembly and were keen to consolidate and further their revolutionary gains. Accordingly, though initially lacking a sophisticated mobilizing apparatus, the new political forces in France were able to consciously sculpt the conditions in which those with revolutionary affinities might converge and thereby have some influence on how the masses might be mobilized.

AN ACTIVIST PRESS

The first move to direct the masses toward some kind of ideological end was the rapid and dramatic reorganization of the revolutionary press into more sophisticated media operations. This began with the transformation of Parisian news from disorganized flurries of pamphlets into an organized, nationwide newspaper system, through which editors proclaimed a variety of revolutionary opinions in line with their allies in the Assembly. Meanwhile, in provincial France, remaining advertising pamphlets, or *affiches*, swiftly transformed into full newspaper endeavors that connected the political and social upheavals in the French capital to provincial citizens in previously impossible ways. As Jeremy Popkin wrote in his history of the French revolutionary press, "By the end of the year 1789... the entire French press system had been altered almost beyond recognition."[19] With its increasing professionalization, the news agenda was swiftly reorganized along the lines of the emergent factions of the Assembly. The revolutionary press became skilled at equating Assembly members' positions with the "public will." "Why debate when everyone is in agreement?" the then incredibly popular *Courrier de Provence* once asked its readership.[20] "Did not the common good clearly manifest itself? The first [member of the Assembly] to display a new tribute to the public interest did no more than express what the others already felt: there was no need for debate or fine speech to have adopted what had already been decided by the majority and commanded by the overwhelming authority of the nation's mandates."[21]

This language of "the sovereign people" and a general will was routinely used to either argue for the legitimacy of a given perspective or even directly call people to action, in both cases by appealing to a collective national identity.[22]

Although there initially existed a plurality of outlets available to the French public, those under the influence of radical factions in the Assembly would eventually dwarf all others, making it exceedingly difficult to get any news at all, except from a revolutionary. By contrast, the limited set of papers and pamphlets aligned to conservative causes struggled to compete with the more sensational and numerous revolutionary communiqués. One very prominent paper, *L'Ami du Peuple*, had, in December 1790, encouraged direct action from its readership without reservation, ordering them to: "Form yourselves into an armed body, present yourselves at the National Assembly and demand that you immediately be given some means of subsistence from the national wealth."[23] Such lines of communication provided the more radical elements of the Revolution's leaders with a means of shaping, however vaguely, the dispositional affinities (identities, attitudes, and perceptions of injustice) held by the ordinary men and women who carried out the revolutionary insurrections that would determine their fate.

THE CLUB MOVEMENT

At the same time as the revolutionary press was becoming more organized in its character, an enormous number of popular clubs and societies spread rapidly across France over the course of 1790 and 1791. Some of these had sprung up in the early days of the Revolution, being converted from popular cafés, salons, and even Masonic lodges.[24] The rollout of clubs across the country allowed the radical movement to emulate spaces that had attracted budding revolutionaries in 1789 while circumventing restrictions on outdoor public gatherings and on local district meetings (put in place by their conservatively minded foes in the Assembly). Unlike the public spaces they had overtaken, these new societies were concerted efforts at political coordination and influence. They proved a compelling alternative to the popular committees and assemblies (which the Assembly had begun to crack down on), while also retaining the popular element found in cafés, wineshops, and public spaces.[25]

The clubs were not initially formally coordinated by a single cause or network. As Alan Forrest noted in his inquiry on this topic, "one of the most salient features of the club movement, indeed, was its diversity: they did not all speak with the same voice, nor did they look consistently to Paris for leadership."[26] Similarly, though ideology was often a reason people chose to visit clubs, they also did so for similar reasons as one might visit a café. This included searching for "sociability, a place to meet friends and kindred spirits. In the early months, indeed, they were often open and welcoming to newcomers, a broad church where men of differing views could mingle and debate." Although later in the Revolution club membership would become more strictly delineated and hierarchical, initially citizens would often be members of multiple clubs and popular societies at the same time. To some extent, then, club membership was driven by two particular categories of affinity: ideological attitudes and personal drives. Of the clubs that would come to prominence in the Revolution, two in particular sought to build an organized movement out of the mobilized masses of France: the *Cordeliers* and *Jacobins*.

It was in the wake of a spate of grassroots mobilizations of workers and the unwaged in the city of Paris that the men of the Cordeliers first sought to bring urban protesters under their auspices by offering them space to meet and associate. Urban tradesmen, workers, craftsmen, and the unemployed were subject to concerted recruitment and radicalization attempts, beginning with offers of material assistance (such as meeting places) in which these groups could assemble, as well as sympathetic coverage in club-controlled presses.[27] Eventually, however, these efforts became part of a move to integrate the masses more concretely into club infrastructures, where they could be instructed and educated in the ways of a revolutionary faction's ideological persuasion, then mobilized accordingly. As the historian Timothy Tackett wrote in his landmark study on revolutionary politics in 1791, "many of the Parisian clubs had been created specifically to attract those 'passive citizens' whom the National Assembly had excluded from voting and office holding by means of property qualifications."[28]

The Jacobins were even more successful than the Cordeliers in supplanting the Revolution's spaces of convergence with ones under their own organizational control. The club expanded from only twenty-three chapters in 1790 to a remarkable nine hundred and twenty-one chapters throughout France by July 1791. The Jacobins adopted a parliamentary structure, providing spaces for structured political engagement with ideological trajectories offered up by its masters in the Assembly and their allies in the presses. This structure proved effective and gave rise to what has been termed the Jacobins' "systematic indoctrination of the *sans-culottes*."[29] Alongside these clubs, various "fraternal societies" were established, intended to expand this model to even broader sections of the French population, such as women and the unwaged.

The clubs and societies of revolutionary France constituted a move from organically occurring contexts of convergence, coupled with the coincidental affinities of a diverse and free-associating *menu peuple*, to the emergence of deliberate manufacturing of the conditions of contention by competing elites. Revolutionary publishers would raise support for the agendas of well-defined and comprehensible revolutionary factions, corresponding with aligned elements in the Assembly. While, in the Revolution's early days, radical publications, popular debates, and discussions in the street helped galvanize participation among people with affinity for revolutionary action, affinities after 1789 were cultivated by a more explicitly structured revolutionary public sphere, subordinated to organized factions. Likewise, factional control over the Revolution's core spaces and avenues of association in which participants would converge allowed a corresponding control over the outcome of this mass participation, effectively availing the bourgeois revolutionary "leaders" with the capacity to loosely shape and even potentially manufacture situations to their advantage.

What emerged in France during the period of 1790–1791 was a shift from largely spontaneous mobilization to quasi-spontaneous mobilization, sculpted and conditioned by activists in the popular press and the rising stars of the country's political clubs and societies. This manifested in a shift from the unpredictable gatherings of 1789 to a form of mobilization "in direct response to the call of leaders."[30] Once these crowds began to manifest, however, they still attracted a great many more spontaneous participants beyond those who were affiliated to distinct revolutionary causes. These were thus neither the more autonomously driven instances of the Revolution's early days, nor fully organized. Instead, what ensued was a form of hybrid mobilization in which frames, grievances, attitudes, and identities were instilled in the public by activists in the popular press, and mobilizations themselves often began in meetings of the political clubs and assemblies. When these marches hit the streets, they were received by a public that had been psychologically prepared to participate, often under circumstances handpicked by their beneficiaries.

It was amid this period of the dramatic expansion of political organizing structures in the capital that there began to emerge a variety of methods by which mobilization could be somewhat more predictably elicited from the revolutionary masses. For those who were not already strongly attached to the patriotic cause, Paris's activists, pamphleteers, and provocateurs would attempt to instill the dispositional affinities upon which their successes in 1789 had hinged. A mass of leaflets, pamphlets, and papers, accompanied by staunch ideological sermons in Parisian clubs and sectional assemblies, provided opportunities to radicalize many of the common people of Paris who had made their way into these newly opened political spaces. While the Jacobins adopted the strategy of opening clubs across the nation, the Cordeliers sought to consolidate power in Paris and, in the spring of 1791, established a Central Committee around which the smaller political clubs and more diverse fraternal societies of Paris could be coordinated. These had become serious organs of influence.[31] A consequence of increasing revolutionary control over these new spaces of convergence was that the creation of the kind of massive insurrectionary journée that had previously only been possible in the context of an outraged and precarious populace became far more readily available.

THE TRIUMPH OF ORGANIZATION

By 1792 organized mobilization would take its place as the vital organ of revolutionary advancement. By this point in the Revolution, France was facing staunch foreign opposition, beset by a harsh famine, and had elected a new Legislative Assembly. On April 20 a declaration of war against Austria launched France into a renewed period of crisis.[32] While the war had initially inspired great popular enthusiasm, a series of mutinies and defeats on the battlefield quickly shattered the nation's confidence.[33] By May it was believed that Louis XVI, a constitutional monarchist revolutionary faction called the *Feuillants*, and a coalition of military generals were conspiring to betray the French people.[34] By May things had worsened further. Nicolas Ruault (the bookseller mentioned in chapter 11) wrote to his brother on the twenty-fourth of the month, decrying that it was widely believed "that the king is betraying us, that the generals are betraying us [and] that we must trust nobody.... Paris will be taken in six weeks by the Austrians," supported by a secret "Austrian Committee" within the French government.[35] The month of June was punctuated by popular disturbance,[36] most notably the storming of the king's Tuileries Palace on the twentieth by thousands of self-proclaimed sans-culottes: now a term of political identification loosely associated with the type of revolutionary, particularly prevalent in Paris, drawn from the working and middle classes who identified with the Jacobin persuasion, at this point more generally driven by passionate speeches and publications more than by clearly given orders.[37]

By July Prussia had entered the war against France, and matters had reached a crisis point. A state of *patrie en danger* (fatherland in danger) was declared: all of the nation's governmental bodies would sit permanently until it was resolved and were urged to recruit volunteers for the coming war.[38] This effectively made permanent a number of spaces of convergence that brought so many of the early revolutionaries together, particularly those in Paris. Accordingly, one of the new groups attracted to these spaces was the growing concentration of *fédérés* in the capital. The fédérés had been (since 1790) a collection of fervent patriots from the French provinces who would attend the yearly *Fête de la Fédération* celebrations (Bastille Day) in the nation's capital and other major cities. In 1792, however, the pressing demands of the war led to the decision to militarize the *fête*, inviting all good patriots to travel to Paris first, for the celebrations, second for military training, and ultimately for deployment for the coming war effort.

In their hometowns, many of the fédérés might not have met the qualification for participation in local political institutions (likely for the same reasons that it was so feasible for them to travel to the capital on such a patriotic whim). This would swiftly change, as their arrival was soon followed by a decree from numerous Parisian sectional assemblies that they would accept all citizens, rather than just those with voting rights. Furthermore, the fédérés quickly became involved with Parisian political clubs, most notably that of the Jacobins, which, as the most prominent club in France, was familiar to the fédérés from their own towns and villages. Accordingly, attendance at the clubs and sections of Paris skyrocketed, and by July 25 Paris's sectional assemblies were also sitting continuously.[39] Parisian popular politics was now open to all: fédérés from all over France, members of political clubs, and men and women at sectional assemblies. Many of these groups were by now well networked with one another, often being coordinated into central committees that gave shape to their activities.

The first serious test of revolutionaries' organized mobilization strategies came with the events that would oust Louis XVI from not only his throne, but the realm of the living. With the vast bulk of Parisian clubs, popular societies, and sections pushing fervently antimonarchical propaganda to their members, there was a rapidly rising tide of antimonarchism (particularly among the fédérés). The sections, in concert with their activist allies in the Legislative Assembly, demanded that Louis XVI be immediately deposed. By the next day, August 10, 1792, the chimes of the tocsin would serve as a call to arms for all of the veritable mélange of sans-culottes, ordinary citizens, National Guardsmen, and fédérés from across France who had by now become familiarized with the symbols, signs, and ideologies of radical revolutionary politics.[40]

Now in possession of an organizational apparatus through which fully fledged mobilizations could be directed, revolutionary activists were no longer dependent on the more spontaneous outpouring of grassroots popular sentiment to effect their desired political outcomes. The combined masses that formed, obeying Jacobin leaders, marched through the capital. Seizing the Hôtel de Ville, they marched on the Tuileries Palace to impose that which the Assembly had not granted. As Doyle concluded, Louis XVI's "authority fell with his palace,"[41] and the next year would begin with the trial and decapitation of the now "Citizen Louis Capet." Events would swiftly progress further, culminating in the ascendance of the Jacobin movement in a "coup d'état against the national representatives."[42]

Until 1792 the bulk of popular mobilizations retained a disordered, unmanaged quality, emerging organically from gatherings in spaces of convergence often outside of the control of regime forces and open to a new form of politics: sometimes they would favor the Jacobins, sometimes the more moderate Cordeliers club, and other times a different faction altogether. This time, however, the Jacobins were unwilling to cede the control they had just gained, electing to take the popular movement firmly under their own direction.[43] Soon enough, the Jacobins began to further consolidate the formerly relatively open spaces of the clubs under their own control, creating a dense network of political clubs, newspapers, and even street corners tightly structured around their factional cause.[44]

By April 1793 the Jacobins were ready. Jacobin leaders issued a public invitation to the Parisian sections to depose or arrest "rogue" deputies of the French legislature belonging to competing revolutionary factions. Of course, the leadership of Paris's sections were already largely in ideological lockstep with the Jacobins, functioning as an organ for popular mobilization. A total of thirty-five of the forty-eight sections mobilized for the day, coordinating with the Paris Commune, a body within which the Jacobins had also consolidated considerable power. All these forces combined to form a "Central Revolutionary Committee" that would formally direct operations between May 29 and June 2, 1793, during which the next major mobilization in the capital was intended to be executed. This committee was possessed of both funds and manpower, even offering monetary reimbursement to some twenty thousand people drafted for the day.[45] Having already captured the revolutionary movement, the insurrection of May to June 1793 would hand radical activists an even greater prize: the revolutionary state. This was far from the end of the Revolution, but it marked the moment after which the Revolution's spontaneous character would be progressively extinguished. August saw the institution of the *levée en masse*, a forced conscription of the male French population into service of the state, and September marked the start of the Revolution's Reign of Terror. The popular movement was over, and France would begin its journey from democracy to empire.

Conclusion

Conclusions are, by necessity, exercises in addressing two different kinds of reader. The first will arrive at a book's conclusion having already read the bulk of its content. Another will have moved far more rapidly to the conclusion—perhaps prior to or even instead of attending to the majority of the chapters—in order to swiftly ascertain what they can learn from the book as a whole. Each approach has its merits, and I have written this conclusion with both sets of reader in mind. So first, let us briefly recap what the last twelve chapters have told us.

Affinity-convergence theory (ACT) is an effort to plug a small but significant gap in what we know about mobilization. It seeks to detail the dynamic through which unaffiliated protesters, those who are not associated with movement organizations or activist networks, come to participate in contentious politics en masse without reliance on these structures, a phenomenon known as spontaneous mass mobilization. Building and detailing this theory was the task pursued in part I. The first task in building ACT was to work out what we already knew about mobilization and how it helps us to understand the phenomenon of spontaneous participation (chapter 1). Drawing on these considerable contributions and placing them in dialogue with the empirical cases discussed in this book, the second chapter detailed how spontaneous mass participation relied not on concrete ties to organizations or activist networks (sometimes termed "structural availability"), but on individual affinity to the movement: the matrix of personal predispositions that encourage someone to seek out or encounter opportunities to participate. On its own, affinity functions as only a very weak mobilizing force; after all, even among those highly predisposed to participate in a movement, there will be all manner of *other* competing things to which they are also predisposed. For people's affinity to a movement to produce mobilization en masse requires conditions that cause movement participation to become far more compelling than it might usually be. I term these, "conditions of convergence": the catalyst in the process of spontaneous mass mobilization.

At its most basic level, ACT posits that where there exists a substantial population with affinity to a movement *and* conditions of convergence that catalyze their participation, spontaneous mass mobilization results. This is expressed in shorthand as:

$$\text{Affinity} \xrightarrow{\text{convergence}} \text{Participation}$$

But what constitutes affinity to a movement, and how are conditions of convergence achieved? Drawing on the literature on mobilization and the research underpinning this book, chapter 2 fleshed out these concepts in greater detail. Affinity to a movement can be broken into a wider number of individual factors, or affinities. Some of these relate to an individual's social position, including their activity patterns, social status, resources, and matrix of obligations. By contrast, others relate to psychological factors such as their disposition toward the movement—spanning their identity, political attitudes, and perceptions of injustice—or personal drives—the interests and needs to which a mobilization in some way caters. Convergence, meanwhile, can be differentiated depending on the mechanism through which participation was being catalyzed: by making it more advantageous (opportune conditions), by making it more available (exceptional conditions), or by making it more important (paramount conditions). Sometimes convergence occurred within a certain structural context (situations), a certain environment (spaces), or at the level of reality construction (frames).

Affinity-convergence theory offers some useful benefits over existing approaches to mass mobilization. Research on mobilization in the political process tradition is certainly highly useful in relation to organized groups and movement networks, but it tells us considerably less about participants who are not integrated into organizations.[1] Similarly, work on social movement networks and communities has been extremely helpful in enriching our understanding of mobilization, but it stops short of providing a complete explanation of participation: many people who join mass protests do not appear to be integrated into or recruited via movement networks.[2] Yet established approaches to the study of spontaneity also have their drawbacks. Classical theories of collective behavior rightly paid attention to participant psychology and emergent social conditions, but they struggled to explain how these intersected at the individual level. The consequence was an approach often dismissive or even pathologizing when it came to ordinary people's decisions to partake in contention.

These traits made it very difficult to extend collective behavior theories from answering "why" questions to addressing more intricate "how" questions. Conversely, rational choice theories have offered very promising models of individual-level participation decisions in spontaneous protests (such as the 1989 German Revolution), but sometimes struggle to capture nonagentic qualities that involve neither choice nor rationality. Meanwhile, spontaneist approaches to collective action offered an inspiring focus on the capacity of social and institutional disruption to trigger mass protest (and vice versa) but left little space for the concerted work of movement organizations and networks in both laying the groundwork for and subsequently capitalizing upon spontaneity.

ACT explains spontaneous mass mobilization by fusing what we already know about organized, networked, and spontaneous mobilization with recent advances in social psychology and in-depth empirical research. In doing so, the theory draws together participant psychology and social circumstances (affinity) with large-scale social shifts (convergence), while acknowledging the agency of activists, organizers, and movement networks, as well as the interplay between spontaneity and organization. This allows us to analyze not only purely spontaneous instances of mobilization but also more mixed cases, such as circumstances in which organization, spontaneity, and networked protest intersect or where spontaneous mobilization occurs over a longer period of time.

Each of the book's four further parts demonstrated ACT in practice through the lens of empirical cases: the 2011 Egyptian Revolution, the Occupy Wall Street movement, the 2020 Black Lives Uprising, and the 1789 French Revolution. Each of these cases tells us complementary things about how affinity-convergence mobilization plays out and how the dynamics of spontaneous mass mobilization interact with the activities of organizers, activists, opponents, and the state.

Part II introduced the book's first empirical case, the Egyptian Revolution. Serving as our empirical introduction to the practical operation of affinity-convergence mobilization, the Egyptian case showed how, despite lacking an organized revolutionary movement prior to the 2011 Arab Spring, a single successfully organized protest on January 25 established the conditions for far larger-scale spontaneous revolutionary mobilization. A paramount frame (prompted by a revolution in nearby Tunisia) had already been hanging over the country, but the spectacle of this first protest and the incredibly violent police response, combined with the subsequent shutting down of internet and telecommunications networks, laid the foundations for spontaneous mobilization on a far greater scale by creating an exceptional situation moments prior to a planned protest on

January 28. In response, Egyptians poured forth from their homes and into the streets, showing up in their hundreds of thousands on January 28, vanquishing the nation's police forces, and occupying Tahrir Square, which became the revolution's central hub. Over the course of the next fifteen days, revolutionaries rebuffed further repression attempts with novel surges in mobilization and maintained an enormous occupation in the center of the capital that persisted until the fall of the regime.

Over the course of the revolutionary period, Egyptians were subject to the full suite of convergence conditions discussed in this book (opportune, exceptional, and paramount situations, frames, and spaces), and acted on the basis of a wide spectrum of affinities, with people's patterns of activity, social status, and dispositions playing a particularly starring role in the early days, after which drives, obligations, and resources also came to the fore. But such a situation was not to last. Once President Mubarak was overthrown, the suite of convergence conditions that buoyed revolutionary mobilization proved impossible to maintain or to reliably restage, and the underlying affinities that had drawn people to participate were no longer commonplace. This period of the revolution shows us how fragile affinity-convergence mobilization can be, vulnerable to severe interruptions whenever convergence conditions fall away or when people's social and psychological affinities undergo shifts.

The Egyptian case shows us how suddenly affinity-convergence mobilization can massively amplify participation in contentious politics in circumstances where activists lack organizational force or large-scale networks of affiliates. This can cause small-scale movements to suddenly balloon, taking activists by surprise in a way that can sometimes be difficult to capitalize on. It should be noted that this case shows an example of convergence at its most extreme. No other case exhibited the totality of convergence conditions (though France in 1789 came close), and it is therefore no surprise that Egyptian revolutionary mobilizations featured perhaps the largest-scale single-day protests of all the cases in this book.

Not all instances of affinity-convergence mobilization are as dramatic and full-throated as the Egyptian case. Part III, covering the fall 2011 Occupy Wall Street protests in New York City, showed how affinity-convergence mobilization can occur without the truly extreme situational dynamics that characterize more dramatic revolutionary processes or mass uprisings. Rather, in the context of Occupy Wall Street, it was the dynamics of spaces and frames that served as the convergence conditions propelling popular participation. After an attempted occupation of Wall Street on September 17, participants were forced instead to begin their occupation in a small park just steps away from the site of the World

Trade Center bombings. Activists successfully created an exceptional and opportune space, in which participation could take an enormous array of forms under the protection of a confusing legal arrangement that seemed to repel law enforcement repression. Steadily, an occupation grew, with gradually increasing crowds of ordinary people finding themselves drawn to the park on the basis of a wide array of social affinities and drives. Following confrontations with law enforcement, high-profile mass arrests, and increasing popular attention in the news media, the occupation also benefited from a powerful paramount frame, presenting the movement as a drastic showdown between the "99 percent" of ordinary people in society and the global "1 percent" who had benefited from the misery induced by the financial crisis. This elicited a renewed flood of participation among ordinary people whose dispositions resonated with this attractive framing now proliferating in the public sphere.

Rather than manifesting as a high-stakes showdown with power holders (as in Egypt or France), Occupy Wall Street was a case of longitudinal mass mobilization, never reaching the short-lived heights of Egyptian revolutionary protests, but instead consistently drawing in thousands of people every day while appealing to a broader spectrum of affinities than any other movement in this book. In stark contrast to Egypt, the case of Occupy involved no structural convergence conditions to speak of, only a paramount frame and an opportune and exceptional space: Zuccotti Park. Consequently, once Occupiers were finally evicted from the park in November 2011, the movement struggled to persist over the next half year as its paramount framing waned, eventually fizzling out after an abortive attempt to organize a general strike on May Day 2012.

While the case of Egypt draws particular attention to the power of convergence, the case of Occupy Wall Street serves as a highly useful study of affinity. Participation in Occupy leveraged an enormous range of affinities, not only drawing on every subcategory of affinity discussed in this book but also exhibiting exceptional diversity within each. Occupiers across the social spectrum (status) came seeking food and shelter (obligations), with supplies and support (resources), or just passing through (patterns of activity). Some sought to protest the financial crisis (injustice), to advance a particular vision of social change (attitudes), or just to show their solidarity with the 99 percent (identity). Others had less-political aspirations, seeking to join the occupation's projects and experiments (interests) or to engage in imaginative, creative, expressive activities (needs). Moreover, the elongated format of mass mobilization (occurring over a stretch of months, rather than a small set of key days) made it possible to carefully trace individual-level mobilization processes. This shed light on how various affinities connected with participation once convergence conditions were in place, making it possible to observe some potential tendencies in the relationship between affinity and convergence.

Part IV examined perhaps the most emblematically spontaneous of all the cases in this book, the 2020 Black Lives Uprising. This is despite the fact that, unlike any other case in the book, there was no shortage of well-known, well-resourced, and well-networked movement organizations concerned with precisely the matters protesters were engaging with: racial justice, police brutality, and latterly, government authoritarianism. Caught by surprise amid a deadly pandemic and likely concerned about the epidemiological consequences of mobilization, these groups were relegated to the sidelines of the uprising's peak in late May and early June. What arose in their place was a torrent of popular mobilization in cities across the United States, fueled by the exceptional situation created by the coronavirus pandemic and an array of opportune and paramount conditions created by harsh police repression, victorious popular reciprocation, and seized urban space. By the time established organizers were fully engaged with the protests, a radically different movement had already been built.

The Black Lives Uprising is a useful demonstration of how affinity-convergence theory helps us understand cases at the height of the present information age, in which any remaining divides between our digital and physical lives are increasingly subsiding. Even amid advancing technology and an increasingly mediated self, the underpinnings of spontaneity appear to be highly consistent. Opportune, exceptional, and paramount situations, frames, and, for a period, spaces all played an important role in catalyzing participation in the uprising, which drew on a dispositional triad constituting a strong sense of injustice, attitudinal alignment around policing reform, and shared antiracist and antifascist identifications. For the many young people whose work lives had been disrupted by the pandemic (status), peaceful and violent protests in their localities (patterns of activity) proved highly attractive avenues to act on their political dispositions and experience catharsis and social stimulation (needs). The pull was especially strong for those with the equipment and skills to help (resources) and the absence of competing obligations, such as shielding from the COVID-19 pandemic and attending in-person work. In the absence of organized leadership, participants in the uprising developed their own distributed patterns of coordination, leveraging information and communications technologies while pursuing trajectories of decentralized movement organization that drew explicitly on notions of affinity and developing sensitivities to the dynamics of popular spontaneity that continue to shape their activities.

Part V turned to the French Revolution, testing the utility of affinity-convergence theory in a wholly different context to the twenty-first century cases that make up the bulk of this book, showing the theory's explanatory power beyond the context of digitally connected modern societies. Despite the considerable contextual differences between France and the other cases in this book, the concepts of affinity and convergence proved well suited to explaining the puzzle of revolutionary spontaneity and proved effective in bridging early spontaneity in 1789 with the subsequent development of revolutionary organization. Aided by these concepts, this part of the book showed how a truly exceptional, highly opportune, once-in-a-lifetime situation generated by the convocation of the Estates General was able to activate long-standing affinities present in much of the French population, drawing those possessed of a certain social status into participation in a variety of popular assemblies and contentious mobilizations that allowed them to act on their dispositions. As these activities generated persistent instability, a wide array of exceptional spaces arose in cafés, wineshops, markets, busy bridges, and Paris's Palais-Royal, further broadening revolutionary participation beyond those officially permitted to participate in electoral activities. With mobilization burbling, conflicts between revolutionaries and their (real or imagined) enemies would often be subject to paramount framing that brought forth new surges of mass participation, whether spread by rumor and the popular press or suddenly announced by the ringing of the tocsin in cities such as Paris. Equipped with affinity-convergence theory, we can see how the Revolution's spontaneous element can be understood as ordinary people responding to extraordinary circumstances in accordance with the confines of their social circumstances and the content of their dispositions and drives. In doing so, they forced a radical reordering of their society in a way that cannot readily be dismissed as irrational or chaotic.

The case of the French Revolution not only reenforces the generalizability of ACT but also shows how savvy organizers can parlay spontaneity into more dependable forms of mobilization. Over the course of 1789, French revolutionary activists moved from the irregular beneficiaries of spontaneous protest to its active cultivators. Soon after they set about crystallizing these spontaneous pathways into more conventional mobilizing structures, building formal movement networks capable of influencing their affiliates and organizational structures to give them the direction and resources necessary for mobilization. As the Revolution went on, organizers asserted control over the outlets that framed public perceptions of reality, the spaces of convergence from which mobilizations emanated, and eventually the structure of French society itself. In doing so, they gained not only organizational control over the masses but also tremendous repressive power, eventually turning the Revolution against itself.

Taken together, the four cases in this book show that spontaneous mobilization is a sophisticated phenomenon that can occur across an incredible diversity of sociological contexts. The concepts of affinity and convergence—drawn together in affinity-convergence theory—help us to understand how spontaneous mobilization occurs and to better describe and comprehend the reasons why. The elements that make up affinity and convergence allow us to account for different forms of this process and how they relate to mobilization's social context. In revolutionary Egypt, for example, a situation taking on exceptional, then opportune, then paramount attributes made protest first more available to ordinary Egyptians, then more advantageous, and finally, more important. With ordinary life totally disrupted and repressive forces on the back foot, people ditched their daily routines and flocked to city centers to defend their country against the Mubarak regime's threatening efforts to regain control, grounded in a shared national identity and a hatred of the ruling party. Eight months later, in downtown New York, an exceptional and opportune space created by the occupation in Zuccotti Park drew in a broad spectrum of participants seeking to fulfill their everyday obligations and psychological drives, precisely because there was so little risk associated with participating and such an easy way to do so.

Besides using the concepts contained within ACT to swiftly synopsize instances of spontaneous protest, we can draw on the theory's framework to develop elementary hypotheses for the investigation of spontaneity in other contentious political cases, even where it does not necessarily constitute the most prominent element of protest. One promising prospective case study is participation in the US anti-Trump resistance, where it has already been established that the structural availability hypothesis has sometimes fallen short, such as in the case of mass marches like the 2017 Women's March.[3] By paying attention to the role of convergence conditions and widely held affinities, we can more readily approach the puzzle of unaffiliated participations in the resistance's many mass marches and reactive mobilizations against the Trump administration. ACT might also yield explanatory power in understanding the success of initially small groups in attracting mass participation well beyond their own networks. One promising case study would be Extinction Rebellion UK's April 2019 protests, which successfully elicited a flood of popular participation by occupying prominent urban spaces in the capital and reconfiguring them in a highly appealing, open-ended fashion while framing mobilization as a response to a "climate emergency" needing attention. Such a case does not look all that different, at first glance, from the exceptional spaces and paramount frames that helped propel participation in Occupy Wall Street.

Comparative Lessons

While the core contribution of this book is a novel, synthetic theory of spontaneous mass mobilization, considering its cases in comparative perspective also yields further knowledge about the factors influencing such a process, as well as its relation to social movement activity. In this section, I detail some of these further comparative lessons touching on the relationship between organization and spontaneity, the role played by disruptive tactics, the impact of state opponents in encouraging and discouraging mobilization, and a variety of emergent patterns in the operation of affinity-convergence mobilization.

ORGANIZATION AND SPONTANEITY: REDUX

Even though this is a book about spontaneous mass mobilization, I have sought to illustrate that investigating this phenomenon is not only compatible with but also highly complementary to the study of movement organizations and networks. Whether it is spontaneous mass protest or the skills and resources of organizers that we judge to be most crucial in achieving a given instance of popular protest, when we turn to the empirical facts of a case, we tend to see both. There is always, as William Gamson and Emilie Schmeidler once astutely observed, a "subtle interplay between spontaneity and organization" in the kinds of acts of mass defiance or protest that characterize much of contentious politics.[4] Not only do the longer-running activities of submerged activist networks and social movement communities often play a key role in shaping the kinds of grievances, demands, and movement cultures to which those with affinity for a cause are drawn, but sometimes activists play a more direct role in cultivating convergence conditions. One of the most apparent means by which activists actively cultivated the conditions of spontaneous mobilization was through framing. In the case of Occupy, framing strategies successfully attracted more participants to the occupation and its activities. This took forms such as the proposition of a US Day of Rage (drawing on parallels with the Egyptian Revolution) and the widespread proclamation of the movement's claim to represent a "99 percent" identity. In the Egyptian case, the activists who proposed the January 25 protests took pains to frame its demands in a way that would help bring ordinary Egyptians out onto the streets, and these frames retained force even once their activities were superseded by spontaneous mass protest. A similar phenomenon could be seen in the French Revolution through the popular press outlets of revolutionary activists.

Not only do activists, organizers, and movement organizations sometimes play important roles in triggering convergence conditions and cultivating affinities, but instances of spontaneous mass mobilization can play a highly important role in creating the next generation of movement organization. As scholars such as Catherine Corrigall-Brown have shown, even brief periods of mobilization can be the beginning of sophisticated and impactful trajectories of participation in contentious politics.[5] This was precisely the kind of phenomenon seen in the case of Occupy Wall Street, the Black Lives Uprising, and even the French Revolution, something sometimes termed a "movement moment" by activists. Many of those who were drawn to these movements through the dynamics of affinity-convergence mobilization went on to become persistent participants and sometimes even leaders in longer-running cycles of contention. In Egypt, by contrast, the combination of dampened communications infrastructures and an exceedingly short-run mobilization window prohibited the forging of relationships on a scale seen in these other cases.

THE VALUE OF DISRUPTION

Every single one of the movements in this book involved clashes with police, illegal tactics, and disruptive methods that had the effect of galvanizing further mobilization. The movements in this book proved so disruptive that all four of them were either accused of terrorism or designated national security threats by power holders in their respective countries. All of these movements seized something from the state in some way: taking space, making gains, and creating conditions that allowed more to join in, furnishing more fertile circumstances for mobilization.[6] In contexts such as the Egyptian and French revolutions, as well as the Black Lives Uprising, disruption took the form of victorious battles with oppressive forces and movement opponents and acts of strategic arson or sabotage. In the case of Occupy Wall Street, other disruptive nonviolent activities, such as the blockading of the Brooklyn Bridge, had a similar function. In the case of Occupy, Egypt, and the 2020 uprising, all three movements seized spaces from power holders, creating occupations that then served to attract participants to the movement.

Another related lesson from the cases in this book is that even if movements were *generally* highly peaceful or nondisruptive in character, select instances of disruptive tactics often proved highly useful in triggering high-tenor contests with governing powers. These often attracted further defensive mobilization by those with affinity to the cause (paramount conditions) or otherwise demonstrated the efficacy of the movement and thereby inspired others to join in (opportune conditions). This is consistent with recent research on riots and disruptive protest that shows violent protest and other unruly radical flank actions can (sometimes) increase movement participation by polarizing issues, demonstrating efficacy, and eliciting regime missteps that increase sympathy with protesters.[7] At least insofar as these four cases are concerned, movement success arose amid the pursuit of a diversity of tactics over adherence to nonviolent discipline.

THE ROLE OF STATE OPPONENTS, MISSTEPS, AND REPRESSION

Another pattern that emerged across the four cases explored in this book was the important role of state forces and political opponents in shaping convergence conditions. In all four cases major movement opponents were, to a greater or lesser degree, also in control of state power. From the Egyptian government's internet shutdown to the NYPD's mass arrests, and from the Ancien Régime's attack on the Third Estate to the Trump administration's deployment of federal paramilitaries, attempts at regime oppression or social control often produced exceptional or paramount conditions that actively spurred further mobilization. In some contexts massive structural alterations to the fabric of social life had the effect of creating exceptional situations more propitious for spontaneous mobilization, as seen in Egypt's internet shutdown. At other times, repression produced moral shocks, which helped establish paramount frames that galvanized further participation.[8]

This pattern bears resemblance to what the late Gene Sharp called "political jiu-jitsu," and others have called repressive "backfire."[9] These are circumstances where botched repression attempts serve to encourage mobilization and cultivate support, resulting in the opposite of state forces' intended effect. Such instances also have a number of effects beyond the immediate context of a mobilization, such as "creating dissent and conflicts among the opponent's supporters, increasing external support... [for the movement] and decreasing external support for the opponent."[10]

However, the repressive activities of state opponents do not always encourage further mobilization. Rather, regime activity can also serve to undo convergence conditions, as seen by the activities of Egypt's military council in the postrevolutionary period and the coordinated evictions of occupied spaces carried under the auspices of the US Department of Homeland Security in 2011. These circumstances usually involved constellations of "hard" (use of force) and "soft" (cultural, social, legalistic, and bureaucratic) forms of repression employed in tandem, a set of techniques well established to have a demobilizing effect.[11]

PATTERNS IN AFFINITY-CONVERGENCE MOBILIZATION

There were also certain patterns emerging across the four cases that related specifically to processes of affinity-convergence mobilization. Of these, two particular patterns are worth reflecting on: the role of spaces of convergence and their relation to the temporality of protest, and the finer-grain interactions of affinity and convergence.

The Efficacy of Spaces

While spaces of convergence played an important role in many of the movements in this book, figuring in some way in every single case, the kind of mass mobilization they catalyzed when present in isolation was considerably slower paced than other conditions of convergence. Spaces such as the Zuccotti Park occupation in 2011 and Seattle's CHOP in 2020 certainly didn't swell in the way that Tahrir Square did during the height of the Egyptian Revolution. This might seem to suggest that spaces of convergence are somehow less effective in mobilizing spontaneous participants than situations or frames. However, such a conclusion is not necessarily the case. Rather, while situations and frames helped to rapidly mobilize a large number of people, spaces tended to catalyze sustained mass participation over longer periods of time.

The appearance of smaller-scale participation in spaces of convergence at any one time is tied to the fact that these spaces were far more flexibly available to participants. This flexibility meant that the total number of people drawn to participate in a given space had the luxury of choosing from a wide array of days and times during which it was possible to participate. This was, if anything, a boon for mobilization, but it had the effect of diluting the apparent scale of occupied protests.

Even if someone considered participation in a space to be an urgent matter, the opportunity to participate occurred in a far wider window than that of, for example, an evening protest. Six thousand participants in an occupation might, over the period between 9:00 a.m. and midnight on a given day, consistently spend three hours each in an occupied space, but the space itself might appear to have had an average of only 1,500 people in it at any one time. Thus, a hypothetical space that consistently mobilized people 42,000 times over the course of a single week might appear relatively sparse compared to a march of 10,000 taking place over the course of a couple of hours.

Finer-Grain Interactions between Affinity and Convergence

There are also a series of more granular observations relating to the interplay of affinity and convergence that constitute fruitful areas for further inquiry. These represent several intriguing tendencies found among the four cases examined in this book.

The first set of tendencies concerns the interplay between subtypes of convergence and varieties of affinity. While all convergence conditions made it easier for people to participate, regardless of their affinities to the movement in question, some conditions seemed to be especially compatible with particular affinities. Paramount conditions, for example, were a regular catalyst for participants mobilized by their dispositions (attitudes, perceptions of injustice, and identity). When the importance of participation was increased, those with strong dispositions toward a cause tended to be strongly affected. Conversely, exceptional conditions were especially effective in mobilizing people with substantial social affinities for participation. When these circumstances radically lowered the impediments to participation, people with compatible activity patterns, a conducive social status, or sets of resources and obligations flocked to participate. Those attracted by drives appeared similarly affected, with such conditions prompting them to pursue movement participation in order to fulfill their needs or interests. Opportune conditions, meanwhile, appear to have a fairly sweeping impact across affinities, rather than an outsized impact in any particular area.

The second set of tendencies refers to the context of convergence. While situations were not especially associated with any particular affinities, there were some interesting tendencies associated with frames and spaces. Frames tended to amplify participation among people with psychological affinities (something that seems fitting, in retrospect), while spaces tended to prove most effective catalysts for mobilization among those with intersecting social affinities, perhaps a side effect of occupied spaces' capacity to play host to resources and coincide with people's patterns of activity.

Though these tendential findings are certainly interesting, their granularity means that they should not be taken as providing any conclusive insight into the scope of interactions between affinities and convergence conditions. As I noted in chapter 2, we should be wary of overtheorizing the intricacies of such interactions. Because convergence conditions are abstractions made from rich, variable empirical conditions, there is likely to be a great deal of qualitative variation in terms of their catalytic impact. Likewise, the scope of affinities (even within a single category, such as resources, attitudes, or needs) is potentially very broad, so certain specific items within each category may potentially exhibit quirks in the way they interact with convergence conditions. In view of this potential analytical friction, I do not intend to suggest that the patterns discussed in this section are generalizable. Rather, I raise these observations as potential starting points for further reflection and research.

Further Puzzles

Amid the various answers I have tried to provide in this book are openings for a plethora of new questions. Some of these arose during the research process for the book but were decidedly beyond its scope. Others were raised by friends, colleagues, and other readers who took an interest in the project and suggested a variety of future lines of inquiry that I or others might wish to take up. For these I am immensely grateful, and I am excited by the prospect of their future exploration. Such further questions include: How do episodes of affinity-convergence mobilization affect countermovements? How does the demobilization of spontaneous protest differ from that of organized causes? What might an improved version of affinity-convergence theory look like?

COUNTERMOVEMENTS AND THE (NON)EXCLUSIVITY OF CONVERGENCE

The discussion of convergence conditions in this book has focused solely on the mobilization of participants in a single movement, but what about the more general impact of convergence conditions on movements across the board? During many of the mobilization trajectories discussed in this book, countermovements also saw increases in their activity, ranging from Mubarak loyalists in Egypt to white supremacist mobilization in the United States. Without sustained investigation focused specifically on these countermobilizations, it is difficult to ascertain the extent to which they were instances of spontaneous mobilization, but the notion that select convergence conditions might have a more generalized impact is worth investigating further.

We might well expect certain convergence conditions to have a more indiscriminate effect on movement activity: exceptional situations, for example, are remarkably open periods that do not appear to circumscribe the kind of cause for which one might potentially mobilize. Paramount situations, meanwhile, seem intuitively liable to mobilize both sides of a given conflict. Even certain opportune conditions may permit people predisposed to a plethora of movements to take advantage of them. By contrast, spaces and frames are more likely to exhibit a more exclusive form of convergence, with spaces restricted to those able to access them, and frames restrained not only to their general audience but also to those with whom those frames resonate.[12]

Recent patterns of protest in the United States constitute an excellent starting place for further inquiry on this topic. This may include drawing on protest event databases, such as the Crowd Counting Consortium's data,[13] or applying similar methods to other events. Alternatively, protest survey methods could be utilized in tandem with qualitative research to investigate spontaneous attendance across an array of movements over a given period.[14]

DEMOBILIZING SPONTANEITY AND SPONTANEOUS DEMOBILIZATION

Another question arising from the cases in this book regards the demobilization of spontaneous participants. While this process was explained by the undoing of convergence conditions and/or the dissolution of affinity—a "reverse process" approach—might there be more intricacies to such a process than we expect?

On the one hand, we might seek to understand precisely how this reversal was achieved. Might there, for instance, be conditions of divergence, which could serve to separate causes from those who have affinities to them, counteracting conditions of convergence that are already in place? We might imagine menacing circumstances, such as terrorist attacks or dangerous weather conditions as potentially prohibitive of participation in collective action.[15] Alternatively, ultranormative spaces, frames, or situations might similarly impede protest participation (one might recall the postrevolutionary collapse in protest attendance during Egypt's election season). Such a topic is ripe for further inquiry.

On the other hand, we might ask whether there exist instances of "spontaneous demobilization," in which those mobilized by conventional social movement organizations rapidly cease their participation for reasons beyond opponents' or activists' control. Why did loyalists of Mubarak's National Democratic Party cease mobilizing during the Egyptian Revolution, against the wishes of the regime? Why do repressive forces fail to mobilize against insurrections or suffer mass defections? Such inquiry is well beyond the scope of what we have discussed here, but constitutes another fruitful avenue for future research.

IMPROVING THE THEORY

A final puzzle concerns the ideas at the core of this book: affinity-convergence theory. What are its limitations, and how might it be improved? One puzzle raised during the book's theoretical chapters concerned factors that might have been eclipsed by my selection of cases or methods of inquiry but that could still play an important role in mobilization under certain circumstances. There are indeed a variety of circumstances not covered by the analysis in this book. One of the most notable constitutes premodern and ultra-early-modern instances of mobilization taking place before the French Revolution.[16] Another notable omission concerns a whole suite of events: civil wars. How might spontaneous mobilization play out in these contexts, and would it obey the same logics as modern revolution, riot, and protest?

Might expanding the analysis of spontaneous mobilization to a greater number of contexts also reveal new elements of affinity or convergence that ACT presently overlooks? What, for example, of the role of language and symbolic resonance in contentious politics?[17] Might communicative or aesthetic affinities play a role in some kinds of mobilization, such as nationalist movements and independence struggles? Likewise, what of the role of self-directed intentions in protest participation? As Doug McAdam and colleagues have recently found, participation in college activism appears to be strongly predicted by behavioral intentions: already-laid plans to act on one's values, over and above the precise content of those values. Might such intentions also constitute an important affinity for participation in spontaneous mobilization in certain settings within and beyond the college campus?[18] And what of other factors that lie beyond or interact with convergence conditions, but which nonetheless help shape the context of spontaneity in some way?

One of the patterns in this book was that regime activity often played an important role in giving shape to convergence conditions, and so one way in which we might wish to expand ACT is to focus more squarely on the role of the state and how it influences populations' capacity for spontaneous mobilization. The godfather of contentious politics, Charles Tilly, once suggested that regimes could be categorized according to two "crude" dimensions: level of governmental capacity and level of democracy.[19] The cases in this book have comprised a high-capacity democratic regime (the United States), a high-capacity nondemocratic regime (Egypt), and a case that, owing to its historical circumstance, is difficult to pin down as belonging to any of the types (France). Looking at cases of low-capacity democracies (Tilly suggested Belgium and Jamaica) and low-capacity nondemocracies (such as twenty-first-century Somalia) might help us to understand a little more about how regimes influence spontaneous mobilization. We might also wish to interrogate more mixed regimes, such as prerevolutionary Armenia (2018) and modern-day Brazil.

Beyond potentially occluded elements of affinity and convergence and the presence of intervening causal factors or agents, how else might affinity-convergence theory be improved? One option would be to further develop ACT into a more precise micro model of spontaneity (reminiscent of work in the rational choice and psychological traditions of research on mobilization), or even to develop a larger-scale micro-macro model, complete with weighted variables. There is certainly some utility in trying to further understand the interaction of the variables involved in spontaneous mobilization, but I fear that unless we are careful, pursuing an exceedingly precise model may well tell us less about spontaneity than we might think. One of the core lessons emerging from the cases in this book is that spontaneity is a dynamic and unfolding process that does not proceed in a regular, easily formularized fashion, but draws from all manner of constituencies and swells from multiplex sociopolitical developments. Not only is it the case that many of the elements of affinity and convergence would be very difficult to simplify into a quantitative measure, but it is also true that the dynamic interactions between convergence conditions and affinities would be hard to quantify without losing considerable analytical resolution.

Even if such a fine-grain model could be built, whom exactly would it serve?

This question prompts another, final puzzle: How might the findings in this book and the theory I develop be put to productive use for social good? Might the theory be even faintly helpful for oppressed peoples mobilizing in contexts where organizations are stultified by regime activity or wrought with passivity? Or might it be used to help social justice campaigners build truly momentous challenges to systemic issues? I should hope so, but to offer an affirmative answer would be hubristic at best. I can only say that for those who wish to try, I would be more than willing to help.

Acknowledgments

I am immensely grateful to so many people for helping make this book a reality.

I was honored to receive intellectual advice, assistance, and guidance from David Andress, Colin Beck, Manuel Castells, Dana Fisher, Jeff Goodwin, John Jost (and his brilliant lab), Hazem Kandil, Neil Ketchley, Richard Lachmann, Michael Mann, Doug McAdam, Richard Mole, Anthony Oberschall, Karl-Dieter Opp, Jo Reger, Eric Selbin, Sidney Tarrow, Jay Ulfelder, and Ed Walker. I was also blessed with some very thoughtful and constructive reviewers to whom I am immensely grateful for their help and support.

I am deeply grateful to my editor at the University of Chicago Press, Elizabeth Branch Dyson, who proved an invaluable guide throughout the review process, a tremendous interlocutor as to the book's shape and format, and an enthusiastic supporter of its mission. Thanks also to Mollie McFee, the senior editorial associate for the book, and Lindsy Rice, my production editor, who were both always readily available to help whenever I needed it.

I couldn't possibly have written this book without the aid of family and friends, who have served variably as proofreaders, confidants, and welcome listeners throughout the process. I am truly grateful to Alice, Dominic, and Zoe Abrams, Roderick Blevins, Tiago Carvalho, Tara Cookson, Hunter Dukes, Lukas Fuchs, Peter Gardner, Mohamed el-Gendy, Isaac Holeman, Diane Houston, Daniel Keim, Nathan Masih-Hanneghan, Joe Mooney, Nicholas Mulder, Ryan Rafaty, Giulio Regeni, Victor Roy, Lera Shumaylova, Emma Vehviläinen, Noura Wahby, and Harald Wydra. I am especially grateful to my partner, Philippa Carveth, for her immense support over the past six years and for preparing the brilliant maps of Zuccotti and Tahrir.

There are some institutions that supported me a great deal during the book's development. King's College, Cambridge, was my academic home between 2009 and 2019, during which I completed the full cycle from undergraduate student to teaching staff. It was there that I conceived the research project that would lead to this book with the incredible support of the Economic and Social Research Council. Since 2019 University College London's School of Slavonic and East European Studies has taken me in, funded by the very generous support of the Leverhulme Trust. I have also been kindly supported in various ways by the City University of New York Graduate Center, the University of Maryland, New York University, St. Catharine's College, Cambridge, and St. John's College, Cambridge.

Finally, I would like to thank the great many people that I cannot name here: the spontaneous revolutionaries, Occupiers, and protesters who were kind enough to speak to me about why they did what they did, as well as the various activists who recalled, frankly and honestly, the bounds of their engagement with the proceedings. Without your trust, patience, and willingness to help, this work would never have been possible. I dedicate this book to you.

Notes

INTRODUCTION

1. Kurt Andersen, "Person of the Year, 2011," *Time*, December 14, 2011, http://content.time.com/time/person-of-the-year/2011/.

2. Eric Trager, "The Cairo Files: Pre-Revolutionary Egypt?," *Commentary*, July 30, 2008, https://www.commentary.org/eric-trager/the-cairo-files-pre-revolutionary-egypt/.

3. George Floyd was a forty-six-year-old Black Minnesotan who, despite peacefully submitting to arrest, was pinned to the ground and forcibly asphyxiated to death by Minneapolis Police Department Officer Derek Chauvin. Floyd's asphyxiation lasted a total of nine minutes and twenty-nine seconds, during which Chauvin kneeled on his neck, while Floyd repeatedly complained that he could not breathe, until ultimately falling silent.

4. My thanks to the anonymous reviewer of this manuscript for recommending this phrasing.

5. Craig Calhoun, "Afterword: Why Historical Sociology?" in *Handbook of Historical Sociology*, ed. Gerard Delanty and Engin Isin (London: Sage 2003), 383–93; Richard Lachmann, *What Is Historical Sociology?* (Cambridge: Polity, 2013), 6.

6. Diana Fu and Erica S. Simmons, "Ethnographic Approaches to Contentious Politics: The What, How, and Why," *Comparative Political Studies*, 54, no. 10 (June 2021): 1695–1721, https://doi.org/10.1177/00104140211025544.

7. Lachmann, *Historical Sociology*, 6.

8. Sidney Tarrow, "Progress Outside of Paradise: Old and New Comparative Approaches to Contentious Politics," *Comparative Political Studies*, 54, no. 10 (July 2021): 1885–1901, https://doi.org/10.1177/00104140211024297.

9. Some observers have used the term "Black Lives Matter" to refer to these protests, but I use the term "Black Lives Uprising." Although participants in the uprising did indeed regularly proclaim that "Black lives matter," there are two key reasons for my using this terminology. First, as we shall see in part IV, the involvement of self-professed "Black Lives Matter" movement organizations in the uprising was relatively minimal. Second, the use of the phrase "Black lives matter" by racial justice protesters has been widespread for a decade, and came to public prominence in a separate, 2014 uprising, which some already dub the "Black Lives Matter Uprising."

10. I investigated archival sources in considerable depth, yet much of their utility was in the clarity that they offered collectively, rather than in their role as singular sources of information. Consequently, there is far from a preponderance of specific archival references in this book.

11. Archival sources, livestreams, and social media data are cited unobtrusively in notes.

12. With respect for individual privacy, I only directly refer to material intended for a public audience and footage shared by public-oriented figures in this book, but the total volume of material I made use of was far greater.

CHAPTER ONE

1. W. Lance Bennett and Alexandra Segerberg, *The Logic of Connective Action: Digital Media and the Personalization of Contentious Politics* (Cambridge: Cambridge University Press, 2013).

2. Many readers will have opened this book without a prior interest in the relatively specialist domain of research on mobilization. As such, I have prioritized accessibility over granularity. The more expert reader will, of course, notice a great deal that has been sacrificed on the altar of clarity and concision. These include theories of breakdown/strain, biographical availability, brokerage, cognitive liberation, contagion, critical mass theories, the dynamics of contention approach, diffusion, emotions, free riders, mass society theories, moral incentives, instrumental and ideological motives, policing, precipitation, and repression. All of these areas of focus have proven highly instructive in my development of affinity-convergence theory. Some are raised elsewhere in the book. Others are, regrettably, omitted. As the sheer length of this list illustrates, to cover the scope of their contribution here is beyond the limitations of this volume.

3. Albion W. Small, "The Meaning of the Social Movement," *American Journal of Sociology* 3 (1987): 349–50.

4. Small, "The Meaning of the Social Movement," 344.

5. Ted Robert Gurr, *Why Men Rebel* (Princeton, NJ: Princeton University Press, 1970).

6. Ted Robert Gurr, "Why Men Rebel Redux: How Valid Are Its Arguments 40 Years On?" *E-International Relations*, November 17, 2011, http://www.e-ir.info/2011/11/17/why-men-rebel-redux-how-valid-are-its-arguments-40-years-on/.

7. Gurr, *Why Men Rebel*, 23–24.

8. These theories have taken a variety of names, including mass society, strain/breakdown, contagion, convergence, and emergent norm theories.

9. Lewis M. Killian, "Social Movements," in *Handbook of Modern Sociology*, ed. Robert E. L. Faris (Chicago: Rand McNally, 1964), 427.

10. Herbert Blumer, "Collective Behavior," in *New Outline of the Principles of Sociology*, ed. Alfred M. Lee (New York: Barnes & Noble, 1951), 171.

11. Ralph H. Turner and Lewis M. Killian, *Collective Behavior* (Englewood Cliffs, NJ: Prentice-Hall, 1957), 29.

12. Kurt Lang and Gladys Engel Lang, *Collective Dynamics* (New York: Thomas Y. Crowell, 1961).

13. Blumer, "Collective Behavior."
14. Killian, "Social Movements."
15. Turner and Killian, *Collective Behavior*.
16. David A. Snow and Deana Rohlinger, "Convergence Theory," in *The Blackwell Encyclopedia of Social and Political Movements*, ed. David A. Snow, Donatella della Porta, Bert Klandermans, and Doug McAdam (Hoboken, NJ: Wiley-Blackwell, 2013), 1.
17. Turner and Killian, *Collective Behavior*, 28–29.
18. A notable exception here is work by Daniel Myers and Pamela Oliver on the diffusion of collective violence, which extends the mission of this literature, seeking to map and model the spread of protests and political violence across urban settings using a contagion model but explicitly stops short of theorizing spontaneous protest. See Daniel J. Myers, "The Diffusion of Collective Violence: Infectiousness, Susceptibility, and Mass Media Networks," *American Journal of Sociology* 106, no.1 (2000): 173–208; Pamela Oliver and Daniel J. Myers, "The Coevolution of Social Movements," *Mobilization* 8 (2003): 1–25; and Daniel J. Myers and Pamela E. Oliver, "The Opposing Forces Diffusion Model: The Initiation and Repression of Collective Violence," *Dynamics of Asymmetric Conflict* 1, no. 2 (2008): 164–89.
19. For an excellent discussion of this trend, including interviews with key figures such as Olson, McCarthy, and Zald and Oberschall, as well as a number of the collective behavior theorists they were responding to, see Aldon Morris and Cedric Herring, "Theory and Research in Social Movements: A Critical Review," 1984, https://www.researchgate.net/profile/Aldon_Morris/publication/30851820 _Theory_and_Research_in_Social_Movements_A_Critical_Review/links/5729fbf 208ae057b0a078384.pdf.
20. William A. Gamson, *The Strategy of Social Protest* (Homewood, IL: Dorsey Press, 1975), 130, 133–34.
21. Gamson, *Strategy*, 139.
22. John D. McCarthy and Mayer N. Zald, "Resource Mobilization and Social Movements: A Partial Theory," *American Journal of Sociology* 82, no. 6 (1977): 1212–41.
23. These included Michael Lipsky's analysis of "Protest as a Political Resource," *American Political Science Review* 62, no. 4 (1968): 1144–58; William Gamson's *Power and Discontent* (New York: Dorsey Press, 1968) and *The Strategy of Social Protest*; Anthony Downs's "Up and Down with Ecology: The 'Issue-Attention' Cycle," *Public Interest* 28 (1972): 38–50; and John McCarthy and Mayer Zald's "The Trend of Social Movements in America: Professionalization and Resource Mobilization," *CRSO Working Paper* 164 (1977), https://hdl.handle.net/2027.42/50939.
24. McCarthy and Zald, "Resource Mobilization," 1218.
25. See, for example, Bob Edwards, John D. McCarthy, and Dane R. Mataic, "The Resource Context of Social Movements," in *The Wiley-Blackwell Companion to Social Movements*, ed. David A. Snow, Sarah A. Soule, Hanspeter Kriesi, and Holly J. McCammon (Bridgewater, NJ: John Wiley, 2018), 79–97.
26. Frances Fox Piven, *Challenging Authority: How Ordinary People Change America* (Lanham, MD: Rowman & Littlefield, 2008); and Frances Fox Piven and

Richard Cloward, *Poor People's Movements: Why They Succeed, How They Fail* (New York: Pantheon Books, 1977).

27. Piven and Cloward, *Poor People's Movements*, 18–25.

28. Mancur Olson Jr., *The Logic of Collective Action: Public Goods and the Theory of Groups* (Cambridge, MA: Harvard University Press, 1965).

29. Karl-Dieter Opp, *The Rationality of Political Protest* (London: Avalon Publishing, 1989), 128.

30. Peter Voss, "The Goals of the Revolution," in *Origins of a Spontaneous Revolution: East Germany, 1989*, ed. Karl-Dieter Opp, Peter Voss, and Christine Gern (Ann Arbor: University of Michigan Press, 1995), 47. See also Anthony Oberschall, *Social Conflict and Social Movements* (Englewood Cliffs, NJ: Prentice-Hall, 1973), and Anthony Oberschall, "Rational Choice in Collective Protests," *Rationality and Society* 6, no. 1 (1994): 79–100.

31. Karl-Dieter Opp, "Soft Incentives and Collective Action: Participation in the Anti-Nuclear Movement," *British Journal of Political Science* 16, no. 1 (1986): 88.

32. Pamela Oliver, "Selective Incentives," in *The Wiley-Blackwell Encyclopedia of Social and Political Movements*, ed. David A. Snow, Donatella della Porta, Bert Klandermans, and Doug McAdam, 2013, https://doi.org/10.1002/9780470674871.wbespm185.

33. Voss, "Goals," 43.

34. Karl-Dieter Opp, "The Blunt Weapons of the Stasi," in Opp et al., *Spontaneous Revolution*, 151. See also Steven Pfaff, "Explaining Protest Mobilization in Repressive Settings: Lessons from East Germany's Spontaneous Revolution," paper presented at the Society for Comparative Research/Center for Comparative Social Analysis Retreat, May 8–9, 1999, Los Angeles, http://www.sscnet.ucla.edu/soc/groups/scr/pfaff.htm.

35. Charles Tilly, *From Mobilization to Revolution* (Reading, MA: Addison-Wesley, 1978). See also Charles Tilly, *Big Structures, Large Processes, Huge Comparisons* (New York: Russell Sage, 1984); and Charles Tilly, "To Explain Political Processes," *American Journal of Sociology* 100, no. 6 (1995): 1594–1610.

36. Doug McAdam, *Political Process and the Development of Black Insurgency, 1930–1970* (Chicago: University of Chicago Press, 1982).

37. Sidney Tarrow, *Power in Movement*, 2nd ed. (Cambridge: Cambridge University Press, 1998) and 3rd ed. (Cambridge: Cambridge University Press, 2011).

38. Tilly, *Big Structures*, 306.

39. Doug McAdam, John D. McCarty, and Mayer N. Zald, "Introduction: Opportunities, Mobilizing Structures, and Framing Processes—toward a Synthetic, Comparative Perspective on Social Movements," in *Comparative Perspectives on Social Movements: Political Opportunities, Mobilizing Structures and Cultural Framings*, ed. Doug McAdam, John D. McCarty, and Mayer N. Zald (Cambridge: Cambridge University Press 1996), 3.

40. Tarrow, *Power in Movement*, 2nd ed., 123.

41. McAdam, *Political Process*, 41.

42. Charles Tilly, Louise Tilly, and Richard Tilly, *The Rebellious Century, 1830–1930* (Cambridge, MA: Harvard University Press, 1975), 254.

43. Doug McAdam, "Conceptual Origins, Current Problems, Future Direction,"

in McAdam et al., *Comparative Perspectives*, 23–40; William A. Gamson and David S. Meyer, "Framing Political Opportunity," in McAdam et al., *Comparative Perspectives*, 275–90; Jeff Goodwin and James M. Jasper, "Caught in a Winding, Snarling Vine: The Structural Bias of Political Process Theory," *Sociological Forum* 14, no. 1 (1999): 27–54.

44. Jack Goldstone and Charles Tilly, "Threat (and Opportunity): Popular Action and State Response in the Dynamics of Contentious Action," in *Silence and Voice in the Study of Contentious Politics*, ed. Ronald R. Aminzade et al. (Cambridge: Cambridge University Press, 2001), 183.

45. Herbert H. Haines, *Black Radicals and the Civil Rights Mainstream, 1954–1970* (Knoxville: University of Tennessee Press, 1988). See also Piven, *Challenging Authority*; and Eitan Y. Alimi, "The Dialectic of Opportunities and Threats and Temporality of Contention: Evidence from the Occupied Territories," *International Political Science Review* 28, no. 1 (2007): 101–23.

46. Jack Goldstone, "Is Revolution Individually Rational? Groups and Individuals in Revolutionary Collective Action," *Rationality and Society* 6, no. 1 (1994): 139–66; Opp et al., *Spontaneous Revolution*.

47. Tilly, *Mobilization*, 134.

48. Doug McAdam, "Recruitment to High-Risk Activism: The Case of Freedom Summer," *American Journal of Sociology* 92, no. 1 (1986): 66.

49. Roger V. Gould, "Beyond Structural Analysis: Toward a More Dynamic Understanding of Social Movements," in *Social Movements and Networks: Relational Approaches to Collective Action*, ed. Mario Diani and Doug McAdam (Oxford: Oxford University Press, 2003), 236.

50. Alan Schussman and Sarah A. Soule, "Process and Protest: Accounting for Individual Protest Participation," *Social Forces* 84, no. 2 (2005): 1086–87. See also Clare Saunders et al., "Explaining Differential Protest Participation: Novices, Returners, Repeaters, and Stalwarts," *Mobilization* 17, no. 3 (2012): 253–80.

51. Maryjane Osa, "Networks in Opposition: Linking Organizations through Activists in the Polish People's Republic," in Diani and McAdam, *Social Movements and Networks*, 105–23.

52. Robert D. Putnam, "Bowling Alone, Revisited," *Responsive Community* 5, no. 2 (1995): 18–33; Ann Mische, "Cross-talk in Movements: Reconceiving the Culture-Network Link," in Diani and McAdam, *Social Movements and Networks*, 281–98.

53. Suzanne Staggenborg, "Social Movement Communities and Cycles of Protest: The Emergence and Maintenance of a Local Women's Movement," *Social Problems* 45, no. 2 (1998): 180–204; Hatem M. Hassan and Suzanne Staggenborg, "Movements as Communities," in *The Oxford Handbook of Social Movements*, ed. Donatella Della Porta and Mario Diani (Oxford: Oxford Handbooks Online, 2015), doi:10.1093/oxfordhb/9780199678402.013.37.

54. Alberto Melucci, "The Symbolic Challenge of Contemporary Movements," *Social Research* 52, no. 4 (1985): 800.

55. Mario Diani, "Networks and Social Movements: A Research Program," in Diani and McAdam, *Social Movements and Networks*, 299–319.

56. Neil Fligstein and Doug McAdam, *A Theory of Fields* (Cambridge: Cambridge University Press, 2012).

57. Bennett and Segerberg, *Connective Action*. See also Daniel Myers, "The Diffusion of Collective Violence: Infectiousness, Susceptibility, and Mass Media Networks," *American Journal of Sociology* 106, no. 1 (July 2000): 173–208; Jennifer Earl and R. Kelly Garrett, "The New Information Frontier: Toward a More Nuanced View of Social Movement Communication," *Social Movement Studies* 16, no. 4 (2017): 479–93.

58. Mario Diani, *The Cement of Civil Society: Studying Networks in Localities* (Cambridge: Cambridge University Press, 2015); David Knoke, Mario Diani, James Holloway, and Dimitris Christopoulos, *Multimodal Political Networks* (Cambridge: Cambridge University Press, 2021), 134–57.

59. Robert D. Benford and David A. Snow, "Framing Processes and Social Movements: An Overview and Assessment," *Annual Review of Sociology* 26, no. 1 (2000): 611–39; Francesca Polletta and James M. Jasper, "Collective Identity and Social Movements," *Annual Review of Sociology* 27 (2001): 283–305.

60. Benford and Snow, "Framing Processes," 611.

61. Doug McAdam, "Culture and Social Movements," in *New Social Movements: From Ideology to Identity*, ed. Enrique Laraña, Hank Johnston, and Joseph R. Gusfield (Philadelphia: Temple University Press, 1994), 39.

62. William A. Gamson, "Bystanders, Public Opinion and the Media," in *The Blackwell Companion to Social Movements*, ed. David A. Snow, Sarah H. Soule, and Hanspeter Kriesi (Oxford: Blackwell, 2004), 249.

63. Jennifer Earl, "The Dynamics of Protest-related Diffusion on the Web," *Information, Communication and Society* 13, no. 2 (2010): 211.

64. David A. Snow and Robert D. Benford, "Ideology, Frame Resonance and Participant Mobilization," *International Social Movement Research* 1 (1988), 198.

65. Snow and Benford, "Ideology," 202.

66. James M. Jasper, *The Art of Moral Protest: Culture, Biography and Creativity in Social Movements* (Chicago: University of Chicago Press, 1997), 106; James M. Jasper and Jane D. Poulsen, "Recruiting Strangers and Friends: Moral Shocks and Social Networks in Animal Rights and Anti-Nuclear Protests," *Social Problems* 42, no. 4 (1995): 493–512.

67. David A. Snow, Daniel Cress, Liam Downey, and Andrew Jones, "Disrupting the 'Quotidian': Reconceptualizing the Relationship between Breakdown and the Emergence of Collective Action," *Mobilization* 3, no. 1 (1998): 1.

68. Snow et al., "Disrupting the 'Quotidian,'" 21.

69. See, for example, Michael A. Hogg and Dominic Abrams, *Social Identifications: A Social Psychology of Intergroup Relations and Group Processes* (London: Routledge, 1988); Henri Tajfel and John C. Turner, "The Social Identity Theory of Intergroup Behavior," in *Psychology of Intergroup Relations*, ed. Stephen Worchel and William G. Austin (Chicago: Nelson-Hall, 1986), 7–24; Steve Reicher, "Social Identity and Social Change: Rethinking the Context of Social Psychology," in *Social Groups and Identities: Developing the Legacy of Henri Tajfel*, ed. W. Peter Robinson (London: Butterworth, 1996), 317–36; Martijn van Zomeren, Tom Postmes, and Russel Spears, "Toward an Integrative Social Identity Model of Collective Action: A Quantitative Research Synthesis of Three Socio-Psychological Perspectives," *Psychological Bulletin* 134, no. 4 (2008): 504–35.

70. Iain Walker and Heather J. Smith, eds., *Relative Deprivation: Specification, Development and Integration* (Cambridge: Cambridge University Press, 2002).

71. John Drury and Steve Reicher, "Explaining Enduring Empowerment: A Comparative Study of Collective Action and Psychological Outcomes," *European Journal of Social Psychology* 35 (2005): 25–58; Laura S. Schrager, "Private Attitudes and Collective Action," *American Sociological Review* 50, no. 6 (1985): 858–59.

72. Van Zomeren et al., "Toward an Integrative Social Identity Model," 510.

73. Sheldon Stryker, Timothy J. Owens, and Robert W. White, "Social Psychology and Social Movements: Cloudy Past and Bright Future," in *Self, Identity and Social Movements*, ed. Sheldon Stryker, Timothy J. Owens, and Robert W. White (Minneapolis: University of Minnesota Press, 2000), 6.

74. Robyn K. Mallett, Jeffrey R. Huntsinger, Stacey Sinclair, and Janet K. Swim, "Seeing through Their Eyes: When Majority Group Members Take Collective Action on Behalf of an Outgroup," *Group Processes and Intergroup Relations* 11, no. 4 (2008): 451–70; Martijn van Zomeren, Maja Kutlaca, and Felicity Turner-Zwinkels, "Integrating Who 'We' Are with What 'We' (Will Not) Stand For: A Further Extension of the Social Identity Model of Collective Action," *European Review of Social Psychology* 29, no. 1 (2018): 122–60.

75. Dominic Abrams and Peter R. Grant, "Testing the Social Identity Relative Deprivation (SIRD) Model of Social Change: The Political Rise of Scottish Nationalism," *British Journal of Social Psychology* 51, no. 4 (2012): 687.

76. Giovanni A. Travaglino, Dominic Abrams, and Giuseppina Russo, "Dual Routes from Social Identity to Collective Opposition to Criminal Organizations: Intracultural Appropriation Theory and the Roles of Honor Codes and Social Change Beliefs," *Group Processes and Intergroup Relations* 20, no. 3 (2017): 317. See also David A. Snow, Louis A. Zurcher, and Sheldon Ekland-Olson, "Social Networks and Social Movements: A Microstructural Approach to Differential Recruitment," *American Sociological Review* 45 (1980): 787–801.

77. Katie E. Corcoran, David Pettinicchio, and Jacob T. N. Young, "The Context of Control: A Cross-National Investigation of the Link between Political Institutions, Efficacy, and Collective Action," *British Journal of Social Psychology* 50, no. 4 (2011): 597–98.

78. Bert Klandermans, "Demand and Supply of Protest," in Snow et al., *The Wiley-Blackwell Encyclopedia of Social and Political Movements*, 175.

79. Bert Klandermans and Jacquelien van Stekelenburg, "Social Movements and the Dynamics of Collective Action," in *The Oxford Handbook of Political Psychology*, 2nd ed., ed. Leonie Huddy, David O. Sears, and Jack S. Levy (Oxford: Oxford University Press, 2013), 19, doi: 10.1093/oxfordhb/9780199760107.013.0024. See also Bert Klandermans and Dirk Oegema, "Potentials, Networks, Motivations, and Barriers: Steps towards Participation in Social Movements," *American Sociological Review* 52, no. 4 (1987): 519–31.

80. Klandermans and van Stekelenburg, "Collective Action," 26–27.

81. McAdam, *Political Process*, 60.

82. McAdam, *Political Process*, 63.

83. Tarrow, *Power in Movement*, 2nd ed., 19.

84. Goldstone, "Individually Rational"; Opp et al., *Spontaneous Revolution*.

85. Fligstein and McAdam, *Theory of Fields*, 20–21.

86. Doug McAdam, Sidney Tarrow, and Charles Tilly, *Dynamics of Contention* (Cambridge: Cambridge University Press, 2001), 46.

87. Diani, "A Research Program." See also Kristin Luker, *Abortion and the Politics of Motherhood* (Berkeley: University of California Press, 1984); Patrick Mullins, "Community and Urban Movements," *Sociological Review* 3 (1987): 347–69.

88. Florence Passy, "Social Networks Matter. But How?," in Diani and McAdam, *Social Movements and Networks*, 34.

89. Dana R. Fisher and Lorien Jasny, "Understanding Persistence in the Resistance," *Sociological Forum* 34, no. 1 (2019): 1065–89.

90. Joris Verhulst and Stefaan Walgrave, "The First Time Is the Hardest? A Cross-National and Cross-Issue Comparison of First-Time Protest Participants," *Political Behavior* 31, no. 3 (2009): 455–84.

91. James M. Jasper, "Social Movement Theory Today: Toward a Theory of Action?" *Sociology Compass* 4, no. 11 (2010): 965.

92. Jasper and Poulsen, "Moral Shocks"; Snow et al., "Disrupting the 'Quotidian.'"

93. Jacquelien van Stekelenburg and Bert Klandermans, "The Social Psychology of Protest," *Sociopedia.isa*, 2010, retrieved January 3, 2017, http://www.sagepub.net/isa/resources/pdf/Protest.pdf.

94. Suzanne Staggenborg, "Entrepreneurs, Movement," in Snow et al., *The Wiley-Blackwell Encyclopedia of Social and Political Movements*; Klandermans, "Demand and Supply."

95. Bert Klandermans et al., "Mobilization without Organization: The Case of Unaffiliated Demonstrators," *European Sociological Review* 30, no. 6 (2014): 702–16.

96. Klandermans and van Stekelenburg, "Collective Action."

97. On the potential promise of this notion, see David A. Snow and Dana M. Moss, "Protest on the Fly: Toward a Theory of Spontaneity in the Dynamics of Protest and Social Movements," *American Sociological Review* 79, no. 6 (2014): 1122–43.

98. William Kornhauser, *The Politics of Mass Society* (Glencoe, NY: Free Press, 1959), 163.

99. Kira Jumet, *Contesting the Repressive State: Why Ordinary Egyptians Protested during the Arab Spring* (New York: Oxford University Press, 2017).

100. Pfaff, "Explaining Protest Mobilization," n.p.; Opp et al., *Spontaneous Revolution*.

CHAPTER TWO

1. James M. Jasper, *Getting Your Way: Strategic Dilemmas in the Real World* (Chicago: University of Chicago Press, 2006); Neil Fligstein and Doug McAdam, *A Theory of Fields* (Cambridge: Cambridge University Press, 2012).

2. This characterization can be found in James M. Jasper, "Social Movement Theory Today: Toward a Theory of Action?," *Sociology Compass* 4, no. 11 (2010): 965–76; and Doug McAdam, "Beyond Structural Analysis: Toward a More Dynamic Understanding of Social Movements," in *Social Movements and Networks: Rela-*

tional Approaches to Collective Action, ed. Mario Diani and Doug McAdam (Oxford: Oxford University Press, 2003), 6.

3. Karl-Dieter Opp, *Theories of Political Protest and Social Movements: A Multidisciplinary Introduction, Critique and Synthesis* (New York: Taylor & Francis, 2009), 3.

4. Albert Bandura, "The Psychology of Chance Encounters and Life Paths," *American Psychologist* 37, no. 7 (1982): 747–55; Albert Bandura, "Toward a Psychology of Human Agency," *Perspectives on Psychological Science* 1, no. 2 (2006): 164.

5. A notable exception is McAdam's "Freedom Summer," discussed later.

6. I have drawn together the theoretical underpinnings of affinity in dialogue with a diverse array of sources, many of which come from everyday activist and organizational practices. Developing a concept that is already used by organizers and activists is, in my view, better than requiring the reader to entertain some novel abstraction entirely of my own making.

7. S11-AWOL, "Preparing for the World Economic Forum," Autonomous Web of Libertians, last modified May 30, 2000, http://www.ainfos.ca/oo/may/ainfos00472.html.

8. "History of Affinity Groups," Rant Collective, last modified May 19, 2006, https://web.archive.org/web/20060519032829/http://www.rantcollective.net/article.php?id=33.

9. Iain McIntyre, *Always Look on the Bright Side of Life: The AIDEX '91 Story* (Canberra, Australia: Homebrew Cultural Association, 2008).

10. Andrea Johnson Meadows and Andrés Tapia, *Global Diversity Primer* (New York: Bonnier, 2009).

11. Interview: OWS/Annie.

12. Matthew Scott Smith, "IAN: Implicit Affinity Networks," Brigham Young University Department of Computer Science, December 22, 2006, http://site.smithworx.com/publications/IANDefense.pdf.

13. Matthew Scott Smith, "Social Capital in Online Communities," PhD diss., Brigham Young University, 2011, 33, https://scholarsarchive.byu.edu/cgi/viewcontent.cgi?article=3729&context=etd.

14. Dirk Oegema and Bert Klandermans, "Why Social Movement Sympathizers Don't Participate: Erosion and Nonconversion of Support," *American Sociological Review* 59, no. 5 (1994): 703–22; Doug McAdam, "Recruitment to High-Risk Activism: The Case of Freedom Summer," *American Journal of Sociology* 92, no. 1 (1986): 64–90.

15. Alan Schussman and Sarah A. Soule, "Processes and Protest: Accounting for Individual Protest Participation," *Social Forces* 84, no. 2 (2005): 1086–87.

16. Dana R. Fisher and Lorien Jasny, "Understanding Persistence in the Resistance," *Sociological Forum* 34, no. 1 (2019): 1065–89; David A. Snow, Daniel Cress, Liam Downey, and Andrew Jones, "Disrupting the 'Quotidian': Reconceptualizing the Relationship between Breakdown and the Emergence of Collective Action," *Mobilization* 3, no. 1 (1998): 1–22; Joris Verhulst and Stefaan Walgrave, "The First Time Is the Hardest? A Cross-National and Cross-Issue Comparison of First-Time Protest Participants," *Political Behavior* 31, no. 3 (2009): 455–84.

17. The dynamics and variety of these are, of course, liable to expand, contract, and shift over time.

18. Alberto Melucci, "The Symbolic Challenge of Contemporary Movements," *Social Research* 52, no. 4 (1985): 789–816.

19. Suzanne Staggenborg, "Beyond Culture versus Politics: A Case Study of a Local Women's Movement," *Gender and Society* 15, no. 4 (2001): 507–30.

20. Just as members of a movement's organized core will also be a part of its supporting networks, affinity is not confined exclusively to participants beyond movement networks. Rather, it is generally (though not necessarily always) superseded by a different form of connection in the context of conventional mobilization.

21. Aldon Morris and Cedric Herring, "Theory and Research in Social Movements: A Critical Review," 1984, https://www.researchgate.net/profile/Aldon_Morris/publication/30851820_Theory_and_Research_in_Social_Movements_A_Critical_Review/links/5729fbf208ae057b0a078384.pdf.

22. Personality is also known to play a role in protest participation decisions, although I do not cover the matter in this book. More detail on the operation of personality as a low-level predictive variable for participation in protest can be found in the work of Brandstätter and Opp. See Karl-Dieter Opp and Hermann Brandstätter, "Personality Traits ('Big Five') and the Propensity to Political Protest: Alternative Models," *Political Psychology* 35, no. 4 (2014): 515–37. Efficacy also plays a role, addressed in the section on convergence.

23. Sophia J. Wallace, Chris Zepeda-Millán, and Michael Jones-Correa, "Spatial and Temporal Proximity: Examining the Effects of Protests on Political Attitudes," *American Journal of Political Science* 58, no. 2 (2014): 433–48; Tyler T. Reny and Benjamin J Newman, "The Opinion-Mobilizing Effect of Social Protest against Police Violence: Evidence from the 2020 George Floyd Protests," *American Political Science Review* 115, no. 4 (November 2021): 1499–1507, doi:10.1017/S0003055421000460.

24. Deana A. Rohlinger and Leslie A. Bunnage, "Connecting People to Politics Over Time? Internet Communication Technology and Retention in MoveOn.org and the Florida Tea Party Movement," *Information, Communication and Society* 18, no. 5 (2015): 539–52. See also Jennifer Earl and R. Kelly Garrett, "The New Information Frontier: Toward a More Nuanced View of Social Movement Communication," *Social Movement Studies* 16, no. 4 (2017): 479–93; Jennifer Earl, "The Dynamics of Protest-related Diffusion on the Web," *Information, Communication and Society* 13, no. 2 (2010): 209–25.

25. W. Lance Bennett and Alexandra Segerberg, *The Logic of Connective Action: Digital Media and the Personalization of Contentious Politics* (Cambridge: Cambridge University Press, 2013).

26. Frances Fox Piven and Richard Cloward, *Poor People's Movements: Why They Succeed, How They Fail* (New York: Pantheon Books, 1977), 21–23.

27. Russell Dalton, Alix Van Sickle, and Steven Weldon, "The Individual-Institutional Nexus of Protest Behaviour," *British Journal of Political Science* 40, no. 1 (2010): 51–73, doi:10.1017/S000712340999038X.

28. Toni Rodon and Marc Guinjoan, "Mind the Protest Gap: The Role of Resources in the Face of Economic Hardship," *PS: Political Science and Politics* 51, no. 1 (2018): 84–92, doi:10.1017/S1049096517001809.

29. Bob Edwards, John D. McCarthy, and Dane R. Mataic, "The Resource Context of Social Movements," in *The Wiley-Blackwell Companion to Social Movements*,

ed. David A. Snow, Sarah A. Soule, Hanspeter Kriesi, and Holly J. McCammon (Bridgewater, NJ: John Wiley, 2018), 79–97.

30. McAdam, "Recruitment," 70.

31. For example, as a "selective incentive" in the parlance of rational choice theories; see Pamela Oliver, "Selective Incentives," in *The Wiley-Blackwell Encyclopedia of Social and Political Movements*, ed. David A. Snow, Donatella della Porta, Bert Klandermans, and Doug McAdam, 2013, https://doi.org/10.1002/9780470674871.wbespm185.

32. Bert Klandermans and Jacquelien van Stekelenburg, "Social Movements and the Dynamics of Collective Action," in *The Oxford Handbook of Political Psychology, 2nd ed.*, ed. Leonie Huddy, David O. Sears, and Jack S. Levy (Oxford: Oxford University Press, 2013), 19, doi: 10.1093/oxfordhb/9780199760107.013.0024.

33. Dominic Abrams and Peter R. Grant, "Testing the Social Identity Relative Deprivation (SIRD) Model of Social Change: The Political Rise of Scottish Nationalism," *British Journal of Social Psychology* 51, no. 4 (2012): 674–89. See also Klandermans and van Stekelenburg, "Collective Action"; Martijn van Zomeren, Tom Postmes, and Russel Spears, "Toward an Integrative Social Identity Model of Collective Action: A Quantitative Research Synthesis of Three Socio-Psychological Perspectives," *Psychological Bulletin* 134, no. 4 (2008): 504–35.

34. Henri Tajfel and John C. Turner, "The Social Identity Theory of Intergroup Behavior," in *Psychology of Intergroup Relations*, ed. Stephen Worchel and William G. Austin (Chicago: Nelson-Hall, 1986), 7–24; Michael A. Hogg and Dominic Abrams, *Social Identifications: A Social Psychology of Intergroup Relations and Group Processes* (London: Routledge, 1988); Steve Reicher, "Social Identity and Social Change: Rethinking the Context of Social Psychology," in *Social Groups and Identities: Developing the Legacy of Henri Tajfel*, ed. W. Peter Robinson (London: Butterworth, 1996), 317–36.

35. Van Zomeren et al., "Social Identity Model." On this topic see also Sheldon Stryker, Timothy J. Owens, and Robert W. White, eds., *Self, Identity and Social Movements* (Minneapolis: Minnesota University Press: 2000).

36. Interview: OWS/Kevin.

37. Ted Robert Gurr, *Why Men Rebel* (Princeton, NJ: Princeton University Press, 1970), 23–24; and more recently, Abrams and Grant, "Relative Deprivation Model," 687.

38. Interview: Egypt/Yusha.

39. Dominic Abrams et al., "Mobilizing IDEAS in the Scottish Referendum: Predicting Voting Intention and Well-being with the Identity-Deprivation-Efficacy-Action-Subjective Well-being Model," *British Journal of Social Psychology* 59, no. 2 (2020): 425–46. See also van Zomeren et al., "Social Identity Model."

40. Doug McAdam, *Freedom Summer* (Oxford: Oxford University Press, 1988), 62–65.

41. David A. Snow, Louis A. Zurcher, and Sheldon Ekland-Olson, "Social Networks and Social Movements: A Microstructural Approach to Differential Recruitment," *American Sociological Review* 45 (1980): 787–801.

42. Dana R. Fisher and Stella M Rouse, "Intersectionality within the racial justice movement in the summer of 2020," *Proceedings of the National Academy*

of Sciences 119, no. 30 (2022); Dana R. Fisher and Michael Heaney, "George Floyd Protests in Multiple Sites: Preliminary Findings" (unpublished manuscript, 2020).

43. Oberschall, "Rational Choice"; Opp, "Soft Incentives"; Oliver, "Select Incentives"; Staggenborg, "Beyond Culture."

44. "U.S. Music 360—2018 Highlights," Nielsen, last modified November 15, 2018, https://www.nielsen.com/us/en/insights/report/2018/us-music-360-2018/; "Hobbies and Interests in the US," Statistica, retrieved May 5, 2020, https://www.statista.com/forecasts/997050/hobbies-and-interests-in-the-us.

45. Andy Newman, "For a Concert That Never Was, a Good Turnout Nonetheless," *New York Times*, October 1, 2011, https://www.nytimes.com/2011/10/01/nyregion/radiohead-concert-at-wall-street-protest-was-just-hoax.html.

46. "Former Five-Star Chef, Now Broke, Feeds Occupy Wall Street," Grub Street, October 26, https://www.grubstreet.com/2011/10/former_five_star_chef_now_brok.html.

47. Interview: Egypt/Gamal.

48. Fisher and Heaney, "George Floyd Protests"; Fisher and Rouse, "Intersectionality."

49. Interview: Uprising/Maria.

50. McAdam, "Recruitment," 65.

51. Charles Tilly, *From Mobilization to Revolution* (Reading, MA: Addison-Wesley, 1978). See also Charles Tilly, *Big Structures, Large Processes, Huge Comparisons* (New York: Russell Sage, 1984); and Charles Tilly, "To Explain Political Processes," *American Journal of Sociology* 100, no. 6 (1995): 1594–1610.

52. Jeff Goodwin, James M. Jasper, and Francesca Polletta, "The Return of the Repressed: The Fall and Rise of Emotions in Social Movement Theory," *Mobilization: An International Quarterly* 5, no. 1 (2000): 65–83.

53. Doug McAdam, Sidney Tarrow, and Charles Tilly, *Dynamics of Contention* (Cambridge: Cambridge University Press, 2001); Fligstein and McAdam, *Theory of Fields*.

54. Robert D. Benford and David A. Snow, "Framing Processes and Social Movements: An Overview and Assessment," *Annual Review of Sociology* 26, no. 1 (2000): 611–39.

55. David A. Snow and Dana M. Moss, "Protest on the Fly: Toward a Theory of Spontaneity in the Dynamics of Protest and Social Movements," *American Sociological Review* 79, no. 6 (2014): 1136; Snow et al., "Disrupting the Quotidian."

56. Jeff Goodwin and Steven Pfaff, "Emotion Work in High-Risk Social Movements: Managing Fear in the US and East German Civil Rights Movements," in *Passionate Politics: Emotions and Social Movements*, ed. Jeff Goodwin, James M. Jasper, and Francesca Polletta (Chicago and London: University of Chicago Press, 2001), 282–302.

57. James M. Jasper and Jane D. Poulsen, "Recruiting Strangers and Friends: Moral Shocks and Social Networks in Animal Rights and Anti-Nuclear Protests," *Social Problems* 42, no. 4 (1995): 493–512.

58. I consider "structural" to refer to the sociopolitical structures of control rather than enduring physical arrangements. This is in line with the literature on

political processes and subsequent theory in social movement studies across a broad range of authors, such as Goodwin and Jasper, Gould, McAdam, and Tilly.

59. These "contexts" are distinct from one another, but certainly not mutually exclusive. For example, the characteristics of a space can be dependent on situational factors, and structural conditions are usually accompanied by a frame that draws attention to them.

60. A key difference is that, while "political opportunity" refers to a favorable political and institutional context, in the long or short run, under which a movement may achieve its goals, "opportune situations" constitute emergent social contexts in which the cost/benefit balance of individual movement participation is made substantially more advantageous for prospective participants. One constitutes a promising setting for building social change, the other a sudden chance to join the fight.

61. Jack Goldstone and Charles Tilly, "Threat (and Opportunity): Popular Action and State Response in the Dynamics of Contentious Action," in *Silence and Voice in the Study of Contentious Politics*, ed. Ronald R. Aminzade et al. (Cambridge: Cambridge University Press, 2001), 183.

62. See, in turn, Snow and Moss, "Spontaneity"; Lewis M. Killian, "Social Movements," in *Handbook of Modern Sociology*, ed. Robert E. L. Faris (Chicago: Rand McNally, 1964); Ralph H. Turner and Lewis M. Killian, *Collective Behavior* (Englewood Cliffs, NJ: Prentice-Hall, 1957).

63. Rebecca E. Klatch, *A Generation Divided: The New Left, the New Right, and the 1960s* (Berkeley: University of California Press, 1999), 74.

64. Jack Goldstone, "Is Revolution Individually Rational? Groups and Individuals in Revolutionary Collective Action," *Rationality and Society* 6, no. 1 (1994): 139–66; Karl-Dieter Opp, Peter Voss, and Christine Gern, eds., *Origins of a Spontaneous Revolution: East Germany, 1989* (Ann Arbor: University of Michigan Press, 1995); Tilly, *Mobilization*.

65. Benford and Snow, "Framing Processes."

66. Peter Grant, Dominic Abrams, Daniel W. Robertson, and Jana Garay, "Predicting Protests by Disadvantaged Skilled Immigrants: A Test of an Integrated Social Identity, Relative Deprivation, Collective Efficacy (SIRDE) Model," *Social Justice Research* 28 (2014): 76–101.

67. Benford and Snow, "Framing Processes," 615–17; William A. Gamson and David S. Meyer, "Framing Political Opportunity," in McAdam et al., *Comparative Perspectives*, 275–90; McAdam et al., *Dynamics of Contention*.

68. Goodwin and Pfaff, "Emotion Work," 293–94.

69. Magda Boutros, "Place and Tactical Innovation in Social Movements: The Emergence of Egypt's Anti-harassment Groups," *Theory and Society* 46, no. 6 (2017): 543–75; Walter Nicholls, Byron Miller, and Justin Beaumont, eds., *Spaces of Contention: Spatialities and Social Movements* (Farnham, UK: Ashgate, 2013); William H. Sewell, "Space in Contentious Politics," in *Silence and Voice in the Study of Contentious Politics*, ed. Ronald R. Aminzade et al. (Cambridge: Cambridge University Press, 2001), 82–85.

70. Charles Tilly, "Spaces of Contention," *Mobilization: An International Quar-*

terly 5, no. 2 (2000): 135–59; Dingxin Zhao, "Ecologies of Social Movements: Student Mobilization during the 1989 Prodemocracy Movement in Beijing," *American Journal of Sociology* 103, no. 6 (1998): 1493–1529.

71. Aldon Morris, "Birmingham Confrontation Reconsidered: An Analysis of the Dynamics and Tactics of Mobilization," *American Sociological Review* 58, no. 5 (1993): 621–36; Nurettin Özgen, "Power-Identity and City Squares: A Sociopolitic Geography Analysis," in *Urban and Urbanization*, ed. Recep Efe, Turgut Tüzün Onay, Igor Sharuho, and Emin Atasoy (Sofia, Bulgaria: St. Kliment Ohridski University Press, 2014), 228–41.

72. James Billington, *Fire in the Minds of Men: Origins of the Revolutionary Faith* (New York: Basic Books, 1980), 31.

73. Sara M. Evans and Harry C. Boyte, *Free Spaces: The Sources of Democratic Change in America* (Chicago: University of Chicago Press, 1986).

74. Hakim Bey, *TAZ: The Temporary Autonomous Zone, Ontological Anarchy, Poetic Terrorism* (New York: Autonomedia, 1991).

75. Lang and Lang, *Collective Dynamics*.

76. Opp, *Political Protest*, 347.

77. Atef Said, "We Ought to Be Here: Historicizing Space and Mobilization in Tahrir Square," *International Sociology* 30, no. 4 (2014): 348–66.

78. Xu Wang Yu Ye and Chris King-chi Chan, "Space in a Social Movement: A Case Study of Occupy Central in Hong Kong in 2014," *Space and Culture* 22, no. 4 (November 2019): 434–48, https://doi.org/10.1177/1206331217751805.

79. We should be wary of overtheorizing the intricacies of this interaction. Convergence conditions' empirical manifestations are contextually specific, and so the exact affinities they catalyze in any one case will vary. While certain subtypes and contexts of convergence might prove to be tendentially aligned with certain affinities—over and above convergence's overall effect—any such relationship would require a great deal of further research to firmly establish. This is further discussed in the book's conclusion.

80. Carl von Clausewitz, *Vom Kriege* (Berlin: F. Dümmler, 1832).

PART II INTRODUCTION

1. "The Arab Awakening Reaches Syria," *Economist*, March 21, 2011, https://www.economist.com/newsbook/2011/03/21/the-arab-awakening-reaches-syria.

2. See, for example, Manuel Castells, *Networks of Outrage and Hope: Social Movements in the Internet Age* (Cambridge: Polity 2012); Paolo Gerbaudo, *Tweets and the Streets: Social Media and Contemporary Activism* (London: Pluto Press, 2012); and Gilad Lotan et al., "The Arab Spring| the Revolutions Were Tweeted: Information Flows during the 2011 Tunisian and Egyptian Revolutions," *International Journal of Communication* 5, no. 31 (2011), http://ijoc.org/index.php/ijoc/article/view/1246.

3. Most famously in Wael Ghonim, *Revolution 2.0* (London: Fourth Estate, 2012).

4. The majority of interviews were conducted in English, with the periodic use of Arabic for precision or clarification. While English is very widely spoken

CHAPTER THREE

1. Tarek Osman, *Egypt on the Brink* (New Haven, CT: Yale University Press, 2010), 169.
2. The broader pattern of discontent in Egypt is masterfully chronicled in Adel Abdel Ghafar, *Egyptians in Revolt: The Political Economy of Labor and Student Mobilizations, 1919–2011* (London: Routledge, 2017).
3. Interview: Egypt/Ahmad.
4. Interview: Egypt/Hazem.
5. Interview: Egypt/Hosni.
6. Osman, *Egypt on the Brink*, 221.
7. Interview: Egypt/Mustafa.
8. "World Development Indicators," World Bank, accessed May 1, 2022, https://databank.worldbank.org/source/world-development-indicators.
9. "الجهاز المركزى للتعبئة العامة والاحصاء" [Labor Force Survey for the Third Quarter (July/August/September)], Central Agency for Public Mobilization and Statistics, 2021, accessed August 6, 2021, https://web.archive.org/web/20110310201759/http://capmas.gov.eg/news.aspx?nid=491.
10. Freedom House, *Countries at the Crossroads 2011: An Analysis of Democratic Governance* (Lanham, MD: Rowman & Littlefield 2012), 203.
11. Except for the Leftist Tagammu or National Progressive Unionist Party, which received five seats.
12. Hazem Kandil, *Inside the Brotherhood* (London: Polity Books, 2015), 134.
13. Interview: Egypt/Anonymous4.
14. Interview: Egypt/Anonymous5.
15. Paul Schemm, "Sparks of Activist Spirit in Egypt," *Middle East Research and Information Project*, April 13, 2002, http://www.merip.org/mero/mero041302; Amira Howeidy, "Dissent on the Fringe," *Ahram Weekly*, September 22, 2004, http://weekly.ahram.org.eg/archive/2004/708/eg2.htm.
16. Eric Robert Trager, "Trapped and Untrapped: Mubarak's Opponents on the Eve of His Ouster" (PhD diss., University of Pennsylvania, 2013), 181–82, https://repository.upenn.edu/cgi/viewcontent.cgi?article=1869&context=edissertations.
17. Jason Brownlee, "A New Generation of Autocracy in Egypt," *Brown Journal of World Affairs* 14, no. 1 (2007): 73–85; Human Rights Watch, "Egypt: Crackdown on Antiwar Protests," March 23, 2003, https://www.hrw.org/news/2003/03/23/egypt-crackdown-antiwar-protests; Daniel Williams, "Egypt Extends 25-Year-Old Emergency Law," *Washington Post*, May 1, 2006, http://www.washingtonpost.com/wp-dyn/content/article/2006/04/30/AR2006043001039.html.
18. Khalil Al-Anani, *Inside the Muslim Brotherhood: Religion, Identity, and Politics* (Oxford: Oxford University Press, 2016), 186.
19. Abdel Moneim Mahmoud, "د. محمد بديع للجزيرة : لا نعارض ترشيح الأستاذ جمال مبارك للرئاسة بشرط ألا يتميز عن أي مواطن ويتم انتخابه دون قهر," [Mohammed Badie to Al Ja-

zeera: We do not oppose Gamal Mubarak's candidacy for the presidency, provided that he is not distinguished from any citizen and is elected without coercion], Ana-Ikhwan Blog, January 22, 2010, http://ana-ikhwan.blogspot.com/2010/01/blog-post_22.html (https://archive.ph/NyZGf#); Kandil, *Inside the Brotherhood*, 136.

20. Mustapha Kamel al-Sayyid, "Kefaya at a Turning Point," in *Political and Social Protest in Egypt*, ed. Nicholas S. Hopkins (Cairo: American University in Cairo Press, 2009), 47.

21. Previously, elections in Egypt were run as referenda on a single presidential appointment made by parliament.

22. Baheyya, "Kifaya—Asking the Right Questions," *Baheyya Blog*, April 2005, http://baheyya.blogspot.co.uk/2005/04/kifaya-asking-right-questions.html.

23. Charles Krauthammer, "The Arab Spring of 2005," *Seattle Times*, March 21, 2005, http://old.seattletimes.com/html/opinion/2002214060_krauthammer21.html.

24. "Kefaya: The Origins of Mubarak's Downfall," *Egypt Independent*, December 12, 2011, http://www.egyptindependent.com/news/kefaya-origins-mubaraks-downfall.

25. The charges were grounded on evidence provided by Nour's codefendant, Ayman Ismail Hassan, who, after recanting his statement on the grounds that it had been coerced by threats to his family, was found hanged in his cell. See Denis J. Sullivan and Kimberly Jones, *Global Security Watch—Egypt: A Reference Handbook* (Westport, CT: Greenwood Publishers, 2008), 9.

26. Facebook in Egypt in 2010–2011 was demographically skewed in a very particular way: its earliest adopters were not only young and tech-savvy, like many of those who used Facebook in its early days, but also economically well-off, having the means to afford comparatively expensive smartphones, laptops, and internet connections that many ordinary Egyptians could only dream of ever owning. For more on this and the facts and figures cited here, see Philip N. Howard, *The Digital Origins of Dictatorship and Democracy: Information Technology and Political Islam* (Oxford: Oxford University Press, 2010), 132–35.

27. Because of the online component of these organizations, the term "membership" is often used flexibly. Generally, membership should not be taken to mean active, involved members but merely people who chose to affiliate by either liking a page on Facebook or signing a petition.

28. Samantha M. Shapiro, "Revolution, Facebook-Style," *New York Times Magazine*, January 22, 2009, http://www.nytimes.com/2009/01/25/magazine/25bloggers-t.html.

29. Abdel Ghafar, *Egyptians in Revolt*.

30. This was particularly pressing, as constitutional reforms implemented in 2007 upheld a ban on independent candidates while also mandating that any party's candidate must be a member of that political party's senior leadership for at least one year prior to running for the presidency.

31. Interview: Egypt/Hakim.

32. Wael Ghonim, *Revolution 2.0* (London: Fourth Estate, 2012), 44.

33. This constituted voting by national ID, with monitoring by civil society groups, judicial oversight, equal media access, and no arbitrary restrictions on who could run.

34. Operating the website http://www.taghyeer.net/, which had obtained 123,052 signatures by the start of 2011. See http://web.archive.org/web/20101230224514/ (http://www.taghyeer.net/).

35. Operating the website https://www.tawkatonline.com/, which had obtained 817,280 signatures by the start of 2011. See http://web.archive.org/web/2011 0130164107/ (https://www.tawkatonline.com).

36. This was an incredibly big risk for those who signed, and consequently many refused to do so. What many suspected, but did not know, was that Egypt's considerably entrenched police intelligence agents were desperately trying to locate the database for its own sinister purposes. Interview: Egypt/Anonymous2.

37. Interview: Egypt/Ibrahim.

38. Interview: Egypt/Anonymous1.

39. Walid Shawky, "How the Margins Became the Center: On Protest, Politics and April 6," Madamasr.com, November 25, 2016, http://www.madamasr.com /en/2016/11/25/opinion/u/how-the-margins-became-the-center-on-protest-politics -and-april-6/.

CHAPTER FOUR

1. Interview: Egypt/Heba.

2. Wael Ghonim, *Revolution 2.0* (London: Fourth Estate, 2012), 131.

3. The originals are no longer available, but the Egyptian newspaper *Ahram Online* reported on their publication and enduring impact. See "Twin Portrait of Mubarak and Ben Ali: Same Regimes, Same Endings," *Ahram Online*, April 6, 2014, http://archive.vn/trXI5.

4. "Twin Portrait," 120.

5. "Twin Portrait," 137.

6. Ghonim, *Revolution 2.0*; "Political Forces in Egypt Preparing for the January 25 Day of Rage Demonstration," IkhwanWeb, January 23, 2011, https://www.ikhwan web.com/article.php?id=27906.

7. "الاخوان: لن نشارك فى تظاهرات 25 يناير" [Brotherhood: We will not participate in the January 25 demonstrations], *AlWafd.org*, January 20, 2011, http://web.archive .org/web/20110321231603/http://www.alwafd.org/index.php?option=com_content& view=article&id=12821&cpage=30; IkhwanWeb, "Egypt Preparing." In defiance of this declaration, a torrent of younger Brotherhood members began unilaterally professing their participation, forcing a last-minute reversal of the organization's official stance in the forty-eight hours before the protests.

8. Ghonim, *Revolution 2.0*, 160.

9. Interview: Egypt/Mahmood.

10. Ramy Raoof, "Egypt: Sequence of Communication Shutdown during 2011 Uprising," *GlobalVoices*, February 9, 2011, https://advox.globalvoices.org/2011/02/09 /egypt-sequence-of-communication-shutdown-during-2011-uprising/.

11. Interview: Egypt/Mariam.

12. Spanning activists from the April 6 movement, Kefaya, and ElBaradei's National Association for Change.

13. Interview: Egypt/Mahmood.

14. Ghonim, *Revolution 2.0*, 132.

15. Midnight in Egypt is not quite as late as it might seem in other countries. During my fieldwork, I often found myself arranging meetings and even conducting interviews well after midnight.

16. Ghonim, *Revolution 2.0*, 120.

17. Ghonim, *Revolution 2.0*, 178.

18. Quoted in Matt Richtel, "Egypt Cuts Off Most Internet and Cell Service," *New York Times*, January 28, 2011, http://www.nytimes.com/2011/01/29/technology/internet/29cutoff.html.

19. Interview: Egypt/Anonymous2.

20. Neil Ketchley, *Egypt in a Time of Revolution: Contentious Politics and the Arab Spring* (Cambridge: Cambridge University Press, 2017).

21. Ketchley's data specifically focus on attacks on police *stations* during the Eighteen Days, rather than police more generally. Boulaq's police station was attacked and set on fire at least once in the revolution's first year, in November 2011, but there exists no newspaper reporting on what happened to the station in January. See الوفد "إحراق نقطة شرطة رملة بولاق أبوالعلا." [The Ramlet Boulaq Abou El-Ela police station was set on fire], *AlWafd.org*, November 16, 2011, https://archive.ph/YK7uu.

22. Outside of Cairo this was also echoed by the wave of supportive strikes that usually would have been met with harsh police repression. See Anne Alexander and Mostafa Bassiouny, *Bread, Freedom, Social Justice: Workers and the Egyptian Revolution* (London: Zed Books, 2014).

23. Interview: Egypt/Gamal.

24. "GeoEye-1 Satellite Image of Tahrir Square in Cairo, Egypt," GeoEye. January 29, 2011, https://www.satimagingcorp.com/gallery/geoeye-1/geoeye-1-tahrir-square/.

25. Pierre Sioufi, "Tahrir Square: A Revolution Minute by Minute (Almost)," *Kikhote Blog*, October 25, 2011, http://kikhote.blogspot.com/2011/10/tahrir-square-revolution-minute-by.html.

26. As more information became available later in the Eighteen Days, this sentiment would reverse, with the swelling occupation in Tahrir Square constituting a place of safety amid an unpoliced and unsecured Egypt.

27. The original reporting has since been removed, but other media organizations still cite it, for example, "Egyptian Protests: Tuesday 1 February 2011 as It Happened," *Telegraph*, February 2, 2011, http://www.telegraph.co.uk/news/worldnews/africaandindianocean/egypt/8297700/Egypt-protests-Tuesday-1-February-2011-as-it-happened.html.

28. White House, "Readout of the President's Calls to Discuss Egypt," January 30, 2011, https://obamawhitehouse.archives.gov/the-press-office/2011/01/30/readout-presidents-calls-discuss-egypt.

29. Quoted in "Egypt Protests—Thursday 3 February," *Guardian*, February 3, 2011, https://www.theguardian.com/news/blog/2011/feb/03/egypt-protests-live-updates.

30. Mine is not the only study of revolutionary participation to emphasize the

role of identity. See Jeroen Gunning and Ilan Zvi Baron, *Why Occupy a Square? People, Protests and Movements in the Egyptian Revolution* (Oxford: Oxford University Press, 2014), 205–6.

31. Interview: Egypt/Yusha.
32. Interview: Egypt/Fatima.
33. Interview: Egypt/Heba.
34. Interview: Egypt/Gamal.
35. Pierre Sioufi, "Tahrir Square."
36. Quoted in Marwa Awad and Hugo Dixon, "Inside a Revolution: Tahrir Square, 2011," *Reuters Special Reports*, April 13, 2011, http://graphics.thomsonreuters.com/specials/tahrir.pdf.
37. This is also corroborated by other scholarship. See Mariz Tadros, "Contentious and Prefigurative Politics: Vigilante Groups' Struggle against Sexual Violence in Egypt (2011–2013)," *Development and Change* 46 (2015): 1345–68, https://doi.org/10.1111/dech.12210.
38. "Egypt Army Steps in, Sign Mubarak Has Lost Power," *Washington Post*, February 10, 2011, http://www.washingtonpost.com/wp-dyn/content/video/2011/02/10/VI2011021003317.html.
39. Maggie Michael, "Egypt's Military Takes Control, CIA Expects Mubarak Will Step Down Thursday," *Chicago Tribune*, February 10, 2011, http://articles.chicagotribune.com/2011-02-10/news/chi-ap-egypt-dupe_1_president-hosni-mubarak-protests-military-rule.
40. Ashraf Khalil, "We Need to Drag Him from His Palace," *Foreign Policy*, February 11, 2011, http://foreignpolicy.com/2011/02/11/we-need-to-drag-him-from-his-palace/.
41. Greg Hounshell, "The Pharaoh Is Dead, Long Live the Pharaoh?," *Foreign Policy*, February 11, 2011, http://foreignpolicy.com/2011/02/11/the-pharaoh-is-dead-long-live-the-pharaoh/.
42. Gunning and Baron, *Why Occupy a Square?*, 206.
43. Interview: Egypt/Yusha.

CHAPTER FIVE

1. James M. Jasper and Jan Willem Duyvendak, eds., *Players and Arenas: The Interactive Dynamics of Protest* (Amsterdam: Amsterdam University Press, 2015). See also Neil Fligstein and Doug McAdam, *A Theory of Fields* (Cambridge: Cambridge University Press, 2012).
2. Interview: Egypt/Mahmood.
3. Gamal El-Din, "Egypt's Constitution: A Controversial Declaration," *Ahram Online*, March 30, 2011, https://english.ahram.org.eg/NewsContent/1/64/8960/Egypt/Politics-/Egypt%E2%80%99s-constitution-A-controversial-declaration.aspx.
4. "Muslim Brotherhood to Establish 'Freedom and Justice Party,'" *Egypt Independent Online*, February 21, 2011, https://www.egyptindependent.com/muslim-brotherhood-establish-freedom-and-justice-party/.
5. Interview: Egypt/Omar.

6. Interview: Egypt/Gamal.

7. David Kirkpatrick, "Crime Wave in Egypt Has People Afraid, Even the Police," *New York Times*, May 13, 2011, https://www.nytimes.com/2011/05/13/world/middleeast/13egypt.html.

8. Interview: Egypt/Anonymous6.

9. Yasmine Fathi, "The Circle of Hell: Inside Tahrir's Mob Sexual Assault Epidemic," *Ahram Online*, February 21, 2013, http://english.ahram.org.eg/NewsContent/1/151/65115/Egypt/Features/The-circle-of-hell-Inside-Tahrirs-mob-sexual-assau.aspx.

10. Interview: Egypt/Fouad.

11. Bryant Ott and Mohamed Younis, "Egyptians Optimistic Post-Revolution," Gallup, June 6, 2011, https://news.gallup.com/poll/147938/egyptians-optimistic-post-revolution.aspx.

12. Interview: Egypt/Abdul.

13. Quoted in Mohamed Abdel-Baky, "Realpolitik," *Ahram Weekly Online*, January 26, 2012, http://weekly.ahram.org.eg/Archive/2012/1082/sc111.htm.

14. Asma AlSharif and Yasmine Saleh, "The Real Force behind Egypt's 'Revolution of the State,'" *Reuters Special Reports*, October 10, 2013, http://uk.reuters.com/article/uk-egypt-interior-special-report-idUKBRE99908720131010; Hazem Kandil, *Soldiers, Spies, and Statesmen: Egypt's Road to Revolt* (London: Verso Books, 2012), 194.

15. Quoted in AlSharif and Saleh, "The Real Force."

16. Neil Ketchley, "Elite-led Protest and Authoritarian State Capture in Egypt," 34–36 in *From Mobilization to Counter-Revolution* (Project on Middle East Political Science, 2016), 36, https://pomeps.org/wp-content/uploads/2016/07/POMEPS_Studies_20_Mobilzation_Web.pdf.

17. See Ketchley, "Elite-led Protest" for further detail on this concept and how it played out in the case of Egypt.

18. There were, of course, various sham "elections" conducted, but these were stage-managed affairs in which only controlled opposition parties were permitted to run, and any real contenders were either jailed or disqualified. Moreover, empirical tests of the country's election results as recently as 2018 found that there were significant "anomalies... consistent with officials manipulating vote counts after the fact." Neil Ketchley, "Fraud in the 2018 Egyptian Presidential Election?," *Mediterranean Politics* 26, no. 1 (2019): 128–29.

19. Interview: Egypt/Anonymous3.

20. Human Rights Watch, "All According to Plan: The Rab'a Massacre and Mass Killings of Protesters in Egypt," August 12, 2014, http://www.hrw.org/report/2014/08/12/all-according-plan/raba-massacre-and-mass-killings-protesters-egypt.

21. Interview: Egypt/Anonymous3.

22. Mona Daoud, "Jailed for Putting Mickey Mouse Ears on Sisi?," *CairoScene*, October 20, 2015, https://web-beta.archive.org/web/20160413071119/ (http://www.cairoscene.com/BusinessAndPolitics/Jailed-for-Putting-Mickey-Mouse-Ears-on-Sisi).

23. These were generally described with the Arabic term *al-Muwāuwā al-sharīf*.

24. This was with the natural exception of my interviewees who gave fully informed consent.

25. "Egypt: 'Officially, You Do Not Exist'—Disappeared and Tortured in the Name of Counter-terrorism," *Amnesty International Reports*, June 13, 2016, https://www.amnesty.org/en/documents/mde12/4368/2016/en/.

PART III INTRODUCTION

1. Interview: OWS/Larry.

2. Interview: OWS/Larry. See also Mark Bray, *Translating Anarchy: The Anarchism of Occupy Wall Street* (Winchester, UK: John Hunt Publishing, 2013).

CHAPTER SIX

1. "#OCCUPYWALLSTREET," *Adbusters*, July 13, 2011, http://www.webcitation.org/63DZ1nIDl.

2. Oleg Komlik, "The Original Email that Started Occupy Wall Street," *EconomicSociology Blog*, December 27, 2014, https://economicsociology.org/2014/12/27/the-original-email-that-started-occupy-wall-street/.

3. Interview: OWS/Owen.

4. Nathan Schneider, "Some Assembly Required," *Harper's Magazine* (February 2012): 50.

5. Interview: OWS/Annie.

6. These included the anarchist anthropologist David Graeber, the filmmaker Marisa Holmes, and the horizontalist writer Marina Sitrin.

7. Nathan Schneider, "Occupy Wall Street: FAQ," *Nation*, September 29, 2011, https://www.thenation.com/article/occupy-wall-street-faq/.

8. A full list of more or less loosely formed pre-occupation working groups formed comprises Arts and Culture Working Group, Facilitation Group, Food Committee, Internet Working Group, Legal Group, Media Group, Outreach Group, Student Outreach Group, and Tactical Group.

9. Interviews: OWS/Annie, OWS/Violent, OWS/Larry.

10. In part, these bonds were developed outside of the larger assembly meetings: each of the working groups formed during the planning process would also meet and work together on particular projects in advance of the seventeenth.

11. Interview: OWS/Owen.

12. For footage, see Reporter World News, "New York City Protest—Occupy Wall Street—September 17, 2011," YouTube video, accessed September 18, 2011, https://www.youtube.com/watch?v=vTmkuzwXWpY.

13. Interview: OWS/Annie.

14. Michael A. Gould-Wartofsky, *The Occupiers: The Making of the 99 Percent Movement* (Oxford: Oxford University Press, 2015), 69.

15. A term used to refer to those who would stay full time in the park, sleeping on the cold, hard ground.

16. "Declaration of the Occupation of New York City," *New York City Gen-*

eral Assembly, September 29, 2011, http://www.nycga.net/resources/documents/declaration/. See also Schneider, "FAQ."

17. Interview: OWS/Annie.

18. Ernesto Castañeda, "The Indignados of Spain: A Precedent to Occupy Wall Street," *Social Movement Studies* 11, no. 3–4 (2012): 309–19.

19. "NYCGA Minutes 10/17/2011," *New York City General Assembly*, October 17, 2011, http://www.nycga.net/2011/10/nycga-minutes-101711/; "Working Group Directory," *New York City General Assembly*, October 25, 2011, http://www.nycga.net/group-documents/working-group-directory/.

20. Interview: OWS/Kevin.

21. Sean Captain, "Inside Occupy Wall Street's (Kinda) Secret Media HQ." *Wired*, November 16, 2011, https://www.wired.com/2011/11/inside-ows-media-hq/. Newshole is a journalistic term, referring to the amount of space available for news on any given day.

22. "USLaw.com's Pepper Spray Video Emboldens Movement," *USLaw.com*, September 28, 2011, http://occupy.uslaw.com/post/11068650072/pepper-spray-video-strengthens-occupy-wall-street.

23. Clyde Hamberman, "No Thank-You Note, but Several Lawsuits for a Pepper-Spraying Inspector," *New York Times*, September 25, 2011, https://cityroom.blogs.nytimes.com/2012/09/25/no-thank-you-note-but-several-lawsuits-for-a-pepper-spraying-inspector/.

24. Tricia Sartor, "Media Coverage of Occupy vs. Tea Party," Pew Research Center, October 21, 2011, http://www.journalism.org/numbers/tale-two-protests/.

25. See, for example, John Doyle and Rich Schapiro, "700 arrested at Occupy Wall Street protest as demonstrators and NYPD shut down Brooklyn Bridge," *New York Daily News*, October 1, 2011, https://www.nydailynews.com/new-york/700-arrested-occupy-wall-street-protest-demonstrators-nypd-shut-brooklyn-bridge-article-1.962107; "700 Arrested after Wall Street Protest on Brooklyn Bridge," *FoxNews.com*, October 2, 2011, http://www.foxnews.com/us/2011/10/01/500-arrested-after-wall-street-protest-on-nys-brooklyn-bridge.html; Nate Rawlings, "Occupy Wall Street: 700 Arrested in Brooklyn Bridge Standoff," *Time*, October 2, 2011, http://newsfeed.time.com/2011/10/02/occupy-wall-street-a-larger-march-and-standoff-on-the-brooklyn-bridge/.

26. Sartor, "Media Coverage."

27. Gould-Wartofsky, *The Occupiers*, 82.

28. Interview: OWS/Clive.

29. Federal Bureau of Investigation, "PCJF OWS FOIA Documents from DHS," 61, last modified March 21, 2012, https://assets.documentcloud.org/documents/549516/fbi-spy-files-on-the-occupy-movement.pdf.

30. Justin Eliott, "Occupy Wall Street Goes Global: 900 Protests around the World, Thousands in Times Square," *AlterNet*, October 16, 2011, http://www.alternet.org/story/152752/occupy_wall_street_goes_global%3A_900_protests_around_the_world,_thousands_in_times_square; Occupy Together, "Occupy Together," *Meetup.com*, December 5, 2012, http://archive.is/Lw1C.

31. Jen Doll, "Transport Workers Union Votes Unanimously to Support Oc-

cupy Wall Street," *Village Voice*, September 29, 2011, http://www.villagevoice.com/news/transport-workers-union-votes-unanimously-to-support-occupy-wall-street-6668782.

32. Chris Garces. "Occupy Wall Street, Open Ethnography and the Uncivilized Slot," *Integraph* 3, no. 2 (April 29, 2012), http://intergraph-journal.net/enhanced/vol3issue2/3.html.

CHAPTER SEVEN

1. "Notice of Cleaning and Upkeep Operations to Commence Friday, October 14," *Brookfield Office Properties*, retrieved March 12, 2016, https://assets.documentcloud.org/documents/256287/zuccotti-cleanup-notice.pdf.

2. Though it is important to note, the representation of these demographics among self-identified Occupiers were certainly skewed toward the young, white, and university educated. See Ruth Milkman, Stephanie Luce, and Penny W. Lewis, "Changing the Subject: A Bottom-up Account of Occupy Wall Street in New York City," *Russell Sage Foundation*, January 2013, retrieved April 3, 2015, https://www.russellsage.org/research/reports/occupy-wall-street-movement.

3. "Occupy Wall Street Divided," *The Daily Show with Jon Stewart* video, broadcast November 16, 2011, http://www.cc.com/video-clips/5510me/the-daily-show-with-jon-stewart-occupy-wall-street-divided.

4. Jonathan Matthew Smucker, "Occupy: A Name Fixed to a Flashpoint," *Sociological Quarterly* 54, no. 2 (2013): 222.

5. Interview: OWS/Kristina.

6. Interview: OWS/Joe.

7. Interview: OWS/David.

8. Interview: OWS/Charlotte.

9. Interview: OWS/Rose.

10. In Rose's case, a "direct" mechanism of recruitment, was actually passed over in favor of affinity-led mobilization. Her brother's friend, who had been staying with them at the time, was involved in the movement but did not attempt to recruit her. Rose was not primarily seeking out Occupy; she was pursuing her drive for art.

11. Interview: OWS/Ernesto.

12. Jen Doll, "Transport Workers Union Votes Unanimously to Support Occupy Wall Street," *Village Voice*, September 29, 2011, http://www.villagevoice.com/news/transport-workers-union-votes-unanimously-to-support-occupy-wall-street-6668782.

13. Interview: OWS/André.

14. Interview: OWS/Jack.

15. In fact, the General Assembly routinely refused any proposition of demands or clear ideology of any kind. Eventually, a "declaration" of the occupation was produced, which offered some notional guidance on how Occupy conducted itself, but this was well after Occupy Wall Street had already gained popularity.

16. Interview: OWS/Charlotte.

17. These included police officers, proprietors of local businesses, charity workers, food vendors, construction workers, and service industry employees, among many others.

CHAPTER EIGHT

1. Interview: OWS/Juan.
2. Interview: OWS/Kevin.
3. The Spokes Council, an attempted remedy for the unwieldiness of General Assembly meetings, was adapted from the organizing traditions of the Global Justice movement, as well as the anarchist Direct Action Network, which had, in turn, drawn its version of the "Spokes" model from anarchist modes of organizing during the Spanish Civil War. See "Spokes Council Proposal," *New York City General Assembly*, October 2011, retrieved May 12, 2015, http://www.nycga.net/spokes-council/.
4. It is worth noting here that these spokespeople were intended only to communicate the decisions already reached within their respective groups, rather than making decisions on their behalf.
5. Adrian Chen, "Wall Street Protesters Now Occupy an Office," *Gawker*, November 16, 2011, http://gawker.com/5860148/wall-street-protesters-now-occupy-an-office.
6. For a discussion see Christian Fuchs, *OccupyMedia! The Occupy Movement and Social Media in Crisis Capitalism* (Alresford, UK: Zero Books, 2014), 31–32.
7. Interview: OWS/Munroe.
8. Federal Bureau of Investigation, "PCJF OWS FOIA Documents from DHS," 61, last modified March 21, 2012, https://assets.documentcloud.org/documents/549516/fbi-spy-files-on-the-occupy-movement.pdf. See also Naomi Wolf, "Revealed: How the FBI Coordinated the Crackdown on Occupy," *Guardian*, December 29, 2012, https://www.theguardian.com/commentisfree/2012/dec/29/fbi-coordinated-crackdown-occupy.
9. Interview: OWS/Liam.
10. Interview: OWS/Emily.
11. Interview: OWS/Noah.
12. Andy Newman, "How Big Was That Protest: The Trickiness of Crowd-Counting," *New York Times*, November 19, 2011, https://cityroom.blogs.nytimes.com/2011/11/19/packed-into-foley-square-but-how-tightly-is-a-mystery/.
13. Interview: OWS/Anonymous1.
14. "May Day Directory: Occupy General Strike in Over 135 Cities," *occupywallst.org*, April 21, 2012, http://occupywallst.org/article/may-day/.
15. Interview: OWS/Anonymous2.
16. Interview: OWS/Joe.
17. Interviews: OWS/Stephanie, OWS/Kevin. See also "OS Income and Expenditures: Public Summary," Occupy Sandy, February 2, 2017, retrieved February 2, 2017, https://docs.google.com/spreadsheets/d/1deBIKIJsuYCmtyONLonHmG6PKiuAG4qSZeLFR4UASNY/.
18. Eric Ambinder and David M. Jennings, "The Resilient Social Network,"

Homeland Security Studies and Analysis Institute, September 30, 2013, https://www.propublica.org/documents/item/1357203-the-resilient-social-network.html.

19. Alan Feuer, "Occupy Sandy, a Movement Moves to Relief," *New York Times,* November 9, 2012, http://www.nytimes.com/2012/11/11/nyregion/where-fema-fell-short-occupy-sandy-was-there.

20. Interview: OWS/Anonymous3.

21. Interview: Uprising/Chloe.

PART IV INTRODUCTION

1. This list can be found in "A Decade of Watching Black People Die," *National Public Radio,* May 31, 2020, https://www.npr.org/2020/05/29/865261916/a-decade-of-watching-black-people-die.

2. "Data Dashboard," Mapping Police Violence, accessed May 12, 2021, https://mappingpoliceviolence.org/.

3. Followed by Boston at 17.6x, Washington, DC, at 13.4x, and Atlanta at 11.7x, "Data Dashboard."

4. Although I have surveyed a much wider volume of material, I directly refer *only* to social media posts and livestreams shared by users with a managed public presence. This is to avoid revealing information that might have been accidentally made public by users unfamiliar with privacy settings For more on the ethical challenges relating to digital ethnographic methods, see Alex Thompson, Lindsay Stringfellow, Mairi Maclean, and Amal Nazzal, "Ethical Considerations and Challenges for Using Digital Ethnography to Research Vulnerable Populations," *Journal of Business Research* 124 (2021): 676–83.

CHAPTER NINE

1. "Investigative Update on Critical Incident," Minneapolis Police Department press release, May 25, 2020, https://archive.ph/SQVwS.

2. Darnella Frazier, "They Killed Him Right in Front of Cup Foods over South on 38th and Chicago!!," Facebook, May 26, 2020, https://www.facebook.com/story.php?story_fbid=1425401580994277&id=100005733452916 (https://archive.is/Wo30E).

3. Police body camera footage later revealed that the total duration was nine minutes and twenty-nine seconds, even longer than the initial video showed.

4. Nekima Levy Armstrong, "Nekima Levy Armstrong Was Live," Facebook videos, May 26, 2020, 7:09, ID: 1386660781504540, https://www.facebook.com/nekima.levypounds/videos/1386660781504540/ (https://archive.is/XK5gb).

5. "I Can't Breathe Nation Wide Protest," Facebook event, May 26, 2020, ID: 570939316949305, https://www.facebook.com/events/570939316949305/ (https://archive.is/AVYQY).

6. "I Can't Breathe: Protest against Police Violence," Facebook event, May 26, 2020, ID: 1287696424910611, https://www.facebook.com/events/1287696424910611/?active_tab=discussion (https://archive.is/OtQut).

7. Levy Armstrong, "Was Live."

8. Trahern Ausar Crews, "Trahern Ausar Crews Was Live," Facebook video, May 26, 2020, ID: 10216902147239146, 1:15:58, https://www.facebook.com/trahern.crews/videos/10216902147239146 (https://archive.is/Jo1eD).

9. Kingdemetrius Pendleton, "Kingdemetrius Pendleton Was Live," Facebook video, May 26, 2020, ID: 1147282135634352, 1:18:13, https://www.facebook.com/demetrius.pendleton.5/videos/1147282135634352 (https://archive.is/BccWI).

10. Pendleton, "Was Live."

11. Pendleton, "Was Live."

12. Pendleton, "Was Live"; Unicorn Riot, "#LIVE: Minneapolis Responds to Police Murder of George Floyd," YouTube video, May 26, 2020, ID: XAa5xb6JitI, 2:07:05, https://www.youtube.com/watch?v=XAa5xb6JitI (https://archive.is/ aEHki).

13. Pendleton, "Was Live."

14. Unicorn Riot, ID: XAa5xb6JitI.

15. Unicorn Riot, ID: XAa5xb6JitI.

16. Unicorn Riot, ID: XAa5xb6JitI.

17. Santa Ana Police Department, "40MM Less Lethal Launcher Guidelines," *Santa Ana PD Procedures Manual*, May 7, 2019, https://www.santa-ana.org/sites/default/files/PD%2520Dept%2520Policies/Dept%2520Procedures/3004.pdf.

18. Unicorn Riot, ID: XAa5xb6JitI.

19. Interview: Uprising/Whitney.

20. Shay Webbie, "Shay Webbie Was Live," Facebook video, May 27, 2020, ID: 557493288528859, 17:41, https://www.facebook.com/shay.webbie/videos/557493288528859 (https://archive.is/TNRSt).

21. Interview: Uprising/Chase.

22. Unicorn Riot, "#LIVE: Minneapolis Responds to Police Murder of George Floyd," YouTube video, May 27, 2020, ID: fHmoqQ86uxU, 25:29, https://www.youtube.com/watch?v=fHmoqQ86uxU (https://archive.is/T4PtJ); Unicorn Riot, "#LIVE: Minneapolis Responds to Police Murder of George Floyd," YouTube video, May 28, 2020, ID: AbohekheQUE, 2:35:47, https://www.youtube.com/watch?v=AbohekheQUE (https://archive.is/8LsKG).

23. Unicorn Riot, "Unicorn Riot Presents Reporter Reflection on Black Lives Uprising, Episode 2," YouTube video, October 21, 2020, ID: no5aazRc_pE 22:32, https://www.youtube.com/watch?v=no5aazRc_pE (https://archive.is/zNhVt).

24. Unicorn Riot, ID: AbohekheQUE.

25. Interview: Uprising/Devin.

26. Levy Armstrong, "Much of Lake Street Is Unrecognizable," Facebook video, May 28, 2020, ID: 1387887694715182 http://www.facebook.com/nekima.levypounds/videos/1387887694715182 (https://archive.is/4v46o).

27. Interview: Uprising/Marley.

28. Interview: Uprising/Anonymous1.

29. Andy Hobday, "George Floyd Protest in Minneapolis, MN Day 3, Part 2," Facebook video, May 28, 2020, ID: 10158266126389491, 2:40:02, https://www.facebook.com/andy.hobday.5/videos/10158266126389491/ (https://archive.is/fEeaQ).

30. Hobday, "Day 3, Part 2."

31. Hobday, "Day 3, Part 2."

32. "Day 50 of Continued Violence in Portland," Department of Homeland

Security, July 20, 2020, https://www.dhs.gov/news/2020/07/19/day-50-continued-violence-portland.

33. Alex Chun, "A Close Look at the Outside Agitator Trope," *Daily Northwestern*, November 13, 2020, https://dailynorthwestern.com/2020/11/12/multimedia/defining-safe-defining-the-outside-agitator/.

34. Aren Aizura, "A Mask and a Target Cart: Minneapolis Riots," *New Inquiry*, May 30, 2020, https://thenewinquiry.com/a-mask-and-a-target-cart-minneapolis-riots/; Brooke Cain, "Raleigh Mayor: Don't Judge Peaceful Protesters by Those Who Came for 'Destruction,'" *Raleigh News and Observer*, September 28, 2020, https://www.newsobserver.com/news/local/article246045220.html.

35. The exact definition of violence is debatable, but for the sake of simplicity, I am using the definition of violence found in US criminal law (US Code 18 I 1 § 16), which includes property damage within its remit.

36. Max Chillin, "Minneapolis Protests Live Pt. 5," YouTube video, May 29, 2020, ID: EJnclb6Y6q0, 2:36:28, https://www.youtube.com/watch?v=EJnclb6Y6q0 (https://archive.is/PY8io); Unicorn Riot, "#LIVE: Minneapolis Responds to Police Murder of George Floyd, Day 3, Part 2," YouTube video, May 29, 2020, ID: Nmv8IReEERs, 1:34:37, https://www.youtube.com/watch?v=Nmv8IReEERs (https://archive.is/kgyO3).

37. Cardi B (@iamcardib), "Spread," Twitter post, May 29, 2020, https://twitter.com/iamcardib/status/1266274385142231041 (https://archive.is/grlvw).

38. Interview: Uprising/Cameron.

39. Interview: Uprising/Mason.

40. Interview: Uprising/Avery.

41. Interview: Uprising/Peyton.

42. Audra D. S. Burch et al., "How Black Lives Matter Reached Every Corner of America," *New York Times*, June 13, 2020, https://www.nytimes.com/interactive/2020/06/13/us/george-floyd-protests-cities-photos.html.

43. 11Alive, "11Alive Reporter Shares Her Experience Covering the Atlanta Protests," YouTube video, June 3, 2020, https://www.youtube.com/watch?v=cQoh2azbq5E (https://archive.is/74hWS).

44. 11Alive, "Reporter Shares."

45. 11Alive, "Atlanta Protests for Ahmaud Arbery, George Floyd, Breonna Taylor: Live Stream," YouTube video, May 30, 2020, https://www.youtube.com/watch?v=xXGRR8rJNso (https://archive.is/AXDe7).

46. "Demonstrations and Political Violence in America: New Trends for Summer 2020," Armed Conflict Location and Event Data, September 3, 2020, https://acleddata.com/acleddatanew/wp-content/uploads/2020/09/ACLED_USData Review_Sum2020_SeptWebPDF.pdf.

47. "March for Justice #GeorgeFloyd," Facebook event, May 30, 2020, ID: 565450260835002, https://www.facebook.com/events/565450260835002/ (https://archive.is/DXAqo).

48. "The Defiant Walk of Resistance against Injustice," Facebook event, May 30, 2020, ID: 268024694396827, https://www.facebook.com/events/268024694396827/ (https://archive.is/L8Dfd).

49. The only involvement from established organizations occurred when the

overwhelmed organizer of the 12:00 p.m. Facebook event reached out to the local chapter of the NAACP and invited them to bring a list of speakers, after which the chapter publicized it on its Facebook page.

50. Washington Poor People's Campaign: A National Call for Moral Revival, "Urgent Info re: #GeorgeFloyd Protests/Call for Clergy," Facebook post, May 30, 2020, https://www.facebook.com/WashingtonPPC/posts/urgent-info-re-georgefloyd-protests-call-forclergydear-friends-supporters-and-ac/2399734520324328/ (https://archive.is/vhNNo).

51. "Statement from Black Lives Matter Seattle/King County on Recent Protests and Actions of City of Seattle Mayor Durkan," Black Lives Matter Seattle/King County, June 3, 2020, https://blacklivesseattle.org/blm06032020statement/.

52. As time went on, the group would reverse this stance and, despite being comprised of only a small group of activists, organized a singular, very successful protest numbering in the tens of thousands on June 12, accompanied by a call for a statewide general strike.

53. Seattle Police Department, "Timeline of Events on May 30th, 2020," *SPD Blotter*, June 1, 2020, https://spdblotter.seattle.gov/2020/06/01/timeline-of-events-on-may-30th-2020/.

54. Nicole Hong and William K. Rashbaum, "The 2 Lawyers, the Anti-Police Protests and the Molotov Cocktail Attack," *New York Times*, June 7, 2020, https://www.nytimes.com/2020/06/07/nyregion/molotov-cocktail-lawyers-nyc.html.

55. Seattle Police Department, "Timelines of Police Responses to Demonstrations," *SPD Blotter*, June 7, 2020, https://spdblotter.seattle.gov/2020/06/07/timelines-of-police-responses-to-demonstrations/.

56. Eric Scigliano, "Seattle's Riot Geography: 11th and Pine and a History of Protest," *Post Alley*, June 3, 2020, https://www.postalley.org/2020/06/02/the-fire-those-times-the-line-from-rodney-king-and-the-wto-to-todays-police-public-showdowns/.

57. Omari Salisbury, "Omari Salisbury Was Live," Facebook video, June 1, 2020, ID: 10220021035848747, https://www.facebook.com/omarisal/videos/10220021035848747 (https://archive.is/M7LjI).

58. Salisbury, "Was Live."

59. Sometime after people settled on the acronym CHOP, the wording was slightly changed to avoid references to occupations that were seen as potentially insensitive to indigenous groups. Thus, "occupied" became "organized."

60. See, for example, Andrew O'Hehir, "Is This What Democracy Looks Like? With Federal Goons in the Streets, History Hangs in the Balance," *Salon*, July 19, 2020, https://www.salon.com/2020/07/19/is-this-what-democracy-looks-like-federal-troops-are-in-the-streets-history-hangs-in-the-balance/.

61. Katherine Fung, "Hillary Clinton Joins Biden in Warning Trump May Retaliate If He Loses 2020: 'Be Ready,'" *Newsweek*, July 14, 2020, https://www.newsweek.com/hillary-clinton-joins-biden-warning-trump-may-retaliate-if-he-loses-2020-ready-1517713.

62. Luke O'Brien, "Trump Has Unleashed Authoritarian Violence in Portland. What City Is Next?," *HuffPost*, July 21, 2020, https://www.huffingtonpost

.co.uk/entry/tear-gas-kidnappings-trump-authoritarian-violence-portland_n_5f166610c5b615860bb6803d?ri18n=true.

63. "Trump to Send 'Surge' of Hundreds of Federal Agents to Cities," *BBC News*, July 23, 2020, https://www.bbc.co.uk/news/world-us-canada-53507660.

64. Jeff Merkley (@SenJeffMerkley), "Authoritarian governments, not democratic republics, send unmarked authorities after protesters," Twitter post, July 16, 2020, https://twitter.com/SenJeffMerkley/status/1283852273089683464 (https://archive.is/JHw7e).

65. Michelle Goldberg, "Opinion: Trump's Occupation of American Cities Has Begun," *New York Times*, July 21, 2020, https://www.nytimes.com/2020/07/20/opinion/portland-protests-trump.html.

66. Some among this new cohort even publicly and explicitly stated that they were not showing up for Black Lives Matter, much to the chagrin and frustration of the protesters they had shown up to protect. See Robert Evans, "The Fed War, Part 2," 2021, in *Uprising, a Guide from Portland*, podcast mp3, 49:51, https://www.iheart.com/podcast/1119-uprising-a-guide-from-por-73255667/.

67. "The Fed War."

CHAPTER TEN

1. Nicholas Bloom, "How Working from Home Works Out," Stanford Institute for Economic Policy Research, June 1, 2020, https://siepr.stanford.edu/research/publications/how-working-home-works-out.

2. Melanie Hanson, "College Enrollment and Student Demographic Statistics," Education Data Initiative, June 8, 2019, https://educationdata.org/college-enrollment-statistics.

3. Elise Gould and Melat Kassa, "Young Workers Hit Hard by the COVID-19 Economy: Workers Ages 16–24 Face High Unemployment and an Uncertain Future," Economic Policy Institute, October 14, 2020, https://www.epi.org/publication/young-workers-covid-recession/.

4. Interview: Uprising/Chase.

5. Interview: Uprising/Maria.

6. Interview: Uprising/Gray.

7. At this point the phenomenon of "long COVID" affecting younger people had not yet been widely recognized in public discourse.

8. Interview: Uprising/Riley.

9. For more on this, see Jonathan Pinckney and Miranda Rivers, "Sickness or Silence: Social Movement Adaptation to COVID-19," *Journal of International Affairs* 73, no. 2 (2020): 23–42.

10. "This Is the Right Call: Officers Involved in Fatal Minneapolis Incident Fired, Mayor Says," KSTP-TV, May 26, 2020, https://kstp.com/minnesota-news/minneapolis-police-george-floyd-death-/5741256/?cat=1.

11. Robert Klemko, "Former Atlanta Police Chief Walked with Protesters to Demand Change. She Resigned after an Officer Fatally Shot a Black Man," *Washington Post*, June 15, 2020, https://www.washingtonpost.com/national/former

-atlanta-police-chief-walked-with-protesters-to-demand-change-she-resigned-after-an-officer-fatally-shot-a-black-man/2020/06/15/ae6fe890-ae87-11ea-8758-bfd1d045525a_story.html.

12. Interview: Uprising/Lennon.
13. Interview: Uprising/Blake.
14. Interview: Uprising/Billie.
15. Interview: Uprising/Whitney.
16. Interview: Uprising/Hayden.
17. "Transcript: Trump to Mobilize Federal Resources to Stop Violence, Restore Security," *ABC News*, June 2, 2020, https://abcnews.go.com/Politics/transcript-trump-mobilize-federal-resources-stop-violence-restore/story?id=71008802.
18. Interview: Uprising/Anonymous3.
19. Interview: Uprising/Anonymous4.
20. The former site of Occupy Portland.
21. "The Fed War."
22. Interview: Uprising/Devin.
23. See Monica Anderson, "Teens, Social Media and Technology 2018," Pew Research Center, May 31, 2018, https://www.pewresearch.org/internet/2018/05/31/teens-social-media-technology-2018/; Monica Anderson and Andrew Perrin, "Barriers to Adoption and Attitudes Towards Technology," Pew Research Center, May 17, 2017, https://www.pewresearch.org/internet/2017/05/17/barriers-to-adoption-and-attitudes-towards-technology/; Emily A. Vogels, "Millennials Stand Out for Their Technology Use," Pew Research Center, September 9, 2019, https://www.pewresearch.org/fact-tank/2019/09/09/us-generations-technology-use/.
24. Interview: Uprising/Cameron.
25. Robert Evans, "Resistance through Mutual Aid," 2021, in *Uprising, a Guide from Portland*, podcast mp3, 1:16:54, https://www.iheart.com/podcast/1119-uprising-a-guide-from-por-73255667/.
26. Interview: Uprising/Anonymous2.
27. Interview: Uprising/Maria.
28. Unicorn Riot, ID: AbohekheQUE.
29. This is not to say that racial identities were unimportant, but rather that other identity categories had a more prominent impact on mass mobilization.
30. On this matter, see "The June 2020 AP-NORC Center Poll," Associated Press Center for Public Opinion Research, accessed August 5, 2021, https://apnorc.org/wp-content/uploads/2020/06/Topline_final_release5.pdf; Doug McAdam, "We've Never Seen Protests Like These Before," *Jacobin*, June 20, 2020, https://jacobinmag.com/2020/06/george-floyd-protests-black-lives-matter-riots-demonstrations; Kim Parker, "Amid Protests, Majorities across Racial and Ethnic Groups Express Support for the Black Lives Matter Movement," Pew Research Center, June 12, 2020, https://www.pewresearch.org/social-trends/2020/06/12/amid-protests-majorities-across-racial-and-ethnic-groups-express-support-for-the-black-lives-matter-movement/.
31. Interview: Uprising/Emerson (preuprising field interview).
32. Interview: Uprising/Jordan.

33. This referred to a series of slogans that became popular among protesters in Seattle: Defund the Police, Invest in the Community, Free the Protesters.

34. Lucas Combos, "Seattle Mayor Promises to Meet with Protesters, Consider Changes," Patch, June 3, 2020, https://patch.com/washington/seattle/seattle-mayor-promises-meet-protesters-consider-changes; Elise Takahama, "Durkan Promises to Meet with Seattle Protest Organizers: 'The Plan Has to Come from Community Voices,'" *Seattle Times*, June 2, 2020, https://www.seattletimes.com/seattle-news/durkan-promises-to-meet-with-seattle-protest-organizers-the-plan-has-to-come-from-communty-voices/.

35. Leslie Albrecht, "People Donated Millions of Dollars to the Wrong Black Lives Matter Foundation—Read This Before You Give to Any Charity," *MarketWatch*, July 6, 2020, https://www.marketwatch.com/story/people-donated-millions-of-dollars-to-the-wrong-black-lives-matter-foundation-read-this-before-you-give-to-any-charity-2020-07-01.

36. "Statement from Black Lives Matter Seattle/King County on Recent Protests and Actions of City of Seattle Mayor Durkan," Black Lives Matter Seattle/King County, June 3, 2020, https://blacklivesseattle.org/blm06032020statement/. As time went on, the group would reverse this stance and, despite being composed of only a small group of activists, organize a singular, very successful protest numbering in the tens of thousands on June 12, accompanied by a call for a statewide general strike.

37. Crowd Counting Consortium, "CCC—View/Download the Data," August 4, 2021, https://sites.google.com/view/crowdcountingconsortium/view-download-the-data.

38. This declined to approximately two-thirds of protests in July and about two-fifths in August, reflecting the increasing generation of *new* organizations by protesters, a general decline in spontaneous mobilization by ordinary people, and the resurgent role of established groups.

39. These data are drawn from the Crowd Counting Consortium data set.

40. Interview: Uprising/Anonymous5.

41. BlocBlocPDX, linktr.ee, n.d., accessed July 1, 2021, https://linktr.ee/BlocBlocPDX (https://archive.is/zj8LB).

42. Paige St. John, "Inside the Black Bloc Militant Protest Movement As It Rises Up against Trump," *Los Angeles Times*, February 12, 2017, https://www.latimes.com/local/lanow/la-me-black-bloc-20170212-story.html.

43. Even in the context of the successful occupations of public space achieved in certain US cities, the protesters and activists I talked to almost universally pursued digital coordination (and the anonymity it often availed) over face-to-face organizing.

44. For more information, see Barbara Ortutay and Amanda Seitz, "How Messaging Technology Is Helping Fuel Global Protests," Associated Press, June 6, 2020, https://apnews.com/article/ga-state-wire-american-protests-us-news-ap-top-news-ri-state-wire-76da6597cb481d0486ea7ec6ea192e9a; Rani Molla, "From Citizen to Signal, the Most Popular Apps Reflect America's Protests," *Vox*, June 3, 2020, https://www.vox.com/recode/2020/6/3/21278558/protest-apps-signal-citizen-twitter

-instagram-george-floyd; Amelia Nierenberg, "Signal Is the Messaging App of the Protests," *New York Times*, June 11, 2020, https://www.nytimes.com/2020/06/11/style/signal-messaging-app-encryption-protests.html.

45. Matt Sepic, "A Year after George Floyd's Death, Plans for Minneapolis Police Reform Have Softened," *NPR News*, May 25, 2021, https://www.npr.org/2021/05/25/1000298293/a-year-after-george-floyds-death-plans-for-minneapolis-police-reform-have-soften.

46. Steve Karnowski, "Court OKs 3rd-Degree Murder against 3-Ex Cops in Floyd Death," Associated Press, July 1, 2021, https://apnews.com/article/mn-state-wire-death-of-george-floyd-2ccad4d876d39044eda79402353b6819.

47. Everton Bailey Jr., "Portland Mayor Pledges to Divert Millions from Police Bureau, Ban Chokeholds in City Reforms," *The Oregonian*, June 9, 2020, https://www.oregonlive.com/portland/2020/06/defund-portland-police-units-to-reinvest-in-communities-of-color-among-citys-reform-plans-mayor-says.html.

48. David Kroman, "Defunding Seattle Police by 50% Proving Complicated for Council," *Crosscut*, Cascade Public Media, July 31, 2020, https://crosscut.com/news/2020/07/defunding-seattle-police-50-proving-complicated-council.

49. Sam Levin, "These US Cities Defunded Police: 'We're Transferring Money to the Community,'" *Guardian*, March 11, 2021, https://www.theguardian.com/us-news/2021/mar/07/us-cities-defund-police-transferring-money-community.

50. US House of Representatives, "U.S. House of Representatives—Vote Details," Office of the Clerk, June 25, 2020, https://clerk.house.gov/Votes/2020119.

51. Sepic, "A Year After."

52. Jonathan Levinson and Conrad Wilson, "Oregon Politicians Have Struggled to Keep Promises after George Floyd's Murder," Oregon Public Broadcasting, May 27, 2021, https://www.opb.org/article/2021/05/27/oregon-politicians-struggle-to-keep-promises-after-george-floyd-murder/.

53. General estimates from Crowd Counting Consortium data put 2,344,169 people as the high-end estimate for antiracist mobilizations in June, compared with 30,094 in August.

54. "2020 Impact Report—Black Lives Matter," Black Lives Matter, 22, February 23, 2021, https://blacklivesmatter.com/2020-impact-report/.

55. Black Lives Matter Seattle/King County, "Statement."

56. The group reported fewer than twenty branches in its report, and at least ten chapters broke away.

57. Black Power Media, "The #BLM10 Speak: It's Time for Accountability," YouTube video, February 10, 2021, https://www.youtube.com/watch?v=if_IAZpFm7w (https://archive.is/niqax).

58. "'It Is Time for Accountability': Statement from the Frontlines of BLM," BLM10+, March 29, 2021, https://www.blmchapterstatement.com/no1/.

PART V INTRODUCTION

1. George Rudé, *The Crowd in the French Revolution* (Oxford: Oxford University Press 1959), 231.

2. Rudé, *Crowd*, 281.

3. Hillel Soifer, "Shadow Cases in Comparative Research," *Qualitative and Multi-Method Research* 18, no. 2 (2020): 9–18.

4. The sole exception is the absence of paramount space.

CHAPTER ELEVEN

1. Edmund Burke, *Reflections on the Revolution in France and on the Proceedings in Certain Societies in London Relative to That Event* (London: James Dodsley, 1790), 352.

2. Quoted in John Hardman, *Robespierre* (London: Longman, 1999), 13. This was a theme that would continue throughout the revolution, as well as throughout the life of its ambitious and radical author, Maximilien Robespierre.

3. With regard to professions, exceptions were often made for professional groups not in guilds that asserted their desire to participate, except for the unemployed and landless. See Malcolm Crook, *Elections in the French Revolution* (New York: Cambridge University Press, 1996), 12.

4. Crook, *Elections*, 12.

5. John Markoff, *Abolition of Feudalism: Peasants, Lords, and Legislators in the French Revolution* (University Park: Penn State University Press, 1996), 20.

6. David Andress, *French Society in Revolution, 1789–1799* (Manchester, UK: Manchester University Press, 1999), 50; Friedemann Pestel, "French Revolution and Migration after 1789," *European History Online*, July 11, 2017, http://www.ieg-ego.eu/pestelf-2017-en.

7. Quoted in Robert Barrie Rose, *The Making of the Sans-Culottes: Democratic Ideas and Institutions in Paris, 1789–92* (Manchester, UK: Manchester University Press, 1983), 25.

8. M. J. Mavidal and M. E. Laurent, eds., *Archives parlementaires de 1787 à 1860*; Série 1/Tome 6, Volume 5 [Parliamentary Archives from 1787 to 1860; Series 1 / Tome 6, Volume 5] (Paris: Librarie Administrative de Paul Dupont, 1879), 601–3, http://gallica.bnf.fr/ark:/12148/bpt6k495219.

9. Crook, *Elections*, 12–13.

10. Rose, *Sans-Culottes*, 25.

11. Andress, *French Society*, 42.

12. John T. Gilchrist and William Murray, eds., *Press in the French Revolution* (London: Cheshire & Ginn, 1971), 4.

13. George Spencer Bower, "Camille Desmoulins," *Westminster Review* 188, no. 233 (1882): 42, https://www.proquest.com/docview/8311721.

14. Jeremy Popkin, *Revolutionary News: Press in France, 1789–99 (Bicentennial Reflections on the French Revolution)* (Durham, NC, and London: Duke University Press, 1990), 33.

15. Nicolas Ruault, *Gazette d'un Parisien sous la révolution: Lettres à son frère, 1783–1796* [*Journal of a Parisian during the Revolution: Letters to his brother, 1783–1796*], ed. Anne Vassal (Paris: Librarie Académique Perrin, 1976), 211, https://archive.org/details/gazettedunparisioooooruau.

16. Camille Desmoulins, *Fragment de l'histoire secrète de la révolution* [Part of the secret history of the revolution] (1793), 11, https://gallica.bnf.fr/ark:/12148/bp t6k6220649j/f19.item.

17. *Arrêtés concernant le choix des électeurs de Paris qui doit être fait le mardi 21 avril 1789, pris dans une assemblée de citoyens de Paris, le 19 du même mois* [Orders concerning the selection of the electors of Paris which must be made on Tuesday, April 21, 1789, taken in an assembly of citizens of Paris, on the 19th of the same month] (1789), https://gallica.bnf.fr/ark:/12148/bpt6k40187z.texteImage.

18. Rose, *Sans-Culottes*, 31.

19. Bailey Stone, *The Genesis of the French Revolution: A Global Historical Interpretation* (Cambridge: Cambridge University Press, 1994), 226–27. See also Bailey Stone, *Reinterpreting the French Revolution: A Global-Historical Perspective* (Cambridge: Cambridge University Press, 2002).

20. Peter M. Jones, *The Peasantry in the French Revolution* (Cambridge: Cambridge University Press, 1988), 67.

21. Lynn A. Hunt, "Committees and Communes: Local Politics and National Revolution in 1789," *Comparative Studies in Society and History* 18, no. 3 (1976): 321–46.

22. Norman Hampson, *A Social History of the French Revolution* (London: Routledge, 1963), 139–40.

23. See Jones, *Peasantry*. See also Anatoli Ado, *Paysans en révolution: terre, pouvoir et jacquerie, 1789–1794* [Peasants in revolution: land, power and rebellion, 1789–1794] (Paris: Société des études Robespierristes, 1996); Jean Boutier, "Jacqueries en pays croquant. Les révoltes paysannes en Aquitaine (décembre 1789–mars 1790)" [The Croqant Rebellions: The peasant revolts in Aquitaine (December 1789–March 1790)], *Annales. Économies, Sociétés, Civilisations* 34, no. 4 (1979): 760–86.

24. William Doyle, *Origins of the French Revolution* (Oxford and New York: Oxford University Press, 1980), 31.

25. Andress, *French Society*, 53.

26. Katie L. Jarvis, "Allez, Marchez Braves Citoyennes: A Study of the Popular Origins of, and the Political and Judicial Reactions to, the October Days of the French Revolution" (PhD diss., Boston College, 2007), 22, http://hdl.handle.net/2345/523.

27. Hunt, "Local Politics," 324.

28. Georges Lefebvre, *The Coming of the French Revolution*, trans. Robert R. Palmer (Princeton, NJ: Princeton University Press, 1947), 142.

29. This uneasy alliance could only last so long as a common enemy remained. As Jones notes in *Peasantry*: "The alliance of townspeople and country dwellers... was not automatic" (1988, 70). In regions such as Strasbourg, once the feudal classes had been disposed of, bourgeoisie and peasant turned on one another, prefiguring the later conflicts of the revolution.

30. Denis Richet, "Revolutionary Journées," in *A Critical Dictionary of the French Revolution*, ed. François Furet and Mona Ozouf, trans. Arthur Goldhammer (Cambridge, MA, and London: Harvard University Press, 1989), 125.

31. Emmet Kennedy, *A Cultural History of the French Revolution* (New Haven, CT: Yale University Press, 1989), 6.

32. Kennedy, *Cultural History*, 9.

33. Arlette Farge and Jacques Revel, *The Vanishing Children of Paris: Rumor and Politics before the French Revolution* (Cambridge, MA: Harvard University Press, 1991), 664.

34. Hampson, *Social History*, 139–40.

35. Richard Cobb, *The People's Armies: The Armées Révolutionaires Instrument of Terror in the Departments April 1793 to Floreal Year II* (New Haven, CT: Yale University Press, 1987), 333.

36. David Garrioch, "The Everyday Lives of Parisian Women and the October Days of 1789," *Social History* 24, no. 3 (1999): 231–49. See also Katie L. Jarvis, "'In the Name of Humanity': Redefining Socio-economic Assistance in the Revolutionary Marketplace," *French History* 33, no. 4 (2019): 530–36; Darline Gay Levy, Harriet Branson Applewhite, and Mary Durham Johnson, eds., *Women in Revolutionary Paris, 1789–1795* (Champaign: University of Illinois Press, 1979).

37. Garrioch, "Everyday Lives," 239–41.

38. Garrioch, "Everyday Lives," 242.

39. Jones, *Peasantry*, 68.

40. For a detailed discussion on the Third Estate, its composure, and political engagement with the king, see Timothy Tackett, *Becoming a Revolutionary: The Deputies of the French National Assembly and the Emergence of a Revolutionary Culture (1789–1790)* (University Park: Pennsylvania State University Press, 1996).

41. Lefebvre, *Coming*, 116–17. See also Rudé, *The Crowd*, 47.

42. Rudé, *The Crowd*, 47.

43. Though the insurgency accompanying the Grande Peur (Great Fear) is sometimes depicted as having largely subsided by the autumn of 1789, these endeavors show a more persistent pattern of contention, finding that "a little over a hundred chateaux were invaded by peasant bands drawn from at least 330 different parishes," between December 1789 and March 1790. Jones, *Peasantry*, 70.

44. Jones, *Peasantry*, 74.

45. Jones, *Peasantry*, 74.

46. Kennedy, *Cultural History*, 31–32.

47. Lefebvre, *Coming*, 144. See also Jones, *Peasantry*, 74.

48. Markoff, *Abolition*, 376–77.

49. Richard Cobb, *Paris and Its Provinces, 1792–1802* (Oxford: Oxford University Press, 1975), 27.

50. Lefebvre, *Coming*, 150.

51. Kevin Hetherington, *The Badlands of Modernity: Heterotopia and Social Ordering* (London and New York: Routledge. 1997), 15.

52. Translation is mine. The original French quotation can be found in Ruault, *Gazette*, 151.

53. As Rudé put it in *The Crowd*, 48: "In the early days it was the Palais Royal alone that gave a positive direction to the popular movement."

54. Billington, *Minds and Men*, 31.

55. Micah Alpaugh, *Non-violence and the French Revolution: Political Demonstrations in Paris, 1787–1795* (Cambridge: Cambridge University Press, 2015), 61–62.

56. Alpaugh, *Non-violence*, 61.

57. Archives nationales de France, C 26, unnumbered, July 12, 1789, quoted in Alpaugh, *Non-violence*, 61.

58. Hans-Jürgen Lüsebrink and Rolf Reichardt, *The Bastille: A History of a Symbol of Despotism and Freedom* (Durham, NC, and London: Duke University Press, 1997), 38–78.

59. Farge and Revel, *Vanishing Children*, 63.

60. Andress, *French Society*, 59–60.

61. Jones, *Peasantry*, 68.

62. Louis Gottschalk and Margaret Maddox, *Lafayette in the French Revolution: Through the October Days* (Chicago: University of Chicago Press, 1969), 329.

63. Sigismond Lacroix, *Actes de la Commune de Paris pendant la révolution*, vol. 2 [Acts of the Paris Commune during the revolution, vol. 2] (Paris: Sigismond Lacroix, 1895 [1789]), 165, https://gallica.bnf.fr/ark:/12148/bpt6k49128m.r.

64. Jarvis, *Allez, Marchez*, 45.

65. *Procédure Criminelle, Institute au Chatelet de Paris: Sur la dénonciation des faits arrivés à Versailles dans la journée du 6 Octobre 1789* [Criminal proceedings, heard at the Châtelet in Paris: on the denunciation of the facts that occurred at Versailles on October 6, 1789] (1790), LXXXI, https://www.google.co.uk/books/edition/Procédure_criminelle_instruite_au_Chate/.

66. William Doyle, *The Oxford History of the French Revolution* (Oxford: Oxford University Press, 1989), 121.

67. Doyle, *Oxford History*, 121–22.

68. *Révolutions de Versailles et de Paris, dédiées aux dames françoises* [Revolutions of Versailles and Paris, dedicated to the French ladies], no.1: 1, https://gallica.bnf.fr/ark:/12148/bpt6k42479n/f3.item.

CHAPTER TWELVE

1. Not featured in figure 12.1 are people's identities and drives, as well as paramount spaces, all three of which came to play important roles later in the revolutionary process (especially identity, discussed later) but which were not as prominently involved in mobilization during this early stage.

2. Bailey Stone, *The Genesis of the French Revolution: A Global Historical Interpretation* (Cambridge: Cambridge University Press, 1994), 226.

3. Translation from Darline Gay Levy, Harriet Branson Applewhite, and Mary Durham Johnson, eds., *Women in Revolutionary Paris, 1789–1795* (Champaign: University of Illinois Press, 1979), 49.

4. This deposition and those subsequently quoted can be found in *Procedure Criminelle, Institute au Chatelet de Paris: Sur la denonciation des faits arrives à Versailles dans la journée du 6 Octobre 1789* (1790), https://www.google.co.uk/books/edition/Proc%C3%A9dure_criminelle_instruite_au_Chate/. The verbs *forcée* and *entraînée* are used frequently in the depositions, and often ambiguous. In some cases, women reported being physically coerced by the crowd into joining, and here the translations "forced" and "dragged" might be most appropriate. Usually, however, they are used by women who quite clearly had a choice in the matter and generally partook in events with a degree of enthusiasm. One deposition even

refers to how a woman, *"également arrêtée et forcée d'aller à Versailles,"* took a trip to a tavern en route, where, needing to return to her young son who was waiting at home, "in order to obtain her freedom, she proposed that she would drink a bottle of wine." *Journée du 6,* LXXXII.

5. *Journée du 6,* CII.

6. *Journée du 6,* XC.

7. George Rudé, *The Crowd in the French Revolution* (Oxford: Oxford University Press 1959), 62–63.

8. William Doyle, *The Oxford History of the French Revolution* (Oxford: Oxford University Press, 1989), 159–61.

9. John Markoff, "Peasant Grievances and Peasant Insurrection: France in 1789," *Journal of Modern History* 62, no. 3 (1990): 446–76.

10. Stone, *Genesis,* 233.

11. Stone, *Genesis,* 233.

12. See, for example, Jean-Paul Bertaud, *The Army of the French Revolution: From Citizen Soldiers to Instrument of Power,* trans. Robert R. Palmer (Princeton, NJ: Princeton University Press, 1989), 22; Richard Cobb, *The Police and the People: French Popular Protest, 1789–1820* (Oxford: Oxford University Press, 1970); Samuel F. Scott, *The Response of the Royal Army to the French Revolution: The Role and Development of the Line Army, 1787–93* (Oxford: Oxford University Press, 1978), 27.

13. Georges Lefebvre, *The Coming of the French Revolution,* trans. Robert R. Palmer (Princeton, NJ: Princeton University Press, 1947), 212.

14. Steve Bradshaw, *Café Society: Bohemian Life from Swift to Bob Dylan* (London: Weidenfeld & Nicolson, 1978), 27.

15. Lynn A. Hunt, "Committees and Communes: Local Politics and National Revolution in 1789," *Comparative Studies in Society and History* 18, no. 3 (1976): 345.

16. Hunt, "Local Politics," 344.

17. Micah Alpaugh, *Non-violence and the French Revolution: Political Demonstrations in Paris, 1787–1795* (Cambridge: Cambridge University Press, 2015). See also Micah Alpaugh, "A Self-Defining 'Bourgeoisie' in the Early French Revolution: The Milice Bourgeoise, the Bastille Days of 1789, and Their Aftermath," *Journal of Social History* 47, no. 3 (2014): 696–720.

18. Rudé, *The Crowd,* 63.

19. Jeremy Popkin, *Revolutionary News: Press in France, 1789–99 (Bicentennial Reflections on the French Revolution)* (Durham, NC, and London: Duke University Press, 1990), 33–34.

20. Quoted in John T. Gilchrist and William Murray, eds., *Press in the French Revolution* (London: Cheshire & Ginn, 1971), 13.

21. *Le Courrier de Provence,* no. 24, in Gilchrist and Murray, *Press in the French Revolution,* 60.

22. A considerable number of reports, constituting an excellent representative sample of the French press, can be found in Gilchrist and Murray's *Press in the French Revolution.* See also Hugh Gough. "The French Revolutionary Press," in *Press, Politics and the Public Sphere in Europe and North America, 1760–1820,* ed. Hannah Barker and Simon Burrows (Cambridge: Cambridge University Press, 2002).

23. Quoted in Gilchrist and Murray, *Press in the French Revolution,* 79.

24. Alan Forrest, *Paris, the Provinces and the French Revolution* (Oxford: Oxford University Press, 2004), 108.

25. Hunt, "Local Politics," 344.

26. Forrest, *Paris, the Provinces*, 109–10.

27. Rudé, *The Crowd*, 81–82.

28. Timothy Tackett, *When the King Took Flight* (Cambridge, MA, and London: Harvard University Press, 2003), 114.

29. Rudé, *The Crowd*, 213.

30. Rudé, *The Crowd*, 220.

31. Tackett, *The King*, 94.

32. Doyle, *Oxford History*, 183.

33. David Andress, *The French Revolution and the People* (London: A&C Black, 2004), 158.

34. François Furet, *The French Revolution, 1770–1814* (Oxford: Blackwell Publishing, 1988), 108; Doyle, *Oxford History*, 184.

35. Nicolas Ruault, *Gazette d'un Parisien sous la révolution: Lettres à son frère, 1783–1796*, ed. Anne Vassal (Paris: Librarie Académique Perrin, 1976), 284–85, https://archive.org/details/gazettedunparisioooruau.

36. Furet, *French Revolution*, 108–9.

37. Patrice Higonnet, "Sans-culottes," in *A Critical Dictionary of the French Revolution*, ed. François Furet and Mona Ozouf, trans. Arthur Goldhammer (Cambridge, MA, and London: Harvard University Press, 1989), 393–99.

38. Doyle, *Oxford History*, 187.

39. Doyle, *Oxford History*, 188.

40. Rudé, *The Crowd*, 105.

41. Doyle, *Oxford History*, 189.

42. Furet, *French Revolution*, 128.

43. Rudé, *The Crowd*, 120.

44. Forrest, *Paris and the Provinces*, 109–10.

45. Rudé, *The Crowd*, 121.

CONCLUSION

1. Doug McAdam, *Political Process and the Development of Black Insurgency, 1930–1970* (Chicago: University of Chicago Press, 1982).

2. Florence Passy, "Social Networks Matter. But How?," in *Social Movements and Networks: Relational Approaches to Collective Action*, ed. Mario Diani and Doug McAdam (Oxford: Oxford University Press, 2003); Dana R. Fisher and Lorien Jasny, "Understanding Persistence in the Resistance," *Sociological Forum* 34, no. 1 (2019): 1065–89; Joris Verhulst and Stefaan Walgrave, "The First Time Is the Hardest? A Cross-National and Cross-Issue Comparison of First-Time Protest Participants," *Political Behavior* 31, no. 3 (2009): 455–84.

3. Fisher and Jasny, "Understanding Persistence."

4. William A. Gamson and Emilie Schmeidler, "Organizing the Poor," *Theory and Society* 13, no. 4 (1984): 567.

5. Catherine Corrigall-Brown, *Patterns of Protest: Trajectories of Participation in Social Movements* (Stanford, CA: Stanford University Press, 2012).

6. This pattern is reminiscent of the advantages of disruption promoted by Frances Fox Piven and Richard Cloward in *Poor People's Movements: Why They Succeed, How They Fail* (New York: Pantheon Books, 1977).

7. See Benjamin Case, "Riots as Civil Resistance: Rethinking the Dynamics of 'Nonviolent' Struggle," *Journal of Resistance Studies* 4, no. 1 (2018): 9–44; Benjamin Case, "Molotov Cocktails to Mass Marches: Strategic Nonviolence, Symbolic Violence, and the Mobilizing Effect of Riots," *Theory in Action* 14, no.1 (2021): 18–38; Cathy Lisa Schneider, *Police Power and Race Riots: Urban Unrest in Paris and New York* (Philadelphia: University of Pennsylvania Press, 2014).

8. James M. Jasper and Jane D. Poulsen, "Recruiting Strangers and Friends: Moral Shocks and Social Networks in Animal Rights and Anti-Nuclear Protests," *Social Problems* 42, no. 4 (1995): 493–512.

9. Brian Martin, *Justice Ignited: The Dynamics of Backfire* (Lanham, MD: Rowman & Littlefield, 2007).

10. Erica Chenoweth and Maria J. Stephan, "Why Civil Resistance Works: The Strategic Logic of Nonviolent Conflict," *International Security* 33, no. 1 (2008): 11.

11. Jules Boykoff, "Limiting Dissent: The Mechanisms of State Repression in the USA," *Social Movement Studies* 6, no. 3 (2007): 281–310; Erica Chenoweth, Evan Perkoski, and Sooyeon Kang, "State Repression and Nonviolent Resistance," *Journal of Conflict Resolution* 61, no. 9 (2017): 1950–69; Tijen Demirel-Pegg and Scott Pegg, "Razed, Repressed and Bought Off: The Demobilization of the Ogoni Protest Campaign in the Niger Delta," *The Extractive Industries and Society* 2, no. 4 (2015): 654–63.

12. David A. Snow and Robert D. Benford, "Ideology, Frame Resonance and Participant Mobilization," *International Social Movement Research* 1 (1988), 198.

13. Jay Ulfelder, "Hello, World!," *Crowd Counting Consortium*, February 9, 2021, https://countingcrowds.org/2021/02/09/hello-world/.

14. See, for example, Fisher and Jasny, "Understanding Persistence."

15. However, we can never quite be sure what impact such events will have. A draft of this paragraph written many years ago posited that epidemic disease might have been just such a factor, and yet, by 2020, it helped to encourage youth participation in the Black Lives Uprising.

16. A topic attended to masterfully by Jack Goldstone in *Revolution and Rebellion in the Early Modern World* (Berkeley: University of California Press, 1991).

17. Sidney Tarrow, *The Language of Contention: Revolutions in Words, 1688–2012* (Cambridge: Cambridge University Press, 2013). See also Benjamin Abrams and Peter R. Gardner, *Symbolic Objects in Contentious Politics* (Ann Arbor: University of Michigan Press, 2023).

18. Doug McAdam, Priya Fielding-Singh, and Krystal Laryea, "Predicting the Onset, Evolution and Postgraduate Impact of College Activism," *Mobilization* 27, no. 2 (2022) 125–47.

19. Charles Tilly, *Regimes and Repertoires* (Chicago: University of Chicago Press, 2006).

Index

Page numbers in italics refer to figures and tables, and page numbers followed by *n* refer to endnotes.

action: direct, 188–89, 191–92, 223; versus organization, 114–15; strategic, 3; theory of, 28
activists, 31, 92, 237–38; Black Lives Uprising, 157–58, 187–95; Egyptian, 1–2, 55–56, 71–79, 81–83, 85–86, 91–95, 99; French Revolutionary, 48, 201–3, 218, 221–27, 236; Occupy Wall Street, 107, 112–17, 148–50
Adbusters, 108, 111–12, 116, 135
affiliates, of movements, 3, 22, 141, 143, 235; absence of, 73, 232
affinities (categories), 37–44, 50–53; in the Black Lives Uprising, *181*, 181–87; difference between social and psychological, 37, 50–51; in the Egyptian Revolution, 86–88, *87*, 97–99; in the French Revolution, *216*, 217–19; in Occupy Wall Street, 123–37 passim, *124*, 233. *See also* psychological affinities; social affinities
affinity (concept), 4–6, 32–44; background to, 33–35; conceptualization of in context of contention, 35–36; without convergence, 51, 229; definition of, 36; dissipation of, 97–99; interaction with convergence, 44, 50–54, *52*, *53*, 128, 130, 134, 241–42; summary of, 230

affinity-convergence mobilization, 4–6, *5*, *36*, 50–54, *53*; in the Black Lives Uprising, 154, 175–89, *181*, 234; and conventional mobilization, 5, 50–51; in the Egyptian Revolution, 85–89, *87*, 232; fragility of, 221, 232; in the French Revolution, 198, 215–21, *216*, 235; in Occupy Wall Street, *124*, 124–37, 233; patterns across cases, 240–42. *See also* mobilization; spontaneous mobilization (concept)
affinity-convergence theory (ACT), 2, 29, 31–57; benefits of, 230–31, 236–37; development of, 3; intended uses of, 52–54; limitations of, 54, 241–42; potential improvements to, 243–54; summary of, 4–6, 32–33, 229–31. *See also* affinity (concept); convergence
affinity groups, 33–34, 189–91; corporate affinity networks, 34
African Americans. *See* Black people
age, 39, 80, 159, 175. *See also* status (affinity)
agency, 4, 6, 17, 28–29, 31–32; and affinity, 137, 231; and convergence, 42; and framing, 23; and structures, 54
aggregate behavior, 6, 32–33, 52–54, 137
Al Jazeera, 62, 79

INDEX

Alpaugh, Micah, 211
anarchism, 34; and the Black Lives Uprising, 166, 195; and Occupy Wall Street, 108–9, 112–13, 127, 135, 149–50
Ancien Régime (France), 239; mobilization against, 206–13; state of, 199–206
anticapitalism, 118–19, 132
Antifa, 190–91
antifascism, 49, 190–91; as an identity, 186
antipolice, 68–69, 172, 195–96; sentiment, 72, 77, 132
antiracism, 51, 154, 187–89; antiracist identities, 185–86; gestures of, 176–77
antiseigneurialism, 198, 203–4, 206–9, 215
apps, 182, 191–92. *See also* internet; social media
April 6 movement (Egypt), 67, 69, 73; banning of, 103
Arab Spring: of 2011, 1, 231; of 2005, 65. *See also* Egyptian Revolution (2011); Tunisian Revolution
armed protest. *See* weapons
arrests, 158; ability to risk, 39; mass arrests, 64, 117–18, 128, 233, 239
arson, 161, 179; of National Democratic Party headquarters, 77; of police stations, 77, 165–67, 266n21
Atlanta, Georgia, 166–68, 176–77, 189–90, 193–94
attitudes (affinity), 41–42; in the Black Lives Uprising, *181*, 187; in the Egyptian Revolution, 61, 70, 72, 86–87, *87*, 99; in the French Revolution, 204, *216*, 217–19; in Occupy Wall Street, 121, *124*, 131–32, 136. *See also* psychological affinities
Australian International Defense Exhibition of 1991 (AIDEX), 33–34
autonomous organization, 33, 108, 112–13, 115–16, 194, 201
autonomous zones, 46, 49, 171

Bandura, Albert, 32
Ben Ali, Zine el-Abidine, 1, 72
Benford, Robert, 2, 45
Billington, James, 210
biographical availability, 40, 136, 176, 183. *See also* social affinities
black bloc, 190–91
Black Lives Matter: agenda, 42; chapters, 158, 188; distinction from Black Lives Uprising, 249n9; precursors to, 108, 149; Seattle/King County, 168, 188
Black Lives Matter Global Network Foundation, 188, 193; role in protests, 193–94
Black Lives Uprising, 2, 7, 8, 10, 42, 51, *181*; in Atlanta, 167–68, 176–77, 189–90, 193–94; consequences of, 192–96; decline of, 192–95; distinction from Black Lives Matter, 249n9; glamorization of, 154–55, 165–66; in Minneapolis, 157–66, 176–78; most likely participants in, 187; pattern of protest in, 167, 169; in Portland, Oregon, 171–73, 178–79, 184, 190; scale of early protests, 168; in Seattle, 168–71; summary of part IV, 153–55
Black people: brutality against, 153–57, 178; identity as, 185–86; partial list of Black victims of police violence, 151–52; participation in protests, 186
blocs (Black Lives Uprising), 190
Bloomberg, Michael, 112, 142; Bloombergville, 112
Boyte, Harry C., 49
Bread and Puppet, 128–29
bridges, 38, 209, 217, 235; Brooklyn Bridge, 117–18, 238; Pont Neuf (France), 38, 205, 220
brokerage (mechanism), 22
Brookfield Office Properties, 108, 123; John Eugene Zuccotti, 108
Brooks, Rayshard, 155

cafés (France), 201–2, 206–7, 209–10, 216, 218, 235; and clubs, 219, 223–24; and convergence, 220
cahiers de doléances, 199–201; assemblies, 205–6, 208, 215–16, 221
Cairo (Egypt), 38, 55–56, 74; Boulaq Aboul Ela, 77; High Court, 65. *See also* Tahrir Square (Egypt)
Calhoun, Craig, 6
Camel Battle (Egypt), 47, 79–81; aftermath, 83–84, 87
Capitol Hill Occupied Protest (CHOP) (Black Lives Uprising), 170–71, 179–80, 240; compared with Zuccotti Park, 171
censorship, 39, 66, 103, 202
Central Security Forces (Egypt), 69, 76, 78
civil wars, 33, 244; Spanish Civil War, 33
class, 39; antagonisms, 282n29; in the Egyptian Revolution, 66–67, 72, 75, 77, 82–84, 92; in the French Revolution, 203–9, 215–17, 219, 226. *See also* status (affinity)
Cloward, Richard, 18
coalitions, 65, 71–72, 75, 93, 144, 158; collapse of, 94–95, 282n29
cognitive conditions of convergence. *See* frames (convergence)
collective action, 3–4, 19, 24–25; social identity model of collective action (SIMCA), 24–25; supply/demand model of collective action, 25–26, 28. *See also* collective behavior theories
collective behavior theories, 3, 16–17, 28–29, 31–32, 230–31; contagion, 3, 251n18; criticism of, 17
comparative history plus, 6–7. *See also* research methods
conditions of convergence, 4–5, 44–53, 239; in the Black Lives Uprising, 175–80, *181*; combined effect, 137, 154, 179–80; contexts, 5, 46–50, 261n59; in the Egyptian Revolution, 72–73, 77, *87*, 88–89, 95–97, 232; external versus internal sources of, 52; in the French Revolution, *216*, 219–21; in Occupy Wall Street, 109, 119, 121, *124*, 124–29, 133–37, 233; subtypes, 4, 45–46, 51. *See also* exceptional (convergence); frames (convergence); opportune (convergence); paramount (convergence); situations (convergence); spaces (convergence)
convergence, 4–6, 44–53; dissipation of, 52, 95–97, 145; interaction with affinity, 44, 50–54, *52*, *53*, 128, 130, 241–42; (non)exclusivity of, 242–43; prior theories of, 17, 28–29, 31; summary of, 230; taxonomy of, *46*, 52. *See also* conditions of convergence
Cordeliers, 224, 226, 228
Corrigall-Brown, Catherine, 238
corruption, 55, 61, 72–75
countermovements, 242–43
COVID-19 pandemic, 2, 31, 38, 43–44, 47, 149, 234; impact on protest participation, 175–76, 182–83; mitigation methods, 158, 168, 188, 191
Crook, Malcolm, 200, 281n3
Crowd in the French Revolution, The (Rudé), 197
culture, 22–24, 28–29, 50, 126; in the Egyptian Revolution, 81–82, 87, 92; in the French Revolution, 218–19; within movements, 237; in Occupy Wall Street, 111, 126, 133. *See also* framing; moral shocks

Day of Rage: in Egypt, 75–77; in the United States, 237
demobilization: of the masses 95–99, 240, 243–44; movement-led, 94–95. *See also* repression
Democratic Party (United States), 108, 147; Working Families Party, 193. *See also* Obama, Barack; Sanders, Bernie

Department of Homeland Security (DHS), 142, 148, 239–40
Desmoulins, Camille, 202, 210
Diani, Mario, 22
dispositions (affinity), 25, *41*, 41–42, 50–51; in the Black Lives Uprising, *181*, 185–87; in the Egyptian Revolution, 61, 72, 86–87, *87*; in the French Revolution, 203–4, *216*, 217–19; in Occupy Wall Street, *124*, 131–36. *See also* attitudes (affinity); identities (affinity); perceived injustice; psychological affinities
disruption, 18–19, 79, 175–76, 182–83, 231, 238–39. *See also* quotidian disruption
divergence (concept), 243
Doyle, William, 219, 228
drives (affinity), 4, *41*, 42–44, 51; in the Black Lives Uprising, *181*, 184–85; in the Egyptian Revolution, 82, 87, *87*; in the French Revolution, 284n1; in Occupy Wall Street, *124*, 127–30. *See also* interests (affinity); needs (affinity); psychological affinities
Durkan, Jenny, 187–88, 192. *See also* Seattle
Dynamics of Contention (McAdam, Tarrow, and Tilly), 26

efficacy, 24–25, 48, 128, 178, 239. *See also* needs (affinity); opportune (convergence): frames
Egyptian: national identity, 92; people as "revolutionaries in waiting," 60–62; revolutionaries, 48
Egyptian military, 83–84, 93–100; fraternization with, 98; popularity of, 97–98. *See also* Supreme Council of the Armed Forces (SCAF) (Egypt)
Egyptian Revolution (2011), 1, 2, 8, 9, 42, 43, 47–49, *81*; affinity and convergence in, 57, 85–89, *87*; aftermath of, 91–105; "Facebook revolt" and "Twitter revolution" hypotheses, 56; inevitability of, 55–56; peak of, 71–89; prehistory of, 59–70; summary of Part II, 231–32
Eighteen Days (Egypt), 55, 71–89
ElBaradei, Mohamed, 67–68, 70
elections: demobilizing effect of, 96; Egypt (2005), 62, 64–66; Egypt (2010–2011), 62, 67–68, 93; Egypt (2011 onward), 95, 99–101, 268n18; in the French Revolution, 198–201; United States (2012), 145; United States (2020), 178
elites: Egyptian, 62, 81, 84; local government, 176; revolt against, 42
email. *See* messaging
emergent norms. *See* norms, and rules
emotions, 3, 41, 45, 77, 125, 127, 163–67 passim; betrayal, 185; despair, 143; fear, 43; joy, 166–67; rage, 43, 161
encounters, 32, 93, 132, 134, 216–17
Estates General (France): convocation, 198–201, 205, 208, 219, 221, 235; further reading, 283n40. *See also* Third Estate (France)
ethnicity. *See* race, and ethnicity
Evans, Robert, 172
Evans, Sara M., 49
eviction, 195; of CHOP, 171; of Occupy Wall Street, 44, 51, 123, 130, 141–44, 233, 239; of Tahrir protesters (attempted), 100
exceptional (convergence), 45, *46*, 52, 219, 241; frames, 48, 84, 96–97, 219; situations, 47, 76, 88, 175–76, 179–80, 219, 231, 234, 239, 242–43; spaces, 49–50, 84, 89, 119, 125–29, 133–37, 179–80, 210, 220–21

Facebook, 2, 103; Egyptian users, 264n26; events, 73–75, 158, 168; livestreams, 158, 162, 182, 191; pages, 67–68, 73–75; posts, 157
Farge, Arlette, 205, 221
February 2, 2011. *See* Camel Battle (Egypt)
Federal Bureau of Investigation (FBI), 119, 142

federal officers (Black Lives Uprising), 171–73, 178, 239
fédérés, 227
Fed War (Black Lives Uprising), 171–73, 178–79, 184
Fête de la Fédération, 227
15-M Indignados movement, 1, 112, 115, 120, 140
Fligstein, Neil, 26
Floyd, George, 2, 7, 152, 179; dying words, 157; George Floyd Justice in Policing Act, 192; reactions to murder of, 175–76
food, 40, 43, 62, 83, 99, 126, 129, 133, 180; bread and grain, 203–4, 219
Forrest, Alan, 223
frames (convergence), *46*, 47–49, 79, 96, 241–42; exceptional, 48, 84, 96–97, 219; opportune, 48, 77, 79, 88, 176–77, 208; paramount, 48–49, 72–73, 79, 88, 100, 119, 121, 129, 131–37 passim, 144–45, 172, 179, 220, 239
framing: breakdown of, 143–46, 193; misinformation, 78–79; narrative, 100–101, 103; shifts in, 118, 209; strategic use of, 48, 73–74, 78–79, 235, 237; theories of, 3, 23
free spaces, *46*, 49, 221
French Revolution (1789), 2, 8, 10, 48; affinity-convergence mobilization in, 215–21, *216*; clubs and societies, 223–24; early phases of, 199–209; initial recognition of, 211–12; July days, 209–12; October days, 212–13; organized mobilization in, 221–28; *patrie en danger*, 226–28; revolutionary press, 222–23, 225; second revolution, 213; summary of Part V, 235–36
friction (concept), 53
Friday: of Departure (February 11), 85; prayers (Egypt), 38, 75–76; of Rage, 77 (*see also* January 28, 2011)
frustration–aggression hypothesis. *See* relative deprivation
Fu, Diana, 6

Gamson, William A., 17, 237
gender, 39, 84, 88. *See also* identities (affinity); status (affinity)
general assembly. *See* New York City General Assembly (NYCGA)
generalizability, 54, 137, 236–37, 242
German Revolution (1989), 19, 29, 50, 231
Ghonim, Wael, 67–69, 73–76; arrest of, 76
Global Justice movement, 112, 272n3
Goodwin, Jeff, 48
Gould, Roger V., 21
Gould-Wartofsky, Michael, 114, 118
Grande Peur (Great Fear), 207–9, 283n43
grievances. *See* attitudes (affinity); perceived injustice
Gurr, Ted, 16, 42

Hetherington, Kevin, 209–10
historical moment (concept), 45, 48, 79
homelessness, 127, 129, 133–35, 143, 195; activism, 190; becoming homeless, 130. *See also* eviction
human rights, 72–73; organizations, 79, 104
Hunt, Lynn, 203, 220
Hurricane Sandy. *See* Occupy Sandy

identities (affinity), 22, 24; in the Black Lives Uprising, *181*, 185–86; in the Egyptian Revolution, 80, 87, *87*, 93, 98; in the French Revolution, 218, 223, 225, 284n1; in Occupy Wall Street, *124*, 129–33, 136, 147–48. *See also* psychological affinities
ideology, 42, 84; plurality of, 123–24, 131. *See also* attitudes (affinity)
incentives, 19, 32
institutions, 19; politics within, 92
interests (affinity), 43–44; in the Black Lives Uprising, 184; in the Egyptian Revolution, *87*, 89; in Occupy Wall Street, *124*, 127, 130, 133. *See also* drives (affinity)

International Socialist Organization, 107
internet, 182–83; blogs, 64, 66; discussion, 62; email, 34, 139, 141; organizing, 279n43; shutdowns, 2, 39, 74, 76, 231, 329. *See also* social media
InterOccupy, 141
Iraq invasion (2003), 65, 107–8
Islamism/Salafism, 81, 93, 101–2. *See also* Muslim Brotherhood (Egypt)

Jacobins, 224–28
January 25, 2011 (Egypt), 2, 55–56, 60, 71–75, 237–38
January 28, 2011 (Egypt), 38, 71, 75–78, 232
Jasper, James M., 23, 28
Jones, Peter, 208, 212
journalists. *See* reportage
Jumet, Kira, 29

Kefaya (Egypt), 64–66, 67
Ketchley, Neil, 77
Killian, Lewis M., 16
Klandermans, Bert, 25–26, 27, 28
kleptocracy. *See* corruption
Krauthammer, Charles, 65

Lachmann, Richard, 6
Lefebvre, Georges, 204, 208, 220
Les Halles (France), 205, 212, 218
Liberty Plaza. *See* Zuccotti Park
Louis XVI (king), 199–200, 207, 211–13; downfall of, 226–28
Luxemburg, Rosa, 19

magazines. *See* newspapers, and magazines: *Time*
Maher, Ahmed, 66–67
mainstream media, 94, 100–101, 116; coverage of Occupy Wall Street, 116–17; coverage of the Black Lives Uprising, 165–67, 171–72. *See also* newspapers, and magazines; television

maps. *See* Tahrir Square (Egypt); Zuccotti Park
marches, 38; in the Black Lives Uprising, 153, 158–59, 162–65, 167, 180; in Egypt, 74–76, 88, 103, 111; in the French Revolution, 211, 212, 217–18, 225, 227; frustration with, 107–8, 162; in Occupy Wall Street, 113–14, 117–18, 139, 146, 148; 2017 Women's March (United States), 236; women's march on Versailles (France), 47, 217–18, 284n4
Markoff, John, 208
mass mobilization, *See* mobilization
McAdam, Doug, 20, 21, 26, 40, 244
McCarthy, John D., 18
Melucci, Alberto, 22
menu peuple, 218, 221–22, 225
messaging: email, 34; encrypted, 34; text, 34, 73, 80
Metropolitan Anarchist Coordinating Council (MACC), 149
Ministry of Interior (Egypt), 76, 101, 104
Minneapolis: Police Department, 2, 157, 160–62, 164; Third Precinct, 158–61; 38th and Chicago intersection (George Floyd Square), 157–59
mobile phones, 73, 76
mobilization, 1, 4–6, 31–32; avenues/types of, 5, 5, 27, 36, 36–37; elite-led, 102, 268n17; hybrid, 198, 215, 225–26; longitudinal mass mobilization, 108–9, 233, 240–41; mobilization potential (theory), 28; mobilizing structures, 20–23, 92, 191–92; process of, 31; scholarly problems of, 26–29; short-run, 238; what we know about, 1, 15–26. *See also* affinity-convergence mobilization; spontaneous mobilization (concept)
Mohammad Mahmoud Street (Egypt), 100–102
moral shocks, 23–24, 28, 45
moral values, 42, 179

Morsi, Mohamed, 101–2. *See also* Muslim Brotherhood (Egypt)
mosques, 38, 75, 82; Omar Makram, 81; Rabaa al-Adawiya, 102–3
movement building, 92–94
movement moments, 92, 238
Mubarak, Gamal, 1, 59, 64
Mubarak, Hosni, 1, 47, 55, 59, 72
Mubarak regime (Egypt), 59, 66, 78–80; aftermath of, 51, 91–100, 232; bureaucracy, 81; loyalists, 61, 79–80, 83, 242, 243
music, 43–44, 89, 126, 135; Radiohead (band), 43
Muslim Brotherhood (Egypt), 59, 63–64, 67–68, 70, 74, 84; Hassan Abdel Rahman, 64; Abdel Monem Aboel Fotouh, 64; Mehdi Akef, 64; electoral campaign (2005), 64; electoral campaign (2011–2012), 95; pact with State Security, 62–63; youth wing, 74–75, 265n7. *See also* Morsi, Mohamed
mutual aid, 149–50, 180, 190, 195

National Assembly (France), 218, 221–25; declaration of, 207–8; relocation to Paris, 47, 213
National Association for Change (Egypt), 67–68, 70; petition, 67–68
National Democratic Party (NDP) (Egypt), 59, 65; burning of headquarters, 77; party chief Hossan Badrawi, 85
National Guard: France, 211–13, 227; United States, 169, 177–78
needs (affinity), 42–43; in the Black Lives Uprising, *181*, 185; in the Egyptian Revolution, *87*, 98–99; in Occupy Wall Street, *124*, 127, 129–30. *See also* drives (affinity)
network(s): analysis, 21–22; communications networks, 22, 38, 66; interpersonal social networks, 63, 86, 92–93; in Occupy Wall Street, 135, 149–50; social movement networks, 3, 21–22, 27, 36–37, 86, 141, 229; submerged networks, 22, 37
newspapers, and magazines, 1, 8, 23, 81, 101, 238; in the French Revolution, 201–2, 218–19, 222–25; *New York Times*, 117; online, 72; *Time*, 1. *See also* pamphlets
New York City, 34, 40, 42, 107–8; Bowling Green, 112; Chase Plaza, 108, 113; City Hall, 112; Ground Zero, 108; Tompkins Square Park, 34, 112–13; Trinity Church, 144; Wall Street, 108. *See also* Zuccotti Park
New York City General Assembly (NYCGA): later reforms, 140; after the occupation, 144; during the occupation, 115–16, 126; before September 17, 34, 112–13. *See also* Spokes Council
New York City Police Department (NYPD): Anthony Bologna, 116–17, 132; and Occupy, 114, 116–18, 123, 239
New Yorkers Against Budget Cuts, 108, 112
9/11 attacks, 107–8
99 percent, the, 42, 119, 121, 129, 233, 237
nonviolence, 164, 211, 238–39; in the absence of police, 80, 163
norms, and rules, 5, 22, 95, 119, 125; breakdown of, 45, 46, 84; emergent, 3, 17; framing of, 48. *See also* exceptional (convergence)
Nour, Ayman, 65–67, 264n25
November 15, 2011. *See* eviction: of Occupy Wall Street

Obama, Barack, 48, 79, 107
Oberschall, Anthony, 19, 29
obligations (affinity), *38*, 40; in the Black Lives Uprising, *181*, 184; in the Egyptian Revolution, 78, 82–83, *87*, 88; in the French Revolution, *216*, 216–17; in Occupy Wall Street, 123, *124*, 126, 129, 133, 142
Occu-Evolve, 146

occupations (protest tactic), 3, 51, 238–39, 240–41; in the Black Lives Uprising, 154, 173, 179–80; in Egypt, 81–84. *See also* Capitol Hill Occupied Protest (CHOP) (Black Lives Uprising); Occupy Wall Street

Occupiers, 123–34 passim; hardgrounders, 114, 143, 269n15; as an identity, 147–48

Occupy Democrats, 145. *See also* Democratic Party (United States)

Occupy May Day, 144–45, 233. *See also* strikes

Occupy Sandy, 148–50

Occupy Together, 141

Occupy Wall Street, 8–10, 34–35, 42–44, 49–50, 107–50, *124*, *126*; comparison with Egypt, 136–37 passim; diffusion of, 1–2, 108, 119–21, 141; early development of, 111–21; fragmentation of, 141–46; legacy of, 146–50; participants in, 123–37; summary of Part III, 232–34. *See also* New York City General Assembly (NYCGA); October 1, 2011 (Occupy); September 17, 2011 (Occupy); Spokes Council

October 1, 2011 (Occupy), 116–19, 238. *See also* bridges: Brooklyn Bridge

Olson, Mancur, 19

online. *See* internet

Opp, Karl-Dieter, 19, 29

opportune (convergence), 26–27, 45, *46*, *52*, 238–39, 241–43; collapse of, 96–97; frames, 48, 77, 88, 176–77, 208; situations, 26, 46–47, 77, 88, 177, 180, 200, 219, 261n60; spaces, 49, 80, 88–89, 119, 121, 127, 131–37 passim, 179–80, 208, 221

opportunities, 19–21, 32, 44. *See also* political opportunity theories

opposition parties, 66; El-Ghad Party (Egypt), 66, 74; Freedom and Justice Party (Egypt), 95; interaction with movements, 66–69; Liberal Democratic Front (Egypt), 74; Tagammu (Egypt), 74. *See also* Democratic Party (United States)

oppression, 42, 66. *See also* perceived injustice; police brutality; repression

organizations (and organized groups), 3, 20–23, 31, 36, 236; in the Black Lives Uprising, 188–95; in Egypt, 63–69, 73–75, 83; failure of to capitalize on mobilization, 91–92; in the French Revolution, 222–28; in New York, 107–8, 145; weakness or passivity of, 2–3, 66, 73–74, 188, 201–2. *See also* human rights: organizations; social movement organization (SMO); trade unions

organizers. *See* activists

Osman, Tarek, 61

Palais-Royal (France), 49, 211, 216, 220, 236; description of, 209–10; ownership, 209

pamphlets, 199, 201–2, 210, 222–23; pamphleteers, 207, 225–26. *See also* newspapers, and magazines

paramount (convergence), 45, *46*, *52*, 137, 238–39, 241; frames, 48–49, 72–73, 79, 88, 100, 119, 121, 129, 131–37 passim, 144–45, 172, 179, 220, 239; situations, 47, 80, 88, 95–96, 177–78, 220, 243; spaces, 50, 89

Paris (France): Commune, 211, 212, 228; *faubourgs*, 217; Hôtel de Ville, 205, 212–13, 227; in the July days, 210–12; markets, 205, 212, 216–18, 235; mobilization of, 209–13; in the October days, 212–13; Parisians, 38, 201–2, 204–5, 217–26 passim; revolutionary activism in, 202, 207, 210. *See also Fête de la Fédération*; Les Halles (France); Palais-Royal (France)

participants/participation: absence of, 6, 135–37; barriers to, 48, 78, 127, 142; peripheral, 129–30; persistence of, 238; remote, 120–21, 183; small-

scale, 126–27, 240; unaffiliated, 27–28, 32–33
parties. *See* Democratic Party (United States); National Democratic Party (NDP) (Egypt); opposition parties
Passy, Florence, 27
patterns of activity (affinity), *38*, 38–39; in the Black Lives Uprising, *181*, 182–83; digital, 38–39, 182–83; in the Egyptian Revolution, 75, 82–83, *87*, 88, 98–99; in the French Revolution, 205, *216*, 217–18; in Occupy Wall Street, *124*, 135; physical, 38, 182
peasants, 204, 207–8, 217, 220. *See also* class
perceived injustice, 16, 24–25, 41–42; in the Black Lives Uprising, 176, *181*, 186–87; in the Egyptian Revolution, 61–62, 72, 86–87, *87*, 98; in the French Revolution, 203–4, 208, *216*, 217–19; in Occupy Wall Street, 121, *124*, 131, 136–37. *See also* psychological affinities; relative deprivation
personality (traits), 17, 258n22
Pfaff, Steven, 48
physical conditions of convergence. *See* spaces (convergence)
Piven, Frances Fox, 18
police and security forces, 47, 66, 176–77, 239–40; confrontations with, 69, 87, 233, 238; defeat of, 232–33; defunding, 181, 187, 192–93, 279n33; need for, 99; protests against, 68–69, 153–96 passim. *See also* antipolice; Central Security Forces (Egypt); federal officers (Black Lives Uprising); Minneapolis: Police Department; National Guard; New York City Police Department (NYPD)
police brutality: in Egypt, 68–69, 74–75, 77; in the United States, 42, 149, 169–70
police state: in Egypt, 7, 72, 86; in the United States, 172, 186, 195
political context, 19, 20, 26
political opportunity theories, 19–21, 26, 91; discursive and cultural opportunities, 23; versus opportune situations, 261n60
political process theories, 20–21, 26–27
Poor People's Movements (Piven and Cloward), 18
Popkin, Jeremy, 222
Portland, Oregon, 39, 171–73, 184, 190; Riot Ribs, 180, 184. *See also* Wheeler, Ted
Power in Movement (Tarrow), 26
predisposition. *See* affinity (concept)
privately owned public spaces (POPS), 114, 119, 125, 233
profession(s), 39, 40. *See also* status (affinity); workers
psychological affinities, 4, 37, 40–44, *41*, 50–51, *52*; in the Black Lives Uprising, 154, *181*, 184–87; in the Egyptian Revolution, 86–87, *87*; in the French Revolution, 203–4, *216*, 217–19, 225; in Occupy Wall Street, *124*, 127–34. *See also* attitudes (affinity); dispositions (affinity); drives (affinity); identities (affinity); interests (affinity); needs (affinity); perceived injustice

quotidian disruption, 23–24, 28, 45

Rabaa massacre (Egypt), 102–3
race, and ethnicity, 39, 44. *See also* identities (affinity); status (affinity)
radical flanks, 21, 239
rallies, 43, 107, 112
Rashid, Esraa, 66–67
rational choice theories, 6, 19–20, 29, 32; shortcomings of, 32, 231
recruitment, 15, 21–22, 35–37, 145–46, 224–26; absence of, 31–32, 44, 51, 92–94, 123–24
Regeni, Giulio, murder of, 104
regimes, 239–40, 244–45. *See also* Ancien Régime (France); Mubarak regime (Egypt)

reign(s) of terror, 103–4, 228
relative deprivation, 16–18, 24–25, 42, 62, 203
religion, 84, 88. *See also* Islamism/Salafism
reportage, 38–39, 85, 132, 160–61, 169–72
repression, 5, 16, 239–40; collapse of, 45, 170–71, 207, 220, 243–44; in Egypt, 66, 70, 71, 79–80, 95, 102–5; hard and soft, 77–78, 240; in the United States, 107, 147
repressive backfire, 47; in the Black Lives Uprising, 160–73, 177–79 passim, 239–40; in Egypt, 74–75, 76, 79–80, 96; in Occupy Wall Street, 116–18
research methods, 6–9; archival, 8; case selection, 7; comparative (and historical), 6–7; ethics, 8; ethnography, 7, 56–57; fieldwork in Egypt, 91, 103–4, 262n4; fieldwork in New York, 135; future research questions, 242–45; historical sociology, 6–7; interview details, 8; "plus" approaches, 6; positionality, 154–55; primary data, 6–7; research on the Black Lives Uprising, 153–55, 273n4; research on the French Revolution, 197–98; triangulation, 6; within-case methods, 7–8. *See also* comparative history plus
resistance: to Mubarak, 55–56, 67; to Trump, 149–50, 236
resource mobilization theories, 18–20
resources: of movements, 18, 39, 127, 202; of participants, 39–40, 82. *See also* resources (affinity)
resources (affinity), *38*, 39–40; in the Black Lives Uprising, *181*, 183–84; in the Egyptian Revolution, 82, *87*, 88; in Occupy Wall Street, *124*, 127
Revel, Jacques, 205, 221
revolutionaries. *See* activists
Revolutionary Communist Party (United States), 107

revolutionary movements, 51, 55, 70, 89, 91–92, 231; capture of, 228
Revolutionary Youth Coalition (Egypt), 93–94, 100
revolutions, 3, 19, 71; as a minoritarian phenomenon, 60–61; role of mass mobilization in, 91. *See also* Egyptian Revolution (2011); French Revolution (1789); German Revolution (1989); Tunisian Revolution
riots, 3, 161–73 passim, 205, 239; justifications for, 177–78, 185; mobilizing effect of, 164–66, 178; versus revolutionary mobilization, 221
Rose, Robert Barrie, 201
routines. *See* patterns of activity (affinity)
Ruault, Nicolas, 210, 226
Rudé, George, 197, 218

Saeed, Khaled, 68. *See also* "We Are All Khaled Saeed"
Sanders, Bernie, 147
sans-culottes: definition, 205–6; efforts to organize, 224–27
Schmeidler, Emilie, 237
Schneider, Nathan, 112
Seattle, 166–69, 175–79 passim, 182–84, 187–88, 192; East Precinct, 169–71, 187; Police Department, 168–70. *See also* Capitol Hill Occupied Protest (CHOP) (Black Lives Uprising); Durkan, Jenny
September 17, 2011 (Occupy), 113–14, 232–33; planning, 111–12
1789. *See* French Revolution (1789)
Sharp, Gene, 239. *See also* nonviolence
Simmons, Erica S., 6
Sioufi, Pierre, 78, 84; apartment of, 82
Sisi, Abdel Fattah el-, 91, 94; coup of (2013–2014), 91, 101–2
situations (convergence), *46*, 46–47, 96, 241; exceptional, 47, 76, 88, 175–76, 179–80, 219, 231, 234, 239, 242–43; opportune, 26, 46–47, 77, 88, 177,

180, 200, 219, 261n60; paramount, 47, 80, 88, 95–96, 177–78, 220, 243
Small, Albion W., 16
Smith, Matthew Scott, 34
Smucker, Jonathan Matthew, 125
Snow, David A., 23, 45
social affinities, 37–40, *38*, 51, *52*; in the Black Lives Uprising, 154, *181*, 182–84; in the Egyptian Revolution, 75, 83, *87*, 87–88, 98–99; in the French Revolution, 205–6, *216*, 217–18; in Occupy Wall Street, *124*, 124–27; tabulated summary, *38*. *See also* obligations (affinity); patterns of activity (affinity); resources (affinity); status (affinity)
social cognition, 32. *See also* social psychology
social media, 8–9, 22–23, 38, 56, 66–67, 82, 158, 182, 191–92; Bambuser.com, 74; livestreaming, 116, 120–21, 158–61, 182; Twitter, 74, 116, 189; WhatsApp, 158. *See also* Facebook; internet
social movement communities, 22, 26, 37; in the Black Lives Uprising, 191–92; in Occupy Wall Street, 107, 117, 135
social movement organization (SMO), 18, 36. *See also* organizations (and organized groups)
social movements: early definitions and theories of, 16–17; scholarship on, 3, 15–33. *See also* mobilization; revolutionary movements
social psychology, 17, 24–26, 28, 41–42. *See also* psychological affinities
social status. *See* status (affinity)
social structures, 5, 6, 16, 26, 235–36, 260n58
social ties, 5, 27, 108, 144, 147, 229; lack of, 92–93. *See also* network(s)
spaces (convergence), 45, *46*, 49–50, 81–86, 88–89, 171, 179–80, 220–22, 240–41; exceptional, 49–50, 84, 89, 119, 125–29, 133–37, 179–80, 210, 220–21, opportune, 49, 80, 88–89, 119, 121, 127, 131–37 passim, 179–80, 208, 221; paramount, 50, 89
Spokes Council, 140, 272n3
spontaneity, 2, 18–19, 197, 230; interplay with organization, 221–23, 237–38; spontaneism, 18–20, 231; spontaneous coordination, 19, 82, 170–71, 234
spontaneous mobilization (concept), 5–6, 31–32, 231, 236; definition of, 2–3; necessary and sufficient conditions for, 50–54; participants in, 32–33, 44; as a puzzle, 15–16. *See also* mobilization; spontaneity
squares, urban, 31, 81–84; Chapman Square (Portland), 184; Duarte Square (New York), 144; Karl Marx Square (Leipzig), 50; Rabaa al-Adawiya and al-Nahda squares (Cairo), 102–3; Tompkins Square Park (New York), 34. *See also* Cairo (Egypt); New York City; Tahrir Square (Egypt); Zuccotti Park
Staggenborg, Suzanne, 22
state(s). *See* regimes
status (affinity), *38*, 39; in the Black Lives Uprising, *181*, 181–83, 186; in the Egyptian Revolution, 72, 75, 84, *87*; in the French Revolution, 205–6, *216*, 217; in Occupy Wall Street, *124*, 127–28. *See also* age; class
Stone, Bailey, 203, 217, 219
strategies: of Egyptian activists, 69–70, 92–94; of French revolutionaries, 198, 201–2, 225–28; of Occupy Wall Street, 125, 140; of police, 117–18, 169. *See also* action: strategic; framing: strategic use of; tactics
strikes, 66–67, 266n22; May 1 general strike (2012), 145–56
structural availability hypothesis, 21–22, 27, 229, 236
structural conditions of convergence. *See* situations (convergence)

Stryker, Sheldon, 24
Suleiman, Omar, 85
Supreme Council of the Armed Forces (SCAF) (Egypt), 84–85, 91, 93–100, 239; coup against Mubarak, 97–98; General Hassan al-Roueini, 85
surveillance, 46, 88, 102–4; movement use of, 191

Tackett, Timothy, 224, 283n40
tactics, 31, 111, 113, 148, 166, 170, 201–2; development of, 188, 190–91; diversity of, 162, 166, 188–89, 195, 238–39. *See also* marches; nonviolence; occupations (protest tactic); rallies; strategies; strikes; violence
Tahrir moment, 111, 149
Tahrir Square (Egypt), 38, 40, 49–50, 55–57, 75–85, 88–89, 232; Egyptian Museum, 82; as an exceptional space, 84–85; international visitors to, 111; July 2011 sit-in, 111; map of, 81; the Mugamma, 81; November 2011 sit-in, 100; 2003 sit-in, 65, 69
Tamarrud (Egypt), 101–2
Tantawi, Mohamed Hussein, 83–84, 91
Tarrow, Sidney, 20, 26
taxi drivers (Egypt), 39, 83, 103–4
television, 23, 39, 56, 78, 131, 161, 182; *The Daily Show*, 117, 125. *See also* Al Jazeera
Theory of Fields, A (Fligstein and McAdam), 26
Third Estate (France), 207, 208; elections to, 199–203. *See also* Estates General (France); National Assembly (France)
threats, 21, 26, 44, 47, 132; absence of, 84, 127; to authorities, 68–69, 212, 238–39; in the Black Lives Uprising, 172, 178, 186–87, 191; in the French Revolution, 216
Tilly, Charles, 20, 26, 244–45
tocsin (France), 48–49, 212–13, 216, 220, 227, 235

trade unions, 108, 120–21, 141
Trager, Eric, 63–64
Trump, Donald, 2; administration, 166, 171–73, 178–81 passim, 186–87; coup attempt, 195; resistance to, 149–50, 236
Tunisian Revolution, 1, 48, 55, 60, 72–73, 231
Turner, Ralph, 16
2008 financial crash, 62, 107, 131, 134, 233

Ultras (Egypt), 69, 76

vandalism, 158–60, 188–89
van Stekelenburg, Jacquelien, 25–26, 27, 28
van Zomeren, Martijn, 24, 41
Versailles, 217; march to Versailles, 212–13, 217–18, 284n4
violence: criminal assaults on protesters, 39, 84; definition of, 275n35; violent protest, 183, 238–39. *See also* arson; police brutality; vandalism
von Clausewitz, Carl, 53

Wall of Dads (Black Lives Uprising), 39, 184
weapons, 40, 47, 74, 80, 102; "less lethal" munitions, 161–62, 167; Molotov cocktails, 77, 80; pepper spray, 116–17, 167, 169–70; tear gas, 160–63, 167, 170, 173, 180, 183–84
"We Are All Khaled Saeed," 68–69, 73–75
Wheeler, Ted, 192
Why Men Rebel (Gurr), 16
women, 39, 84, 97, 116; in the French Revolution, 206, 212, 217–18, 284n4. *See also* gender; marches
workers, 39, 66–67, 120, 209–10, 217, 219, 226. *See also* trade unions
Workers World Party, 107, 111–12
working groups (Occupy), 113, 115–16,

139–40, 269n8; Facilitation Working Group, 115; long-term persistence, 116; Media Working Group, 116, 120, 144; Movement Resources Group, 139–40; Tech-Ops Committee, 141

Year of the Protester, 1, 7

Zald, Mayer N., 18
Zuccotti Park, 40, 43, 44, 49–50, 108; attempted reoccupation, 144; compared with CHOP, 171; loss of, 142–43; map of, *126*; as a space of convergence, 119, 126–28, 144. *See also* eviction: of Occupy Wall Street